USBORNE

BUSINESS

FOR BEGINNERS

Contents

I don't think I'm the type of person who goes into business.
Anyone can run a business – there's no such thing as the right type of person to do it!
I'd like to run my own business, but I don't know where to begin!
Well, read on! You'll find out how businesses work. And by the end of Chapter 3, I think you'll have the confidence to start one yourself.

What is a business?

Whether it's one person running a market stall or a big, well-known company with thousands of people working for it, all businesses make and do things people need, in exchange for something – usually money.

To be successful, a business has to make more money than it spends. This is known as making a **profit**.

What do businesses do?

Businesses make products and sell them. A product can be something you hold, such as a book or a cuddly toy. This is known as a **good**.

A product can also be an action, such as delivering groceries or cutting someone's hair. This is known as a **service**.

Some businesses offer products that are a mixture of goods *and* services.

Why do we need businesses?

Imagine a world without businesses. You'd have to make or get everything you needed by yourself – and everyone else would too.

But imagine having to make and grow all the ingredients as well. You'd have to...

Splitting work is a more effective way of satisfying people's needs. An individual person, or group of people, can specialize in the things they are good at, and turn those into **businesses.**

Business is everywhere

Here are some examples of the range of needs that people have, and the kinds of businesses – and business people – that meet them.

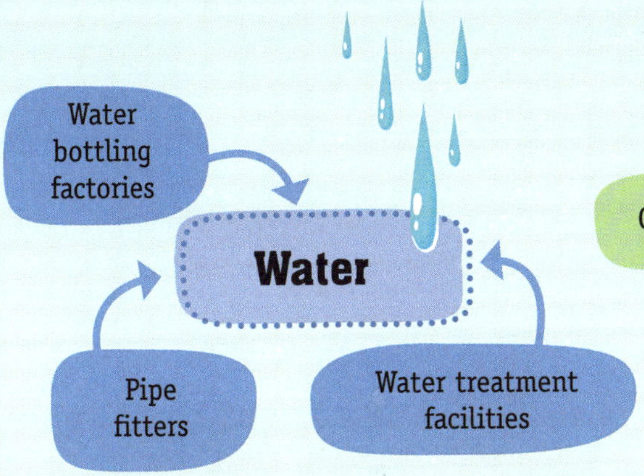

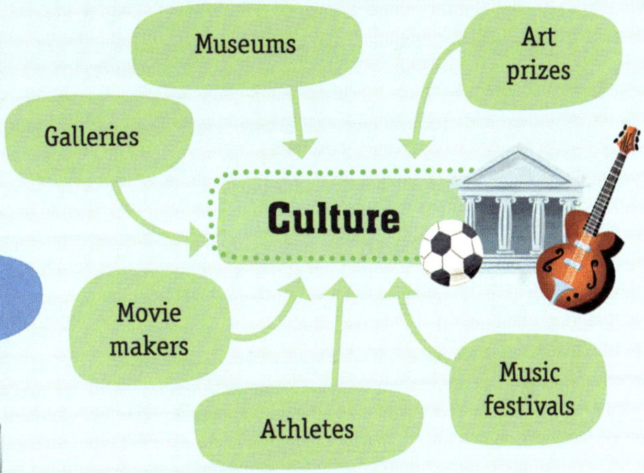

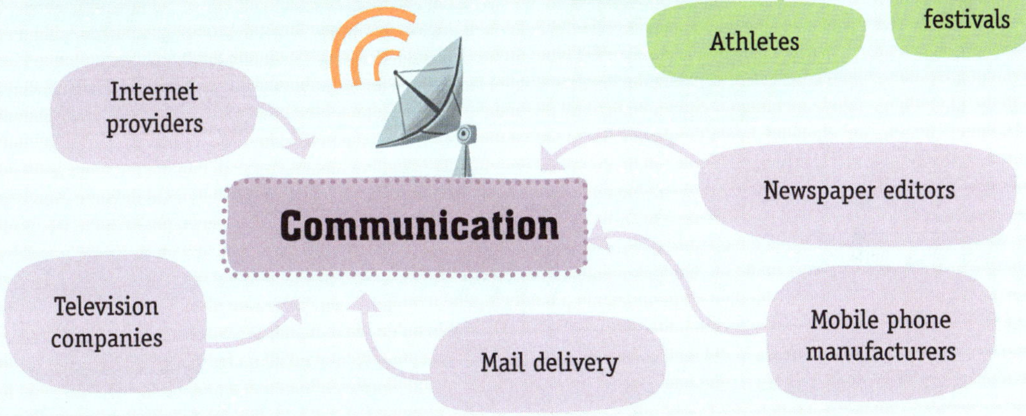

...but not quite everywhere

Some goods and services are provided by *governments* instead of businesses. This might be because the government has decided to make something available to everyone – whether they can pay for it or not – such as healthcare, education or street maintenance.

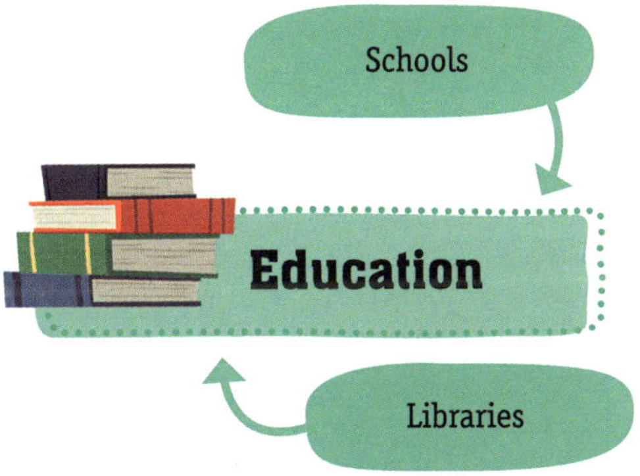

Why set up a business?

Someone who sets up a business is often called an **entrepreneur**. There are all kinds of reasons why people become entrepreneurs.

Some people do it to make money...

Sometimes, someone spots a problem, and wants to fix it...

Some people start a business to make the world a better place...

Some entrepreneurs get a buzz from turning ideas into products...

Entrepreneurs tend to start businesses for a combination of these reasons. They often get huge satisfaction from offering the best possible product or service.

Chapter 1: How to start a business

Do **you** want to be an entrepreneur? You can be. Absolutely anyone can start their own business. All you need to do is think it through a little. The next chapter will show you how.

First you need to come up with an **idea**.

Next, you have to test it. This is to make sure there is a **market** for your good or service, and that it will stand out against the **competition**.

Then, you can create a **business plan** to help you set your goals and persuade people to support you.

Your idea

All businesses start with an idea. If nothing comes to mind straightaway, you could try making a 'mind map' to help you. To do that, write these questions in bubbles on a sheet of paper, then scribble as many ideas you can think of around each one.

After you've finished your mind map, read it through carefully and pick out the business ideas you like the most.

If you have come up with some promising ideas, the next step is to find out whether anyone will *actually buy* the things you want to sell. It's also useful to work out whether you will be *competing* with existing businesses.

Does anyone want your stuff?

Even if you know that *you* would buy a good or service, it's important to find out if anyone else would be willing to pay for it.

To avoid wasting money developing products or services that no one wants, businesses do **market research**. This means talking to the group of people you hope will become customers – your **market**.

Businesses define their market by grouping people together that have something in common. For example, they might aim their goods or services at people who live in one specific place, or are of a particular age, or who have a similar income, or who share a hobby.

Nathan's market is students at his school, so these are the people that he needs to research. He does this in a number of ways.

Observations

Interviews

It's better to ask questions that people can answer however they like. If you ask a question such as, "do you like my idea?", they might just say, "yes" to make you feel good.

Surveys to find the top choice...

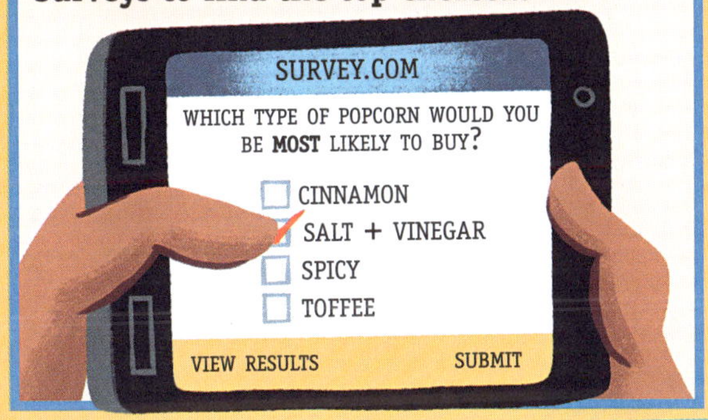

...and bottom choice

Testing sessions

The more research, the better

The more people you ask from within your market, the more useful the information you gather will be. Market research takes time, but it allows you to develop a good or service that is just what your customers want. This makes it much easier to persuade people to buy it.

Be the best!

Rivalry between businesses for customers is called **competition**. Competition can come from different places. For example, if Martha starts a business selling T-shirts at the Saturday market in her town, she may have several competitors. Here are some of them.

Ways to get ahead

In order to get ahead of the competition, businesses try to be better than their rivals in one or more ways.

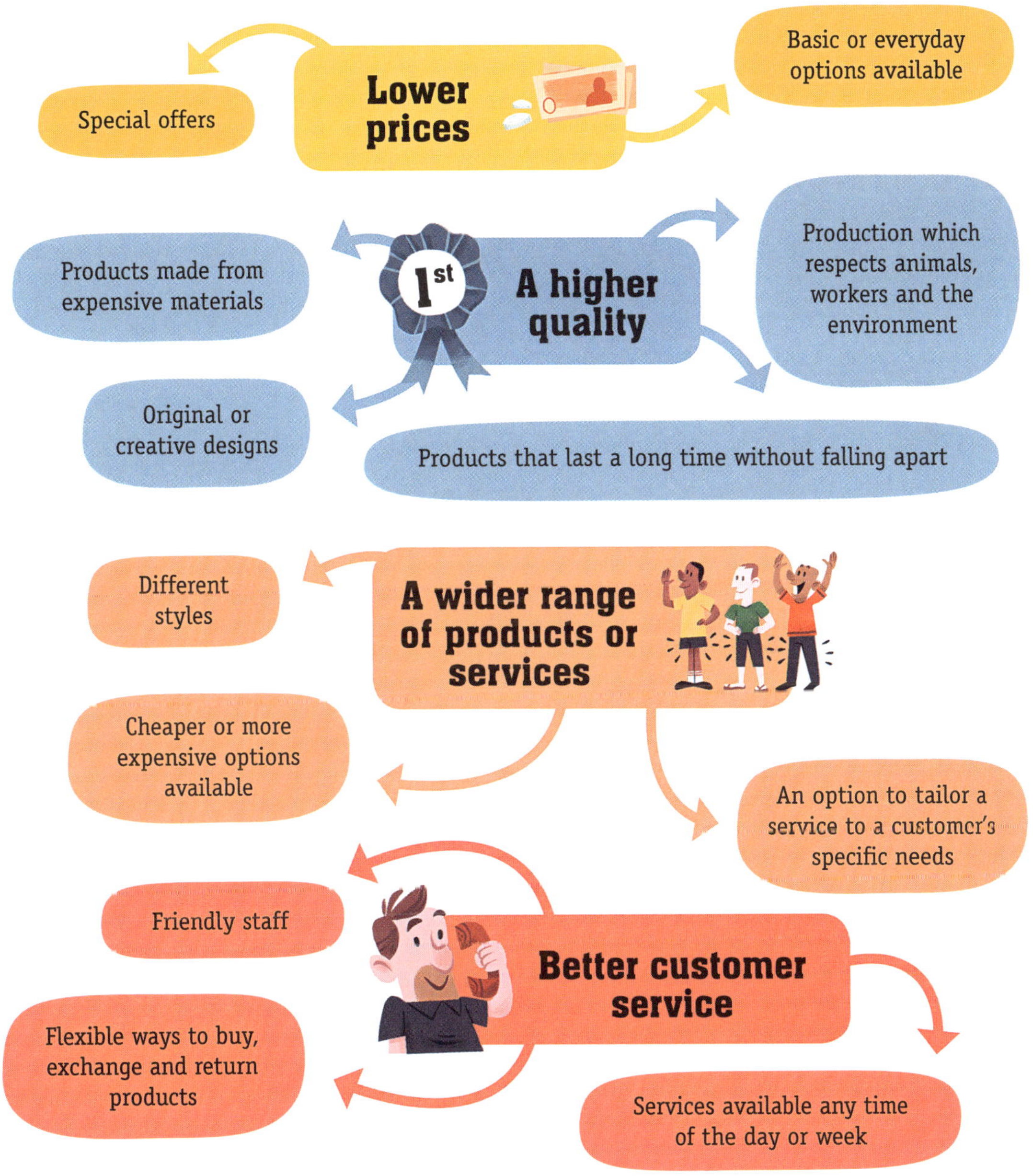

Healthy competition

From a customer's point of view, competition is a good thing, because it can push businesses to offer better products at lower prices. Most countries have laws to *ensure* businesses compete. For example, it's illegal in many places for businesses to agree among themselves to set a fixed price.

How to beat the competition

To win customers, you either need to be first on the scene with a good or service, or to offer something better than your rivals. This flowchart could help you work out how.

Is another business already selling what you want to sell?

NO

YES

You should try to make your product or service stand out from the competition.

Higher quality
Google™ wasn't the first internet search engine. In 1998, the market was dominated by other businesses. *Google* soon took over the market because their search gave more useful results.

REAL EXAMPLE

REAL EXAMPLE

New features
Mp3 players already existed when *Apple* launched the iPod ®. But iPods were the first to come with software – iTunes ® – to organize and transfer music more easily.

Does your market research definitely show that customers need or want your new product or service?

YES

NO

If no one wants it, that explains why there is no competition! Think of a new idea instead.

If you are the first to sell an exciting new good or service, you have an advantage. Even if competing businesses start up, your customers may stick with you because they know and like you.

REAL EXAMPLE

First
Amazon was the first ever online bookshop. This won it loyalty from its early customers. But *Amazon* still has to improve its service constantly to keep its large share of the market.

Find the gap in a crowded market

If you have lots of competitors, it can be hard to get your product noticed. So it helps to find a 'gap in the market', which means something that isn't currently on offer. To do this, you could draw a **market map**, a diagram which arranges existing products, according to their key characteristics.

Sondhya is considering setting up a business selling sunglasses and she's looking for a gap in the market. So she's drawn a market map showing all the sunglasses that are already on sale in her town.

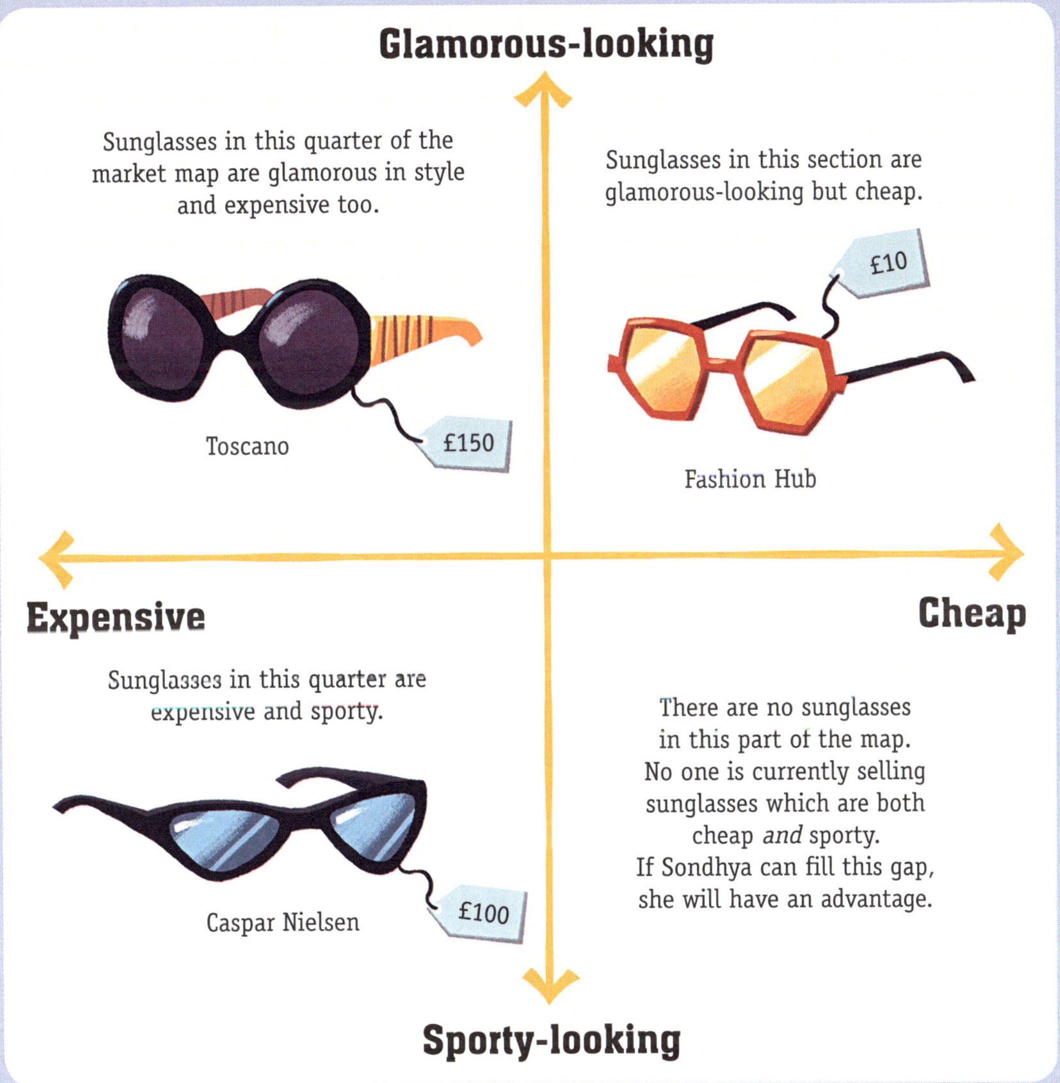

You could make a market map for any product, showing any of its features. For example, you could compare snack bars by mapping the age of the product's target customers on one scale, and how healthy it is on the other scale.

Need money?

Most businesses need *some* money to get started – whether to pay wages, buy equipment, rent a space or pay for advertising. It's often called **startup capital**.

Apply for a grant

A grant is a gift of money. A government may make grants available for businesses that meet certain criteria, such as being a new business – called a **startup**.

Save

Savings can help you get started. But if the business fails, you won't get the money back.

Apply for a loan

Family, friends or the bank might lend you money. But you'll probably have to pay back a bit more than you borrowed. The extra amount is known as **interest** – find out more on page 116.

Crowdfund

This means asking a very large group of people to pay a little bit of money each, often through a specialized website. In return, each person gets a small gift or reward.

Find investors

Investors are people who offer money in exchange for owning part of the company. Choose carefully! They'll expect to have a say in the business and hope to make money by selling their share later on.

Top tips

New businesses often find it tricky to raise money. That's because there is always a risk that the business will fail and not be able to pay the money back. To be taken seriously, here are some things to think about doing:

1. If you're borrowing money from friends or family, draw up a written agreement to avoid misunderstandings later on.

2. Consider how much money you need. Don't spend too much at the beginning, and make sure you only get things you really need.

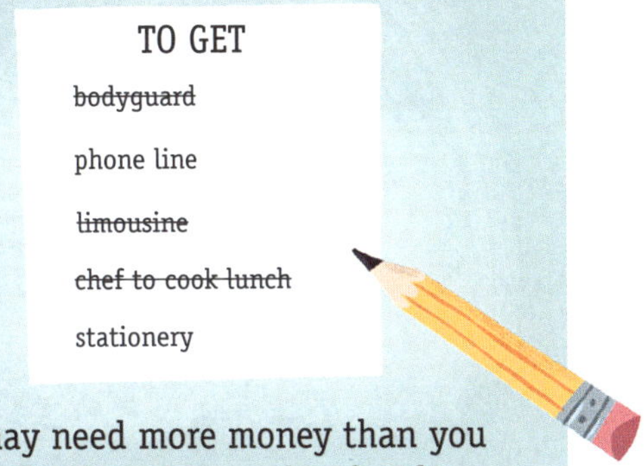

You may need more money than you originally thought, so plan for that too.

3. Make a **business plan** – a booklet that describes your business and how it will make money and achieve its goals. It sounds boring but it's important – it will show that you've thought things through, and help you win other people's support.

Business plan

These are the kinds of questions you need to answer in your business plan.

Describe your business. What's so special about it?

Introduction

We're THE ROCKETTS – three cousins in a band from Montreal, Canada. We write all our own music, and already have a growing fan base.

Picking specific goals makes it easier to measure your progress.

Business goals

Play four concerts this summer, get 50 new people to subscribe to our YouTube channel every month, record an album, and generate enough money from selling tickets and albums to start making a profit.

Who else is selling what you are? How much do they charge? What makes your product better?

Competitors

Our competitors are local bands, such as XYZ and Mashup. They tend to sell their concert tickets for C$5. But we're more popular than they are – we have more subscribers on YouTube.

C$ means 'Canadian dollars' – the money people use in Canada.

What to do with your plan

First of all, get someone to look through the plan to make sure there aren't any mistakes and that you haven't left anything out. Then make several copies to hand out.

Use your plan to try to convince people to support you with money, resources or good advice.

Customers

Our fans are high-school students and some of their parents. They like us because we are fun, creative and cousins – it makes for a good story! They find out about us through word of mouth, posters in schools and our YouTube channel.

Who are your customers and why will they like your product? How will they find out about it?

What you need

We need to raise money to rent professional recording equipment and to pay for transport to concert venues. So we need about C$200 to go to the next level.

Do you need any training, equipment, materials or a location to get started? How much will those things cost?

Making money

We'll charge C$5 for concert tickets. We estimate it will take about four months to pay back the C$200. From then on we hope to be making about C$100 per month as a band.

How much will you charge for the product? How much money do you expect to make? (See more on pages 34 and 54.)

Make it official

It's worth finding out whether there are rules about doing business in the place you live. You may need to register your business with the government, or get permission to sell things in a specific location.

Getting permission

Wherever you're planning to sell, think about who you might need to ask.

Want to sell popcorn at school?

Ask a teacher.

Want to run a lemonade stall in the town square?

Check with the local council.

Want to offer a dog-grooming service at a festival?

Ask the festival organizers first.

Telling the government

Businesses usually have to register with the government. You have to choose a type of business, or **structure**, when you register. The simplest one is called a **sole trader** (or **sole proprietor**).

SOLE TRADER

- Just one person in charge
- Usually the only structure allowed if you're under 18
- Minimal paperwork
- The owner can keep all the profits (minus any **tax** they need to pay - see below).

Businesses have to pay money to the government, known as **tax**. If you have modest sales, you may not need to pay tax when you first start a business, but be sure to check the rules in the place you live. See more on tax on page 58.

Taking on responsibility

Most businesses are sole traders and many are successful. But one downside is that sole traders are entirely responsible, or **liable**, for trying to pay back any money their business loses. This is called **unlimited liability**.

Some business structures protect against this risk. The most common one is called a **limited company** (or **limited liability company**). These businesses have **limited liability**, which means the owners are only partly responsible for any money lost.

In most countries, the ownership of a limited company is split up into equal parts, called **shares**, owned by **shareholders**. Profits from the business are shared between the shareholders. Find out more on page 102.

Other types of business

Partnership – similar to being a sole trader, but business decisions and profits are shared with a partner or partners.

Cooperative – owned and run by its members, which could mean every single person working there. Profits are shared between the members.

Franchise – this is where you pay an existing business to use their idea. It's less risky because the idea has already been shown to work.

Not-for-profit – any money it makes is used to help people in need. This kind of business is usually a charity or a school.

Doing the right thing

Just like individual people, businesses are supposed to act honestly, fairly and with respect for people and the environment. This is known as behaving **ethically**. To make sure a business is ethical, here are some things entrepreneurs need to think about.

How does my business impact on...

...my staff?

How will I treat the people who work for my company?

...the environment?

How much water and electricity am I using? How am I transporting my products to customers? See more on page 93.

...communities?

How does my business affect people living nearby? My local town? The world? See more on pages 80-81.

...customers?

How does my product change customers' lives? Is it in a good way?

If it's legal, is it OK?

A country's laws send a signal to businesses about what's right and wrong. Some businesses make money doing things that are legal, but that many people think are unethical, such as selling cigarettes. What do you think?

Our company makes and sells cigarettes. Would you like some?

Scientists and doctors have proved that they are bad for people. So why are you selling cigarettes to me?

Because you *want* them don't you? And businesses provide things that people want.

So if I wanted a *bomb*, would you sell it to me?

No, because that would be against the law! Cigarettes are unhealthy, but *not* illegal.

Crossing the line

The difficulty with just sticking to the law is that it can't cover every situation. What's more, the line between what's legal and what's illegal isn't always clear. It's sometimes more useful to think about whether or not something seems *fair*.

Ethics isn't just about what a business *does*, either – it's also about how people within a business *behave*. Do you think this manager has crossed a line?

Good ethics is good business

Often, getting managers to behave fairly encourages all staff to work well. When people are calm and happy, they tend to work better, and in turn make more money for the business. So good ethics go hand in hand with good business practice.

Chapter 2: How to sell your stuff

Once you have a great idea, you need to know how to sell it! Ways to persuade customers to buy your good or service are known as **marketing**. Clever marketing will ensure that customers want your product and buy it from *you* and not your competitors.

Giving your business an appealing personality, or **brand**, helps to make customers connect with your business emotionally. Deciding the **price** of your product, where it will be sold and how to **promote** it is also essential.

Where can customers buy it?

Customers are more likely to buy a product if it is on sale somewhere convenient. To help decide *where* to sell, a business has to think about where its customers go and how they like to buy things.

Imagine a business selling a lunchbox called 'Lunchpax'. A potential customer is someone with an office job, who might take a packed lunch to work. Here are some places the business could sell them Lunchpax, in an average day.

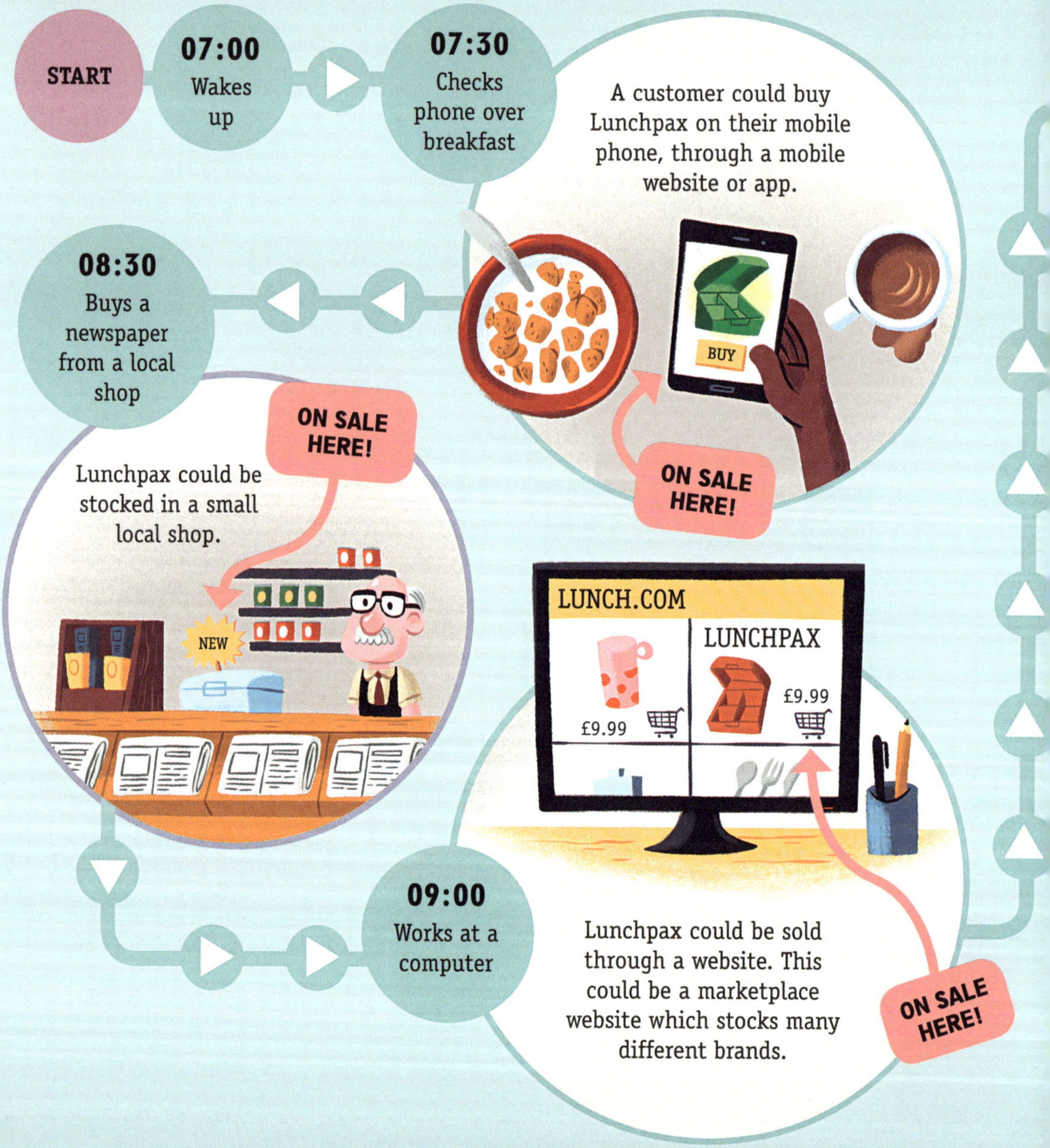

17:00
Goes to a supermarket after work

Lunchpax could be on sale at a supermarket.

ON SALE HERE!

18:00
Arrives home

ON SALE HERE!

The business could sell Lunchpax directly to customers by knocking on doors with samples. It's good to pick a time that lots of people are likely to be at home.

19:00
Opens mail

Lunchpax could be sold through a catalogue. Catalogues can be delivered to customers, then customers ring up or post a form back to order products.

ON SALE HERE!

20:00
Visits a friend for dinner.

ON SALE HERE!

The business could recruit people to sell Lunchpax to friends. This is called a "party" model of selling. The seller invites friends to their home and combines socializing with selling a product.

22:30
Bedtime

FINISH

After selling your product in several places, you can choose the ones which work best and concentrate on them.

What's it worth?

Your good or service is only *worth* what customers are willing to pay. If your price is too high, customers will be put off. If the price is too low, you won't make any money (and you may even lose money).

Price = cost + markup

Remember Nathan, from page 16, with his idea for selling popcorn? He calculates that each box of popcorn will cost him 15p to make. The **price** he charges is the cost, plus an additional amount called the **markup**.

To decide how much markup to add, Nathan thinks about his potential customers and how much they might be happy to pay:

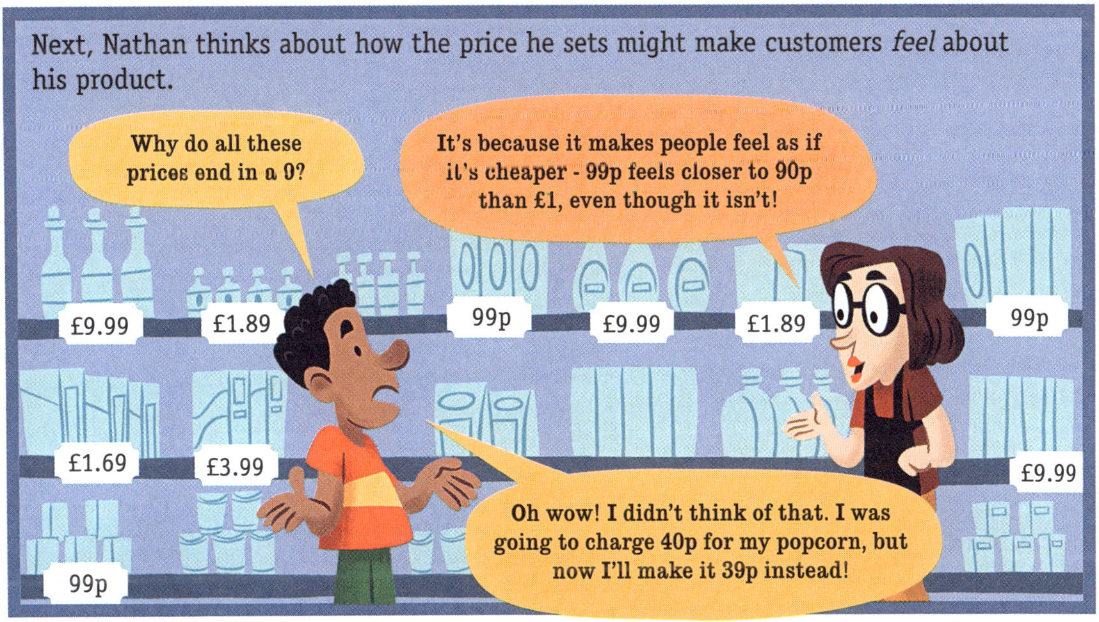

Setting the price at 39p means that Nathan has added a 24p markup to each box of popcorn. This means that for each box he sells, he gets to keep 24p.

Selling to sellers

Sometimes a business sells a product directly to its **consumer** – the person who will actually use it. But businesses can often reach *more* consumers if they sell their product to *another business* instead. This other business could be a shop, or a business that sells to shops.

Mike and his partner Mohan make and sell an electronic device called 'Kid Tracker', which enables parents to track the location of their child in a playground.

So Mike and Mohan decide to get Kid Trackers stocked in shops around the country. They take them to a **wholesaler**, a business selling to other businesses.

Next the wholesaler sells the product on to **retailers**, shops that sell products to consumers. The wholesaler adds a markup to the price when it sells it on.

When the retailer sells the product on, it also adds a markup. *Kev's Kid Zone* sells the Kid Tracker for the same price that Mike and Mohan were originally charging.

Pricing tricks

You might think that price is just about making all the numbers add up. But pricing is part of marketing. It's a way to *persuade* someone to buy stuff. Here are some tricks that businesses often use.

Charge less, win customers

Some businesses set a very low price when they first launch a product. They don't make a profit at first, but they win over customers from competitors. This is called **penetration pricing**, which means it helps businesses enter – or penetrate – a market.

Look fancy, charge more

Some businesses set a very high price for their goods or services, to make people believe that they are superior. This is called **premium pricing**. Sometimes, more expensive things *are* of a higher grade. But not always...

Lose money here, make money there

Another approach is called **loss leader pricing.** A business charges a very low price on one product, in order to attract customers into the store. A customer ends up paying a high price for something else, so the business makes its profit that way.

Make one option look *too* pricey

Within a range of products, one option may have a very high price. This makes the cheaper ones seem like great value. This is called **decoy pricing.** The expensive choice is *only* there to push a customer to another product.

Give your business a personality

One way to attract customers is to create a personality for your business. This is known as a **brand**. The idea is that customers will then continue to buy from your business because they have an emotional connection to it, almost as if it were a friend.

Think about what kind of person you would like your business to be if it was a human being. Here are some characteristics to help you think it through:

approachable TOUGH influential youthful exciting

calm successful thoughtful sophisticated kind

friendly cosy fun outdoorsy serious cheeky

family-loving athletic competent informal sincere

Joe wants his café to have a *cosy* and *approachable* brand. He wants customers to get this impression every time they have contact with his business. For example:

The **name** of his business is informal

The **font** means the style used to write text. Joe has picked a casual font.

A **logo** is a simple image to represent a business, or a distinctive way to write its name. For his, Joe has chosen an appealing hot drink.

The furniture, lighting and decoration is comfy and homely.

Warm **colours** are used in the cafe.

Joe uses a friendly and welcoming **tone of voice** when talking or writing to customers.

Lila is talking about the brand for her new business with her friend Drew:

Watch out for these kinds of pitfalls. Test your brand to make sure the message that it conveys feels consistent across all the ways you will communicate it.

Find words that sell

Successful businesses find a powerful way to describe their product to explain why it is worth buying. These persuasive words are called **marketing messages** and often appeal to people's emotions.

Remember Martha, from page 18? She's launching a business selling T-shirts. Her friend Elise is helping her write her marketing messages.

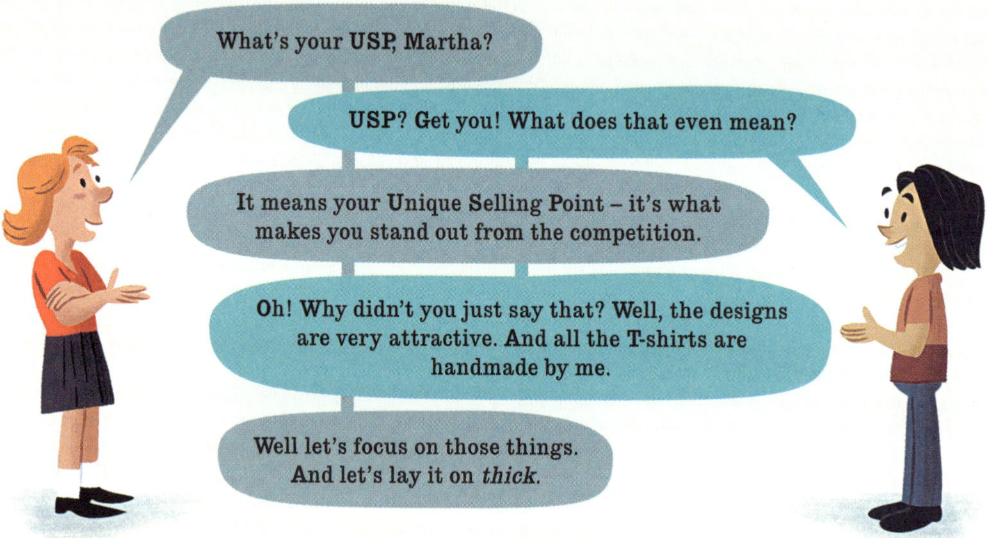

Elise suggests some marketing messages and explains why she's written them.

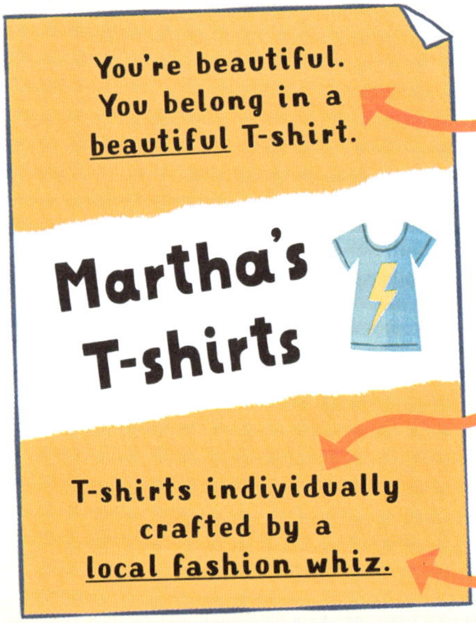

Telling people they are beautiful is flattery, which means making them feel good about themselves.

"Individually crafted" sounds exclusive. Having something that not many others have makes people feel special.

"Local fashion whiz" is a catchy way to describe yourself. People remember catchy phrases.

Businesses hope to trigger emotions that will prompt potential customers to buy their product. This might be a negative emotion, such as fear, or a positive emotion, such as feeling appreciated.

Words can only do so much...

It's hard to sell something useless, however much you work on the words. That's why businesses spend lots of time developing their product so that it matches what customers want (see page 16 about market research).

It's also against the law to lie about goods or services. So in order to make your stuff *sound great*, make sure it *really is great*!

Spread the word

Marketing messages are no use unless potential customers hear or read them. So businesses spread the word in lots of different ways. This is called **promotion**.

Here, Martha and Elise are promoting *Martha's T-shirts* all over their home town of Doxford.

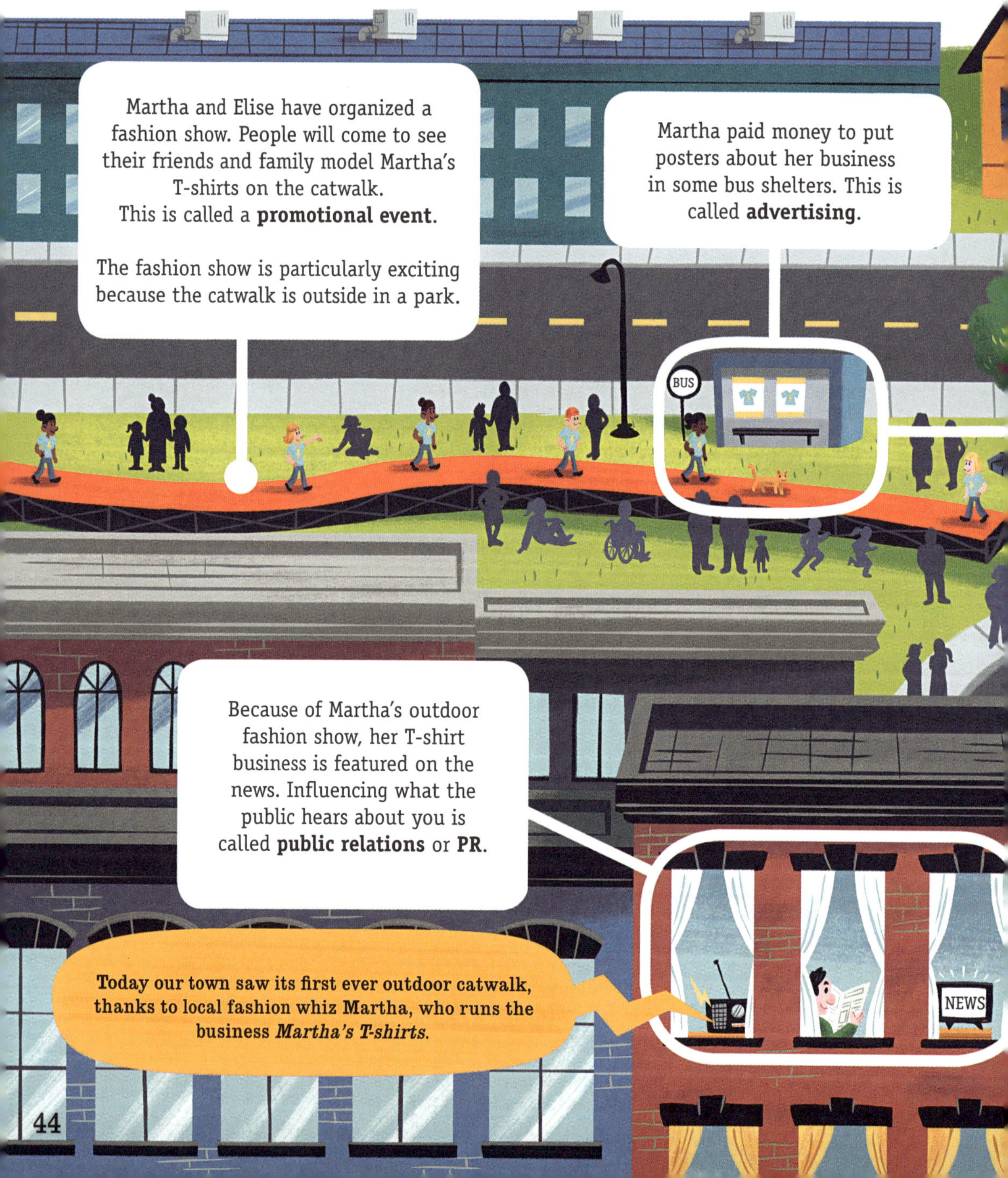

This person has received a letter through his front door about Martha's T-shirts. This is called **direct marketing**.

Unexpectedly, a cat strolls down the catwalk. Someone posts a video of it online, which gets shared 5,000 times. This makes Martha happy because her poster is visible in the video. A video that spreads quickly online is sometimes called **viral**.

Martha has paid for **online adverts**, which only appear when someone types 'T-shirt' and the name of the town into a search engine.

Martha and Elise are handing out coupons giving people money off, called a **discount**, to encourage sales.

People talking casually to each other about the attraction of a product is called **word of mouth** promotion.

Tailored messages

Often, businesses don't send the same marketing messages to everyone. Instead, they find out as much as they can about their customers and then target them personally. To do this, businesses first gather huge amounts of information. This is called **data**.

This is Annie. In the last week, she shopped at a supermarket, used a guitar tuning app, logged on to social media and wore her fitness tracker every day.

This is what businesses know about Annie:

Annie is between the ages of 18 and 25.

She eats lots of granola, eggs and chocolate cookies.

Annie played her guitar last night and spends a lot of time in Ashville.

She is interested in snowboarding and lives in Apricot Creek.

Annie ran eight miles yesterday, and six miles last week.

How can businesses know things about Annie?

What can they do to take advantage of the information they have?

Supermart knows Annie's age because last week she filled in a survey they sent her.

Supermart knows what Annie eats, because she has a loyalty card that she scans each time she shops there.

Supermart sends Annie discount vouchers for products she often buys. They also send her vouchers for cereal bars. She hasn't bought one yet...

...but other granola-eaters aged 18-25 do, according to Supermart's loyalty card data.

Guitar Heaven knows where and when Annie plays her guitar because she uses their tuning app, and she's enabled location services in the app.

Guitar Heaven sends Annie an email about an upcoming Guitar Show in Ashville.

On social media, Annie has liked a page about snowboarding, and has Apricot Creek set as the place she lives.

Snow Mountain Ski Resort – near Apricot Creek – targets Annie with ads through social media. They run ads for day tickets whenever the snowboarding conditions are good.

Active! knows about Annie's runs, as she wears one of their fitness trackers, linked to an app on her phone.

Active! sends Annie motivating tips to her phone. She finds the tips helpful, so feels loyal to *Active!* and might buy more stuff from the business in the future.

Marketing disasters

Some businesses promote their products in ways that are dishonest, unfair or irresponsible. Whether or not a business actually breaks the law, its reputation is severely damaged if it uses unethical marketing tactics. Here are some businesses that got caught.

False promises

A US-based business called *Tarr Inc.* promoted wrinkle creams on the internet using false claims.

It is against the law to mislead people in marketing, and *Tarr Inc.* was ordered to pay $6 million in fines.

Dangerous messages

In Ireland, healthcare company *Omega Pharma* was ordered to remove a TV advertisement for diet pills.

The ad showed a woman complaining about her weight, when she was a normal, healthy size. It could encourage people to lose weight when they don't need to.

Unwanted marketing

A Canadian business called *CompuFinder*, which sold training courses, sent hundreds of people emails without asking their permission. This is often called **spam**.

Under Canada's law against spam, *CompuFinder* was fined C$200,000.

Targeting children

REAL EXAMPLE

A young Swedish vlogger broke advertising rules, when she enthused about a range of dolls in an online video. She failed to say that she was advertising them for the dolls' manufacturer, *GR-Trading AS*.

Children can't always spot when a company is trying to sell to them, so marketing must be *clearly labelled* as marketing.

False price comparisons

An Australian business called *Zamel's* promoted necklaces and bracelets with a big discount.

Customers thought they were getting a good deal, but in fact the products had never been on sale at the higher price. This is against the law and *Zamel's* was ordered to pay a penalty of A$250,000.

REAL EXAMPLE

REAL EXAMPLE

Offensive content

Miracle Mattress was an American business selling mattresses. But in 2016, it made a promotional video with a jokey reference to the 2001 terrorist attack on New York, in which nearly 3,000 people died.

There was a furious reaction to the video, with thousands of people complaining. The reputational damage was so serious that the owner had to close the business.

Wherever you are, you should think about how different groups of people might feel about your marketing. If you're not sure, do some market research.

Chapter 3: Keeping track of money

It might not sound very exciting, but keeping a record of the money coming in and going out of a business is essential for it to succeed. These records are known as **accounts.** They show how much money the business is making and how much tax it should pay to the government.

About a third of businesses fail in the first two years, mostly because they've run out of money. By keeping a close eye on their accounts, businesses can plan ahead, avoid unpleasant surprises and have a better chance of success.

In and out

Money coming *into* a business from selling products is known as **revenue.** The amounts going *out* and being spent on things the business needs to operate are known as **costs.**

Meena has set up a monthly magazine, which she sells at school. Here are the costs involved in making the October edition and the revenue she gets from selling it.

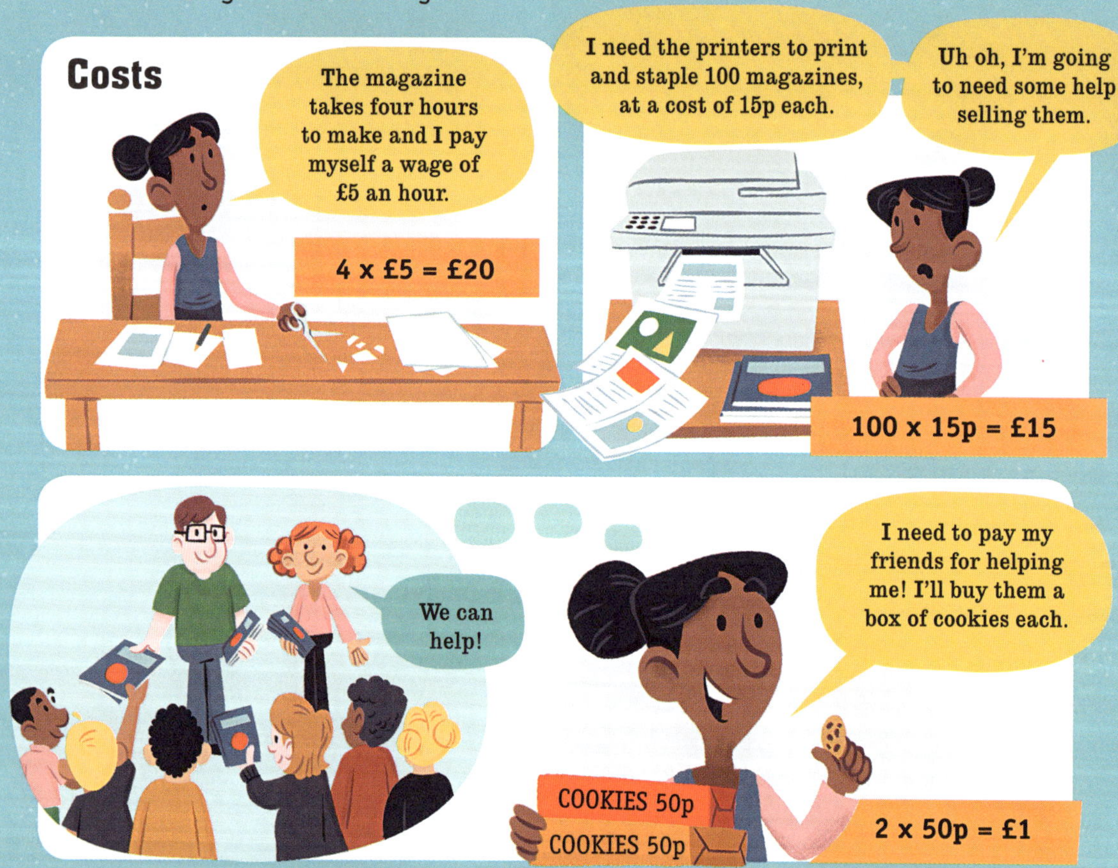

So the total cost for making 100 magazines is: **£20 + £15 + £1 = £36**

Revenue

Price

Revenue

Quantity of magazines → **90 x £1 = £90**

Keeping records

The simplest way of keeping track of costs and revenue is to write them down in a record book as you go along.

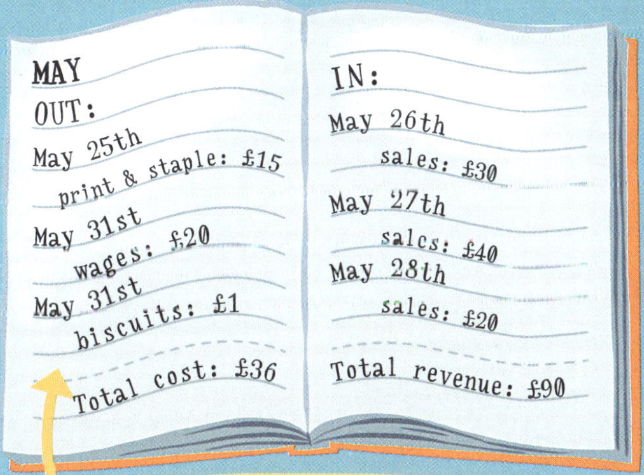

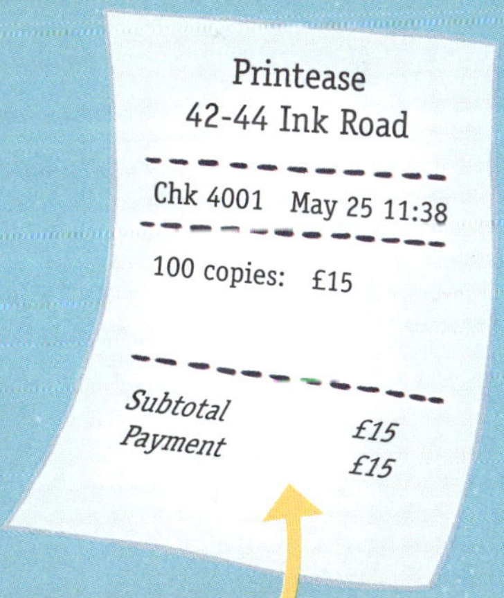

A date and short description will help jog your memory when you come back to that page.

Keep bills and receipts to help you remember exactly what you spent and earned.

Keeping records might seem boring, but it's the only way to know how much money you're making. What's more, you have to make a note of this by law in order to pay the right amount of tax (see more on page 58). Many entrepreneurs hire a person known as an **accountant** to help with their accounts.

Making money

When a business makes more money than it spends, it makes a profit. It's one of the main goals of any business.

Profit = revenue – costs

NOVEMBER: Meena's magazine has been selling well at school.

Meena can use the profit to...

Reward herself for all her hard work.

Invest – spend it on improving and growing the business.

Save in case the business doesn't do so well in the future.

Losing money

Sometimes, businesses don't make enough money from selling their products to cover their costs, so they *lose* money. This might be because they're not selling enough, their prices are too low, their costs are too high or not enough people actually want their product.

DECEMBER: Meena's magazine hasn't been selling well. Lots of her friends need to save their money to buy Christmas presents.

Meena can reduce her losses by...

Changing the way she does business.

Cutting costs

Increasing revenue

Planning ahead

A business has to make enough money to pay its bills, suppliers and workers and these costs often need to get paid before any revenue comes in. Businesses have to keep an eye on **cash flow** – the movement of money in and out of their bank account.

The co-owners of *SunCatcher*, an energy company based in France, are planning to build their next solar farm for some new clients. They keep accounts in Euros, a currency used across much of Europe.

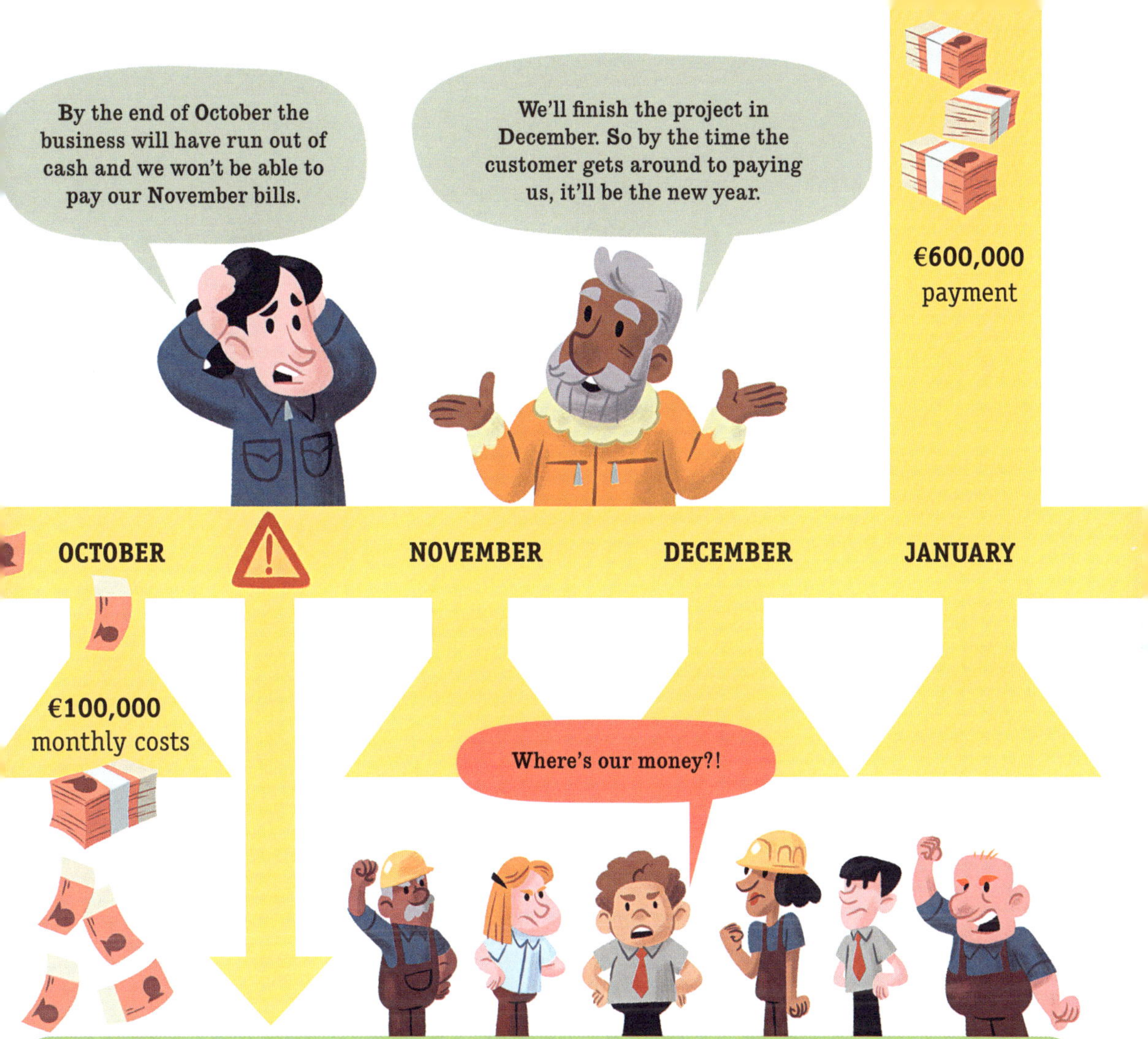

So the business needs to plan ahead to avoid running out of money before January. One or more of these ideas might solve the cash flow problem.

Paying taxes

A business can't simply keep all the money it makes. It has to give some of it back to society, by paying taxes. **Tax** is money a government collects from people, both as individuals and businesses, to pay for **public services** such as roads and schools.

Here's how it works:

1. Businesses pay taxes on...

Buildings

The amount of tax a business pays depends on the type of building it occupies: a shop on a high street is taxed more than one of the same size in the outskirts of a town.

People

This tax goes towards paying for employees' retirement and healthcare.

Profit

This tax is known as **Corporation tax.** The more profit a business makes, the more it pays.

3. The government

It sets the tax rules, which determine the taxes everyone pays.

Police

Fire fighting

Street lighting

Defence

Schools

Libraries

Roads

Hospitals

2. Individuals pay taxes on...

Things you buy

The price of most things includes a tax known as **Value Added Tax (VAT)** or **Sales Tax.**

Money you earn

In nearly all countries, people have to pay an **Income Tax** if they earn more than a certain amount.

Your possessions

In most countries, individuals pay taxes on property, or shares they own and anything they inherit.

Justice system

The government uses taxes to fund public services. Most people agree that taxes help a society work well.

Waste disposal

4. Public services

These kinds of services benefit everyone. Here are some examples...

Keeping honest accounts

By law, every business has to keep accounts which give an honest summary of its activities. This is important, not only for the business itself, but for investors and the government too.

A business needs to keep records of:

- Money spent
- Money received
- Profits and losses
- Debts it owes and is owed
- Things it owns, such as equipment or shares of other companies

Accountants help businesses do their accounts, but it's not always straightforward.

And if a business's accounts aren't honest...

The business can't make sensible decisions as it is basing them on false information.

The government might not receive the right amount of tax.

Investors will be risking their money without knowing how well the business is doing.

So it makes moral sense *and* business sense to keep honest accounts.

Is trying to pay less tax OK?

Businesses often try to pay less tax to save money. Some rules are deliberately designed by the government to help certain businesses pay less tax, for example a lower tax for startups. But sometimes, big businesses escape tax by finding **loopholes**, or ways around tax rules. Some people argue this is cheating the system – even if it's legal. What do you think?

Speek Mobile does most of its business in India, but it is registered in the Cayman Islands, where the government collects fewer taxes. This arrangement is perfectly legal, but it means the Indian government loses out on millions in tax revenue.

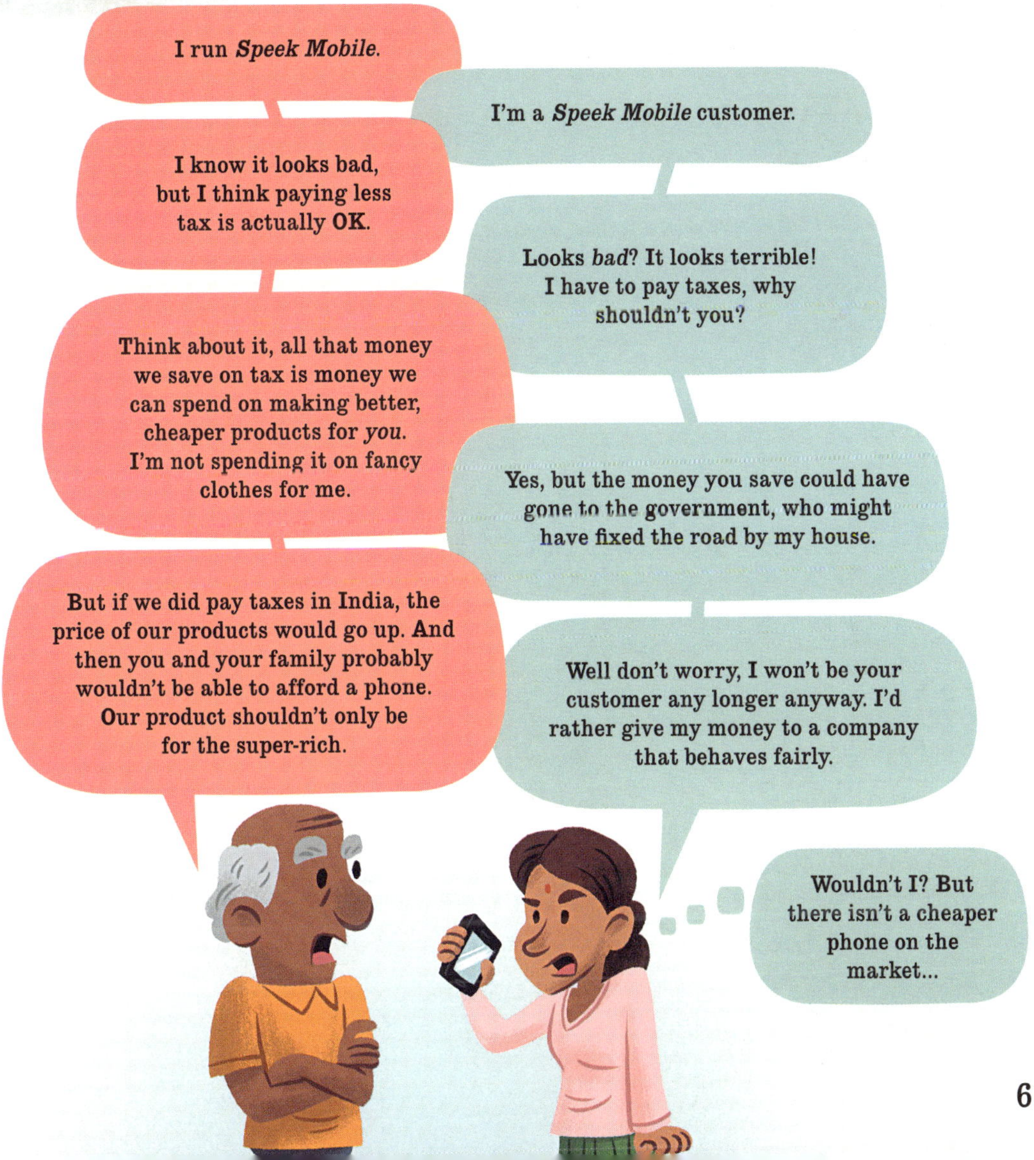

Why businesses fail

The biggest risk of running a business is it might run out of money and fail. Lots do, especially in the first couple of years. Even very successful business people, such as the American inventor and entrepreneur Thomas Edison, experienced failure...

Clever competitors

In 1875, I launched a battery-powered pen that helped make copies of documents. People loved it, but not for long.

Then in 1881, my talking doll, which should have sold well, had to be taken off the market after only a few weeks.

Good idea, badly executed

In 1904, I started a new business that sold my inventions in Germany. When the country found itself at war, people stopped coming to the store, and it had to shut.

Global events

Lots of entrepreneurs have had failed businesses or ideas. They learn from the failure, start again and launch a better business. In some cases, failure can even become an opportunity.

The end of the road

If a business runs out of money and can't repay its debts, it has failed. But the story doesn't just end there. Here's what can happen...

REAL EXAMPLE

HELP!

First, *Transaero* owners tried to make a deal with **creditors**, the people they owed money to. *Transaero* asked for more time to pay its debts.

The creditors said no.

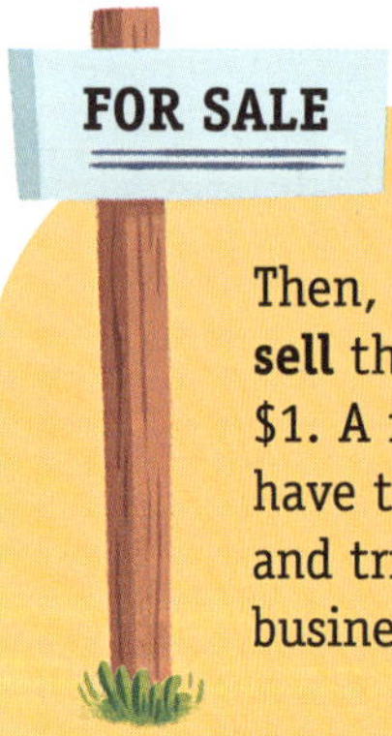

Then, the owners tried to **sell** the business for just $1. A new owner would have taken on the debt, and tried to make the business profitable again.

No one bought it.

Eventually, the airline had to shut down and sell what it owned, in order to pay off as much of the debt as it could. This is known as **liquidation.** (It's called **bankruptcy** for a sole trader.)

It's not always bad

Lots of businesses close without any debts. As long as owners can pay their last bills and taxes, all they have to do is fill in some paperwork and then they're free to move on.

Who loses out?

When *Transaero* had to close, lots of people lost money and even their livelihoods. It took a very long time to sort through the company's finances, and most people were never repaid in full.

Lots of people may depend on a business, so businesses have a responsibility not to take unnecessary risks.

Chapter 4: People in business

Businesses need **people**. Inspiring **leaders** and teams of motivated **employees** can transform a business. A business benefits from a diverse range of skills and experience, which many **managers** keep in mind when they are hiring.

A business is constantly affected by **customers'** decisions about what to buy. And it's the responsibility of a business to protect **consumers** who use its products, as well as the **community** in the local area.

Who's who in business?

It takes many people to run a big business. Here are the different roles involved in a limited company that makes electric bikes.

The **Chief Executive Officer** (CEO), sometimes called a **Managing Director** (MD), is in charge of managing the whole business.

A **Board of Directors** makes long-term decisions about the business. For example, they hire and fire the CEO.

The **staff** is split into different teams, each working in a different area of the business.

Shareholders own a portion of the business, known as shares. The value of their shares increases when the business does well, and decreases when it doesn't. If they sell their shares when the business is doing well, they will make money.

Shareholders elect the Board of Directors at an annual meeting.

EAZY ELECTRIC CYCLES

Managers run a particular team or department.

Managers and staff are **employees**: they work for the business in return for wages.

The CEO and Directors are also paid by the business, but the rules about how this works differ in different countries.

People outside the business – its **customers** and the **community** living nearby – are affected by how well the business is run. See pages 78-81.

How do you lead?

There's a lot to think about if you're in charge. Luana runs a cruise ship business called *Topaz Sailing*. She does all of these things in her role as CEO.

Creates a vision for the future

Luana has a clear, ambitious idea for what the business should be like in five or ten years time.

Inspires people

Luana communicates her vision to her staff and motivates them to make it a reality.

Innovates

She has a flow of creative, exciting ideas that make the business stand out.

Management

Luana organizes projects and staff in a sensible way so the business runs smoothly. She assigns money to different projects, in a plan called a **budget**.

(In some very large businesses, CEOs delegate management to other people, to keep their own minds free for creative and long-term thinking.)

Develops employees

Luana helps staff to gain new skills so they can excel at their jobs.

Makes difficult decisions

To keep the business on track, Luana sometimes has to make herself unpopular.

Leading a micro-business

Leaders of micro-businesses (businesses which employ fewer than 10 people) need to do *all* of the things above. But they may *also* need to do the day-to-day work themselves, from finances, to marketing, to actually making the product.

Diversity

Employing people from different backgrounds is known as **diversity.** Teams can be diverse from the point of view of age, ethnicity, religion, gender, sexuality, disability or level of education. It makes sense for a workforce to include people from **minority groups**, which are groups that can face discrimination. Find out why below.

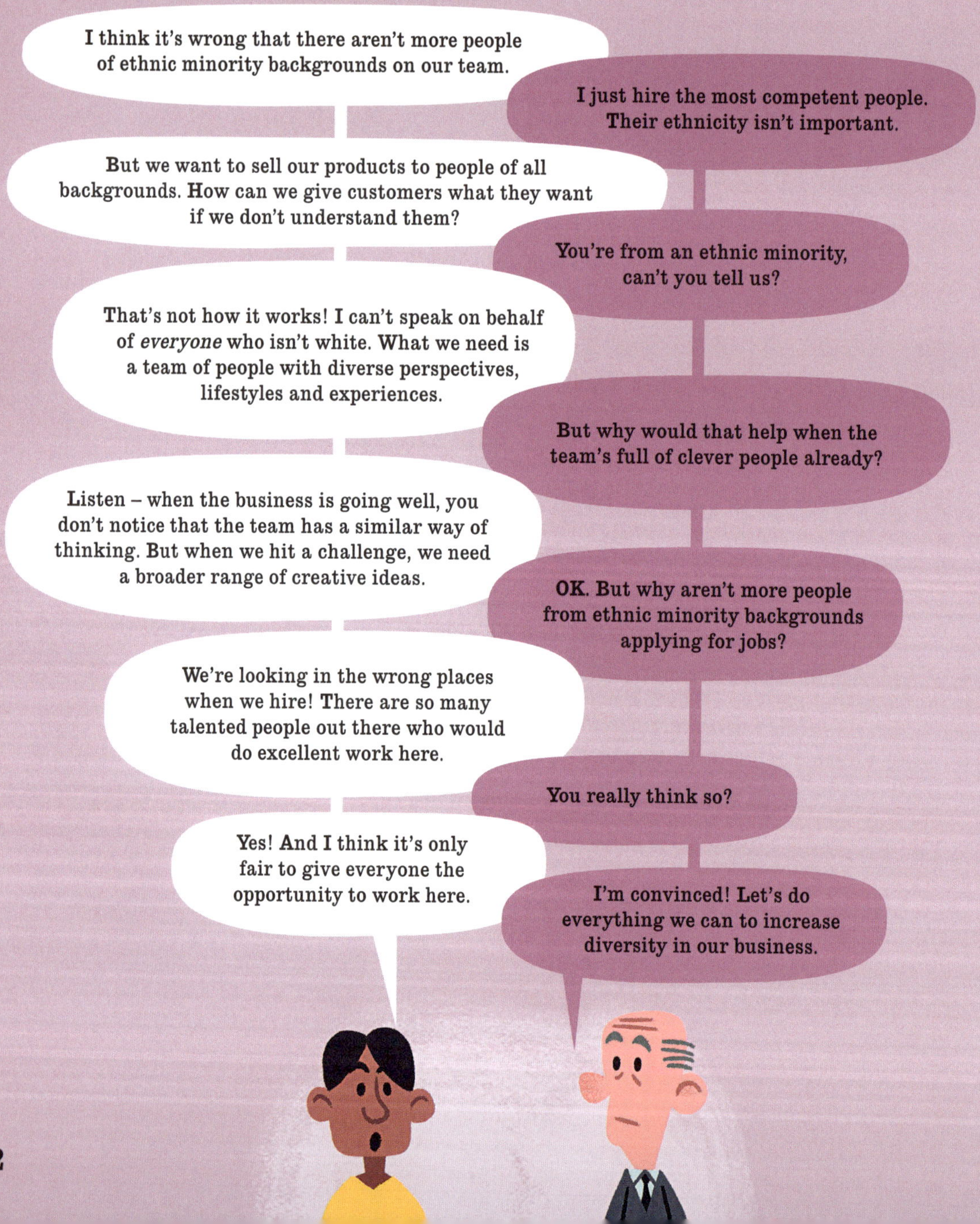

Hiring

When businesses give someone new a job – known as **hiring** – they have to make sure that person is right for the role, and that the process is fair. These are the kinds of steps they go through.

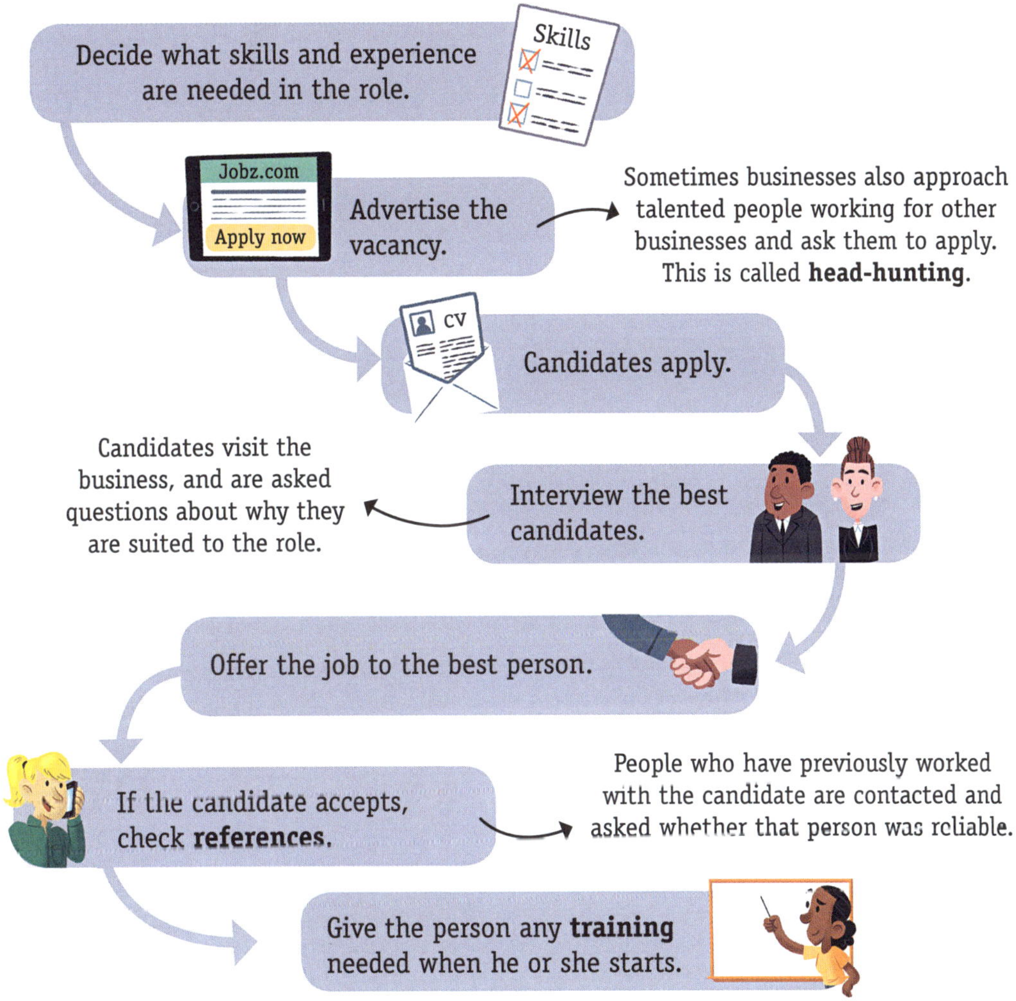

To get the best candidates and hire in a fair way, businesses can do the following:

Advertise jobs on websites and in newspapers which have minority groups as their audience.

Get someone in the business to take people's names and ages off job applications. This stops the person hiring from making assumptions about someone's ability based on their name and age.

Offer paid work placements to help poorer young people get their first step into the business.

Teamwork

Businesses are often structured into teams of employees, who either work in similar roles or on the same project. Working together, people in a team can often achieve more than if they were just getting on with their jobs on their own.

Teams often have a mix of people with different skills and weaknesses.

People improve their ideas by bouncing them around in a team.

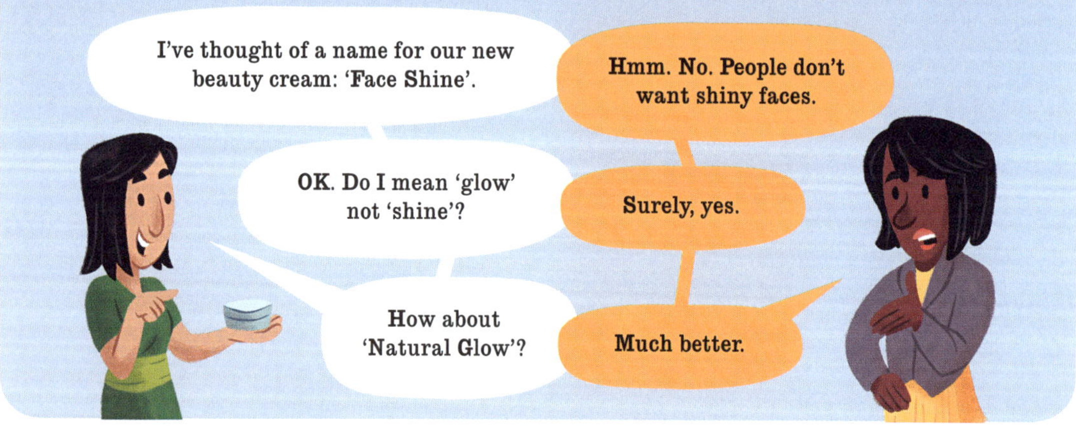

People in a team can support each other.

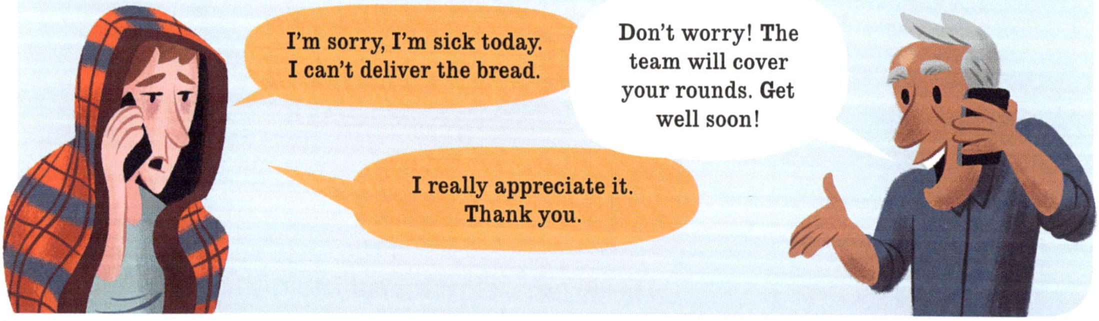

Motivating people

Employees who like their jobs and are committed to the business are usually much more productive. So it's in the interest of managers to keep them happy. Here's one way to approach it.

Step 1: fix bad working conditions

When these conditions are wrong, it demotivates people. But however much you eliminate these kinds of problems, it still won't make people *happy*. It'll just stop them from being *unhappy*.

Step 2: give workers job satisfaction

For workers to be happy, motivated and productive, they need the following:

Good managers aim to achieve as many of these as possible for their staff.

Workers' rights

Business leaders have more power than their employees. This can make employees vulnerable – they can be driven too hard, paid too little or put in danger. To protect them, there are international rules about how to treat workers, known as **workers' rights**.

Everyone has the right...

...to choose whether to work.

People mustn't be forced to work or punished if they don't work.

...to a childhood.

Children mustn't work if it disrupts their education or puts them in danger.

...to fair pay.

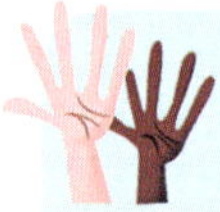

...to be free from discrimination.

For example, a woman or someone from an ethnic minority mustn't be given fewer opportunities than another worker.

...to join a **trade union** (see opposite page).

...to be safe and healthy at work.

...to paid time off every year, known as **paid leave**.

In reality, workers get different rights around the world, depending on the laws in a particular country.

People power

Often workers want better conditions, such as increased pay, more paid time off, or a safer work environment. They have more power if they join together to make their demands to their employer. If the employer refuses, they may go on **strike**...

Organizations called **trade unions** (or labor unions) represent the interests of workers with similar jobs. Trade unions support workers to make their collective demands to their employer, and can help to organize strikes.

In most places, it's illegal for employers to stop workers from joining a trade union. As well as being a legal obligation, it also builds positive relationships within a business if leaders respect union activities.

Consumers and customers

The people *using* the products or services of a business are called **consumers**. They are not always the same as **customers**, who *buy* them. Businesses have very important relationships with both.

Consumers have power. If a baby hates one kind of baby food, the baby's parent won't buy it again. The parent may also influence other customers, for example by writing an online review. This, in turn, will impact on the business's plans.

The best companies don't wait for feedback from consumers. They involve the people who will be buying and using the product as they design it. See page 16, about market research.

Protecting consumers

The law protects consumers from dishonest and careless businesses. There are some things it's illegal to do in most countries.

Sell unsafe products

Sell products that are fakes, such as a fake designer handbag

Deliver services to a poor standard

Advertise dishonestly (see pages 48-49)

In many places, customers have a legal right to return a product and get their money back if it is faulty. This is called a **refund**.

Product recall

If a business realizes it is selling something unsafe, it may ask everyone who bought it to bring it back. This is called **product recall**.

Instead of waiting for an accident to happen, the business can limit the damage to its reputation, and reduce the risk that it will be taken to court by an angry consumer.

Product recall notice

REAL EXAMPLE

Some *Sony* batteries inside *Dell™* notebook computers are at risk of catching fire. If you bought a Dell notebook between April 2004 and July 2006, check the battery model and serial number. Affected batteries will be replaced.

Complaining

Consumers can – and do – complain to businesses when they are disappointed.

But if a business has broken the *law*, consumers can object to the *government*. If many people have been affected, organizations supporting consumers may bring them together to make a joint complaint.

These organizations also give consumers information about their rights, and produce independent reviews of goods and services.

Community impacts

A business impacts the people living around it: the local **community**. This can be positive, bringing money, jobs and services to an area.

The local community benefits from *Blenheim Road Theatre* in multiple ways.

Creating jobs and bringing in new customers to an area are positive impacts that can have a ripple effect:

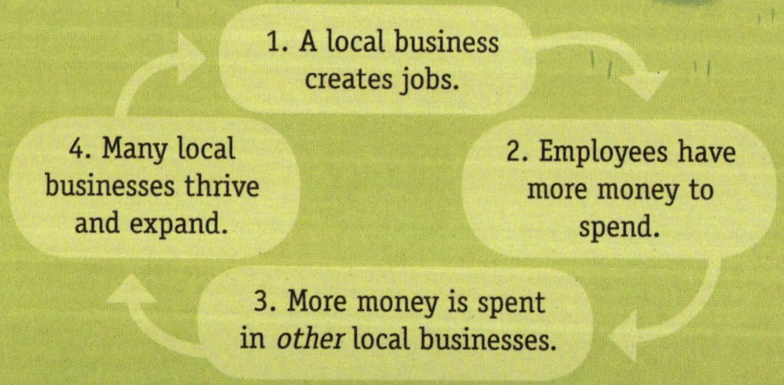

But a business can also have a negative impact on a local community.

It's unethical for business leaders to ignore negative impacts on the local community. It's also shortsighted; a business can be taken to court and forced to pay vast amounts of money to a community for damage it has caused.

Some harmful businesses never even get off the ground. Businesses often need permission from either local or national government to operate, especially for major activities such as drilling for oil. A community can protest against plans, making it less likely for a destructive business to be given permission.

Chapter 5: Making a product

To turn an idea into a **product**, lots of things need to happen. Businesses have to source materials – often from different places around the world. They then need the right people, tools and machines to make the product. Finally, the product has to make its way to somewhere a customer will buy it.

The challenge is to do all that quickly and cheaply, while still creating a product that customers love, and that doesn't cause harm either to people or the environment.

How stuff gets made

The process of creating goods and services is known as **production**. There are lots of ways of making any one thing. So entrepreneurs need to pick the method best suited to their product.

One of a kind

When products are made one by one, it's known as **job production.** It works best for unique, one-off products, where each customer has specific needs.

In batches

Another way to make a product is in groups, or **batches.** It's generally quicker and cheaper than making things individually.

One size fits all

When businesses produce huge quantities of identical goods in a factory with specialized machinery, it's called **mass production.** It's expensive to set up, but once you're up and running, it's a quick and cheap way of making things.

Mass customization

This is a way of producing goods that combines mass production with some element of customization.

How does stuff *really* get made?

Production of day-to-day things often involves complicated, worldwide networks of businesses. This is known as a **supply chain**, and it can make it unclear who is ultimately responsible for making the product, how it gets made and with what materials.

For example, here's how a supply chain works for this pair of shoes:

Here are some reasons why businesses have global supply chains.

Good, low-cost materials

Countries often specialize and become world leaders in making something well and inexpensively.

The cheapest workforce

Businesses can take advantage of lower salaries in some parts of the world.

Don't know, don't care

Global supply chains can bring jobs and money to poorer parts of the world. But they also make it easy for bad working conditions to go unnoticed and unchallenged by big brands and customers.

For example, here are some workers in a factory in Bangladesh:

Vulnerable workers making cheap products for the rest of the world need to be protected. Businesses can help by making sure they know how their products are being made and by whom, and insisting on high standards. Communicating that information then helps consumers buy responsibly.

Making more with less

If a business can make things more **efficiently** – *better, faster* or more *cheaply* than its rivals – it will attract more customers. So businesses are constantly finding ways to improve their production processes.

Lean production

In the 1970s, engineers at *Toyota*, a Japanese carmaker, developed something called **lean production**. This aims to cut costs by reducing different types of waste. Here's what Toyota engineer, Shigeo Shingo, recommended.

REAL EXAMPLE

...waste time

Employees can waste time moving between buildings, looking for tools or materials. Any delays in the process can lead to much bigger delays later on.

So, for example, keeping tools at hand height saves time reaching for them.

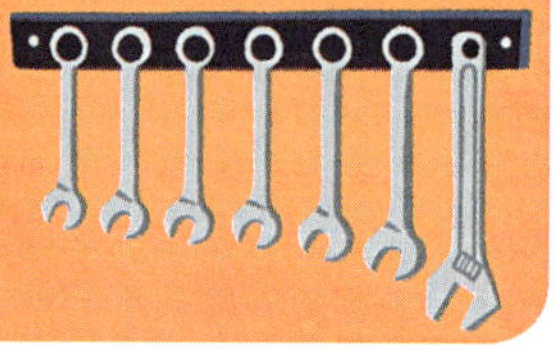

...complicate things

Unless a feature is really important to the consumer, it's not worth adding it. It will create costs without adding extra value.

...overstock

For production to run smoothly, businesses need to have supplies, or **stock**, of materials ready. However, stock costs money to store and maintain.

To minimize the amount of stock, it could be ordered to arrive as it's needed and taken straight to the factory floor.

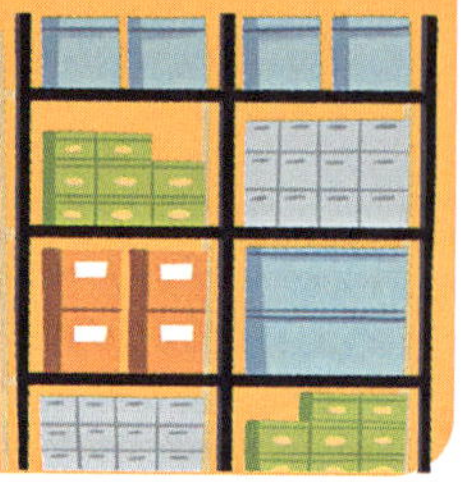

...overproduce

If businesses make things they don't sell, it's a waste of resources and money.

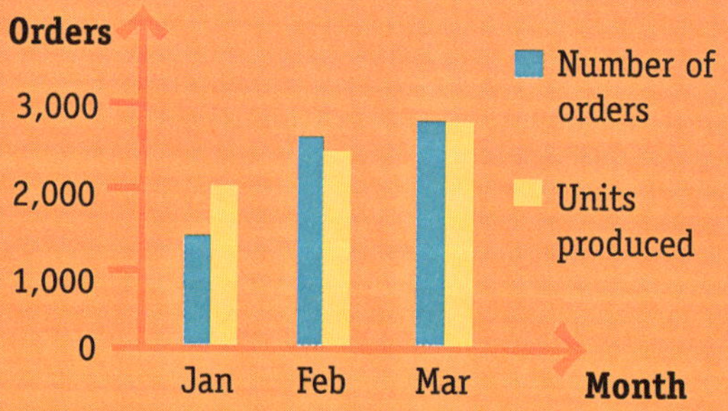

For example, in January this firm overproduced by 500 units. To avoid this, they could wait for customers to place an order before starting production.

Keep improving

If a business stops improving, it's almost inevitable that someone else will come along with a better product or process and win over customers. Providing more training for employees is one way of improving production. Here are some more.

Investing in machinery

Pooling ideas

This system was developed at *Toyota* and is known as **kaizen**, which means 'change for the better' in Japanese.

Learning from the best

Comparing your business to others is known as **benchmarking**.

Quality sells

A **quality** product is one that meets a customer's expectations. If customers love a product, they're more likely to buy it again and recommend it to others. Entrepreneurs value quality, as it helps a product sell itself.

Quality at every step

This internet browser has won lots of loyal customers. Here's why.

SATURN It's the only browser out there!

OVERVIEW | REVIEWS | SUPPORT | RELATED

Easy to access

"Downloading the browser is really straightforward. The instructions are in a big, clear font, and there's an audio version too. I'd recommend it to other internet newbies out there."

Miguel, Canada

Thoroughly tested

"An early version of the browser was released for experienced computer coders. So I was one of the first to test it and point out problems. I loved being involved in the process."

Nina, Germany

Customizable

"It's amazing! You can set the browser up exactly as you want it. If you want a map of the stars and the latest volleyball news on your homepage, you can have it."

Yi Wei, Singapore

Helpful team

"I couldn't work out how to customize the toolbar. I messaged the help team and they got back to me really quickly. They've been trained to be friendly AND helpful. Thumbs up."

Adaeze, Nigeria

Simple to get rid of

"This browser wasn't for me, but at least it was easy to uninstall!"

Iku, Japan

They listen

"I wrote in to complain about download times. Thanks for apologizing and fixing the problem!"

Oliver, Ireland

How much quality?

Quality products cost more to produce. So businesses have to make sure that the customer is willing to pay for it. Sometimes, it makes business sense to sacrifice a little bit of quality to save on price.

Too little

Taste: 5/10
Texture: 4/10
Price: £1.50

Too much

Taste: 9/10
Texture: 9/10
Price: £4.50

Just right

Taste: 8/10
Texture: 7/10
Price: £2.99

Quality products that don't last forever

If a product lasts forever, customers won't ever need to buy a new one. So businesses often produce things they know will eventually look out of date, break or be overtaken by new, better versions. This encourages customers to buy a new product a little sooner than necessary. It's known as **planned obsolescence**.

Production failure

If production isn't properly managed it can have terrible consequences. For example, the Aral Sea in Central Asia has mostly dried up because of intensive cotton production. The lack of water is bad for people, animals and businesses too. Without water it's hard to grow more cotton.

Who's responsible?

It was the decisions of businesses, consumers *and* governments that led to the Aral Sea drying up. Fixing these kinds of problems is tricky, when so many different people and organizations are involved.

The challenge for businesses is to balance satisfying consumers at the same time as producing in a **sustainable** way. That means cutting down on waste and pollution, and using natural resources responsibly. Sustainable production means production that doesn't harm workers or communities.

Sustainable production

One way of producing sustainably is for a business to plan *all* the stages of a product's life cycle right from the start.

For example, here's how this sustainable shampoo from *Lush*, a British cosmetics brand, compares to most other shampoos you can buy:

REAL EXAMPLE

Shampoo in a bottle

Lush shampoo bars

No packaging – so when the shampoo is finished, there's nothing to throw away.

Longer-lasting – the bar can do as many washes as three shampoo bottles.

Smaller – so fewer trucks are needed to transport it, which means less pollution.

More expensive – each bar costs more to make than the average bottle, so it sells at a higher price.

Chapter 6: Growing the business

At the beginning, all a business needs to do is survive. But if it all goes well, it should start making a profit. The next step can be to use that profit to **grow** and make more money. Usually this means growing in every way: hiring more staff, making more things and moving to bigger offices.

Growing is risky as it can cost a lot, but being bigger has lots of advantages, such as getting better deals from suppliers and the power to set prices. And ultimately, bigger businesses tend to make the greatest profits.

Bigger is better

If your business is doing well, it can be tempting to change nothing and keep it the same size. But this means missing out on some of the advantages of being bigger...

It's often cheaper for a big business to do something than a small business. This is known as an **economy of scale.** So bigger businesses can set lower prices but still make a profit.

How to grow

Businesses can grow by producing more of the same thing or selling new products. This is known as growing **horizontally.** Or they can expand into *another* area of their supply chain, called growing **vertically.** To do this they may need more staff, a bigger building or more machinery – all of which cost money.

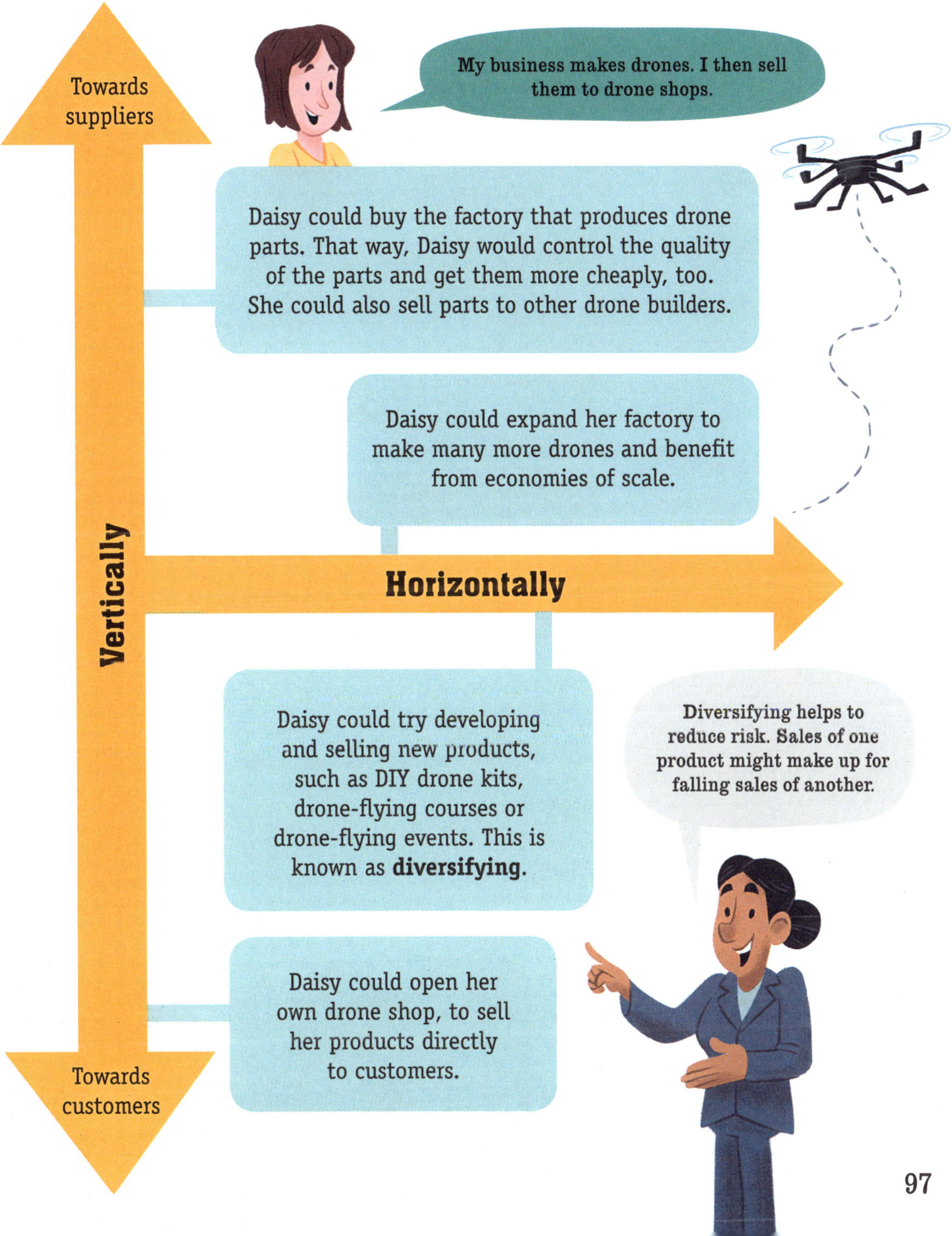

Catching a unicorn

Some new businesses grow extremely fast, reaching a value of a billion dollars in just a couple of years. These kinds of businesses are so rare that they are known as **unicorns**.

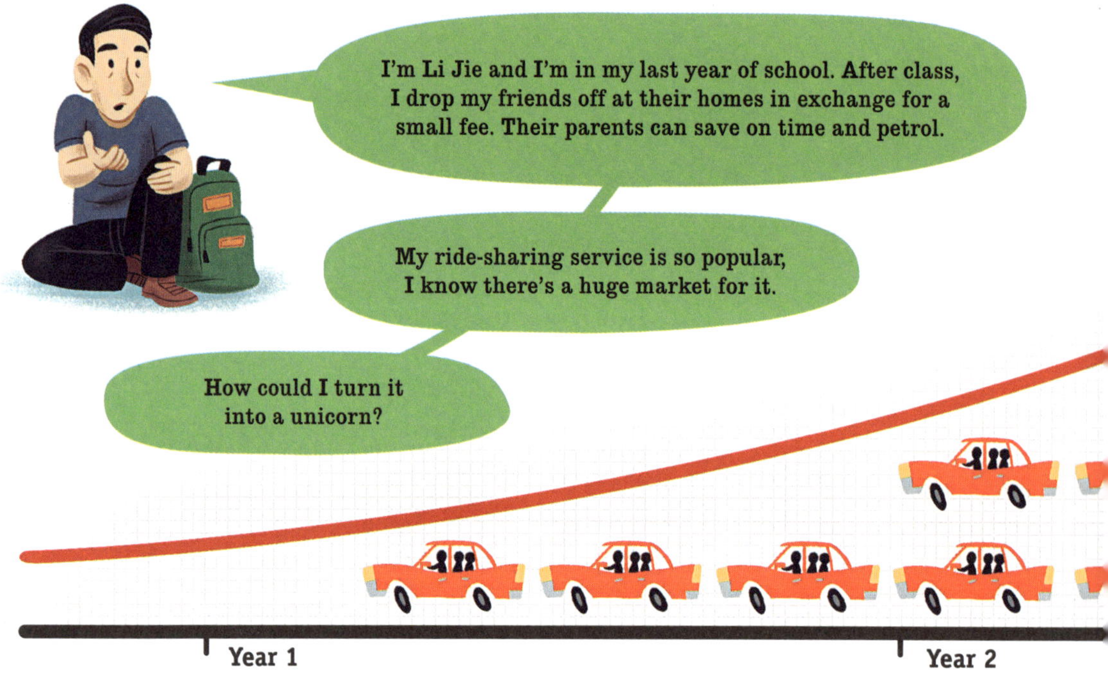

Technology

Businesses that take advantage of new technologies can reach lots of customers quickly.

Get funding

The more money you raise from investors, the lower you can push your prices. This helps win over customers and pushes competitors out of the market.

Two years later, Li Jie's company has become a unicorn. It's been valued at $1 billion.

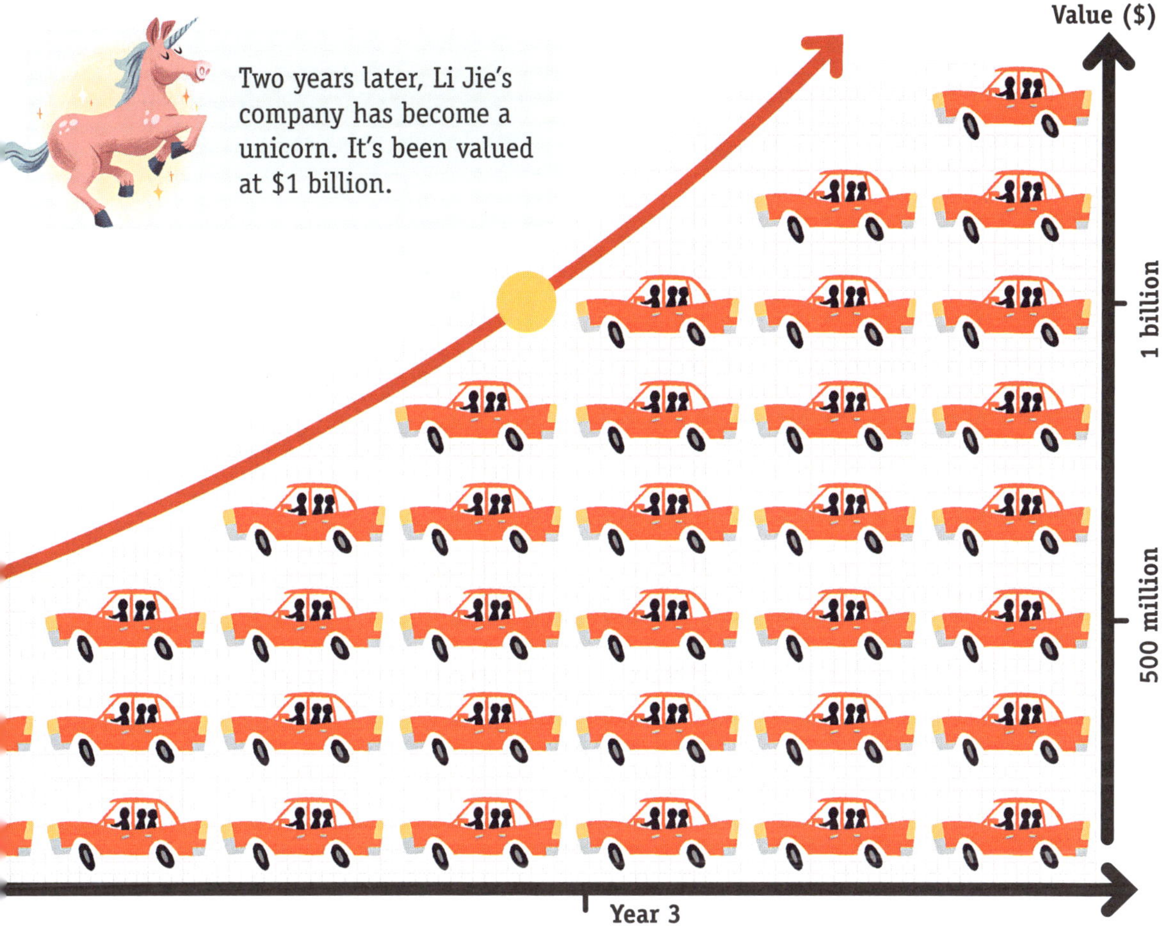

Buy

A quick way to get lots more customers is to buy part of or all of a competitor's company.

Keep innovating

Even the most successful businesses need to keep evolving to stay on top of the competition.

Selling abroad

Selling to other countries is a good way of growing and reaching new customers. But what works in one place might not work elsewhere. To get it right, businesses need to research the new market. Will customers like the product? Where will they find it? Is it affordable?

For example, this book was written in the UK but is sold all around the world, sometimes in English but often in other languages. Here are some of the things the writers, designers and sales team had to think about:

To have the best chance of success, a product needs to be tested on customers of the intended country and adapted accordingly.

Sometimes a product just won't work in another country. People may not want it if competitors in that country are already just as good.

Getting it there

It often takes a lot of time, money and paperwork to get products out of one country and into another. So after taking all those things into account, businesses need to decide if it's still worthwhile.

Some governments might choose to make this process easier or harder on purpose, to encourage or discourage foreign businesses from selling in their country.

Floating the business

Businesses need to spend money in order to grow. One way to raise a *lot* of money is to allow anyone to buy shares in the business. This is known as **going public** or **floating on the stock market**. Once someone buys a share, they are called a **shareholder**.

Stock exchanges

Shares are sold to the public through marketplaces called **stock exchanges** ('stocks' has a similar meaning to 'shares').

After buying shares in one business, a shareholder can later sell them on the stock exchange and buy shares in a different business.

This map shows the biggest stock exchanges around the world.

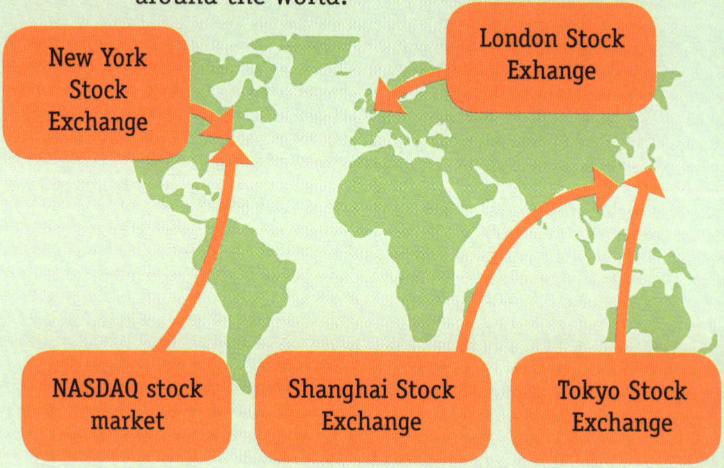

Publicly owned businesses must have limited liability (see page 27). After going public, the business is called a **public company**, **public limited company** or **corporation**. Most of the world's biggest businesses have publicly owned shares:

But floating in itself doesn't *make* a business huge. A business has to reach a decent size and stability before many people will *want* to buy shares.

To float or not to float?

Once a business goes public, it must share more information about itself. These are some of the things that it has to do.

- Reveal any plans to be taken over by another business.
- Announce new product launches in advance.
- Report profits or losses several times a year.

It can help a business's competitors to know this information, which is a downside of being publicly owned. So even very large businesses may choose not to float.

What's the business worth?

When a business goes public, anyone can check its **share price** on the internet. If lots of people want to buy shares in the business, the price goes up. It goes down if lots of people want to sell their shares.

Share price is used as a signal of how well a company is doing. When share prices go up, it's good for the business.

Good publicity 

Easier to attract private investors 

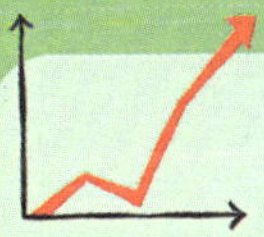 Increased public profile, which can lead to increased product sales

 Easier to get loans from banks

But if share prices drop, the opposite is true.

Shareholders don't like it when share prices fall. If they are very unhappy, they can use their power to demand a change of management. So it becomes a priority for managers to keep shareholders happy.

Scandal

If a business is hit by scandal, share prices often fall. For example, when news broke in 2018 that *Facebook* users' data had been sold, *Facebook* share prices plummeted. Then *Facebook* had to deal with the reputational damage from *both* the scandal *and* the fall in share price.

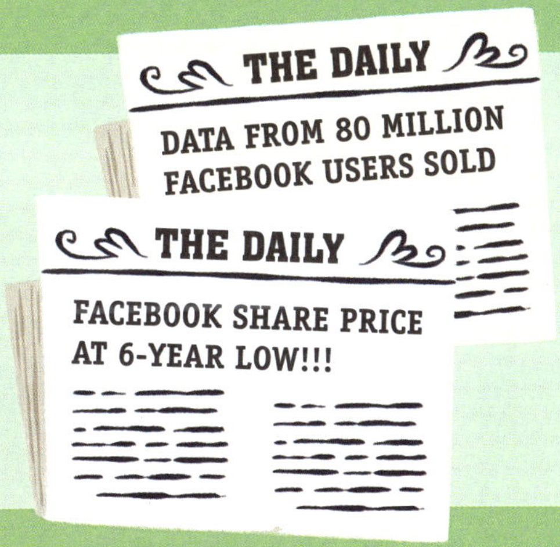

Too big to run?

There are disadvantages to being bigger, too. Eventually the size of a company makes it harder to keep track of everything. For example, here are some of the problems.

It's difficult to communicate effectively with thousands of employees.

When a company gets bigger it's harder to control waste.

People can feel unappreciated and isolated when they work for a huge company, so they become less productive.

Coordinating hundreds of suppliers is tricky too.

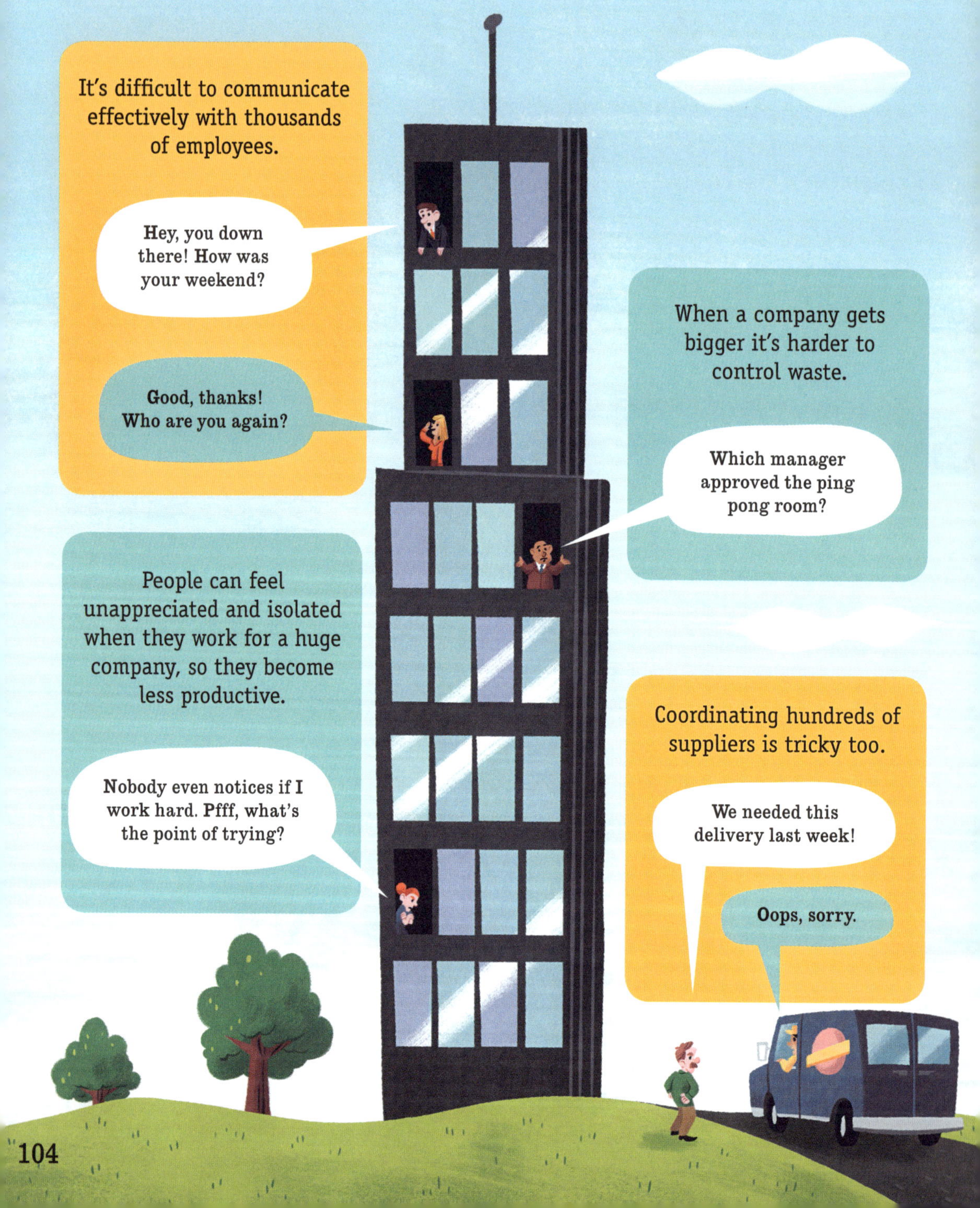

Too big to be fair?

A company can grow so big that it becomes the *only* supplier of a product. This is known as a **monopoly**. The problem with monopolies is the amount of power they have. For example, a milk distribution monopoly could decide to charge high prices to all customers. They could also pay dairy farmers a very low price.

So most governments make laws against monopolies being formed.

Is growth worth it?

Growing a business takes money, time and effort. So entrepreneurs need to weigh up whether the extra money or satisfaction they expect is worth it.

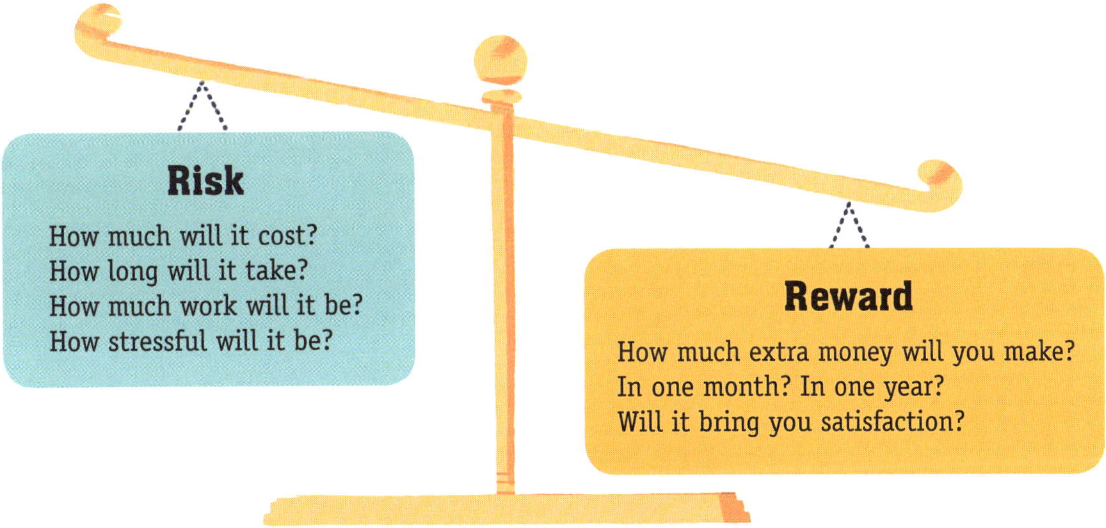

Some entrepreneurs don't want to change their lifestyle, so they decide not to grow their business – and that's ok too.

Too big to fail

When a company is *really big*, lots of people, and even other businesses, depend on it for jobs and revenue. So if the company looks as if it's about to fail, the government might decide to lend it money to prevent jobs from being lost and other businesses from failing too.

Banking crisis

In 2008, lots of American and European banks looked as if they were about to collapse after taking huge risks and losing lots of money. Several national governments decided to step in to prevent a spiral.

REAL EXAMPLE

Many people protested against the decision to save the banks with public money.

Was it worth it?

Banks – and customers' accounts – were saved, but many countries still went into **recession** – a period when businesses sell less, lots of people are out of work and the country as a whole is poorer. Many people think it would have been even worse if the government had done nothing.

To try to prevent a banking crisis from happening again, governments have made banking rules stricter, to stop reckless risk-taking.

Chapter 7: The bigger picture

By now, you'll know lots about how businesses work. But the chances of a business being successful may depend on many things you can't control: the **economy**, the **government**, even the weather.

This chapter explores some of those factors and how businesses can adapt to them.

How easy is it to do business?

Setting up and doing business is different in every country. In some places it takes longer to get things done. In others it might cost more – and sometimes it's not even possible to do business freely at all.

Here are some of the things that make doing business *easier*.

Infrastructure

Things such as roads, electric cables and schools are together known as **infrastructure.** Without them, businesses couldn't distribute products around a country, connect to the internet or employ skilled workers. Usually, infrastructure is taken care of by government and paid for by taxes (see page 58).

Property rights

If businesses don't have the right to own stuff, usually called **property rights**, it's difficult for them to compete fairly. This includes their goods but also their ideas.

Most countries have laws to stop inventions and ideas from being stolen, copied or sold without permission.

Here are some of the things that make doing business *harder*.

Corruption

Business people and politicians sometimes act dishonestly in order to gain power or money for themselves. This is called **corruption**. It gives an unfair advantage to some businesses over others, so governments make rules to stamp it out. Corruption can take many forms. Here are just a few.

Using threats or violence against a business, for example to shut a competitor down, is called **extortion**.

Asking for money in exchange for special treatment, such as processing an application quickly, is called **bribery**.

When a government official is also a business person, this creates something called a **conflict of interest**.

Red tape

Government rules can stop businesses from cheating customers. But excessive rules and regulations slow businesses down – because it makes them spend so much time filling out forms and getting permissions. This is known as **red tape**.

The role of government

In many countries, businesses don't have to worry about simple things such as infrastructure or property rights. That's because the government is working behind the scenes to make doing business *easier*. But sometimes the government can actually make doing business *harder*, by insisting on red tape.

The government's attitude to business – whether they tend to help or hinder – can affect how some people decide to vote in an election.

Supply and demand

Businesses thrive or fail based on their ability to make money. How much a business sells depends on how much it makes available to customers (**supply**) and how much customers are willing to buy (**demand**). In turn, supply and demand affect prices, like this.

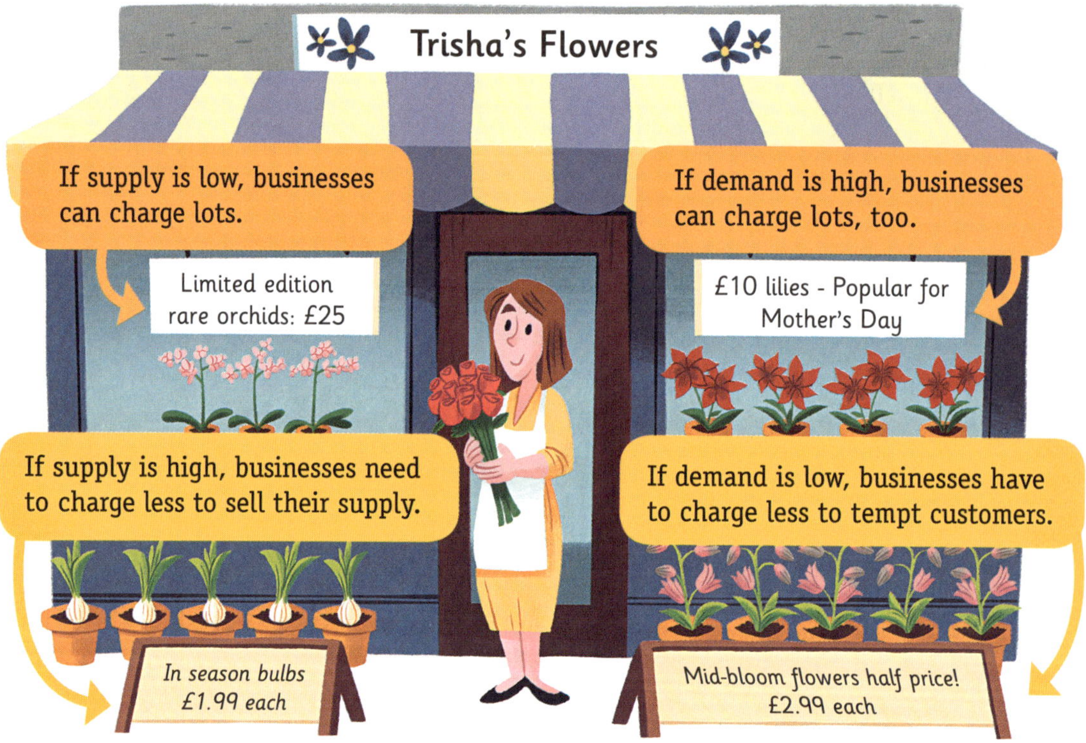

Managing supply and demand is tricky, because lots of things are constantly affecting them. Here are some examples Trisha has to deal with.

Weather
Frost can kill flowers, reducing the supply.

I always try to predict changes to supply and demand. I constantly adjust what I stock and how much I charge for everything.

Trends
There is increased demand for flowers that are in fashion, for example if a celebrity is pictured with them.

Competition
When a competitor lowers their prices, Trisha's become more expensive in comparison. So demand for her flowers goes down.

Price of fuel
If fuel gets more expensive, Trisha has to raise the price of delivery. This in turn reduces demand.

Strong and weak economies

The **economy** of a country is made up of all the things people make, sell and buy from each other. Whether the economy is doing well or doing badly has a big effect on supply and demand for any individual business, too.

Recession

If the economy does badly for more than six months, it's known as a **recession**. Not every business will do badly – supermarkets selling at cheap prices might even do better. Governments and national banks try to prevent recessions, and bring countries out of recession.

Fixing business

A community can be home to bad businesses. In some cases, the problem sorts itself out:

A fall in demand sends a signal to a business, which can encourage them to improve. But often it's not that simple – and the government might need to intervene.

If a problem doesn't affect the consumers of a product, demand and supply can't fix it. This is known as **market failure**. So the government has to step in. For example, they might force a nightclub to move away from people's homes.

Sometimes the government steps in to encourage businesses to produce things that are *good* for consumers or society.

Government toolkit

Pollution is another example of market failure. Suppliers and consumers of goods and services that cause pollution don't suffer individually – but society does. As well as setting laws, here are some of the tools governments can use to tackle it.

Tax incentives

Governments can put a tax on cars that use lots of petrol. By making them more expensive, it discourages people from buying those cars.

On the other hand, by reducing taxes on electric cars, the government can encourage people to switch to less polluting cars.

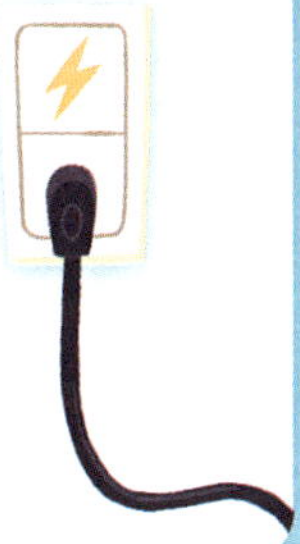

Ownership

Nobody 'owns' rivers, so people don't always take care of them.

The government can give an institution, such as an environment agency, the power to act 'as if' it owns the rivers. This means it's *their* responsibility to police rivers and fine polluters.

Information

Consumers don't always have enough information to know which products cause more harm than others.

To help, a government can force producers to put more information on a product label, such as the distance the product has travelled.

Worldwide agreements

Pollution is a worldwide problem – it doesn't stop at a country's border. What's more, polluting businesses sometimes operate in more than one country. So to tackle the problem, governments from around the world have to work together – but it's not always easy to agree.

The cost of money

Businesses and consumers often need to borrow money from banks. They have to *pay* to borrow money, because banks are businesses too, and money-lending is one of their services. The price to borrow money is called **interest**. The amount of interest is called the **interest rate** – and, just like other prices, it changes all the time.

Citybank agrees to lend the business £100,000, at a current interest rate of 10%.

10% of £100,000 is £10,000

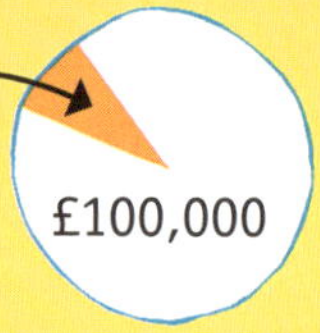

So *Diamond & Sons* will have to repay £100,000 plus an extra £10,000, which is **£110,000**.

The business has decided to repay the amount in chunks of £1,000 per month.

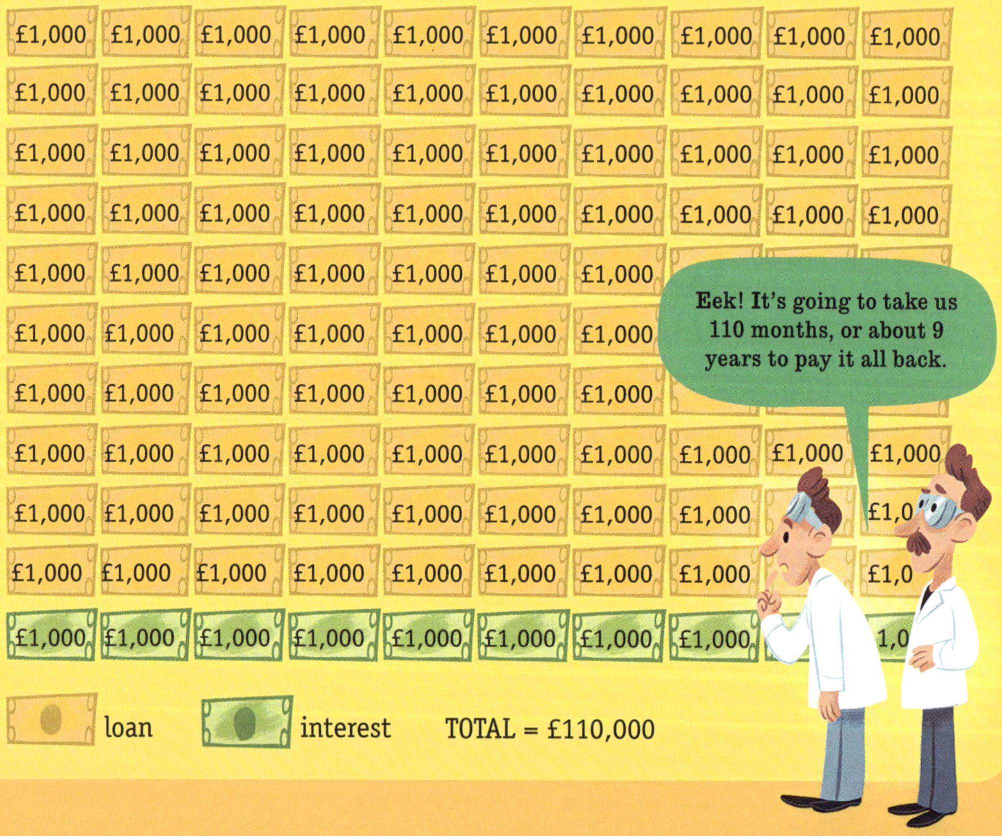

loan   interest   TOTAL = £110,000

When interest rates change

In many countries, a national or central bank is in charge of the central interest rate. It's typical for the bank to raise or lower the rate a few times each year. Other banks who have borrowed from the central bank usually adjust their rates, too.

Businesses

Consumers

Consumers also borrow from banks to buy big things, such as houses or cars. So when interest rates rise, their repayments go up. To save money, they might have to cut back on expensive or non-essential things...

So, businesses selling luxuries can lose customers when interest rates go up.

Governments and central banks don't change interest rates just for fun. They are trying to keep a good economy strong, or to recover from a weak economy (see page 113).

It's a good idea for all businesses to follow the news about anything that will affect them in the near future, especially changes to interest rates.

The power of technology

Breakthroughs in science lead to new technologies, then new products and even new ways of doing business. Here's an example.

DNA and data

DNA is a part of your body that contains a coded 'instruction manual' for how your body builds itself. Scientists have found cheap ways of reading an individual's DNA code, which has created all sorts of business opportunities...

REAL EXAMPLES

DNAFit

This business promises to improve customers' diet and fitness based on their DNA profile.

AncestryDNA

This business reveals customers' unknown relatives, and where distant ancestors came from, just by looking at their DNA.

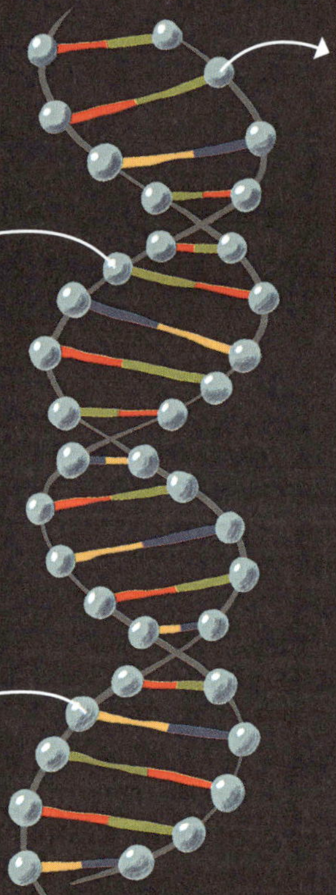

23andMe

By analysing their customers' DNA, this business can warn them if they are at risk of some particular diseases.

With permission from their customers, these businesses can share their findings with DNA researchers. This could lead to more scientific breakthroughs, and more business opportunities.

Technology challenges

New technology often presents big questions for society. For instance, if the technology exists, should parents be allowed to change their child's DNA to make them more intelligent or beautiful?

Rise of the machines

When machines do tasks that humans used to do, or that humans can't do, it's known as **automation**. Businesses that invest in automation can often employ fewer people and lower their costs. That's because unlike employees, machines don't need salaries, time off or pensions.

This pizza business has automated its production process to make it...

As a result, human employees lost their jobs. When this happens, businesses and governments need to help people retrain and find a new job.

But automation doesn't just destroy jobs, it can create them too.

And often machines only take on *certain tasks* rather than *whole jobs.*

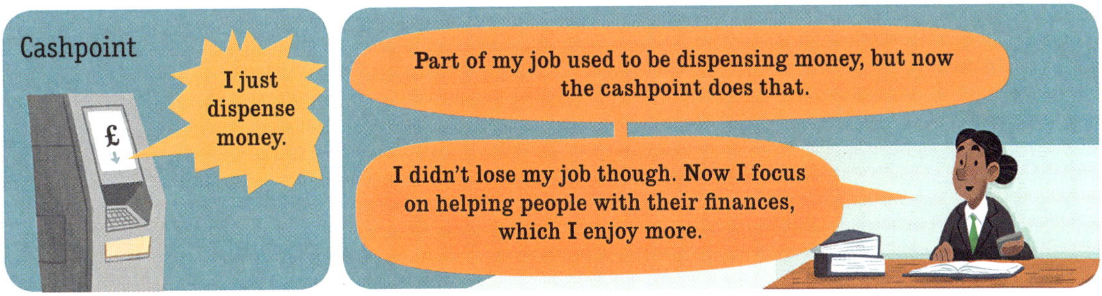

Nobody knows for sure if increased automation technology will lead to fewer jobs overall. Currently people are still better than machines at all sorts of things – from writing a song, defending a victim in a court of law or building personal relations with customers, to fiddly jobs such as stacking books onto a shelf.

What now?

By now, you will understand what a business is, and how businesses fit into the world.

You may be a more shrewd customer, able to spot clever tricks that businesses use.

You might have ideas about how to encourage businesses to be more ethical.

You will have the basic information you need to start your own business, if that's what you want to do. If you are feeling nervous, remember these things:

You don't need to have any particular personality to run a business. You only need to *want* to run a business.

You don't need to know *everything* about running a business before you start, and you don't need any formal qualifications.

You can use things you've learned from being a customer. Copy things that you liked, and avoid anything that put you off.

You don't have to take huge risks. You can start modestly, test your ideas and plan realistically.

It doesn't matter if the first business you try doesn't work out. You can learn from what went wrong. Remember Thomas Edison, from page 62?

If you want to start your own business, you could start with some of these activities:

Join a scheme that offers support and training to young people interested in business. These are often called Young Enterprise Schemes or Business Achievement Programs. Ask if there is one at your school or college, or search online for one in your local area or region.

Look for bargains in second-hand shops, then try selling them on for a profit.

Make something simple and sell it. It could be keyrings, or earrings – or anything!

Sell to your friends and family.

Rent a stall at a market.

Open a shop on an online marketplace such as *eBay* or *Etsy*.

Get to know local business people and chat to them about how they run their businesses.

Read the business section of newspapers, to learn more about why some businesses work and some don't.

Glossary

This glossary explains some of the words used in this book. Words written in *italic* type are explained in other entries.

accountant a professional that businesses pay to check the accuracy of their *accounts*.
accounts records of a business's *costs* and *revenues*.
advertising telling people about a product, for example on TV or a poster. Usually the business pays for this type of *promotion*.

bankruptcy when a person is unable to pay their debts, and his or her possessions are sold off to pay back *creditors*.
Board of Directors a team of experienced people who oversee the running of a business and *hire* and *fire* the *CEO*.
brand the identity of a business, displayed through everything from its name to its packaging materials.
business plan a document that describes a business in detail, usually with the aim of raising money from *investors*.

cash flow money that goes in and out of a business regularly.
CEO short for Chief Executive Officer, the most senior person in charge of running the business day-to-day. Sometimes called an MD, or Managing Director.
competition a rival business that might attract *customers* away from you.
consumer a person who uses *goods* or *services* – not always the same as a *customer*.
costs money a business spends before it can sell a *good* or *service*.
creditor a person or business that *loans* money to another business.
customer anyone who buys a *product*, even if they don't use it themselves.

data information, especially about people and the things they spend money on. Some businesses provide *services* in exchange for data rather than money.
diversity a range of different backgrounds and perspectives.

efficiency making a high quality product quickly and cheaply.
employee someone who works for a business, but is not in charge.
entrepreneur someone who runs their own business, or is starting up their own business.
ethical business any business that puts time and money into protecting the local community or environment.
exporting sending goods or services to another country to sell them.

firing when a *manager* tells an *employee* that they can't work for that business any longer.
franchise a new business that pays an existing business to use their business model.
funding money needed to start or grow a business.

good a physical thing that a business makes and/or sells.
grant money given to a business that doesn't have to be paid back.
growth when a business gets bigger, for example *producing* more and employing more people.

hiring when a business employs someone new.

importing bringing *goods* from another country to sell in your own country.
interest extra money you have to pay back to someone you have borrowed money from.
interest rate the proportion of a *loan* that is charged as *interest*.
investing putting money into a business, hoping to make a *profit* later.
investor a person, business or organization that invests in a business.

liability the responsibility a business has to pay back any money it owes to its *creditors*.
limited liability only the business is responsible for paying back money, not its owners.
unlimited liability the business owners are personally responsible for paying back any money it owes.
liquidation selling off the possessions of a failed business, in order to pay back *creditors*.
loan money given to a business that has to be paid back.

manager an *employee* within a business who is in charge of other employees.
market the potential *customers* that may buy a business's *products*.
market research finding out what your *market* actually wants or doesn't want.
marketing ways that a business persuades people to buy its products, for example through clever *pricing* and *promotion*.
markup the price increase when a business buys a *product* at one price, but sells it for a higher price.
MD see *CEO*
micro-business a very small business, with fewer than ten *employees*.
monopoly when a business is the only provider of a *good* or *service*.

PR when a business influences what the public hears about it, for example by getting coverage on TV. Short for 'public relations'.

pricing deciding what a *product* should cost.
product anything a business sells, whether it's a *good* or a *service*.
production the process of making *goods* and *services* to sell.
profit any money left over after a business subtracts its *costs* from its *revenue*.
promotion publicizing a business's *products* to encourage people to buy them.
public services things such as roads, provided for everybody by a government, and not by a business.

retailer a business that sells *goods* to *consumers*, for example a grocery store.
revenue money that a business receives from selling its *products*.

service an activity that people pay a business to do, such as cleaning.
shareholder someone who owns *shares* in a business, and can receive a portion of any *profits*.
shares parts of the business that are owned by different people.
sole proprietor a person who is the only owner of a business and can keep any *profits* but is *liable* for any losses.
startup a new business, including a business that may not have begun selling anything yet.
supply chain the set of businesses that one business relies on to produce *goods* and *services*.
sustainability when a business or group of businesses ensures that their *production* methods do not harm the environment.

taxes money that individuals and businesses pay to the government, to be spent on *public services*.
trade union an organization that supports *employees* to demand better working conditions from their employer.
unicorn a *startup* with a value of more than one billion dollars.

wholesaler a business that sells large amounts of *goods*, usually to a *retailer*.
workers' rights rules about how *employees* should be treated, including the right to form a *trade union*.

Index

Usborne Quicklinks

For links to websites where you can find out more about how business works, with videos and activities, and tips on how to start your own business, go to the Usborne Quicklinks website at

www.usborne.com/quicklinks

and type in the title of this book. Please follow the internet safety guidelines at the Usborne Quicklinks website.

Here are some of the things you can do at Usborne Quicklinks:

- Play games and quizzes to test your business skills
- Meet young entrepreneurs who have started their own businesses
- Take a virtual tour of a factory
- See inside the New York Stock Exchange in the USA

Acknowledgements

Written by
Lara Bryan & Rose Hall

Illustrated by
Kellan Stover

Edited by
Alex Frith

Series editor: Jane Chisholm

Designed by Jamie Ball
& Freya Harrison

Series designer:
Stephen Moncrieff

Business experts:
Wilson Turkington &
Bryony Henry

Apart from those businesses described as 'real example', all the business ideas and names in this book have been made up by the authors. Any similarities to actual businesses are purely coincidental, and no one associated with this book has received any payment or anything of value to endorse a product or business.

First published in 2018 by Usborne Publishing Ltd., Usborne House,
83–85 Saffron Hill, London, EC1N 8RT, United Kingdom.
www.usborne.com

USBORNE

PHILOSOPHY

FOR BEGINNERS

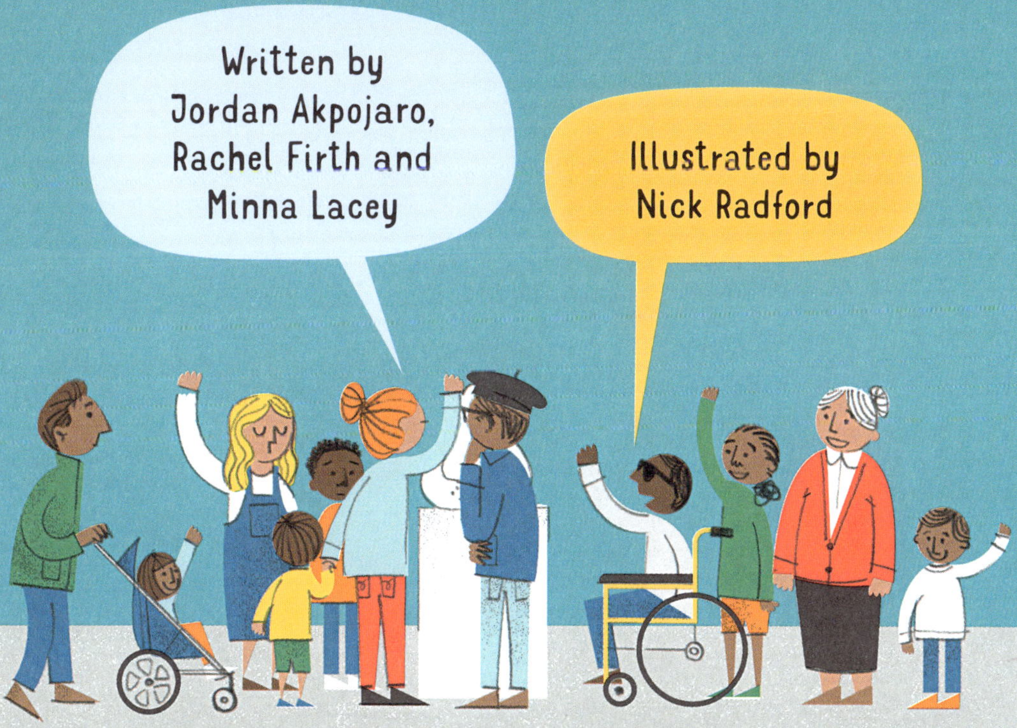

Consultant philosopher: Dr. Alex Kaiserman
Designed by Freya Harrison

CONTENTS

USBORNE QUICKLINKS

For links to websites where you can find out more about philosophy, famous philosophers including Socrates and Plato, and start thinking like a philosopher with videos, games and activities, go to **usborne.com/Quicklinks** and type in the title of this book.

Please follow the internet safety guidelines at the Usborne Quicklinks website. Children should be supervised online.

WHAT IS PHILOSOPHY?

Philosophy is a way of thinking about things – from what the world around us is like, to what beauty is, to the existence of God. These are BIG subjects, and to get to the bottom of them, philosophers ask BIG questions.

But philosophy isn't just for philosophers. Chances are you've asked some of these questions yourself...

Some of these questions may seem like science fiction, but others can and do affect us in our day-to-day lives. This can mean anything from how we behave, to the way governments operate, to the laws we live by.

A WORLD OF PHILOSOPHY

Philosophy covers so many different questions that it's usually broken down into different branches. Here are just some of them, and a few examples of questions they deal with.

EPISTEMOLOGY (KNOWLEDGE)

- What is knowledge and how do we acquire it?
- How can we be sure that our beliefs about the world are true? And if we can't, does it matter?

METAPHYSICS (REALITY, TIME, AND WHO WE ARE)

- Can a cause happen after its effect?
- How much can something change over time, and still be considered to be the same thing?

RELIGION

- Does God exist, and is it possible to prove it?
- If God is good and created everything, how come there's evil?

MIND

- Are we free to make our own choices?
- What does it mean to say that someone has consciousness?

ETHICS (ALSO CALLED MORAL THEORY)

- What is the morally right thing to do?
- Why should we care about the environment?
- Is *anything* right or wrong regardless of what we believe?
- If I don't have free will, can I be responsible for what I do?

AESTHETICS (BEAUTY AND ART)

- What is beauty?
- What is art?

POLITICAL THEORY

- What is freedom?
- What's the best sort of government?
- Is it acceptable for people to own things?

LOGIC AND LANGUAGE

- Can any sentences be both true and false?
- Is it possible to have a language that can only be understood by one person?

DOING PHILOSOPHY

Philosophers question EVERYTHING and ANYTHING. They question ideas and concepts, theories and arguments. They even question the questions that they and other philosophers ask...

The question and answer approach to philosophy has its origins thousands of years ago, in Ancient Greece. It's sometimes known as the **Socratic Method**, after the philosopher Socrates, who was famous for using it. In fact, the word 'philosophy' itself comes from an Ancient Greek word, meaning 'love of wisdom'. Here are two tips on how to do it well.

* say *sock-rat-ease*

HOW TO ARGUE

It's not enough to ask any old question when you're doing philosophy, you need to know how to argue properly. In particular, it's useful to know how to spot different ways an argument can be *true* or *false*.

Arguments are the key tools of philosophy. They're made up of two components: a **premise** and a **conclusion**.

PREMISE

A **premise** is a statement that can either be true or false.

CONCLUSION

A **conclusion** is a statement that's meant to follow from one or more premises.

If an argument is a good one, its premises give you good reasons to believe its conclusion. Here are some examples of arguments. Not all of them are good ones:

	PREMISE 1	PREMISE 2	CONCLUSION
A	All footballs are round.	This is a football. Therefore...	This football is round. 
B	All people with brown hair have brown eyes.	This person has brown hair. Therefore...	This person has brown eyes. 
C	All cats are animals.	My pet rat is an animal. Therefore...	My pet rat is a cat. 

Philosophers examine arguments using a system of rules known as **logic**. If a premise is true, and the conclusion makes sense as a result of that premise, then it's a good argument. Now, you might have noticed that there is something wrong with arguments B and C. They're both *bad* arguments – for two different reasons.

B is a bad argument because one of the premises – premise 1 – is false.

Once you realize that premise 1 is false, you have no reason to believe the conclusion. When an argument fails in this way, it's said to be **unsound**.

C is a bad argument because the conclusion doesn't follow from the premises.

When an argument fails for this reason, it's said to be **invalid**.

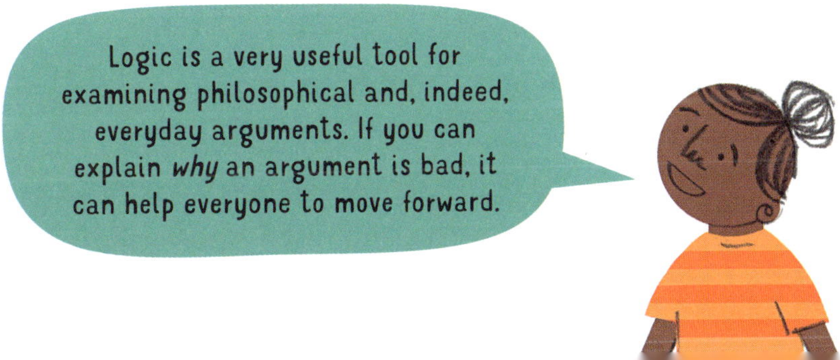

THOUGHT EXPERIMENTS

Another one of philosophy's key tools is known as a **thought experiment.** This is a 'what if' question that sparks a series of further questions. Be warned, thought experiments can get you to imagine some very bizarre situations.

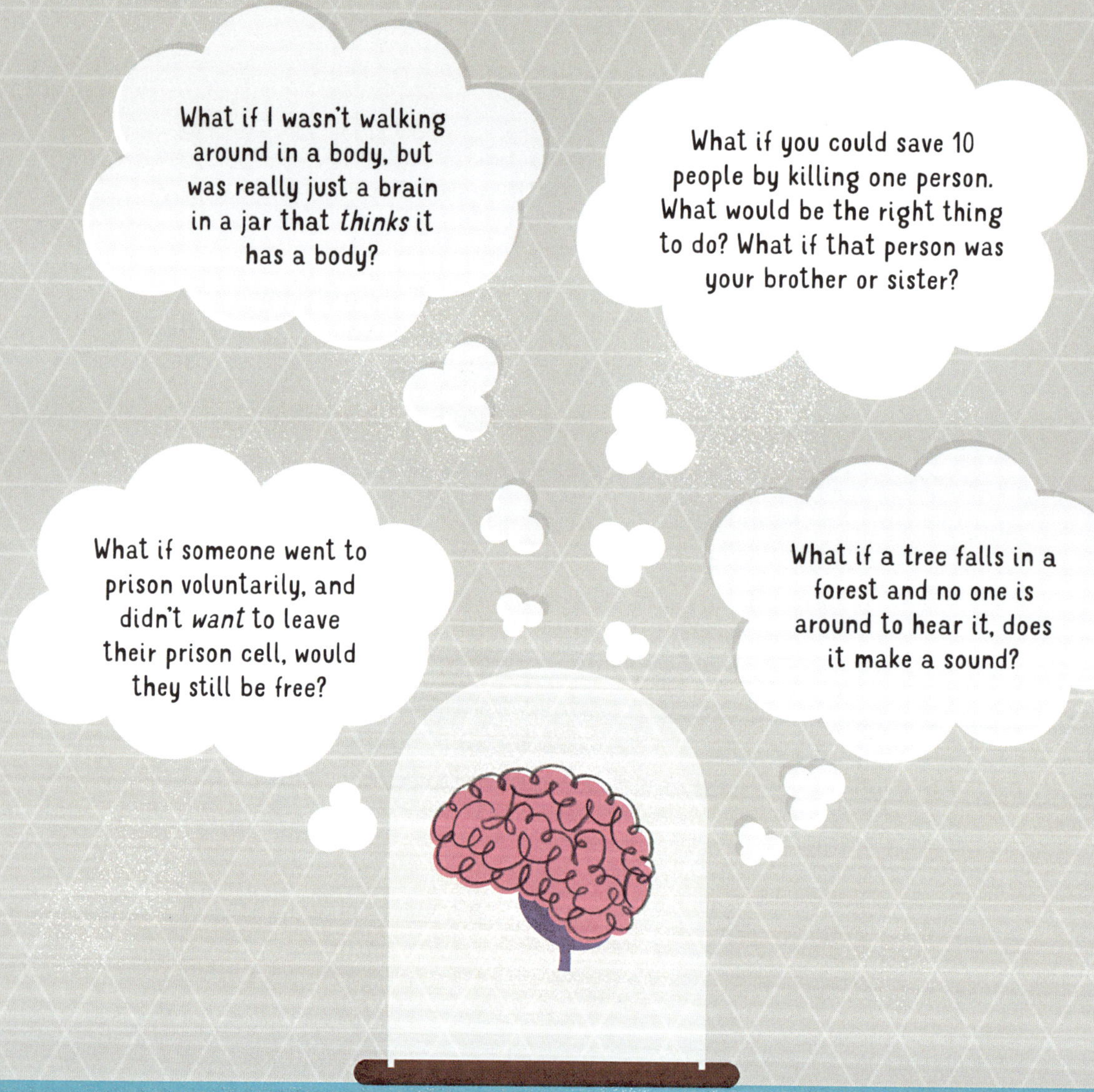

A good thought experiment should lead you onto a path of questions and answers that often challenge your first response to each experiment. The scenarios they describe don't have to be likely, or even physically possible, but they *do* have to make sense. It's no good asking someone to imagine a square circle, for example.

Here's a thought experiment that makes us question our ideas about identity.

You say you've had this teddy bear for a long time. What makes you think it's the same as the one you were given as a baby?

Well it looks the same... it has all the same parts.

Ok, but what if, as time went by, the parts of the original bear wore out. And imagine that, over the years, each old part was replaced by a new part.

Actually that's pretty much what did happen.

Now, imagine this bear has *none* of the original parts. Can we really say it's the same teddy bear?

I'm not sure, but I think so. Surely something can change but still be the same thing.

Alright, but now imagine the original parts hadn't worn out, but were kept in a drawer. Then, years later, they were used to put together *a bear that looks exactly like the original one.*

That would never happen!

But what if it did? *Which* bear is the one you were given as a baby?

The 'original' bear, made from replacement parts?

Or the 'replacement' bear, made of original parts?

Golly, I'll have to think about that...

Instead of a teddy bear, you could ask a similar series of questions about *yourself*.
Find out more on pages 96-99.

WHY DO PHILOSOPHY?

Imagine you're part of a crowd watching someone give a speech. Chances are, a lot of people in that crowd are 'doing philosophy' without even realizing it...

All these people are responding to the news report and to the speech. Some of their questions might not have a clear answer, but just asking them, and debating them, could end up changing the future of society. This is an example of *practical* philosophy.

Not everyone agrees that philosophy can fix problems. But people agree that it gives you thinking tools to sort out good arguments from bad in ANY situation.

IS THERE A REAL WORLD OUTSIDE OF YOUR MIND?

AND CAN YOU *PROVE* IT?

WHAT'S THE MOST BASIC FACT YOU CAN THINK OF?

HOW DO I KNOW IF THE THINGS I BELIEVE ARE TRUE?

KNOWLEDGE

When people talk about knowledge, they don't always mean the same thing. They might be talking about *knowing how* to do something, or *being acquainted* with someone or something, or *knowing that* something is true.

Philosophers are mainly interested in this last type of knowledge – knowledge of **facts**. Questions they ask include: how do we come to know things? What is knowledge anyway? Can we actually *really know anything*?

CAN WE REALLY KNOW ANYTHING?

The chances are you will want to answer, 'Yes, of course we can.' But there are some pretty powerful arguments that might persuade you otherwise. These are known as **sceptical** arguments. Their aim is to force you to doubt even what seems obvious and most certain. Here is an example.

Imagine there is a brain in a jar. The brain is hooked up to a supercomputer which feeds it all the experiences it would have if it were a walking, talking human being. In fact, the brain thinks that it *is* a walking, talking human being.

If the brain in a jar has no way of telling it *is* a brain in a jar, then how do you know that *you* are not a brain in a jar too? You don't.
The point is not actually to make you believe you *are* a brain in a jar, but rather to convince you that you can't be *sure* that you are *not*.

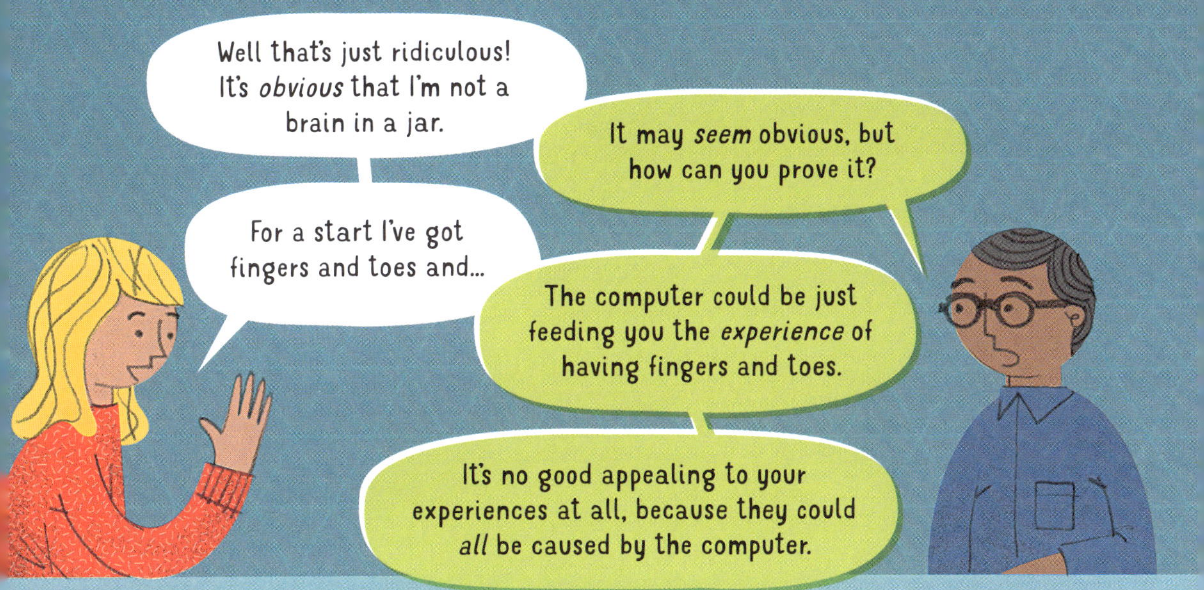

What's the point of sceptical arguments? Well, if you can't *know* that you are *not* a brain in a jar, how can you be sure that reality is anything like what you think it is? And if you can't be sure of this, **how can you really know *anything***?
The answer seems to be that you cannot...

Common sense tells us that this argument just *has to be* wrong. But common sense sometimes gets it wrong, doesn't it? After all, people used to be convinced that the Earth was flat. Can we really rely on common sense to help us?

Here are some suggestions philosophers make *against* the sceptical argument.

What do you think? Do you find any of these responses satisfying? Can you KNOW that you are not a brain in a jar, and if you CAN'T, does it really matter?

HOW DO WE KNOW THINGS?

Let's suppose that knowledge is possible. Although we can still make mistakes, it's likely that quite a lot of the things we *think* we know, we really *do* know. But how do we check whether having particular beliefs can count as knowledge?

The problem is, that this line of questioning needn't stop here. In fact, some philosophers argue that it could just go on forever, and ever and *ever*, in what's known as an **infinite regress**.

When you start to wonder why you believe something... there's always another 'why...?' and the endless chain of whys turns into an **infinite regress...**

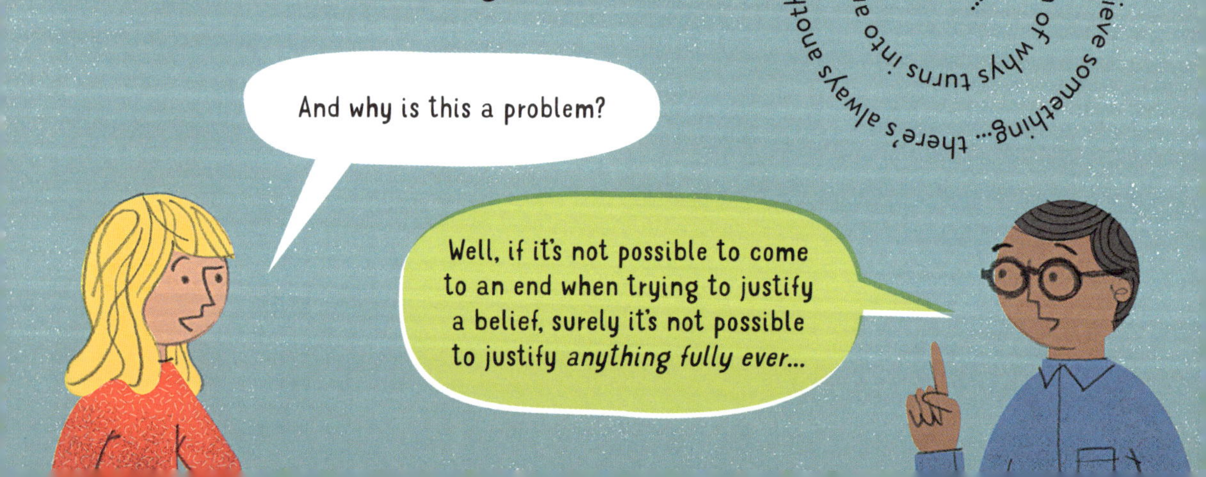

Many philosophers think that we can stop this problem of regress *and* avoid circularity by thinking about the structure of knowledge as a whole.

Knowledge, they argue, is like a building. If everything we know is supported by a strong *foundation* of beliefs that can be trusted, the rest of our knowledge (if we are careful) will be sound.

BUILDING KNOWLEDGE

The theory that knowledge is based on a strong foundation is known as **foundationalism**. Foundationalists don't always agree on exactly *which* beliefs form the foundations, but they *do* agree there must be beliefs that don't need to be justified any further. Such beliefs are known as **basic beliefs**. These can support other beliefs that philsophers describe as **non-basic beliefs**.

However, some philosophers say that knowledge is not a building with foundations – it's more a web-like set of interconnected beliefs. As long as a set of beliefs is *consistent* (beliefs in the same set don't contradict one another) and it's *coherent* (all the beliefs support one another), then it's reasonable to have those beliefs. For instance, here's a set of beliefs belonging to a spider.

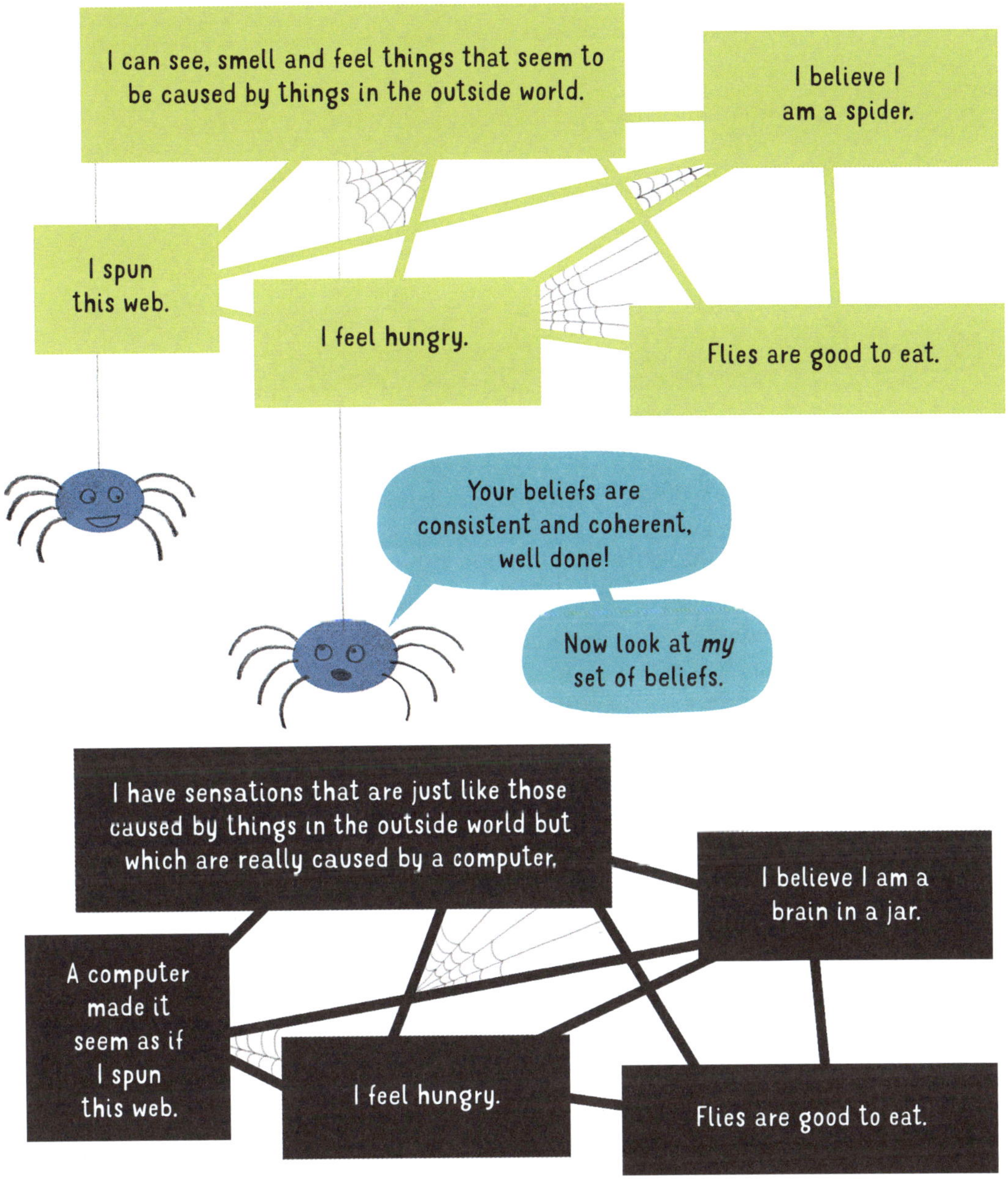

Both sets of beliefs are consistent and coherent. But they lead to two very different conclusions, and there's no way to tell which spider is correct.
So, perhaps, even if all your beliefs are coherent, they could still be false beliefs.

WHAT IS KNOWLEDGE?

Most philosophers agree that in order to *know* a fact, that fact has to be *true*, and you need to *believe* that it's true.

As long as this really *is* Peter, this looks like a clear-cut case of knowledge. But is this all there is to knowledge? Imagine this conversation:

Suppose that Khalid's single really *is* the top-selling song. Does Bill really know this? Do you think Jane knows it?

If you think Bill doesn't know, but Jane does, then what's the difference between their two beliefs? Why does one count as *knowledge*, and the other not? The answer lies in the **reasons** they have given for their true beliefs.

Bill's reason for believing doesn't sound like a good one, while Jane's does. Philosophers would say that Jane's true belief is **justified,** but Bill's is not. So can we use this to give us a new and better account of what counts as knowledge?

To know a fact, that fact must be true, you must believe it and that belief must be justified (you must have good reasons for it).

REASONS TO BELIEVE

Here's a new thought experiment: imagine Henry has dyed his hair blue.

Most people would say that Anna *knows* that Henry has dyed his hair. Seeing him in the street seems like a good enough reason to believe it. So her *knowing* fits the theory of knowledge as **justified true belief**.

But what about Matt? Surely he *doesn't* know. Matt didn't see Henry, so his reason for believing that Henry has blue hair is only true by coincidence. So maybe we just need to add an extra condition to our definition of knowledge:

A justified belief must not depend on other false beliefs.

Or, perhaps we just need to come up with a new approach to describing knowledge. Turn the page to find out more...

KNOWING HOW YOU KNOW

Some philosophers suggest that in order to know something, all you need is a **chain of causes** that links a *fact* to your *belief of that fact*. This is known as the **causal theory of knowledge.**

The causal theory can explain why Anna knows, but Matt doesn't. Anna knows that Henry has dyed his hair because her belief is *caused by* seeing Henry with blue hair. Matt's belief was *not* caused by this (it was caused by seeing Eric), and *this* is why he doesn't really know. The causal theory also lets you say that you know something, even when you can't justify your belief...

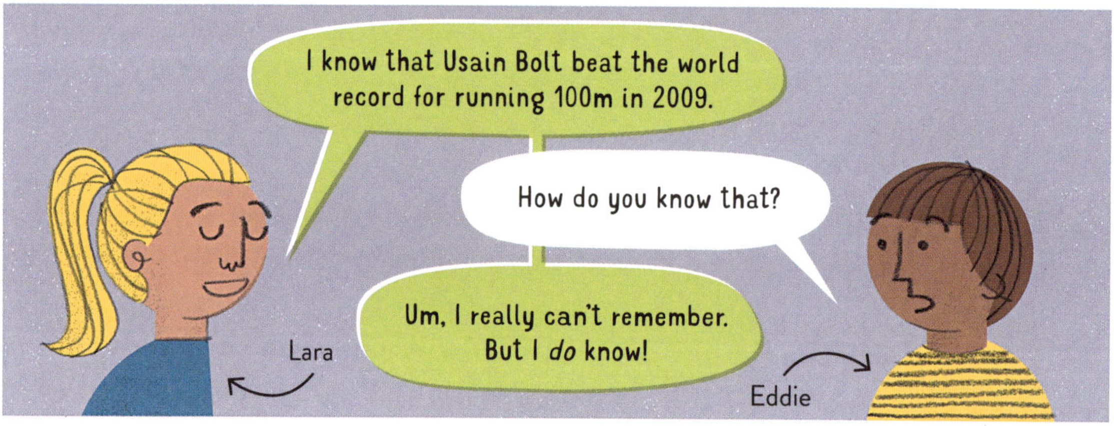

If you think knowlege is just justified true belief, you have to say that Lara *can't* know because she can't give good reasons for her belief.
But according to the causal theory, Lara *can* know as long as there is a chain of causes between the fact and the final belief. Here's an example.

So, so far, the causal theory looks pretty good. But, American philosopher Alvin Goldman came up with this thought experiment:

Amelia is driving through the countryside. She sees a barn and forms a true belief that there is a barn.

Amelia *seems to know* there's a barn because there is a causal chain between the barn and her forming a belief about its existence. Her belief is caused by seeing the barn, and seeing the barn is caused by the fact that the barn is there.

But, unknown to Amelia, there are lots of fake barns in the area, that look just like real barns. The barn Amelia sees *is* a real one, but she could easily have been looking at a fake one. If she had, her belief would have been false.

So the question is, does Amelia really *know* there is a barn over there? It feels as if she only got it right by *luck*. If you think she doesn't really know, then the fact that there is a causal chain between her true belief and the barn being there isn't enough for her to 'know' it. So perhaps there's something wrong with the theory?

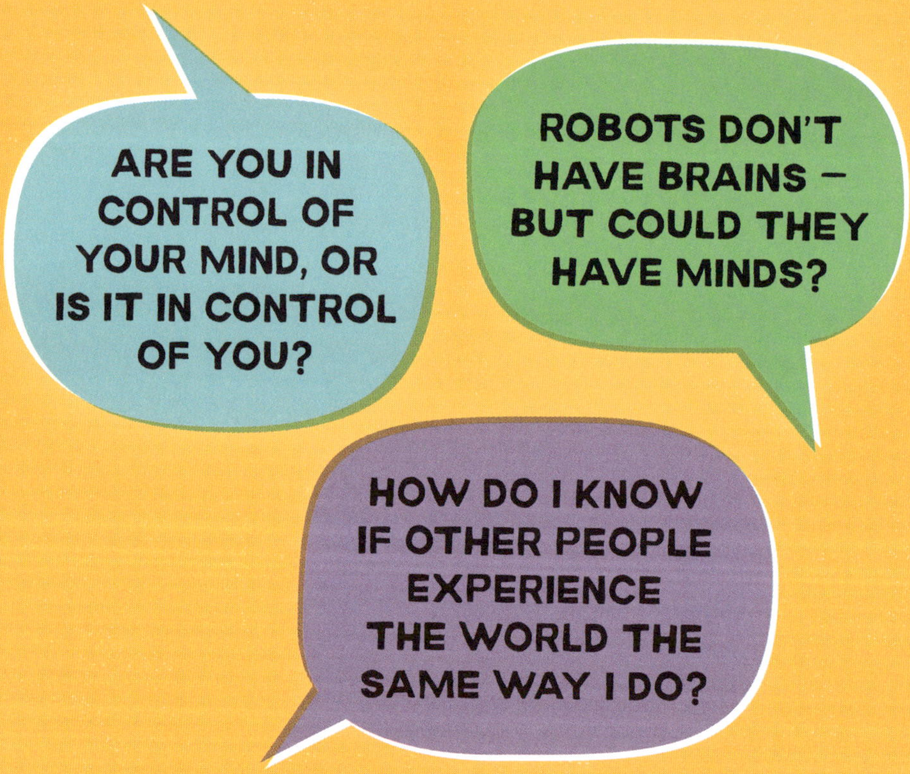
ARE YOU IN CONTROL OF YOUR MIND, OR IS IT IN CONTROL OF YOU?
ROBOTS DON'T HAVE BRAINS – BUT COULD THEY HAVE MINDS?
HOW DO I KNOW IF OTHER PEOPLE EXPERIENCE THE WORLD THE SAME WAY I DO?

THE MIND

Tackling questions about what our minds are, and how they relate to the world, is part of a branch of philosophy known as 'philosophy of mind'. Exploring different ideas about our minds can make us look at ourselves and other people in new ways.

DO OTHER PEOPLE HAVE MINDS?

It's often hard to know what's going on in other people's heads. We can describe what we *think* is going on, but we don't normally believe that we can actually see inside them. Sometimes this can lead to confusion.

Philosophers sometimes describe people's minds as *private*. This means each person's thoughts and feelings are only accessible to *them*. So maybe other people's experiences are totally different from what you might expect.

In fact, how do you know if anyone else *has a mind at all*? People might *look* as if they have thoughts and feelings, but is it possible that they're just bodies with nothing going on in their heads?

You might say "Well, *I* have experiences, feelings and thoughts. Other people look and act like me, so, it makes sense that they have minds too." But this reasoning is actually faulty. To explain why, look at this example.

All dogs *aren't* brown. The point is, it's not possible to make a *general* conclusion from only a *single* example. You need to show that the same thing applies in *multiple* cases. But you can't do that with minds, because you only know for sure that *you* have a mind.

Common sense lets us assume people *do* all have minds because it provides a simple and believable explanation for their actions. But why should we trust common sense? Well, imagine trying to explain people's behaviour at a party.

THE MIND-BODY PROBLEM

Many people would agree there are some clear differences between their minds and their bodies.

BODIES	MINDS
Our bodies exist in space.	Thoughts don't occupy space.
We can measure our bodies and weigh them – and other people can too.	We can't weigh our thoughts or experiences.
We can see and touch our bodies.	Other people can't access our thoughts.

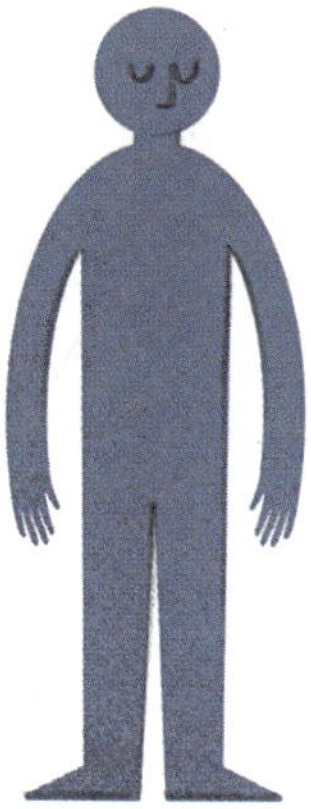

So what is the relationship between your body and your mind? Philosophers call this the **Mind-Body problem**, and they've developed all sorts of theories about it.

1. THE MIND AND THE BODY ARE DIFFERENT SUBSTANCES

According to this theory, the body is a physical substance that takes up space, but the mind is not a physical substance, and it doesn't take up space. But then you might ask: how can a non-physical thing cause changes in a physical thing?

Some philosophers say that something that doesn't take up space cannot affect something that does. So, for them, saying that the mind and the body are different substances doesn't solve the problem.

2. THE MIND *IS* THE BRAIN

Another way to describe the mind is to say that it's the *same thing* as the brain. Philosophers call this **identity theory**. The idea is that we can link what's going on in someone's mind (their **mental states**) to particular processes that are going on in their brain. Here are two rough examples.

When a person said they felt desire for cake (a mental state), *this* part of the brain was being used.

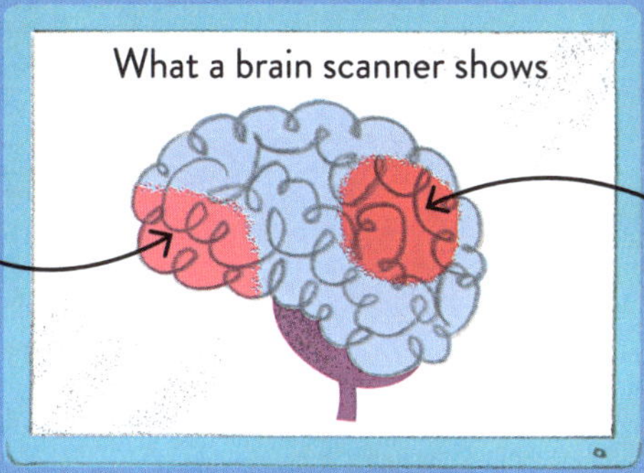

When a person said they felt pain (another mental state), *this* part of the brain was being used.

The idea is that every mental state is identical to a *specific* process in the brain. However, philosophers have pointed out a problem.

Many animals show signs that they feel mental states such as pain. But their brains can be very different to ours.

Since identity theory defines pain as a *specific* brain process, this logically implies that animals can't feel pain – or at least, the pain they feel isn't the same as the pain humans feel.

Here's a thought experiment. Imagine an alien with a completely different body. Do you think it could also feel pain?

Maybe it wouldn't even have a brain; maybe it'd have glowing goo in its head. But does that mean it can't feel the very same kind of pain we feel?

To solve the Mind-Body problem, philosophers need a definition of mental states, such as pain, that can work for *all things* that experience them. But if pain is linked to a specific part of the brain, it might suggest that things that *don't* use or have that part don't feel pain. Maybe identity theory is too specific.

3. THE MIND IS WHAT IT DOES

An alternative to identity theory is **functionalism**. According to this view, mental states should be defined in terms of what they *do*, or what their *function* is. We describe many everyday objects in this way.

For example, you might describe a clock as something that tells the time, regardless of what it's made from, or exactly how it works.

Mechanical clock Digital clock Sundial Talking clock

But how can this be applied to mental states? Functionalists often compare minds to computers. Like a computer, the mind receives **inputs**, and responds with **outputs**. A mental state is just whatever causes an output in response to an input. In other words, what it *does* – its function – is to cause an output.

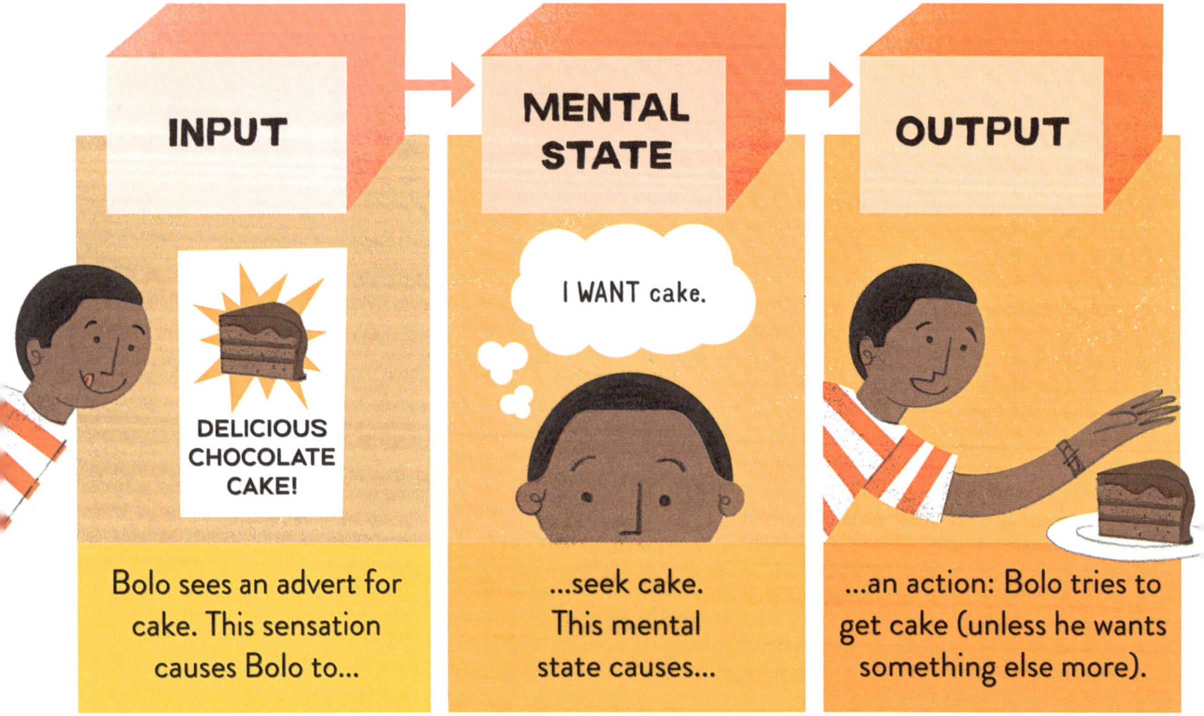

What makes a mental state what it is – here, wanting cake – is not some specific brain activity, but the fact that it *causes* a certain output – trying to get cake.

So, a functional description should work for *any* mind, whether it's a person, an animal, an alien or even a robot. Just as all clocks tell the time, different things can carry out the functions of minds using different materials. Here are some things that might carry out mental functions.

But there are things functionalism *doesn't* explain. Desire and pain aren't *just* functions that bring about certain situations – they are things we *feel*. Ideally, functionalism could explain the connection between how mental states feel and their function – but it doesn't.

Some philosophers think it's impossible to explain the experience of mental states. Imagine trying to explain what pain is to an alien who can't feel it.

If it's impossible to explain how things feel, then maybe it doesn't matter if functionalism doesn't explain feelings.

ARE YOU REALLY IN CONTROL?

Everyone makes choices every day. You *chose* to read this book (we hope). The idea of choice plays a big part in how we all think about our lives. Philosophers call this having *free will*. We often blame or praise people for their actions because they *chose* to do them.

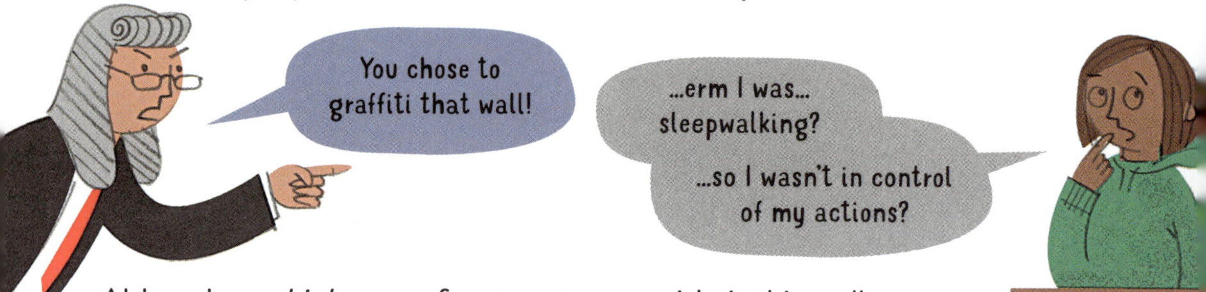

Although we *think* we are free to act as we wish, is this really true? Some philosophers argue that we aren't free at all. If you think about the world around you, you might think that the present and the future are caused by past events. We explain all sorts of things by referring to past events.

This idea is called **determinism**. If current and future events are determined by what's happened before, then that includes your actions and even who you are.

We can't change the past. But if the past *determines* the future...

...that means *we* can't control the future either.

In our own lives, there are many things that we tend to think we have no control over, because they were caused by events from long ago.

How you look depends on your parents, and how *they* look depends on *their* parents.

The language you speak depends on where you grew up.

Your ideas, beliefs and personality depend on what you've learned at school, from your parents, friends, or your surroundings.

Some people take this a step further. What if *everything* about you, and the world around you, depends on the past? If so, it must apply to your *choices* too. This is important. If none of your choices are made freely – if they're all determined by past events – it could affect how judges carry out justice.

So here is the problem:
If we couldn't ever have acted or chosen to act otherwise, how can we have free will?

IS EVERYTHING DETERMINED?

If everything we do is determined by the past, it looks as if we can't have free will. But what if the present and the future *aren't* determined by the past?

The science of how everything works is called physics. Some physicists argue that if you look really closely at the world, it turns out that *everything* that happens from one moment to the next is at least *in part* a matter of chance. Here's an example: flip a coin.

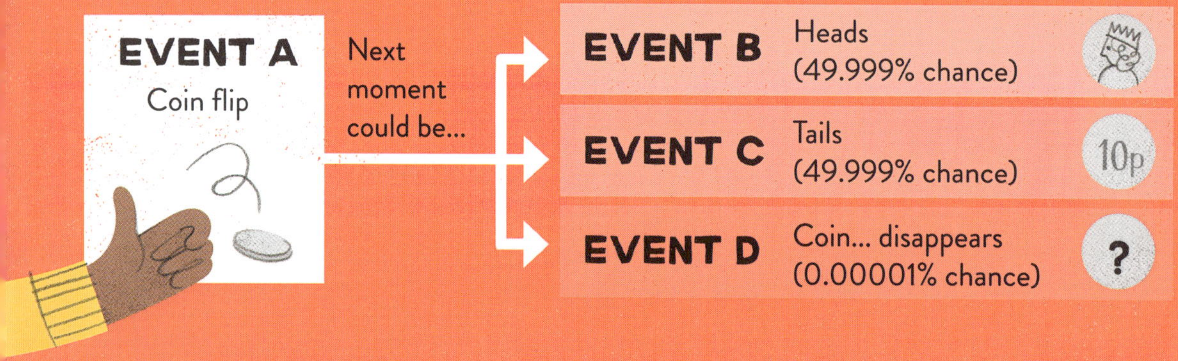

What this means for *philosophers* is that it's always possible for something random to happen, even something very, very unlikely. If so, then determinism is false, because *some* events are not directly caused by previous events – they can happen at random.

So does that mean you have free will? Not necessarily. If determinism is false, your actions could be *completely* random. You might have no more control over them than you would if you made all your decisions with the help of a dice.

If your actions are random, this is essentially the same as having no control. So if your actions are determined, or completely random, you can't have free will.

However, it's very likely that in your experience you feel you *are* free to choose your actions. Is there a way to explain this? Well, what does 'free will' really mean? The simplest explanation is probably that you're free if you make a choice *without being constrained or limited* by the events of the past.

WHAT IS ART?
WHAT IS *GOOD* ART?
CAN A POEM OR A SONG BE AS BEAUTIFUL AS A ROSE?

BEAUTY AND ART

Questions about beauty and art fall into a branch of philosophy known as **aesthetics** (pronounced es-thet-iks). This comes from the Ancient Greek word *aisthesis* (es-thee-sis), which means knowledge through your senses: sight, hearing, touch, taste and smell.

WHAT IS BEAUTY?

Beauty can be applied to all sorts of things: people, music, poetry, art, mountain views, science, flowers, sunsets... but is it possible to pinpoint the meaning of a word that refers to so many different things?

Beauty could be...

MULTIPLE MEANINGS

One idea suggested by philosophers is that the meaning of beauty varies according to the kind of thing it applies to. For instance, a song may have one kind of beauty that inspires a direct, immediate response.

But a poem could have a different kind of beauty that requires more time to understand and appreciate it.

IS BEAUTY JUST IN THE MIND?

Some philosophers argue that beauty is purely in the mind of the beholder – making it what's called a *subjective* value. Others suggest that beauty is *objective* – it depends on qualities that exist *within* things. But if beauty is objective, what are the qualities that define it?

IF BEAUTY WERE OBJECTIVE...

In ancient times, philosophers identified qualities, such as proportion and symmetry, that appeared to define many beautiful things. They believed if you could find a formula for the proportions of a beautiful human form, for instance, you could find a formula for beauty.

Architects in Ancient Greece used mathematics to construct beautiful buildings with specific proportions too.

They used a width-to-height ratio of roughly 1.62, known as the Golden Mean.

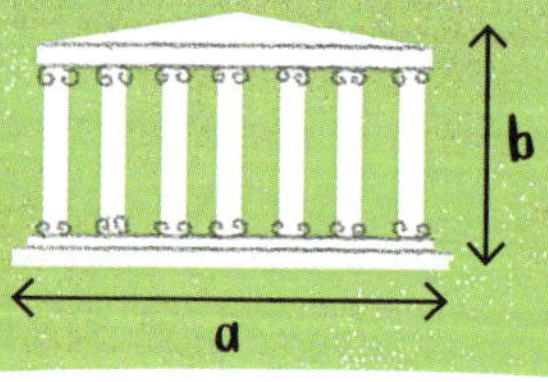

$$\frac{a}{b} = \frac{a+b}{a} = 1.62...$$

But the Golden Mean doesn't explain the beauty of buildings with *other* shapes and proportions. So far, no one has found a rule that works for ALL beautiful buildings – let alone all beautiful things.

IF BEAUTY WERE SUBJECTIVE...

Now let's assume that beauty is subjective, and depends more on our own response to something. After all, there is huge variation in people's opinions about what is and isn't beautiful.

The problem with this argument is that if beauty depends purely on the viewer's perceptions, and it varies for each person, then two people can never know for sure whether they mean the same thing by 'beauty'.

But there still *is* a lot of agreement about what is and isn't beautiful. Few people would doubt the beauty of a dramatic sunset, for instance. This suggests that beauty *does* in fact have *some* kind of universal, recognizable meaning. We're back where we started.

WHO JUDGES BEAUTY?

German philosopher Immanuel Kant believed that beauty is subjective, but he also recognized that people use the term beauty in a meaningful way. Although it's impossible to find qualities common to *all* beautiful things, he argued that you *can* list the qualities *a person* needs to be a good judge.

Kant argued that experienced critics tend to agree with each other and can be trusted to make good judgements. They tell us what is good in literature, art, music and theatre, and select winners in competitions. Although there is variation in their taste, people tend to trust their opinion.

IS BEAUTY REAL?

Ancient Greek philosopher Plato linked 'beauty' to 'goodness' and placed both in an imagined ideal world outside our own. He thought beauty was an ultimate, objective value for people to strive for and that it didn't depend on anyone's views.

But it seems odd to separate 'beauty' from 'beautiful things'. We *do* appear to experience beauty in our world and often share our experience of it with others.

PLEASURE AND THE SENSES

Ancient philosophers defined beauty by the pleasure or emotional response it inspired, which came from the senses.

But the meaning of pleasure, like beauty, changes in different circumstances. Eating ice cream is a sensory pleasure, but it's not the kind of pleasure that comes from beauty. Other kinds of pleasure come from the mind, not the senses, such as reading or solving a puzzle.

WHAT IS ART?

In the past, art was often linked with beauty and the creation of beautiful things. Whether they find it beautiful or not, many people today have a general understanding of 'art' and refer to it happily in conversation.

Art here refers to drawing, painting... anything you might do during an art class at school. But 'art' can mean lots of different things...

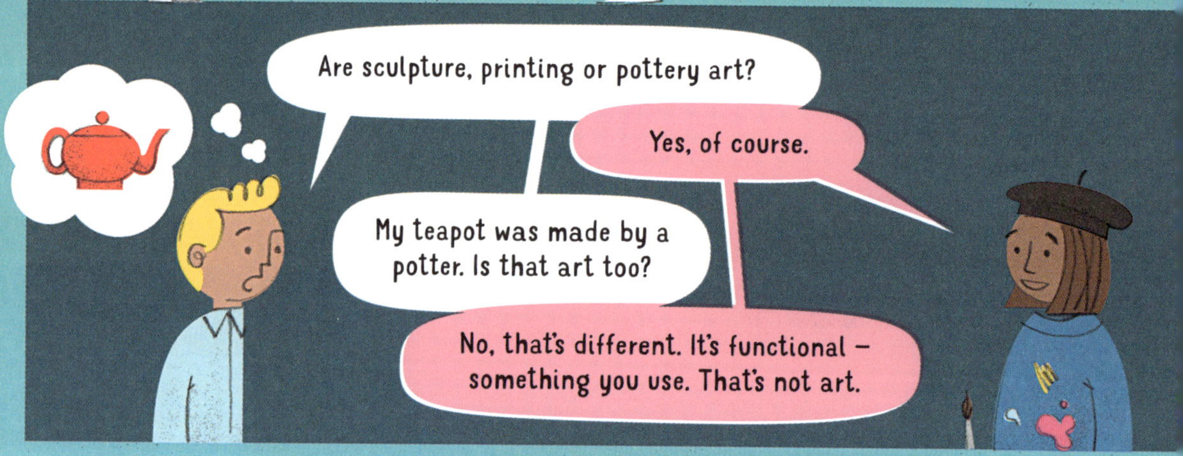

Some people draw a distinction between objects that are *intended* to be art – such as a picture on a wall – and objects created for a function, such as a teapot or chair. But what happens if you put a functional household object in an art gallery? Can it *become* art?

The 'art gallery test' is one way of defining art, but it doesn't cover everything. Lots of art is displayed outside galleries, on trees, hillsides or even in the swirls on the top of a cup of coffee. However you define art, it's always possible to think of an example that lies outside that definition.

ART AND MEANING

Over a hundred years ago, good art was often considered to be art that was beautiful, or art that showed subjects that looked very like things in the natural world. It was this that gave the art *meaning*.

But as artists began experimenting with abstract ideas, and painting pictures that didn't *look* like *things*, the meaning or subject became less clear. Some art, for instance, could be interpreted in lots of different ways.

As non-representational art became more accepted, people began to ask whether art needed to have any meaning at all.

Despite these changes, art was still considered to be some kind of object created, or hand-made by an artist. But this idea was soon to be turned on its head...

PUSHING THE BOUNDARIES

In 1917, French-American artist Marcel Duchamp rocked the art world by submitting an upside-down urinal for an art show in New York. The urinal was titled 'Fountain' and signed 'R. Mutt, 1917'.

The gallery rejected 'Fountain' because it was not considered a true work of art. One reason was because it was not *made* by the artist. Others argued that it *was* art because Duchamp had given it artistic *meaning*.

Artists began to create work that wasn't necessarily intended to be pleasing, but to make people *think*.

This sparked a huge debate about what is and isn't art. This discussion returns every time new work is exhibited that pushes the boundaries of what art is considered to be. Consider a canvas painted blue or boxes printed to look like packets of soap you can buy in a shop. Do you think those would be art?

More recently, some artists have focused on themes of death, decay and horror, creating works of art that shock viewers. The publicity created is sometimes included in the work itself.

Imagine an artist displayed a bucket of animal blood in a gallery. Is that art? People now suggest art can be *anything* – anything an artist chooses to call art. It doesn't even have to be a 'thing'. Some artists put on a show, called **performance art**, that only lasts a few seconds.

When trying to make sense of new art, it's easy to forget that many well-loved artists were highly criticized when they first showed their work. This suggests that whatever art *is*, its definition is sure to have changed by the time you've read this chapter.

IF GOD IS GOOD,
HOW CAN
THERE BE EVIL
IN THE WORLD?

IS THERE
ANY PROOF
FOR GOD'S
EXISTENCE?

DO WE NEED GOD
TO EXPLAIN WHY
THE WORLD EXISTS,
OR WHY IT IS THE
WAY IT IS?

GOD

Many religions are based around the idea that there is a God (or gods). Philosophical debates about God often focus on two basic, but very BIG questions: can we prove that God exists? And, conversely, can we prove that God does *not* exist? The answer to either question will depend partly on what your idea, or concept, of God is.

Often, philosophers think of God as a single, superior being. Of course this *isn't* the *only* way to think of God, and you may not believe in God at all. But it's still worthwhile – and fun – to flex your philosophical muscles and examine the arguments.

THE IDEA OF GOD

God is often defined by theists (philosophers who believe in God) as a **perfect being.** But what does this mean? Does the idea of a perfect *being* even make sense?

In fact, theists *have* typically put forward a number of qualities that they think a perfect being should have. For example, God should be...

You might want to question whether these qualities really *do* make God perfect. But there are other questions to be answered too. What do these qualities involve? Are they compatible with each other? Do they even make *sense*? For example, let's take a closer look at *omnipotence*.

OMNIPOTENCE

Imagine there is a being called Bob. Bob is not God, but he *is* omnipotent. Bob can create things, change things, move things... You name it, Bob can do it!

Bob *seems* to be able to do anything, *but* can he... create a stone that's too heavy for him to lift?

If Bob *can* make a stone he cannot lift, then there is something he *cannot* do – namely, lift that stone.

But if he *can't* make the stone, well, that's also something he cannot do.

Either way, it looks as if he can't *really* be omnipotent. This problem is called the **paradox of omnipotence.**

A **paradox** is a statement which seems false, even though it seems to follow logically from true premises (see pages 10-11).

WORKING AROUND A PARADOX

At this point, you could say, well, you can't expect even an omnipotent being to be able to do just *anything*.
Take Bob's friend, Bodyless Bob. Bodyless Bob can do pretty much anything too, but since he doesn't have a body, he can't blow his nose, or drink a glass of water, or anything else that requires a body...
...but does that mean he can't be omnipotent?

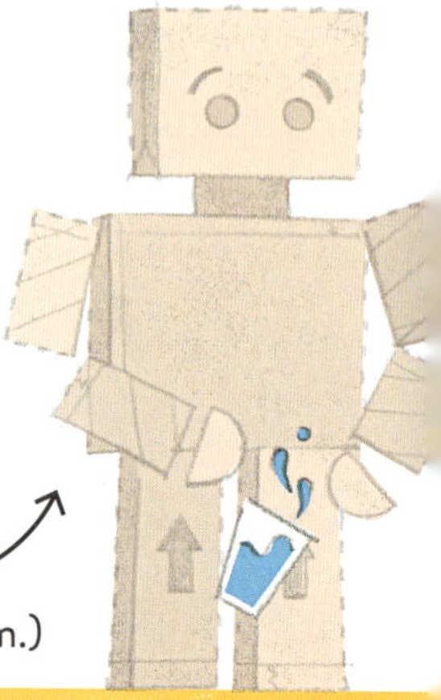

Bodyless Bob
(You'll just have to imagine you can't see him.)

Meet Absolutely Impossible Bob

He can do absolutely *anything* – even the impossible.

Suppose you could agree on what it means for God to be omnipotent. It won't help you solve another problem – how do you combine omnipotence with God's other qualities? One of the most famous examples of this is known as the **problem of evil**. Turn the page to find out more...

THE PROBLEM OF EVIL

God is often said to be wholly good and kind. This seems to imply that God would never do bad things, or let bad things happen. But people do bad things all the time. If God exists and God is good, then how can he let them? This issue is known as the **problem of evil**.

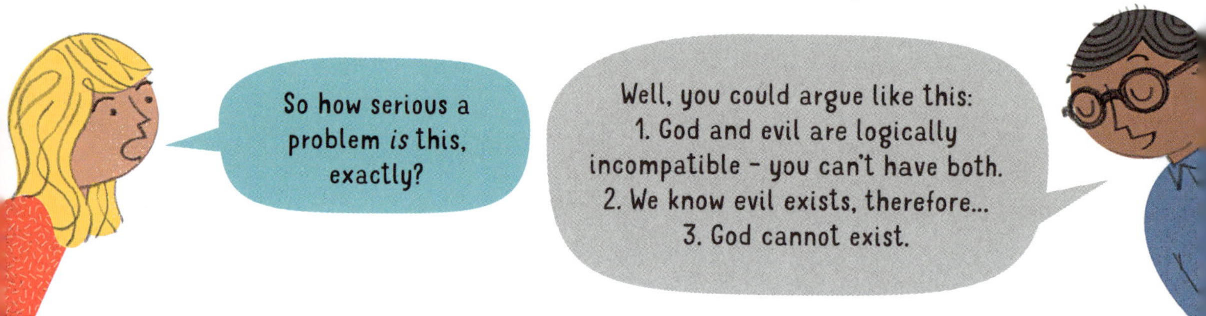

The problem of evil is actually only a problem, though, if you also believe that God is omniscient (knows everything) and omnipotent, as well as wholly good.

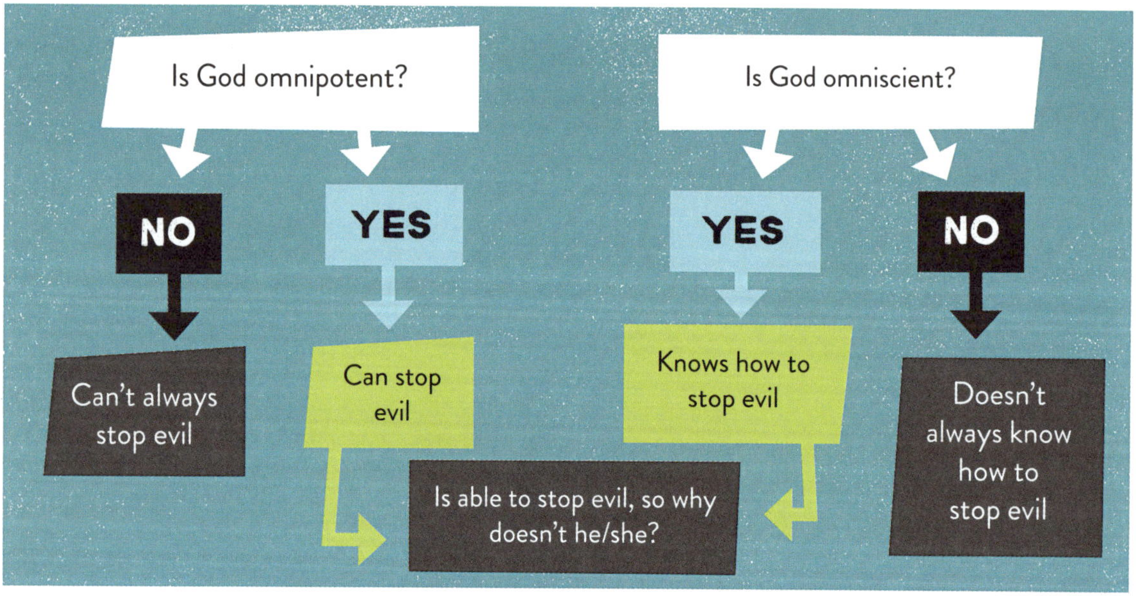

What if being good and allowing bad things to happen *aren't* always incompatible?

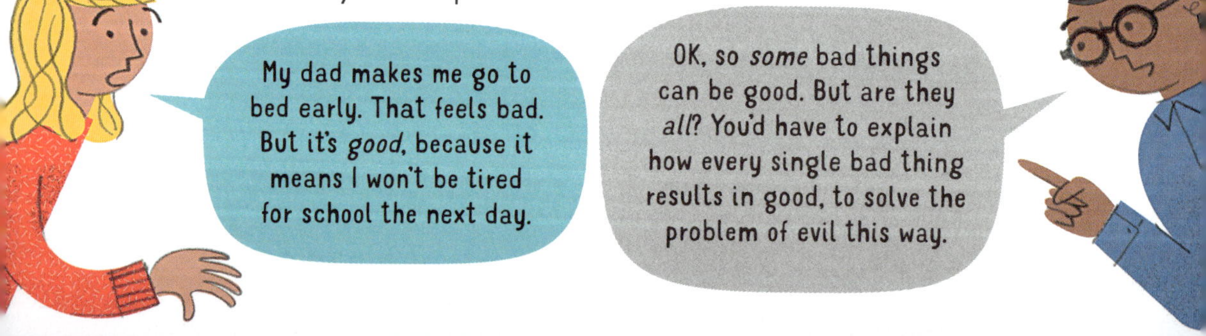

Some religious people DO say that bad things happen because God knows that a greater good will be the result. It doesn't matter if we just aren't clever enough to see it. But if you don't feel happy with this response, there's another version of the argument which altogether avoids the need to justify every instance of evil...

BEING FREE TO CHOOSE

In many religions, the idea of **free will** – people's ability to choose what they do with their lives – is very important. Some philosophers argue that free will is a great good in itself, and is so important that God wants people to have it. But as long as people have free will, it means they are able to choose to do bad things.

REASONS TO BELIEVE

Over the centuries, many philosophers have tried to show that there are good arguments, based on reasoning, for believing in God. Here's one that people sometimes give.

ARGUMENT FROM DESIGN

The world is beautiful and filled with creatures that seem to fit their environment extraordinarily well. It seems *incredible* that all of this could have come about by chance. Surely a better explanation is that someone intended things to be this way – and that could only be a being as powerful as God.

This line of thinking has given rise to the...

FINE-TUNING ARGUMENT

1. If the laws of nature had been even ever so slightly different, our reality would not have existed.

2. The probability of things being the way they are is very very very small. In other words, it's amazing that our reality exists at all.

3. It seems unbelievable that something with such a tiny probablility of existing could come into existence just by chance.

4. It seems more likely that something *intentionally* caused it to exist - and that is God.

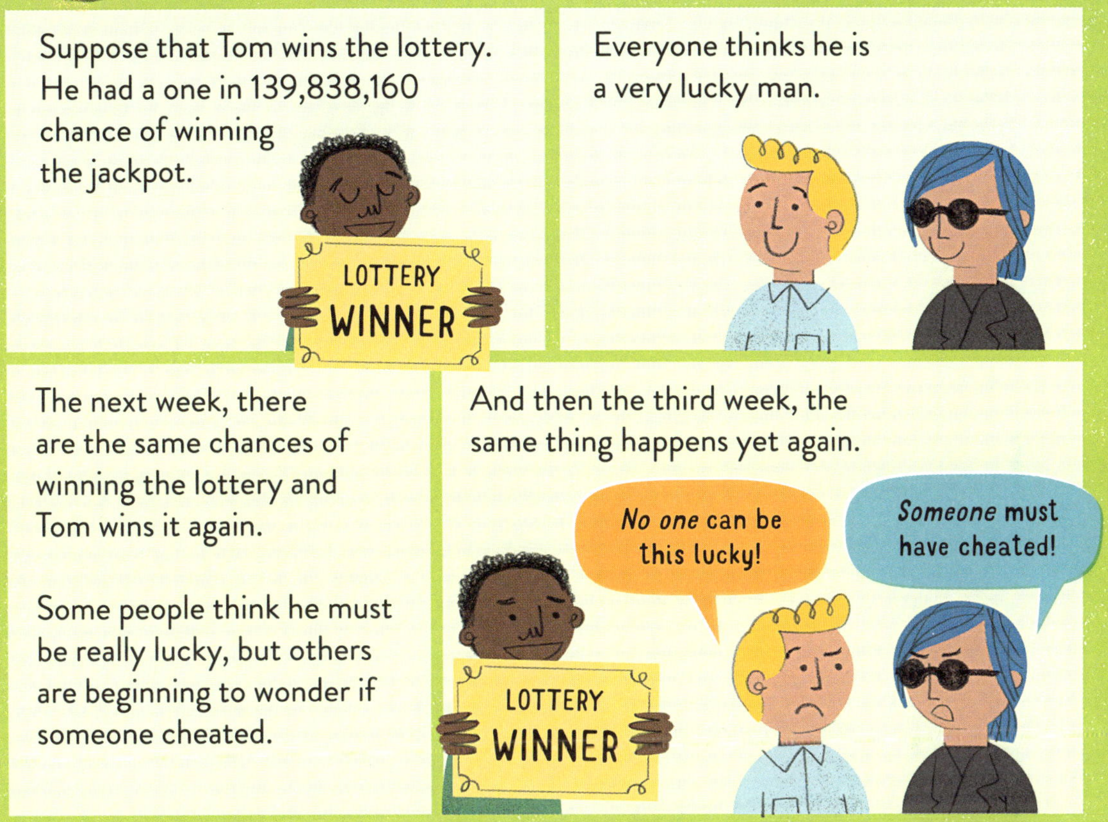

When highly unlikely things happen, we often find it hard to believe that it's all down to chance, and tend to look for an alternative explanation, or reason.

This isn't the end of the matter, of course. But if the argument from design for God's existence isn't convincing enough, there are several other arguments. Turn the page to find out about some of them.

ONTOLOGICAL ARGUMENT

Nearly a thousand years ago, a philosopher and monk called Anselm of Canterbury put forward what's known as the **ontological argument**. He said that there was something about the very *idea* of God that compels you to agree that God *must* exist. If you struggle to get your head round it, don't worry. The language is tricky:

Anselm's Proof

1. God is the greatest possible thing you can imagine.
2. Things can exist just in our imagination, or, in our imagination and in reality.
3. Things that exist in reality are greater than things which exist only in the imagination.
4. Suppose God exists only in the imagination.
5. This God cannot be the greatest possible thing.
6. So God must exist in reality as well as in people's imaginations. God must exist!

Apart from being difficult to understand, this argument is almost certainly wrong. But what, exactly, *is* wrong with it? Here are some suggestions:

Do we have to define God as the greatest possible being?

In what sense is *existing in reality* greater than *existing only in the imagination*? Does this even make sense?

If you swap the word 'God' for, say, ice cream, couldn't you prove the greatest possible ice cream must exist?

Isn't this argument just *defining* God into existence?

Here are some other arguments for the existence of God.

RELIGIOUS EXPERIENCE

Many people believe they have had religious experiences – experiences that *seem* to have been caused by God. These can be taken as evidence for the existence of God.

THE COSMOLOGICAL ARGUMENT

Everything must have a cause. But we can't have an infinite chain of causes. The causes have to stop somewhere, and with something that doesn't *need* a cause. The only possible candidate for that is God.

Another argument came from a 17th century French thinker called Blaise Pascal. He tried to convince people that believing in God was the most rational thing to do, even though it wasn't possible – in his opinion – to prove that God exists.

Pascal, like many people at the time, believed that if God existed and you didn't believe, you'd be punished after you died. If you did believe (and you were a good person), you'd be rewarded. Bearing this in mind, he invited people to look at all the possible outcomes of believing versus not believing.

Pascal's Wager	GOD EXISTS	GOD DOESN'T EXIST
BELIEVE IN GOD	When you die: eternal bliss	When you die: nothing
DON'T BELIEVE IN GOD	When you die: eternal suffering	When you die: nothing

Pascal felt that the possibility of eternal suffering was too great to risk. According to him, a rational person would bet on it being true that God exists, and do their best to believe it even if they didn't...

HOW CAN YOU TREAT ALL PEOPLE EQUALLY?
WHY SHOULD I LISTEN TO THE GOVERNMENT?
IS THE WHOLE IDEA OF 'PRIVATE PROPERTY' FAIR?

POLITICS

Politics is about how groups of people make decisions and work together. Whether it's a government running a country, people living together in a society, or some friends trying to organize an event – it all counts as politics.

Political philosophers are interested in what makes groups work in a peaceful and fair way. They explore different views about how society should be organized. It's not just about exploring ideas, though – political philosophers can and do influence how governments run their countries.

SHOULD WE OWN ANYTHING?

When people talk about things they own, whether it's a book or a bicycle or a house, they normally mean **private property**. This is stuff that a particular person or group uses. It's called 'private' because other people aren't allowed to use it without the owner's permission.

People often have disagreements about who owns what. Since private property causes so many disagreements, philosophers ask if it actually makes society better for everyone.

Here's one argument *for* private property. Imagine a group of fishermen are all fishing in the same spot.

At first, everyone catches loads of fish and business booms – but all too soon, there are no fish left. This isn't *just* a thought experiment. This has actually happened in seas around the world.

People in favour of private property claim that the fish ran out because the space wasn't privately owned – so no one took responsibility for it. If each fisherman (or group of fishermen) had their own private area, they'd have fished it responsibly, making sure there were always some fish left. Are these claims actually true?

1ST OBJECTION

The claim is that the space was ruined because it was shared. But actually, common property has been used responsibly throughout history. One of many examples is a Swiss mountain village that has shared a meadow for over 500 years – without ruining it.

2ND OBJECTION

You might also object that you think that private property doesn't make things better for *everyone*. Consider this counter-argument.

This argument doesn't prove that private property is always *bad* – just that we might not *need* it. And in fact some governments have tried to set up societies where some property – such as food and housing – is shared out. But deciding how to share things *fairly* is a whole new problem...

WHAT IS EQUALITY?

Most people agree that we *should* treat everyone equally. But it's not so clear what that means. While many people are unhappy with the inequality we see around us, it's not obvious what an equal society would look like.

STRICT EQUALITY

There are lots of different ways to look at equality. The most obvious idea is to treat everyone in *exactly* the same way and give everyone the *same* things.

But everyone is different and has their own needs, so a one-size-fits-all approach doesn't make sense. *Equal* doesn't mean *identical* – we can treat people equally without necessarily treating them in exactly same way. Suppose we want to make sure everyone can enjoy a movie equally, we could...

This makes sense when all you're doing is watching a movie – we know we want everyone to be able to enjoy a movie. But what about a whole society? We know we want equality, but what *sort* of equality?

MEETING EVERYONE'S NEEDS

Here's one suggestion – meet everyone's needs equally. This doesn't mean giving everyone the same things, it means treating all people's needs as equally worth satisfying. According to this view, if someone doesn't already have access to something on the list below, it *should* be provided for them.

Many people think that as long as no one has to struggle to survive, some kinds of inequality *are* acceptable – such as some people having more money than others. But others think just satisfying *basic* needs isn't enough. Other important things should be equal, too. Turn the page to explore other approaches to equality.

EQUALITY OF WELLBEING

Some philosophers think it's best to make everyone equally happy. This usually means meeting people's basic needs, then adding more things on top. Of course, each person's happiness will depend on different things, so different amounts of support would be given. But the aim is that everyone should be equally satisfied.

Sounds sensible? Well, consider this...

EQUALITY OF OPPORTUNITY

How about making sure everyone has the same opportunities? Some people don't have access to chances in life because of things that are beyond their control – such as where they were born. So the aim is to remove any barriers to opportunities so that everyone has a fair chance.

Here are some ways in which you could help everyone access education.

ACCESSIBILITY

Schools should be easy to access for students with disabilities.

GOOD LOCATION

Everyone should be able to get to school easily.

FREE SCHOOL MEALS

People shouldn't have to miss out on learning because of hunger.

SPECIAL NEEDS

Schools should provide trained teachers to help anyone with special needs.

NO FEES

People should be able to learn whether they're rich or poor.

Once these opportunities are in place, if things end up being unequal – some people get better grades, say – then that must simply be down to each person and... luck. Or is it? Consider this situation. Kay's parents are bilingual, so Kay learned to speak both English and Mandarin...

Kay has an advantage over lots of people, but it's not right for a government to stop parents from speaking to their children in their own language – is it?

Working out how to share things fairly isn't easy. But there's one thing most people agree on. Even if we don't know exactly what equality looks like, it's unacceptable for some people to suffer and struggle to survive when we CAN do something about it.

LIMITING FREEDOM

In most societies, there are things no one is allowed to do. And many philosophers argue that it's OK to limit someone's freedom, if it's for their own good. This is called **paternalism**.

Some of these laws seem so sensible that you probably don't object. But you might feel differently about laws which limit your choice in other ways. Most people want to *choose* how they live their lives – even if it's not good for them. Here's an example:

Some philosophers say it's simply not possible to do something good for someone against their will. But there seem to be cases when paternalism might well help people.

Creating hard rules, such as traffic light laws, is known as **hard paternalism**. According to another idea, known as **soft paternalism,** it's only OK to limit someone's freedom if that person is *unaware* of what they are doing.

Soft paternalism lets adults have their freedom and protects them when they don't know what they are doing. One reason you might object to this, is if you think something else might be more important than an individual's freedom.

Most people are OK with *some* paternalism. But others worry that if rules limit people's freedom to choose too much, society can become too controlling and even dangerous. All societies limit people's freedom a little, since everyone has to follow *some* rules. But who sets the rules?

WHO SHOULD SET THE RULES?

Most countries are run by governments – people with the job of creating new laws, or getting rid of old ones. They're also allowed to use force to make people do what they say. But why is it OK for the government to do this, and not other groups? Consider this scenario.

Very few people would accept a random group of people making laws and forcing everyone to follow them. But the government does this, so what's the difference? The difference is a matter of **legitimacy** – the government is *allowed* to make laws and enforce them. But why? What makes them so special?
Why *should* you obey the law and listen to the government?

NO, WE *SHOULDN'T* OBEY THE LAW

Some people, often known as **anarchists**, believe that we have no duty to obey the government. They think there's no real difference between a government-run police force and random law-makers.

YES, WE *SHOULD* OBEY THE LAW

Some philosophers think that a government is legitimate because citizens have *agreed* that it is. They argue that citizens voluntarily agree to obey laws, and allow the police to enforce them, for their own protection. This is often known as **the social contract.**

While it's hard to define what counts as an agreement, this idea explains why most of us accept the rule of law. Put simply, if you think it's better to live with other people, rather than going it alone, it makes sense to agree to follow some rules.

IS IT EVER OK TO LIE?
IS FIGHTING EVER JUSTIFIED?
ARE THERE SOME MORAL RULES THAT EVERYONE SHOULD OBEY?

HOW TO BE GOOD

How should we live our lives? How should we act with friends, family, strangers, people who give us orders or people who serve us?

In all areas of life, there are accepted ways of behaving, known as **moral codes**, that define how we are supposed to act and treat the people around us. The branch of philosophy that examines these codes and helps us make decisions about the right thing to do is called **ethics**. Ethics looks at values, such as rights and duties, that help make the world a better, fairer place.

MORALS – ARE THEY ANY USE?

Moral codes are like rules that tell us what to do and how to behave. They give us tools for making decisions, taking responsibility for our actions and dealing with all sorts of tricky issues.

Fred has made a promise – a commitment to do something, which is a kind of moral rule. He now has to decide whether he's going to keep the promise or not.

Some people think that there is a moral rule against breaking promises, or even asking to do so. But others suggest it depends on the situation.

In this example, Fred has asked to break his promise, but his mother is happy to change their plans. Having a rule helps you make decisions, but it doesn't always give you a clear answer about what to do.

WHY SHOULD I?

'Ought' or 'should' are words that often appear in rules or moral statements. Some of these 'oughts' and 'shoulds' are practical, not moral.

But other 'ought' statements *are* moral. They are also trickier to justify.

You ought not to kick people.

Why not?

Because it's wrong to hurt people.

I know people say that, but *why* is it wrong?

Well, if you go around hurting people, they might do the same to you. Imagine if everyone did that...

So the reason for not hurting people is to protect myself?

Not just that - how other people *feel* matters, too. The world is a *better place for everyone* if people don't go around hurting each other.

So *if* I care about others and want to live in a world that's a better place for everyone, *then* I ought not to hurt other people.

Yes.

Here, the final reason given for not kicking people depends on a belief, or assumption, about the world. Wanting to live in a world where people don't harm one another is a good reason for following a moral code.

WHERE DO MORALS COME FROM?

Most people pick up moral codes throughout their lives – from family, school, religion, books and the media. But is it reasonable to judge things merely on the grounds that someone *says* that's how it is? Can you trust that person as a source of moral knowledge? Or is it better to work out what's right and wrong for *yourself*?

Some philosophers argue that religion is like a giant thought experiment. People assume that morals come from God or some kind of higher being, who automatically has more authority than someone's aunt.

Some people do think moral rules are true simply because God says so. Others think morals are weaker if they are true *only* because God says so. It's as if morals are valued more highly if they already exist somewhere out there, so we can learn to recognize them. But is it possible that morals exist independently of humans, or God? Surely someone has to create them?

WHY BE GOOD?

Most people tend to try to do the right thing, at least *some* of the time. Acting selflessly – caring for others more than ourselves – is considered morally good. But is it possible to act truly selflessly, or do we always do things that will help ourselves in some way? Some philosophers argue that many acts that appear selfless can hide a selfish motive.

If you believe that any act of generosity will be returned, can it be morally good? Helping others can make you feel good inside, but does that mean it's *not* morally good? If the reward is no more than a sense of goodness, then most people would agree that a selfless act is morally good – and that there *are* plenty of *selfless* acts.

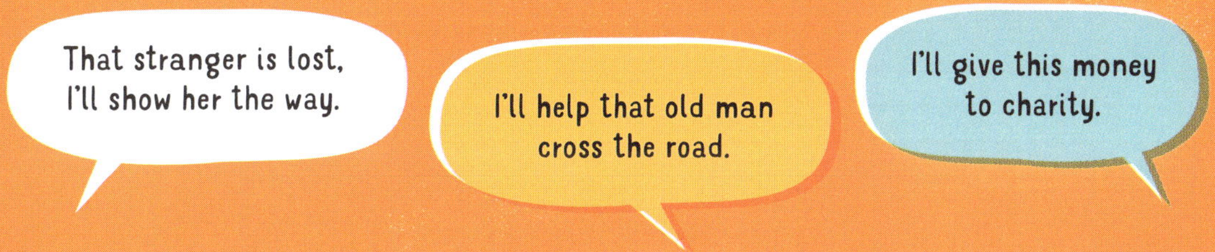

To help decide if an action is right or wrong, philosophers have developed ways of looking at morality. Some have very formal names, such as **utilitarianism**, **deontology** and **virtue ethics**. Read on to find out more about them.

THE PURSUIT OF HAPPINESS

When faced with a moral dilemma, how *do* you decide on the right course of action? One solution is to choose what causes the greatest benefit, or the greatest happiness, for the greatest number of people. This idea is known as **utilitarianism**.

Utilitarianism focuses on the *consequences* of an action, in particular, the *number* of people that will benefit from it, and *how much* they will benefit.

If the total amount of happiness gained outweighs some sadness by a smaller group of people, then a utilitarian would say it's morally right to do this thing.

WHAT ARE ITS ADVANTAGES?

It provides a clear way to judge whether an action is morally right or wrong.

It doesn't treat different groups of people differently – it's purely about numbers.

It makes people more morally responsible, to consider the *consequences* of their actions.

Most people agree that increasing happiness and reducing harm overall is a worthwhile outcome.

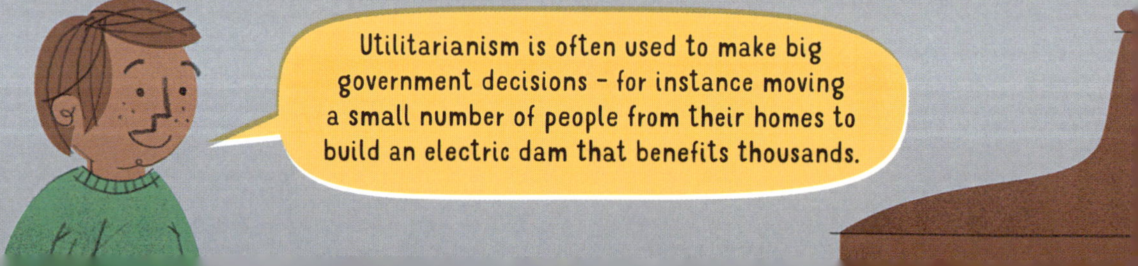

What utilitarianism doesn't do is consider the rights or implications for the few, the people who might not benefit from an action.

WHAT ARE ITS DISADVANTAGES?

It justifies the suffering of a few, to achieve the happiness of the many.

Happiness means different things to different people.

How do you define happiness, let alone compare one person's happiness to another's?

How much happiness will result is not always easy to predict.

Surely all individuals have rights. Utilitarianism doesn't consider anyone's rights.

JUDGING ACTIONS

Another way to make a moral decision is to focus on the action, not the consequences. This is known as **deontology**. It's about following rules and doing the right thing. Imagine you had to decide whether to betray your best friend to save the class from being punished.

Deontologists who believe strongly in loyalty might choose *not* to betray a friend, even if it leads to 30 people being punished. One problem with this philosophy is how rigid it can be. It doesn't allow for your opinion about what is right or wrong to change, depending on the circumstances.

Focusing on actions, the choice is between betraying a friend or not. But if the class received an extreme punishment, or if your friend had done something worse than you'd imagined, being loyal might not *feel* like the right choice any more. Maybe sometimes we have to judge morals on *intuition*, or *what feels right*.

DO WHAT GOOD PEOPLE DO

Another way to make a moral choice is to imagine how a good or virtuous person would act. This is known as **virtue ethics**. For this to work, it's necessary to define what it means to be good. Here's a list of things a good person might be expected to be or do:

Even if you could agree on what qualities a good person should *have*, here's another problem. Virtue ethics doesn't provide a reliable method for finding out what would be the right thing to *do*.

If Alan is not there, it's not clear exactly how to come to a decision.

RULES ARE RELATIVE

Different families have different ways of doing things. So do different schools, regions and countries. Some philosophers suggest that moral judgements are only true or false in relation to the community you belong to. So a moral rule can be true for one place, and false for another.

Is having two husbands wrong? If you are a moral relativist, you think there is no single answer to this question. Having two husbands can be wrong from one perspective, and right from another.

But couldn't two people from different communities disagree about what the right thing to do is? It's a bit like disagreeing with someone about which way is left. You both understand what 'left' means. You might both be pointing left. But if you're facing each other, you'll be pointing in different directions.'

One problem with moral relativism is that there are some actions that seem wrong *regardless* of what anyone else thinks. For instance, even if stealing or torture are accepted in some places, most people would want to say that they're wrong, not just *for us*, but wrong *full stop*.

The opposite of relativism is the idea that moral beliefs are either true or false. This is known as **absolutism**. For an absolutist, it makes no difference which community you belong to. If cannibalism is wrong, for example, then it's wrong whichever community or time in history you are from.

ARE SOME RULES FOR EVERYONE?

The belief that there are at least some universal moral rules that should be upheld across all communities has led to many international agreements, including **The Universal Declaration of Human Rights** (UDHR).

Created in 1948, the UDHR sets out a list of rights for *everyone*. It aims to make the world a fairer place, where humans can live with dignity and respect. Agreements like this are often backed up by international laws. However, these laws only apply to the countries that sign up to them.

TEST YOUR ETHICS

Here's a thought experiment. A runaway train is hurtling along towards ten people who are tied to the track. **You** control a switch that can send the train onto a different track. But if you do, one person will die.
WHAT SHOULD YOU DO?

You can make the choice harder by imagining that the single person is a relative or friend. Or, instead of pulling a switch, what if you had to push a person onto the track to stop the train? Could you do it? **Perhaps there is no right answer here?**

PHILOSOPHY ON THE ROAD

Self-driving cars need programs to instruct them how to react in different situations. Designers of self-driving cars are working with philosophers to write those programs.

Most people answer 'Yes' to the first question and 'No' to the second, even though the consequences are the same. Should a self-driving car act in a utilitarian way that saves more people, or in a way that protects the passenger first? Or should self-driving cars simply be banned? Philosophers are hard at work looking for solutions to these problems.

DIFFICULT DECISIONS

Life is full of moral questions that people – including philosophers – disagree on. Here are some examples.

THE RIGHT TO DIE

Some people believe that if you are very ill you should have the right to die sooner with the assistance of a doctor. Others say this is suicide, which many people believe is wrong. Does your belief depend on the action, the consequences, or on something else?

I am dying of cancer and in great pain. I want the doctors to help me die.

What if the pain and sadness is temporary? The doctors may find a new treatment...

A doctor could abuse the system to commit murder.

Assisted suicide is against my religion.

Life is a fundamental 'right' and no one should have the power to take it away.

The kindest solution is to relieve the patient of their pain and suffering.

CAPITAL PUNISHMENT

Should the state have the right to take a person's life if they have been convicted of murder?

What if a prisoner really is innocent? Innocent people have been wrongfully accused of crimes.

If someone commits a serious crime, they lose their rights, including their right to life.

The threat of execution is the best way to scare people into not committing serious crimes in the future.

The state has a duty to help convicted criminals become better people, no matter how serious their crime.

No one, not even the state, has the right to take someone's life.

MEDICAL ETHICS

Doctors have to face all sorts of ethical dilemmas on a daily basis.
There are groups or committees in hospitals that help make these decisions.

This child needs emergency treatment, but his parents are not here to give permission for the operation. Should we wait?

My patient told me she had committed a crime. Should I inform the police?

PRIVACY

My emails, phone and internet use should be private. I have the right to privacy.

I don't mind what the state does if it helps prevent a terrorist attack.

WAR

Is it ever ok for one country to declare war on another?

War is justified if it's the only way to stop a country from attacking and killing my fellow citizens.

Violence always leads to more violence. Countries should always look for a peaceful solution.

Killing is wrong. War is never justified.

Innocent people always die in wars.

We should go to war if it's the only way to stop an evil dictator from killing thousands of people.

MAKING LAWS

It's hard to find answers that everyone agrees on. Every country has to consider the arguments for and against these types of things, in order to make decisions and laws about them. Laws can differ widely from country to country. At times, your personal viewpoint may be different from the laws of the country you live in. Some people who disagree with laws campaign to get them changed.

HOW DO I KNOW THAT YOU ARE THE SAME PERSON I MET YESTERDAY?

WHAT IS TIME?

DOES IT MAKE SENSE TO THINK I COULD GO BACK IN TIME AND CHANGE THE PAST?

TIME AND IDENTITY

Time and identity are two thorny subjects that are discussed in a branch of philosophy known as **metaphysics**. Metaphysics deals with all sorts of problems – some of them very BIG ones – including the idea of existence, reality, space, the properties of things, and cause and effect. In this chapter, you will just get a small taste of this wide-ranging area of philosophy.

IDENTITY

What makes one thing the same as another? How do you explain how something can change and still be the same thing? These are questions about **identity**.

'The same' can mean two things, and it's important not to confuse them. The first type of identity is known as **qualitative identity.** Imagine two cars that have just rolled off the production line.

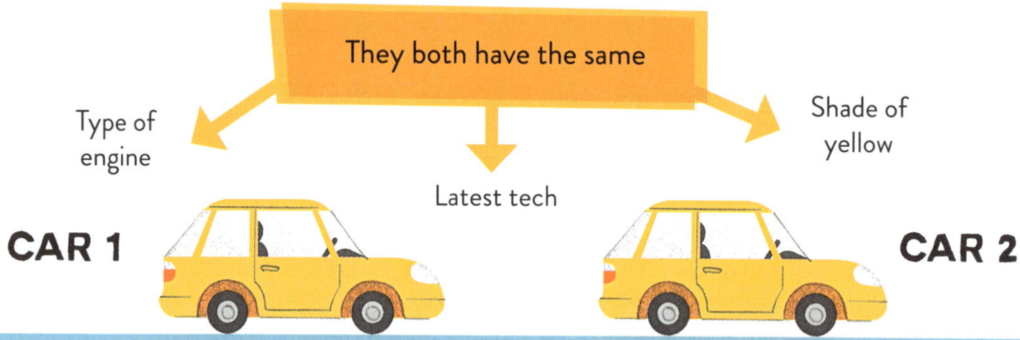

These cars have all the same qualities. They are exactly alike, or *qualitatively* identical. But they are *still* two separate cars.

Now, imagine you buy Car 1, but then it's stolen. One day, the police tell you they've found your car. It doesn't *look* like your car, but they assure you that it *is*. The thief has...

This car looks slightly different so it's *not* **qualitatively identical** to the original car. But it *is* **numerically identical** to it. This means there is only one car and it is the very same as the car you bought. What enables us to say that the car at one point in time is the same car as at another time – especially when it has changed?

Perhaps you might think that as long as something changes *gradually*, it can continue to exist, even if it changes a lot. Remember the thought experiment about the teddy bear on page 13? Here it is again, using the car.

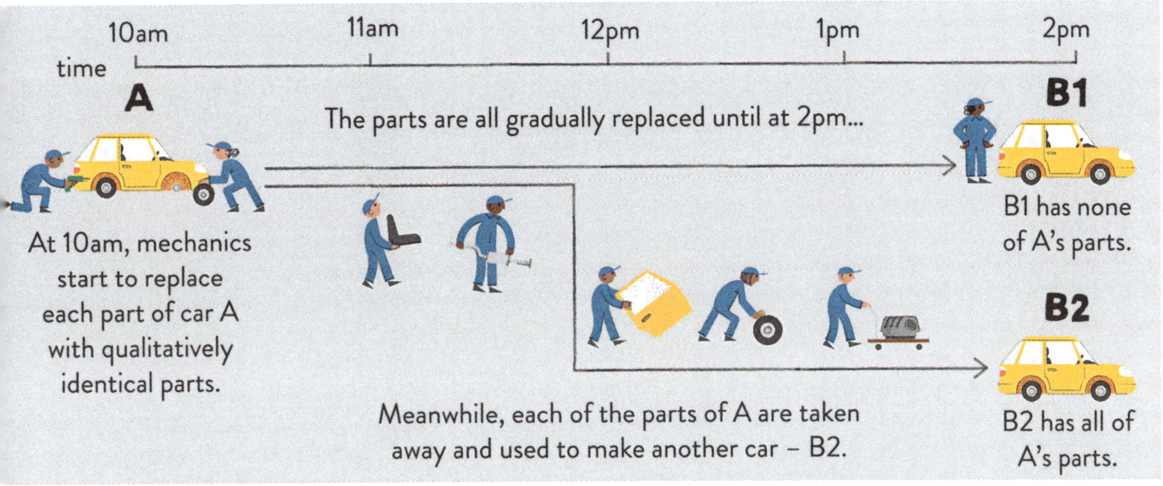

By 2pm, there are two cars, B1 and B2. These two cars are qualitatively identical to each other. They are also both *exactly like* the original car, A. But which one is *numerically* identical to A? They can't *both* be, can they?

If this all seems tricky, things get even trickier when you start to think about identity in relation to *people*. Turn over the page to find out how and why.

PERSONAL IDENTITY

When it comes to people, the problem of identity gets a bit more complicated. For a start, what counts as a person? A human being? A brain? A mind? Or something else...? Here's a simple-sounding question that philosophers ask: How do I know that I am the same person as the person who started reading this book? Answering it, though, is far from simple.

SAME BODY?

We tend to assume that if someone's *body* continues to exist, then *that person* continues to exist too. This is how we *tell* that someone is the same person from one moment to the next. But does this mean that what *makes* you the same person, from one time to another, is that you have the same body? Is **personal identity** the same as **bodily identity**?

Here's a thought experiment to help you test out this idea.

Sam has a serious accident. Her brain is fine, but the rest of her body is dying.

New techniques make it possible to remove her brain without damaging it...

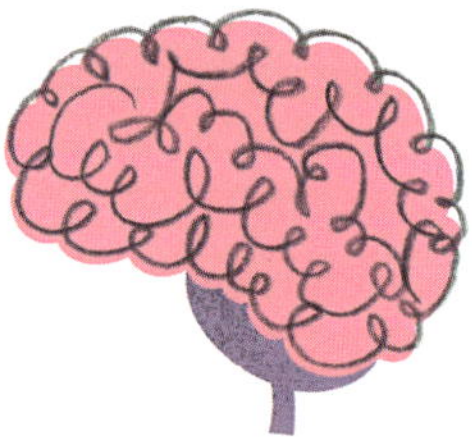

...and transfer it into a new body, where it works as well as it used to. But is this still Sam?

If you think it *is* still Sam, the chances are it's because you don't think that she – or what makes Sam *Sam* – is the same as her body. Or, not her *whole* body, at least. Some philosophers have suggested that what makes someone the same person from one time to another is *having the same brain.*

SAME BRAIN?

If Sam is identical to her brain, then the person who wakes up after the operation is still Sam because they have the same brain. Sam goes wherever her brain goes. But here's a fact to chew on. Our brains are made up of two parts, or hemispheres, that can operate independently.

Which of the resulting people, if either, would be Sam?

But what if you don't need this very brain in order to be you? What if you could have your mental states in a different brain, or a computer, even? Would you *be* that computer or brain? If you think the answer is yes, then this probably means you think that what makes a person the same person at different times is not brain identity, but something to do with the *mind*. But what does this involve? Turn the page to find out.

SAME MIND?

Some philosophers have argued that **continuity of consciousness** is what makes someone the same person from one time to another. But what on earth does this mean? One argument says it's all to do with your memories.

How does this work?

Imagine that Ruth – in 2031 – claims that she's the same person as someone who was called Jo in 2011. On the continuity of consciousness view, Ruth can only be the same person as Jo if she can remember experiences had by Jo in 2011.

But there's a problem with using memories to define identity – it's circular.

Ruth = Jo, if and only if Ruth has memories of things Jo experienced.

What makes a memory a memory is that the person who has it is *the same person* who had those experiences.

We need to understand personal identity in order to understand memory.

The idea of memory assumes you already have an idea of what personal identity involves. You'd be using personal identity to *explain* personal identity.

Here's another thought experiment. At the moment it's science fiction, but one day it might become possible.

Of course, the procedure is only a success if you think that copying Sam's mental states has kept her alive. If you don't believe this, then you'd have to say that Sam has died and been replaced by a very good copy. If *you* were Sam, wouldn't you want to know the answer before you agreed to the procedure?

TIME

People often talk about time as if it were a thing. It flows, it passes, and we move through it. It also *seems* to go in one direction – from past to present to future. But do these common-sense ideas about time make philosophical sense?

We think of events using the terms **past**, **present** and **future**. We also say that time flows in one specific direction: event A must happen first, *then* event B, *then* C.

Events also *change* their positions. When I was drinking tea, reading this book was future. Later on it became present, then past. Similarly, texting my friend will eventually be present, and then later on, past.

So far so good... or is it? British philosopher J.M.E. McTaggart argued that this idea of time involves a **contradiction**. If something involves a contradiction, it means it's saying two things are true that can't *both* be true. This suggests that time itself doesn't make sense! In fact, time must be *unreal*.

Philosophers have suggested various ways out of this. For example, some say that only the present exists. It doesn't make sense to say that things are past or future. Others suggest that *nothing* is past, present or future *full stop*. It's just all relative to where *you* are in time. Confused? You are not alone. As medieval philosopher, St. Augustine said,

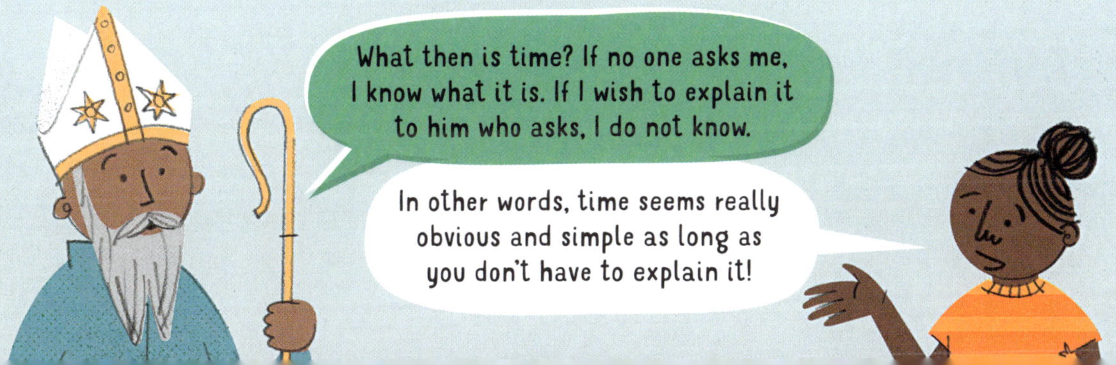

TIME TRAVEL

Time travel makes for exciting stories. But the idea of time travel brings up serious philosophical problems, which suggest that it's not logically possible. And if it's not logically possible, it's not *physically* possible either (whatever physicists say).

So what counts as time travel? Well, technically we are all travelling through time. Since you started reading this book, you have travelled into the future. But what people usually mean by time travel is travelling in the wrong direction – into the past – or into the future at a faster rate than everyone else. It's this sort of 'time travel' that creates **paradoxes** – scenarios that seem both possible and impossible.

ROUND AND ROUND AND ROUND AND...

Arthur travels to the future in a time machine and steals the blueprint for a time machine. He then goes back and gives it to Professor Wells, who uses it to build the time machine that took Arthur to the future. This scenario involves something called a **causal loop**. That's when events ultimately seem to cause themselves.

THE GRANDFATHER PARADOX

Imagine Arthur travels back to a time before his grandfather had children, with the intention of killing him. But, if Arthur kills his grandfather, Arthur's *father* will not be born and nor will *Arthur*. So how *can* he kill his grandfather?

Some people say they have solved the Grandfather Paradox. Arthur *can* travel to the past and kill his grandfather, if the act of murder creates a *new* universe in which events happen differently. In this universe, Arthur will not be born, but he can exist in *this* universe, if he travels there from the universe in which he was born.

But even if time travel *is* logically possible, we still have another question to ask:

WHERE ARE ALL THE TIME TRAVELLERS?

In June 2009, physicist Stephen Hawking sent out invitations welcoming 'all future time travellers' to a party. But, the party had already happened and, not surprisingly, no one had turned up. Hawking's point was that if time travel *is* possible, at some point, someone will do it – so we'd expect to meet people from the future in the present. Simple, isn't it?

ARE SENTENCES ALWAYS EITHER TRUE OR FALSE?

IS THE MEANING OF 'DOG' THE OBJECT IT REFERS TO?

IS IT LOGICAL TO BELIEVE THAT SOMETHING WILL HAPPEN AGAIN IF IT'S HAPPENED MANY TIMES BEFORE?

LOGIC AND LANGUAGE

At the heart of philosophy are the words and language we use to express an idea or argument. But our choice of words and the way we use them can differ from one person to the next. So how do we know what *anyone* really means? And how can we rely on philosophy, if its central tools – words – can be so easily misunderstood?

To find the answers, many philosophers look closely at language itself. They break it down into parts and use the tools of logic – premises, conclusions and so on – to see if one thing truly does follow from another.

DIFFERENT WAYS OF REASONING

Philosophy, like mathematics, follows certain rules. It often involves reasoning from a set of **premises** to a **conclusion** that follows logically from them. Consider this simple conversation:

A philosopher might break down this conversation using logic (see pages 10-11), or, to use another phrase, **deductive reasoning**. It works like this...

PREMISE 1	PREMISE 2	CONCLUSION
Fuzzy always barks when someone is at the door.	Fuzzy didn't bark.	No one is at the door.

The advantage of deductive reasoning is its certainty. If the premises are true, and the overall argument is valid, then it follows logically that the conclusion must be true.

Of course, if one or even both premises are *false*, then the argument fails. For example, maybe Fuzzy doesn't *always* bark when someone is at the door...

REASONING BASED ON EXPERIENCE

Inductive reasoning is another form of argument. It uses evidence from the world around us, and observations from our senses, to lead to *probable* conclusions.

The statement that 'the cafe has been quiet before midday' is based on observing this many times. From this, you can conclude the same will *probably* happen again.

In the 18th century, Scottish philosopher David Hume gave an argument against inductive reasoning...

Just because something has happened in the past *doesn't* always mean it will happen again. But the fact is that we *do* believe the Sun will rise tomorrow. Although inductive reasoning doesn't give us certainty, it seems we can't help using it in our day-to-day thinking.

THE PROBLEM WITH TRUTH

Does language follow logical rules? If it does, some philosophers argue, then it should be possible to break it down into sentences that are true or false. Looking for truth, however, can lead to contradictions. Consider this riddle, known as **the liar's paradox**...

In this example, it's tricky – perhaps impossible – to say whether the sentence itself is either true or false. Perhaps logic doesn't work for all sentences?

THE MEANING OF A WORD

What is the meaning of a word? Perhaps it's the physical object that the word refers to. On this view, the meaning of 'Everest' is a mountain. But you might suggest that the meaning of 'Everest' is also an idea, or a piece of information about it, such as 'the world's highest mountain'.

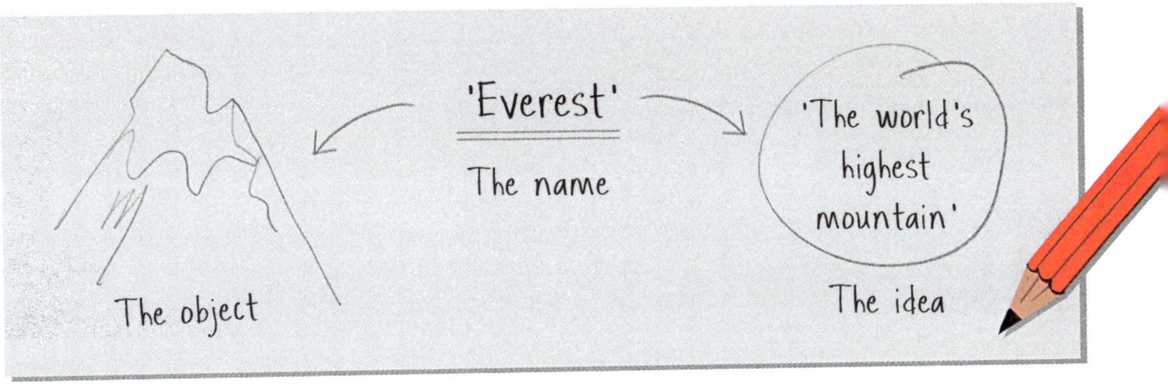

Both types of meaning are acceptable, but they are very different. 'Everest' refers to a mountain in the Himalayas, whereas the phrase 'the world's highest mountain' *could* have referred to a mountain elsewhere.

Consider a cat called Basil. Basil likes to chase cars.
He also likes to sleep on people's doorsteps.

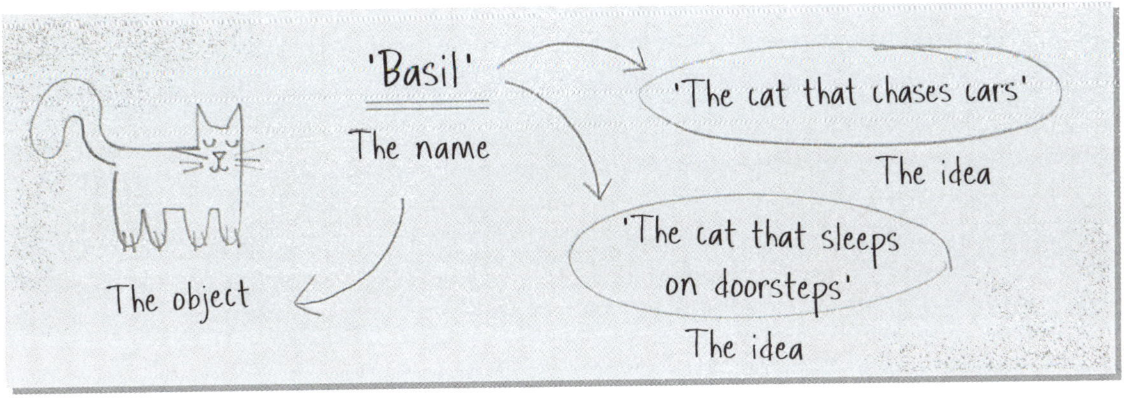

'The cat that chases cars' has a different meaning from 'The cat that sleeps on doorsteps'. Yet both sentences refer to the same thing, Basil. This shows how meaning can be looked at in multiple ways. But does it make sense to seek the precise meaning of a word? Turn the page to see another way of looking at it.

MEANING IS USE

Some philosophers have rejected the idea that words and language have a fixed meaning. They argue that the meaning of a word depends on its *use* in a sentence, the way it's expressed, the language itself...

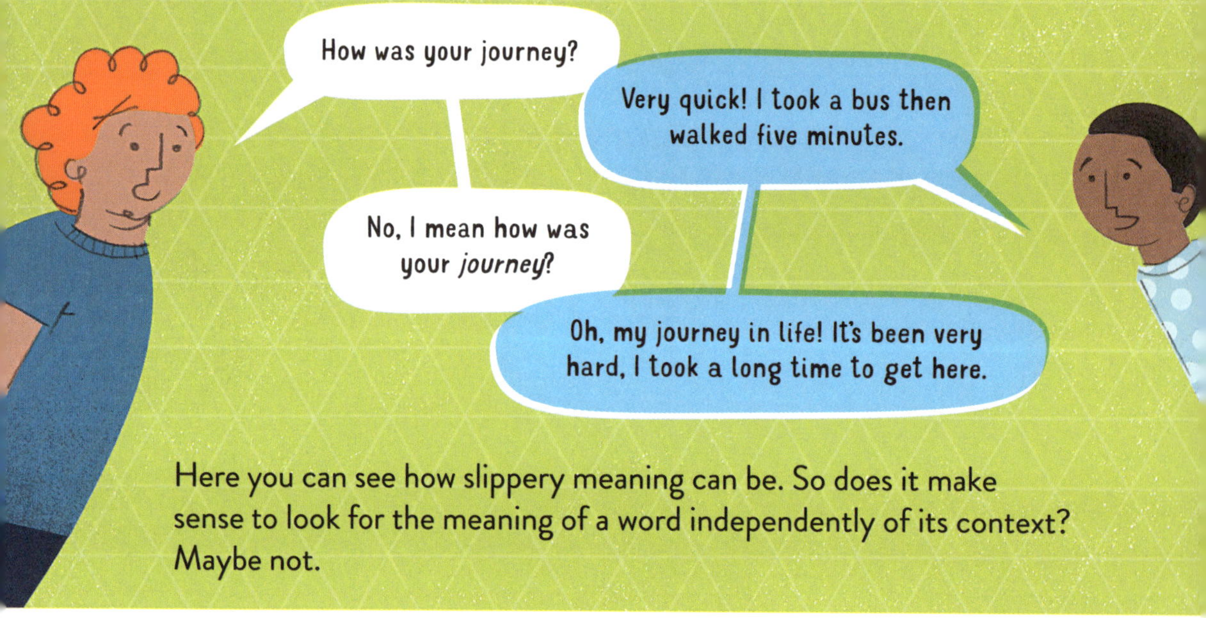

Here you can see how slippery meaning can be. So does it make sense to look for the meaning of a word independently of its context? Maybe not.

The meaning of a word can also depend on the audience. One person's idea of a party might look very different to someone else's. So how do we ever really know we are talking about the same thing? The answer is, perhaps we don't.

MEANING AND THE AUTHOR

Any words you *read* have been written by someone: an author. When trying to understand a piece of writing, can you do so without considering what the author really means? Some people believe you *can*. They believe that meaning is based purely on the writing, NOT the writer.

Many books contain hidden and multiple meanings that can be endlessly interpreted. So perhaps it doesn't matter what the author intended, as long as the reader can back up their own opinion of what the book is *really* about.

But sometimes knowing something about an author can change your point of view – so maybe it does matter.

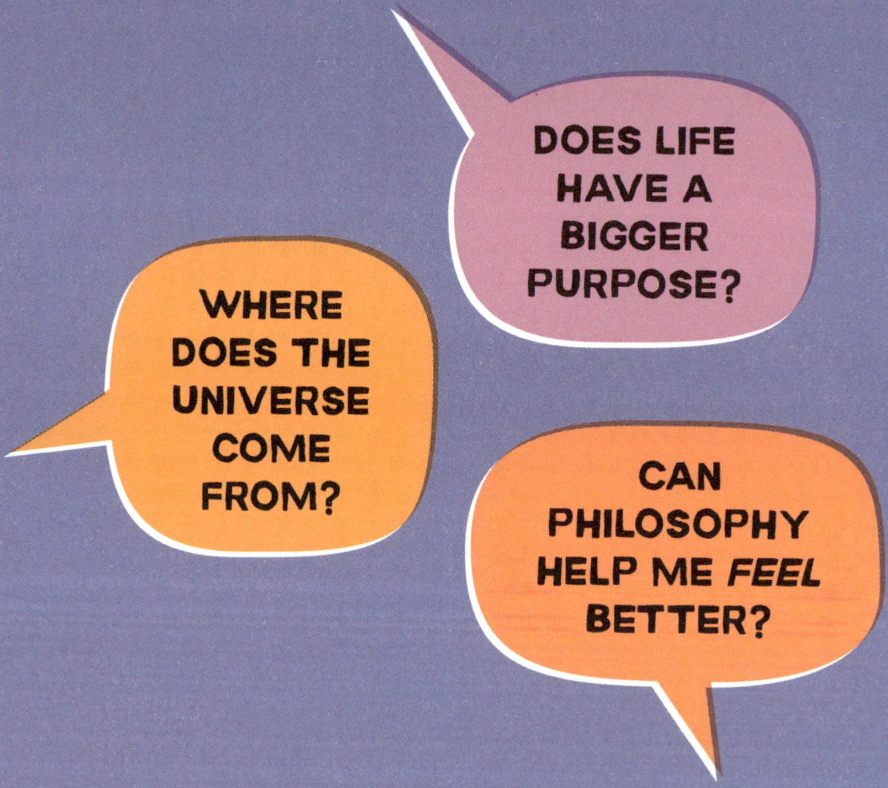
DOES LIFE HAVE A BIGGER PURPOSE?
WHERE DOES THE UNIVERSE COME FROM?
CAN PHILOSOPHY HELP ME *FEEL* BETTER?

THE MEANING OF LIFE

Philosophy often looks at aspects of life, such as art, ethics or knowledge. But what about how it all fits together? So far we have looked at philosophy as something to do – a hobby or perhaps a job. But for some people, philosophy isn't just an activity or a way of thinking – it can provide a code to live by. For many people, philosophy is a way of living.

THE GOOD LIFE?

In pursuit of wisdom and a life of virtue, some ancient philosophers gave up their wealth, or left their homes, to live very disciplined lives. For them, philosophy was a practical way to transform themselves into, they hoped, better people.

This isn't just something people did thousands of years ago. Philosophers from the last century also sought to change their lives with philosophy – but with a little less discipline.

Perhaps the most famous example of a philosopher who *lived* his philosophy is Socrates. He didn't earn a living. He didn't participate in city politics. He didn't even wear shoes. Instead, he spent his life wandering around the city, challenging people's beliefs and pursuing knowledge.

If you're interested in pursuing philosophy as a way of life, you don't have to walk around barefoot or give up your belongings. You just have to examine your beliefs. Make your life a process of exploration.

It's OK to admit that you're unsure or that you don't know something. In fact, the moment you do, you've taken the first step towards knowledge and discovery. And you've found something to do – discover answers to new questions.

WHAT IS THE MEANING OF LIFE?

When people think of philosophy, this is often *the* question that comes to mind.

Some people look for meaning by trying to understand why we exist at all. And that means explaining what the universe itself is.

Some explain it in terms of its history – or where it came from.

Others talk about its purpose – or where it is going.

But, if anything, these explanations leave us with more questions. *Why* was there a big bang? *What happens after the universe collapses*? Is there any purpose to this whole mess?

Most explanations need *further* explanation. Whatever story you are told about life's meaning, you can always ask why *that* story is the case and be told *another* story.

Or, as philosophers might put it, it's a problem of infinite regress.

WHAT'S THE MEANING OF... A POTATO?

Seems like a pointless question, right? I can tell you stories about a potato, but ultimately, it's just a potato. The universe is like a potato, in the sense that, asking what it's all about, is like asking what a potato means. It's just *there*. At some point you have to stop asking *why*.

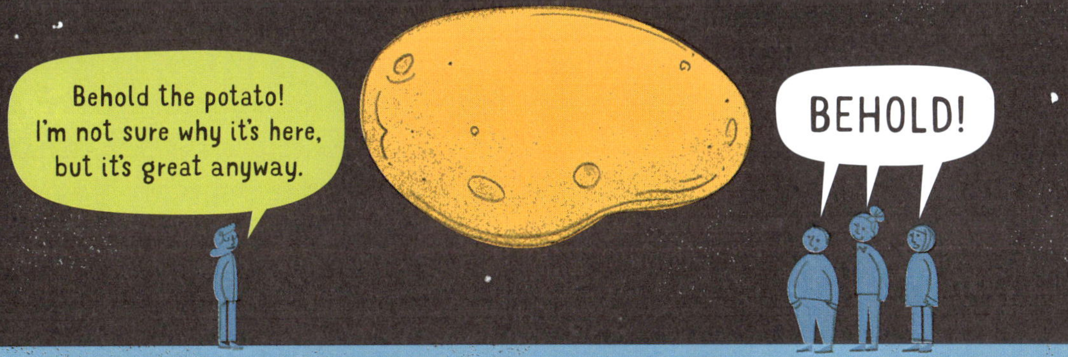

Maybe this isn't a satisfying answer to the question. But there's a reason for this. Usually when people ask, what is the meaning of life, they're actually asking something else. Turn over to explore the *real* question.

WHAT MAKES *MY LIFE* MEANINGFUL?

Some experiences in our lives are *so* interesting and engaging that it's as if nothing else matters. At times when we *don't* feel engaged, we might wonder why we're here. So what makes life *feel* meaningful?

YOU MAKE IT MEANINGFUL

One idea is that YOU decide what makes your experience feel rich and vivid. You decide why you're here. You decide the meaning of *your* life.

It seems we don't have the freedom to choose just *anything* for our lives. Perhaps some choices are more sensible, or meaningful, than others.

DOING THE RIGHT THINGS

Some philosophers think there are certain things that make life meaningful, and some things that *don't*. But, they rarely agree on what those things are.

Creativity

Improving people's lives

Connecting with people and animals

Finding yourself

Being a good person

Growing as a person

Discovering something new

Learning

Being authentic

I think it's possible to do these things and still not have a sense of wonder or engagement...

...and I'm not sure what some of this advice *actually* means.

THERE IS NO MEANING – AND THAT'S OK

These approaches both assume that life must be *made* meaningful – that unless you do *something*, your life is meaningless. But is this true? Maybe life is already rich enough. Maybe our expectations of what life *could* be gets in the way of what life already *is*.

Typically, people consider some things to be meaningful, but not others.

But are we right to do this? Even simple events can be magical experiences.

Experiment and see for yourself. Pay attention to something simple, such as the feel of the pages of this book, or the path of a raindrop. When you pay close attention, what is your experience like? Is it engaging?

WHAT NEXT?

Philosophy can be difficult. If it were easy, we'd already know the answers to life's big questions. So, if you've found yourself scratching your head a few times while reading this book, congratulations! It means you've been reading it correctly.

But now that you know a little about what philosophy is, and how it works, what can you actually *do* with it? Apart from annoying your family and teachers, that is...

If you really want to get into philosophy, a simple way to start is to read more books. Turn to page 125 for a list of some of the most influential thinkers in history, then see what you can find out about their ideas.

But the best way to *do* philosophy is to argue with people. Remember, an **argument** is the word philosophers use to describe a set of premises and a conclusion. It doesn't mean they like shouting at each other – although plenty of real philosophers do that, too. If you have an argument, test it out on someone. If they say it has an error, try to defend your argument, or improve it – but be polite. Where? Well, your school or local library might have a philosophy society you can join, or you might be able to start one up yourself.

WHY BOTHER?

After reading this book, we hope you've been persuaded that philosophy is interesting, fun and sometimes even useful.

Here are a few quotations from philosophers about their subject.

MULTIPLE MYSTERIES

If there's one thing philosophers love, it's coming up with mysteries, puzzles and paradoxes. Here are just a few to test your philosophical skills. Some are thought to be unsolvable – but people have suggested possible answers to almost all of these questions.

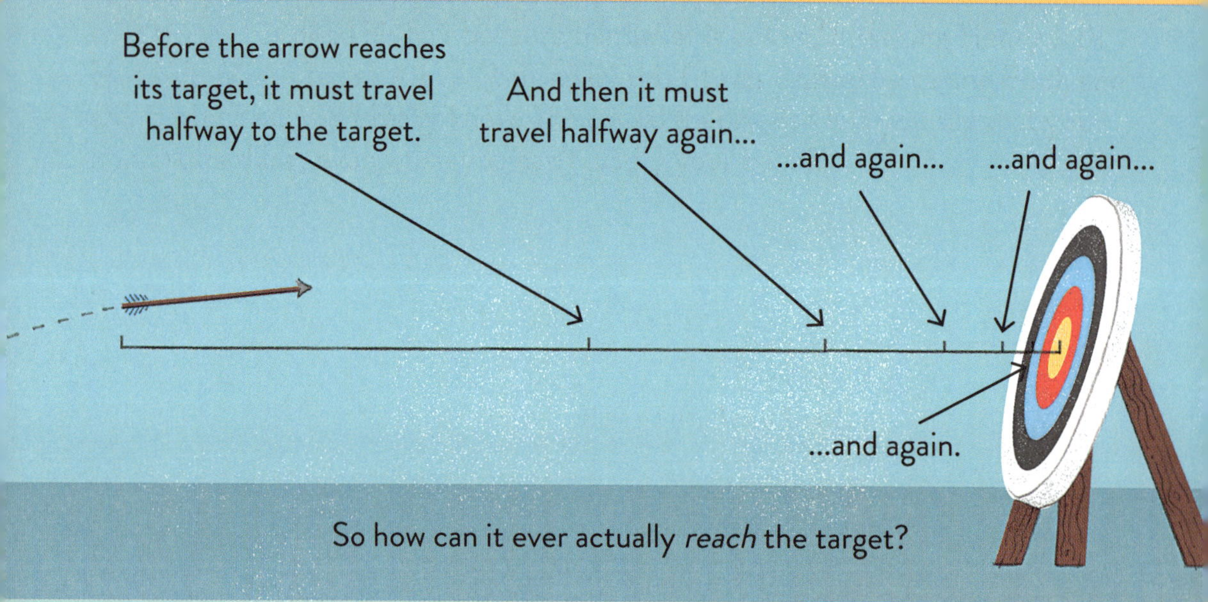

How could you tell if your family was replaced by incredibly lifelike robots?
And would it matter if they were?
If the universe and everything in it was doubling in size every second, would it be possible to tell?
Argh! My measuring tape keeps getting bigger!
Imagine there's a town with one barber in it. He *only* shaves people who *don't* shave themselves.
Is that barber allowed to shave himself?
Wait, if the barber doesn't shave himself, then he needs to go to a barber to be shaved. And he's the only barber in town.
But if he *does* shave himself, then he's breaking his own rule. I'm so confused!
Would it be right to make littering a crime punishable *by death*...
...if you knew *for certain* that this would stop people from ever littering?

GLOSSARY

This glossary explains some of the words used in this book. Words written in *italic* type are explained in other entries.

aesthetics the study of beauty and art.

argument an attempt to reach a particular *conclusion*, usually based on a set of *premises*.

circular argument an *argument* whose *premises* start off by assuming that the conclusion is true.

coherent when a set of ideas or beliefs all support each other.

conclusion the result of an *argument* after following through its *premises*.

consistent when a set of claims do not contradict each other.

deductive reasoning arriving at a *conclusion* based purely on *logic*.

determinism a belief that everything that happens is predictable, based on the laws of nature, and on the state of the Universe when it began.

ethics the study of right and wrong, good and bad, duties and responsibilities.

free will the ability to choose to do one thing rather than another.

identity what makes a thing itself, or a person who they are.

inductive reasoning arriving at a *conclusion* based on past experiences.

infinite regress an *argument* that has no firm *foundation*, but always relies on some further piece of *justification*.

invalid an *argument* whose *conclusion* does not *logically* follow from the stated *premises*.

justification an explanation for why something is the case.

legitimate in politics, something that people agree has a right to be the way that it is.

logic a formal system for testing that *arguments* are valid.

meaning how words are used by some and understood by others.

morals ways of acting and behaving that most people in a society agree are good or proper.

objective truly independent of any one person's point of view.

paradox a statement that appears to be true, but that also contradicts itself.

paternalism setting rules that limit people's freedom, supposedly for their own good.

premise a statement that claims to be true.

scepticism taking the view that nobody knows anything for certain.

sound an *argument* whose *premises* are true and whose *conclusion* follows *logically*.

subjective true only relative to one person's point of view.

unsound an *argument* whose *premises* are not all true, or whose *conclusion* is not *logically* implied by the premises.

valid an *argument* whose *conclusion* follows *logically* follow its *premises*.

FAMOUS PHILOSOPHERS

Throughout this book, we've described ideas developed by lots of philosophers. Chapter by chapter, here are their names, and the times and places where they lived. Some appear more than once.

WHAT IS PHILOSOPHY?

David Hume (Scotland 1711-1776); **Socrates** (Athens, roughly 470-400BC)

KNOWLEDGE

Al-Ghazali (Seljuk Empire 1053-1111); **George Berkeley** (Ireland and England 1685-1753); **René Descartes** (France and the Netherlands 1596-1650); **Gottlob Frege** (Germany 1848-1925); **Edmund Gettier** (USA 1927-present day); **Bertrand Russell** (UK 1872-1970)

MIND

Elisabeth of Bohemia (Saxony 1618-1680); **René Descartes; Hilary Putnam** (USA 1926-2016);

BEAUTY AND ART

Alan Goldman (USA 1945-present day); **Immanuel Kant** (Germany, 1724-1804); **Plato** (Athens roughly 425-370BC); **John Ruskin** (UK 1819-1900)

GOD

Anselm of Canterbury (England, roughly 1030-1100); **Augustine of Hippo** (North Africa 354-430); **Blaise Pascal** (France 1623-1662)

POLITICS

Thomas Hobbes (England 1588-1679); **Hannah Arendt** (Germany and USA 1906-1975); **John Locke** (England 1632-1704); **Karl Marx** (Germany and UK 1818-1883); **John Stuart Mill** (UK 1806-1873); **Mary Warnock** (UK, 1924-2019)

HOW TO BE GOOD

Aristotle (Athens roughly 385-320BC); **Jeremy Bentham** (UK 1748-1832); **Confucius** (China roughly 550-475BC); **Philippa Foot** (UK 1920-2010); **Immanuel Kant; Søren Kierkegaard** (Denmark 1813-1855); **John Stuart Mill; Judith Jarvis Thomson** (USA 1929-present day)

TIME AND IDENTITY

Elisabeth of Bohemia; John Locke; J. M. E. McTaggart (UK 1866-1925); **Bernard Williams** (UK 1929-2003)

LOGIC AND LANGUAGE

Roland Barthes (France 1915-1980); **Noam Chomsky** (USA 1928-present day) **Jacques Derrida** (Algeria and France, 1930-2004); **Gottlob Frege; David Hume; Bertrand Russell; Ludwig Wittgenstein** (Austria and UK 1889-1951)

THE MEANING OF LIFE

Siddhartha Guatama, the Buddha (India, roughly 480-400BC); **Jean-Paul Sartre** (France 1905-1980); **Simone de Beauvoir** (France 1908-1986)

INDEX

ACKNOWLEDGEMENTS

Written by
Jordan Akpojaro, Rachel Firth
and Minna Lacey

Illustrated by
Nick Radford

Edited by
Alex Frith

Designed by
Freya Harrison

Philosophy consultant:
Dr Alex Kaiserman,
University of Oxford

Series editor: Jane Chisholm

Series designer:
Stephen Moncrieff

First published in 2020 by Usborne Publishing Ltd., Usborne House, 83-85 Saffron Hill, London, EC1N 8RT, United Kingdom.
usborne.com

USBORNE

ECONOMICS

FOR BEGINNERS

Written by
Lara Bryan and
Andy Prentice

Illustrated by
Federico Mariani

Economics experts: David Stallibrass and Pedro Serôdio

Designed by Jamie Ball and Freya Harrison

Contents

Usborne Quicklinks

For links to websites where you can find out more about economics, from supply and demand to price bubbles and globalization, with video clips, games, activities and quizzes, go to the Usborne Quicklinks website at **Usborne.com/Quicklinks** and type in the title of this book.

Here are some of the things you can do at Usborne Quicklinks:

- Play games to control inflation or manage the national debt
- Try test-yourself quizzes on economic terms
- Watch video clips on trade, markets and more

Please follow the internet safety guidelines at the Usborne Quicklinks website. Children should be supervised online.

What is economics?

Some people think that economics is all about money, banks and very complicated graphs. But it's actually a lot simpler than that – much of economics is really about **understanding choices**.

Imagine there are two chocolate and two pineapple cupcakes. There's enough for four of you to have one cupcake each. How do you share them out?

When there isn't enough of something, it's **scarce**. Scarcity is an important idea in economics – it's what forces people to make choices. You might be surprised how often you make choices about things that are scarce.

What is an economy?

When a group of people is making choices about what to do, buy or sell it creates an **economy**. An economy can be very small or really big, depending on the number of people making choices.

An economy is created by...

A BIG economy, such as the economy of a country or the world, is a network made up of lots of *smaller* economies – all the households, villages, towns and cities within it.

What do economists study?

Economists are the people that study economies. Some focus on individuals or small groups, while others zoom out to look at the bigger picture. And some economists end up asking – and trying to answer – some surprising questions...

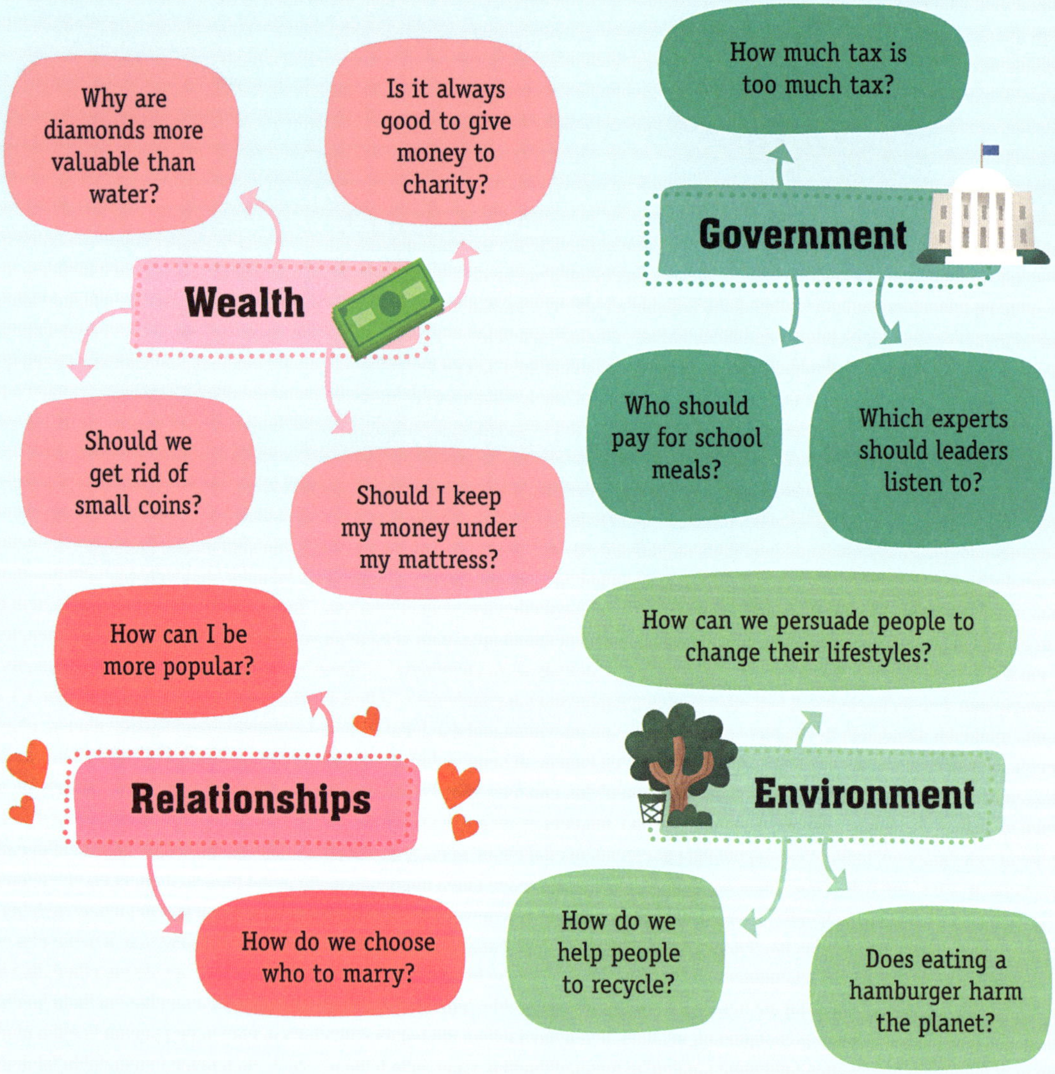

Economics for good

By finding answers to all these questions, economists hope to encourage people, businesses and governments to make better choices – and, hopefully, make the world a better, fairer place. Economics isn't about labelling people or governments as 'good' or 'bad' – it's about observing the choices that people make and trying to understand why they've made them.

Work

- Should *everyone* have a job?
- At what age should people stop working?
- Are people who work longer hours more productive?
- Why are women often paid less than men?

Crime

- What's the best time to rob a bank?
- Why does poverty breed crime?
- Is putting criminals in prison a good idea?

Businesses

- Why do some businesses have January sales?
- Are big businesses dangerous?
- How can I sell more of my product?

Families

- How expensive is having a child?
- Is it better to leave home or live with your parents?

Trade

- How can I trust someone in another country?
- Does free trade make the world richer?
- Does it matter if children make my shoes?

Sports

- Do crowds affect the outcome of games?
- Is there such a thing as a hot scoring streak?

The future

- Can we eliminate poverty?
- Will robots take my job?
- Would mining on Mars fix the world economy?

How do you *do* economics?

Why do people make certain choices? What are the consequences of those choices? To investigate these kinds of questions, economists usually start by coming up with an explanation, or **model.**

Here's a question

Here's a model

Modelling

A model is a simplified way of explaining how something works – in this case the relationship between quantity and price. Economists often show models using graphs, instead of words.

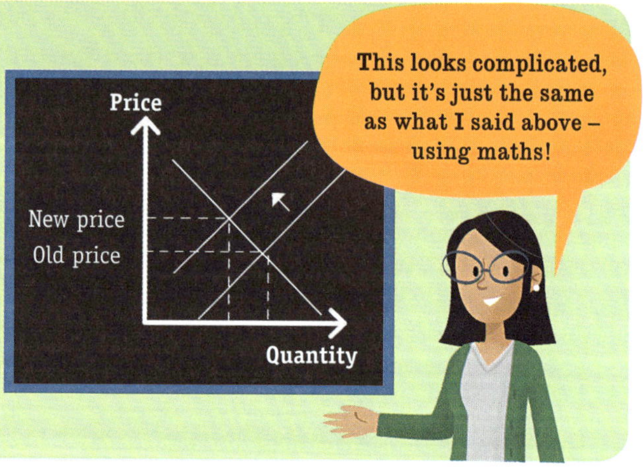

Models can be helpful for making predictions, or **forecasts.**

Test it out

Economists can test a model by collecting information, or **data,** and seeing whether it matches the model or not.

Economics is an argument

Even though all economists study data – sometimes exactly the same data – they often come to different conclusions about what it's saying.

Just like everyone else, economists often have different ideas about how societies *should* work, or a different sense of what's fair. Even in this book, the way we describe economics and the examples we've chosen show our **biases** – the things *we* think are important. Here are some different ways of seeing the world. You might strongly agree or disagree with some of them.

There are economists to back up all of these opinions.

British economist Joan Robinson once said...

Chapter 1: Not enough to go around

If everyone could have anything they wanted, at any time, with no effort needed to get it – there probably wouldn't be any economists. But the world we live in isn't like that.

Every day, everyone must make choices about how to keep on living in a world where **resources** such as food, materials and energy are **scarce** and everyone's time is limited. Studying this challenge is the fundamental task of economics.

The challenge of survival

Our need for food, water, and shelter hasn't changed since our earliest ancestors walked the Earth. Economists talk about us using up, or **consuming**, the Earth's resources to fulfil these needs.

Let's have a look at some of the resources our distant ancestors consumed...

On some days, getting these resources might have been pretty easy. But you can be sure that there were other days when resources were scarce.

Everything around us is a potential resource. Modern economies consume many *different* kinds of resources in ways that our ancestors didn't – not just things to eat, drink or use as tools. Here are some of them...

Sunshine

Manure

Oil

Uranium

Sand

Wind

The cost of choice

Every choice has a cost even if you don't pay money for it. This is because any choice you make makes other choices impossible. Economists call this an **opportunity cost.** The cost to you is all the other things that you chose *not to do* instead.

Most resources can only be used once. The *opportunity cost* of consuming a resource is all the other ways you might have used that resource.

Your time is scarce too. If you spend time doing one thing, that means you've chosen not to spend time doing other things. That's an opportunity cost too.

Frequently, it is very hard to know what the right choice is. You might have to choose between what you want and what you need, or between a short-term gain and a long-term benefit.

To make a choice, people often weigh up how much benefit they will get. Economists call this **utility**.

The utility of something varies from person to person.

People are complicated, so they may make some interesting decisions. Lots of different factors go into deciding what gives you the most utility.

The safest option was to run away, but the girl decided to risk her life to save her dad. Luckily for him, she thought a living dad benefitted her the most.

Turning resources into products

Sometimes we use resources to make other things. This is called **production**. Economists usually break down the process of production into four main parts.

1) In order to produce something, you first need an **idea**. What do you want to make and how do you want to make it?

2) Then you need **resources.**

3) Economists call the work you have to put into producing something **labour**.

Labour isn't just the manual effort that goes into making something, but all the other work too. This includes thinking up ideas and leadership. Anything that takes time is labour.

4) Tools and technology help us to work faster, better or more safely – in other words more efficiently. Economists call these things **capital**.

This is how production works.

Production = idea + resources + labour + capital

New ideas, tools or technology make people more **productive**. This means making more things more efficiently. Economists study productivity because it helps improve people's lives – thanks to the wall, the family is now safer.

From resources to economies

Imagine you had to make everything you needed to survive yourself. Then imagine everyone else having to do the same. It wouldn't be very efficient. This is why it makes sense to divide up most tasks.

Economists call this division of tasks **specialization**.

Some people specialize in gathering or producing **goods**.

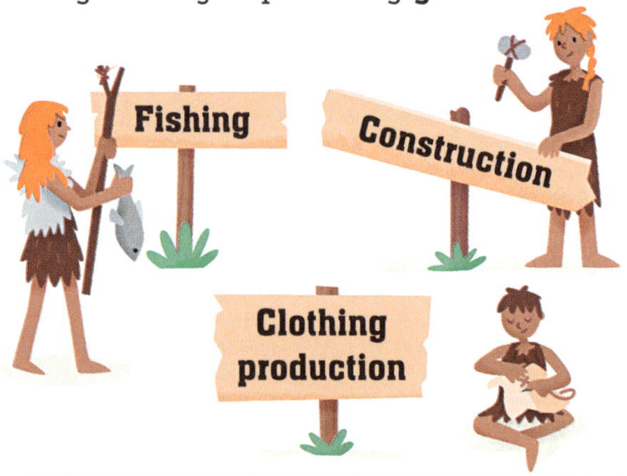

Some people specialize in doing things for others. These jobs are known as **services**.

When people spend a lot of time specializing in just one job, they become more efficient. They often invent new technologies and get faster at producing things.

People who specialize in a task usually produce more of a good or service than they need for themselves. This extra production is known as a **surplus**.

Surpluses are vital to the economy. People can exchange or **trade** their surplus with each other to get all the other things they need.

When you exchange goods directly like this it's known as **bartering**.

Today, we tend to trade using money.

Specialization and trade are the foundation of all **economies**, no matter how big or small. That's how it was thousands of years ago, and it's still like that today.

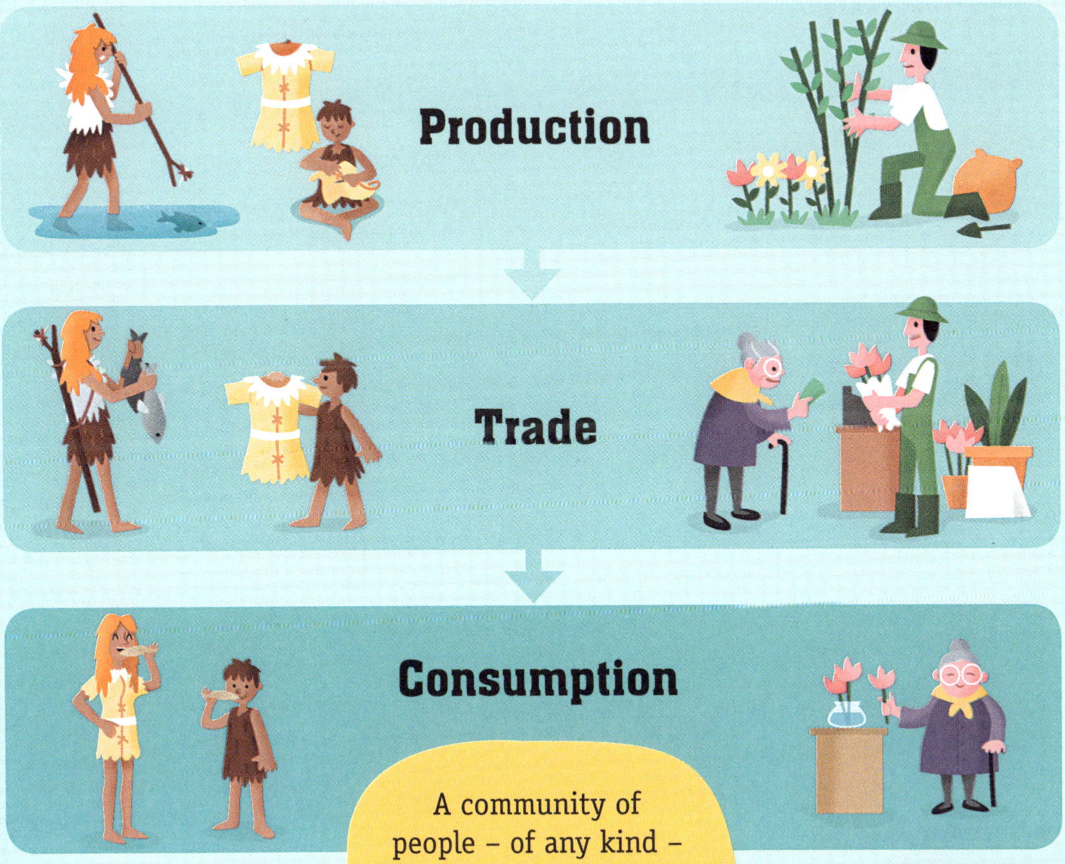

A community of people – of any kind – that produces, trades and consumes is **an economy**.

Chapter 2: Markets

Everything people do – from making ice cream to performing surgery – depends on exchanges of knowledge, goods, services and ideas. A place where people meet to exchange things is known as a **market**.

Over the centuries, economists have analyzed all sorts of markets and discovered various patterns that describe how they work. They've also put forward ideas on how to make sure people trade fairly and efficiently.

Making, buying and selling

All the making, selling and buying in an economy allows people to get the things they want and need. It sounds simple, but at every stage of the process something magical happens – *value* gets created.

Take this rock, around 2,000 years ago...

Making something out of the rock adds value to it.

Trading the statue creates value, too.

For the *seller*, the value is the difference between the price and the cost of making the product.

Price: 40 coins
Cost: 15 coins (tools + time spent)

For the *buyer*, the value is harder to measure. It's the difference between the utility the buyer gets from the purchase and the price paid.

For trading to work, both sides need to believe they're gaining something. They also need to **trust** the other person to supply the promised goods or pay the agreed amount of money.

However much people need each other's goods and services, if they can't *find* each other, trade won't happen. This is the origin of the **market**. The Greek *agora*, the Chinese *shìchâng*, or this Persian *šūqā* are all examples of ancient markets.

Many, many markets

As well as marketplaces with stalls, there are all kinds of markets around you. This scene shows six examples of everyday markets.

A **shop** is a marketplace.

A market can be an online space such as a **website** or **app**, which connects buyers and sellers worldwide.

In the **informal market** for sports stickers, the buyer paid with a snack bar and a card instead of money.

A **workplace**, such as a school, is also a market, where people exchange their work for a salary.*

A stock exchange is a place where people buy and sell parts of companies, known as **shares,** through a computer. The market for shares is called the **stock market**.

If things are bought or sold illegally, it's known as a **black market**.

*Well, the teachers do. The children have to work and don't get paid. Is that fair?

Supply and demand

If you look at any market, you'll notice that the amount people want to buy and sell – known as **demand and supply** – usually follows certain patterns. Economists call these patterns the **laws of supply and demand.**

See if you can spot the pattern in this market for sandwiches of the same quality, but different prices.

More people want to buy the cheaper sandwiches and fewer people want to buy the expensive ones. That's because the lower the price, the more people think it is worth buying it.

Economists show the relationship between price and demand on a graph like this:

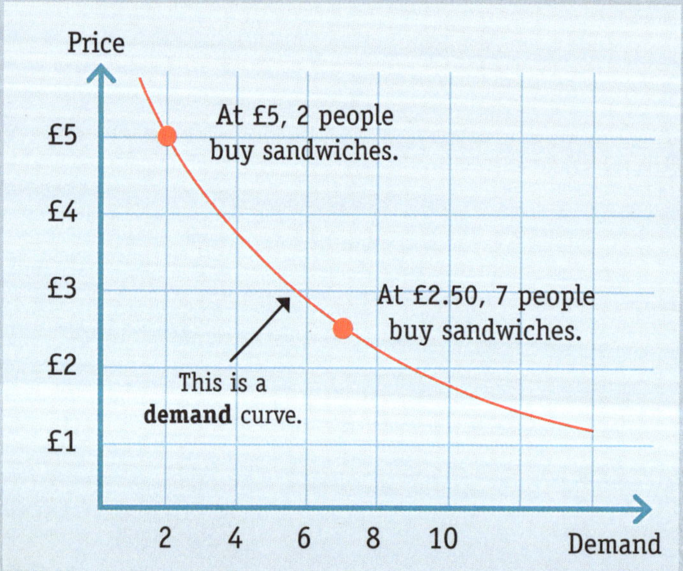

Law of demand

The amount people are willing to **supply** also changes depending on the price, or reward. Take this poetry competition – more poems were submitted in the year with the higher reward.

A higher reward, or price, encourages more poets to supply poems. This graph shows the relationship between price and supply:

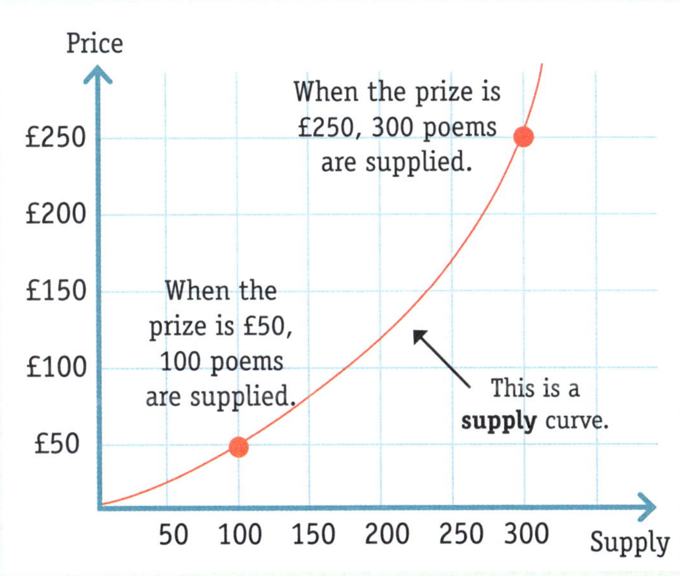

Law of supply

How prices respond to people

Prices influence how much people want to buy and produce. But it also works the other way around – how much people buy and produce makes prices change too.

If there's more supply than there is demand, it sends a signal to a seller to lower prices.

If there's less supply than there is demand, it sends a signal to a seller to increase prices.

Over time, the price changes until it reaches a point where there's as much demand as there is supply. This is known as the **equilibrium price**.

The price is just right – it's high enough for the seller, and low enough for customers. It also means there's no wasted mangoes.

In this kind of market, no one person is responsible for making the price change. It's the result of all the decisions made by buyers and sellers seeking to make a living and get the best deal. Here's how economists have tried to make sense of this process.

In the 18th-century, Scottish economist Adam Smith, described this process as the **invisible hand** of the market.

About a century later, British economist Alfred Marshall developed Smith's idea of the invisible hand.

Marshall came up with the idea of showing the way supply and demand work *together* on a graph.

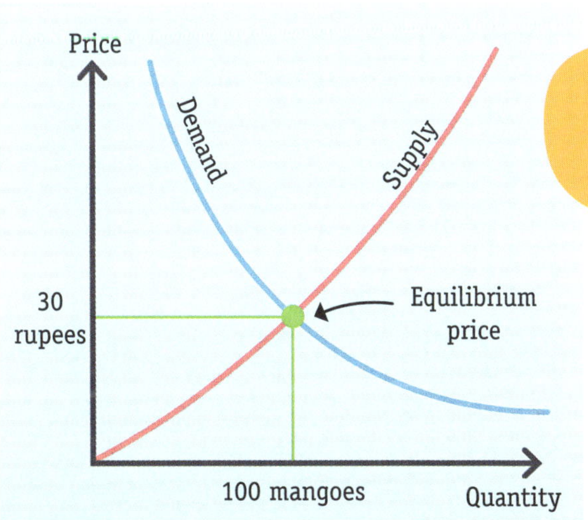

Changing markets

Supply and demand don't just change because of prices. Take bicycles – there are all sorts of reasons why the demand and supply of bikes might change...

Trends

People are trying to live more healthily, so *demand* for cycling is going up.

Costs of making

If the price of electricity goes up, it will cost more to make the bike, so *supply* is likely to go down.

Other prices

If bus tickets get more expensive, more people might switch to cycling. So *demand* goes up.

Weather

If it's cold, the *demand* for cycling is likely to go down.

Number of suppliers

If a new bike shop opens, the *supply* of bikes will go up.

It's hard to tell, looking at all these changes, if the overall demand and supply of bikes has gone up or down. This makes it tricky for businesses to manage supply and demand.

How much change?

Some things respond more to changes than others. Imagine what would happen to the demand for bread and bikes if their prices doubled.

The demand for bread would drop but not by much. It's big part of people's diets, so they will continue to buy it. Demand is said to be **inelastic**.

The demand for bikes would drop by a lot. People don't need to buy bikes every day, so they're likely to put off the purchase. The demand is said to be **elastic**.

Businesses often work out how sensitive their customers are to changes in prices before making a decision about changing them.

Market model

A **model** is an explanation for how something works. The laws of supply and demand are models: they provide a simple explanation for the complicated process of how prices are set. *Real life* is usually not as smooth as models suggest – for example, it can take time for buyers and sellers to respond to each other's signals. But the laws are still useful, because they help to explain all sorts of situations...

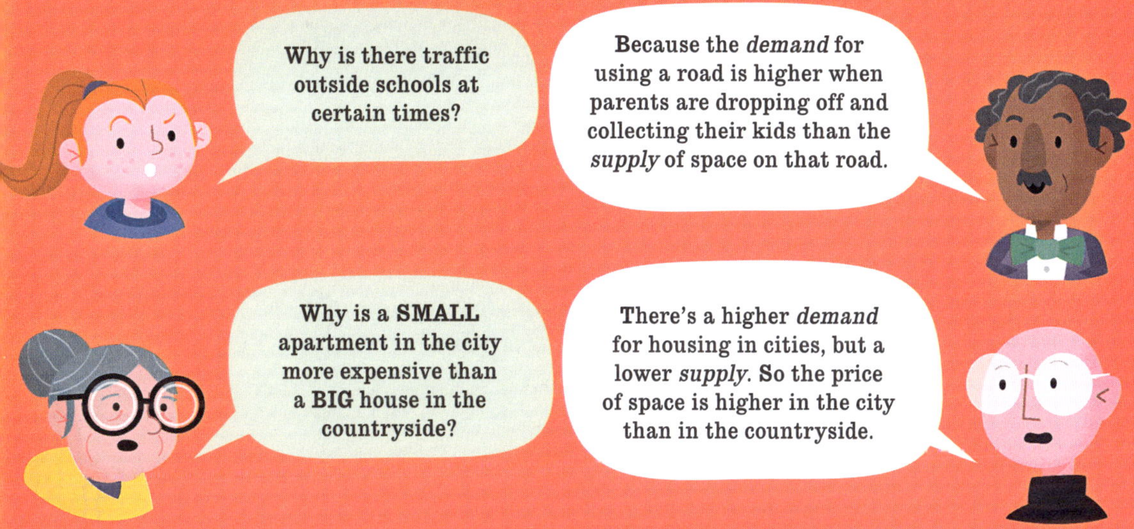

The model even helps to solve problems.

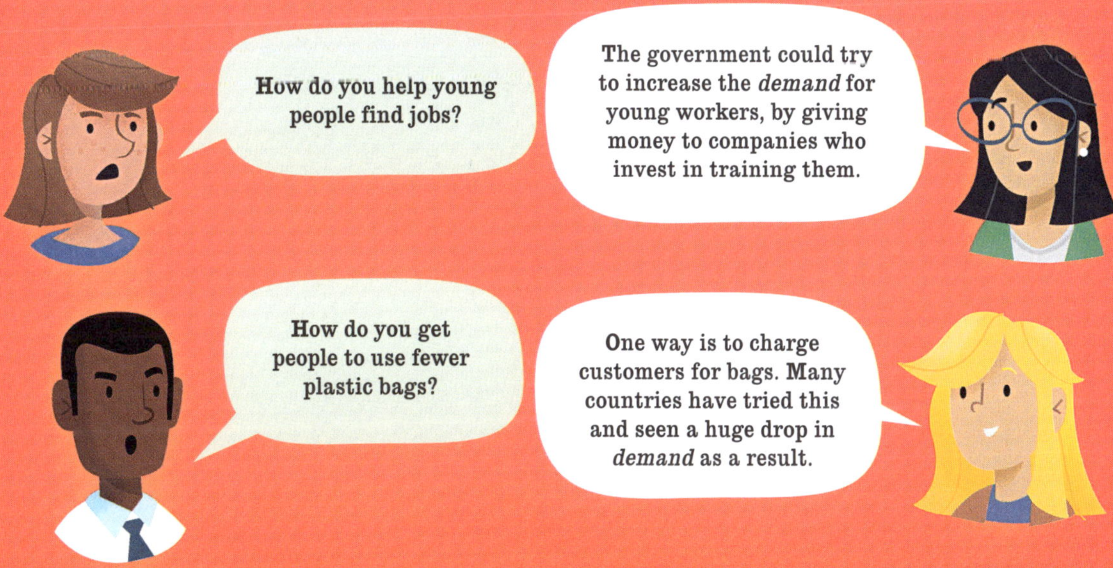

Fixing markets

In any market, businesses sell things to people who can afford them. This might *sound* reasonable, but it's not always fair, safe or even practical to put into practice. When this happens, it's known as **market failure**. The government often steps in at this point.

FAILURE

When there's a **shortage** of something, the price goes up and up. This is a disaster for anyone who can't afford it – especially if it's something essential such as water.

FIX

In a drought, the government might decide to give everyone a certain amount of water for free every day.

FAILURE

Schools and firefighters are **important** services but lots of people wouldn't be able to afford them if they had to pay for them.

FIX

Governments often provide these things for everyone, whether they can pay for them or not.

FAILURE

When a business is the main or only supplier of a resource, it gives it a huge amount of **power** over consumers.

FIX

Governments set rules to protect customers of very big companies, and also to stop businesses from getting too powerful. See more on page 60.

FAILURE

It's **impractical** to charge people individually for some resources such as streetlights. This means businesses can't make money from providing them.

FIX

So governments tend to provide them for everybody.

FAILURE

Sellers often **know more** about a product than consumers, so it's easy for consumers to get caught out.

FIX

Governments can set rules to make businesses share information about a product.

FAILURE

Producing and consuming sometimes have negative **side effects** that nobody pays for, such as pollution from a car factory.

FIX

One solution is a pollution tax, to encourage the factory to find a way to reduce its pollution.

Find out more about this kind of market failure on pages 64-65.

FAILURE

If people want something enough, there will be a business willing to supply it, no matter how **dangerous** that thing is to the buyer or other people.

FIX

The government might restrict who can buy dangerous things such as fireworks.

Chapter 3: Making choices

Some economists like to use simplified **models** to make it easier to understand the messy reasons behind human choices. These models usually assume that people behave selfishly to get the most utility they can. The market models in the previous chapter work this way.

Since the 1970s, however, other economists have tried to explain the mess, in order to understand how people *actually* make choices. They believe that people are often illogical, badly informed and full of superstitions and biases. This field is known as **behavioural economics**.

Model behaviour

Many useful economic theories are based on the idea that people consider each choice carefully and always seek out the most utility. To illustrate this, economists use a model called ***Homo economicus***, which means 'economic man' in Latin, the language of ancient Rome.

Homo economicus is a calculating machine. When it makes a decision, it carefully adds up the costs and benefits of all its options.

What would happen if *Homo economicus* found a wallet in the street?

Economists know that such precise analysis is not how most people make every decision. But they believe that it can accurately predict how a large number of people, on average, will make choices.

A few economists even argue that *all* our decisions, however small, are based on a selfish calculation – how much each of us personally stands to gain.

Ultra-selfish?

Behavioural economists think using *Homo economicus* to explain every choice is unrealistic. They use tests to show how people aren't actually thinking selfishly all the time. One famous test is known as the 'Ultimatum Game':

Frank is acting like a true *Homo economicus,* as he would get to keep the maximum amount of £99 with his £1 offer. If Nancy were just as money obsessed, she would *accept* his offer too. After all, having £1 is better than having £0.

However, test after test has shown that while playing the Ultimatum Game, proposers usually offer far more than £1, and responders often reject offers as high as £40. For many people it is more important to behave fairly, and to be treated fairly, than to gain any money at all.

The Ultimatum Game has even been played with chimpanzees. The chimps displayed a similar desire for fairness as humans did.

Incentives

Whether it's the promise of a reward or the threat of punishment, *anything* that motivates you to make a choice is an **incentive**.

Some incentives come from other people, society or the government.

Some incentives are personal. A way to understand is to ask: what motivates me?

Everyone must decide how to balance out these different incentives. For example, some people might prefer a well-paid, boring job. Others might want a job that was less secure, but more entertaining or rewarding.

Influencing choices

Governments and businesses use incentives all the time to try to influence people's choices. Here are some examples.

Coffee shop loyalty cards reward returning customers.

Celebrity endorsements are an incentive to buy a product for people who admire that celebrity.

The government could raise taxes on businesses that pollute. This incentivizes the use of greener technologies.

A government that wanted to encourage new technologies to be developed could set up prizes to reward inventors.

Governments that use incentives to change behaviour have to be very careful. When incentives are poorly designed, they may not change behaviour in the way they were intended.

Blood donation is a very important part of modern medicine, but it is often hard to get enough donors to step forward.

You might think that *paying* people to give blood would encourage more donations...

...but several studies have shown that when blood donors are paid, blood donation actually goes down.

For most people, the incentive for donating blood is the satisfaction of a kind, charitable act. This feeling was undermined when payment became the main incentive for donation.

So how *do* we make choices?

Imagine that you want an ice cream. You might think carefully through a whole range of decisions.

Now imagine that you went through the same process for every choice you made. You'd never get anything done!

This is why, usually, people don't reason out their choices. They rely instead on simple **rules of thumb** to make their choice quickly, without thinking about it too much at all.

It's more efficient to make choices fast – but there is a cost. Behavioural economists have identified many biases that creep into quick thinking. Biases affect the choices that people make, but they aren't necessarily bad.

Availability bias

People tend to choose the easiest thing – or the first thing they can think of.

Similarity bias

People tend to go for a choice that fits with what they've experienced or seen before.

Herding

People feel more comfortable making the same decision as other people.

Bias in action

Herding can cause **price bubbles**, when everyone tries to buy the same thing at the same time. This causes the price to rise dramatically.

It can also lead to **price crashes,** when everyone tries to sell the same thing at the same time. Find out what can happen after a crash on page 84.

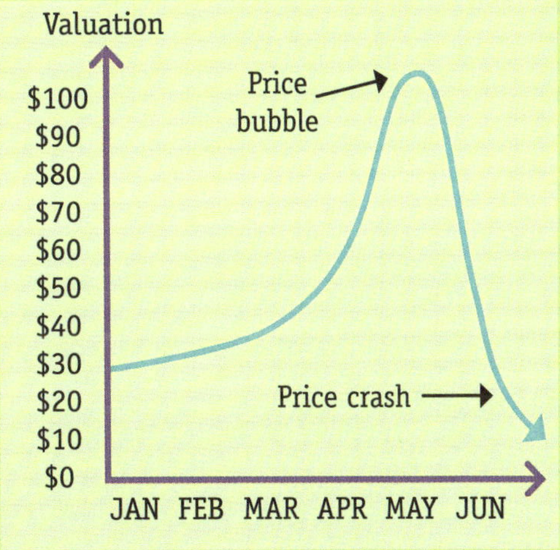

Human judgement

Some biases are present even when people believe they're carefully considering every option before making a choice. For example...

People's choices are also hugely affected by *how* information about their choices is presented to them. This is known as **framing bias**. Sellers use this all the time to get customers to spend more money.

When offered the choice between two popcorn brands, two thirds of customers preferred the cheaper option, while one third chose the more expensive.

But when a third, higher-priced "decoy" option was added to the menu, 90% of people now chose to buy the middle-priced popcorn, even though it had been the most expensive before.

By offering an expensive product as a distraction, businesses trick people into buying something only a little cheaper – and make you feel you are getting a better deal as well.

Nudging

There are (arguably) nicer ways that our biases can be used against us. By framing people's choices, you can also get them to make decisions that are better for them. This is known as **choice architecture**, or **nudging**.

In an experiment to help students eat more healthily, economists found that they didn't need to ban junk food in a school. Instead, they realised that placing good, fresh food at eye level helped the students *choose* salads rather than their usual helping of fried food.

Risk

When you make a choice, there's a chance it won't turn out as you'd hoped. This is called a **risk**. For example, this person is weighing up the risks of a new haircut.

When people make choices they compare the risk to the potential reward.

My haircut	pixie cut	dye blonde	a little trim
My risk of regret	huge	medium	small
My reward	dream look	big change	safe

For this person, although the pixie cut was a big risk, the potential reward was too great to ignore.

The amount of risk you will tolerate is your individual choice. Some people and companies are risk-loving, while others avoid risks. But the prospect of a really big reward can sometimes tempt the most cautious to chase their dream.

How do you really feel about risk?

Although people always weigh up risks and rewards, they don't always do it in a consistent way. For example, people change their attitude to gambling depending on whether they are gaining or losing money.

Try this experiment:

Results

Most people choose the less risky Box A for the first game. When playing the second game, however, most people choose to take a bigger risk. In the hope of avoiding *any* loss, they gamble by choosing Box D.

People seem to *hate* losing much more than they *like* winning. So they are willing to take bigger risks to avoid it. This is why it can be more effective for governments to punish bad behaviour than reward good behaviour.

Making group decisions

A group of people making choices that make sense for themselves can cause trouble when they all share a resource with each other. Take this example of a sheep-farming village:

Bad outcomes like this do happen in the real world. When a group of people, towns or even entire countries share a resource, they often overexploit it. Economists call it the **tragedy of the commons**. Here are some examples.

In the 20th century, North Atlantic cod supplies were almost wiped out by overfishing.

Roads fill up when too many people drive to work so no one goes anywhere.

Countries make so much carbon dioxide, they're dangerously changing the Earth's atmosphere.

American economist Elinor Ostrom researched ways to prevent these kinds of situations. In 2009, she became the first woman to be awarded the Nobel Prize for Economics. Her solution was to get people talking.

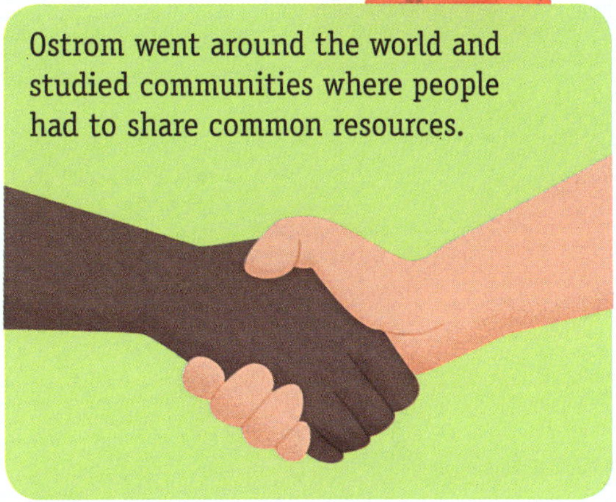

Strong communities help their members make better choices. If people know and trust each other, and know how they are expected to behave, then they are less likely to behave selfishly.

Chapter 4: Production, profit and competition

Most people buy what they want and need from other people or **businesses**. Businesses **compete** with each other to attract the most customers. A successful business makes more money than it spends. This is known as making a **profit**.

Business owners have to make all sorts of choices if they hope to compete successfully and make decent profits...

What do businesses do?

Businesses come in all shapes and sizes, but they all have this in common: they produce goods and services that people need or want, and they exchange what they produce for money.

All businesses spend money...

The money a business spends on producing and selling their product is known as a **cost**.

Once a cost has been paid for, it is known as a **sunk cost**.

Some costs are **variable** depending on how much of a product the business produces. If they produce more, these costs will go up.

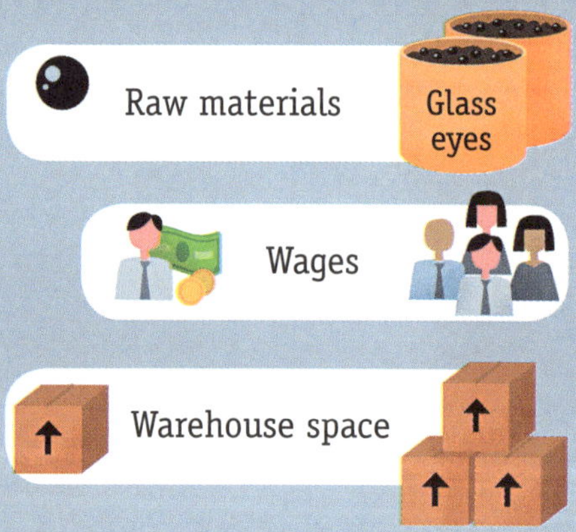

Some costs are known as **fixed costs**, because they remain the same regardless, no matter how much of a product a business produces.

...and try to make money too.

The money a business receives when it sells its product is its **revenue**.

All businesses want to make a profit

Profit is the money left over from a business' revenue, after all costs are paid. It's the incentive for all the risk and hard work involved in running a business.

revenues - costs = profit

All businesses face competition

In most markets, businesses must **compete** fiercely with each other to attract customers. They want customers to choose *their* product rather than a rival's.

Big and small

Every size of business has its advantages and disadvantages.

Small businesses...

...are easier to run because they are less complex.

...adapt quickly to changing markets.

...can make highly specialized products to escape competition.

A drawback of small businesses is they often have to pay other businesses to do some things for them.

Big businesses...

...can produce and control everything they need themselves, from design to advertising and distribution – which can save a lot on costs.

This is because the more of something you produce, the cheaper it gets. It's one reason why big businesses can generate big profits. It happens because...

...more specialized workers and processes are more efficient.

...raw materials are cheaper in big quantities.

...fixed costs such as taxes and rent are spread out over more sales.

These are all known as **economies of scale.**

Is bigger always better?

After a certain point, expansion stops being worth it – costs begin to rise again and revenues fall. This is known as a **diseconomy of scale.** Some common problems for bigger companies are...

...they are hard to run and slow to change.

...different departments don't know what the others are doing.

...workers in big companies can feel unappreciated and work less hard.

Knowing when to stop

To make the biggest profit, you might think that every business would choose to produce as much of their product as possible. But as usual, it's not that simple.

Many businesses fail because they don't know when to stop getting bigger. To decide how much to produce, well-run businesses look at the cost and potential profit of producing just *one* more thing. Studying the next tiny step down the road like this is known as **marginal analysis**.

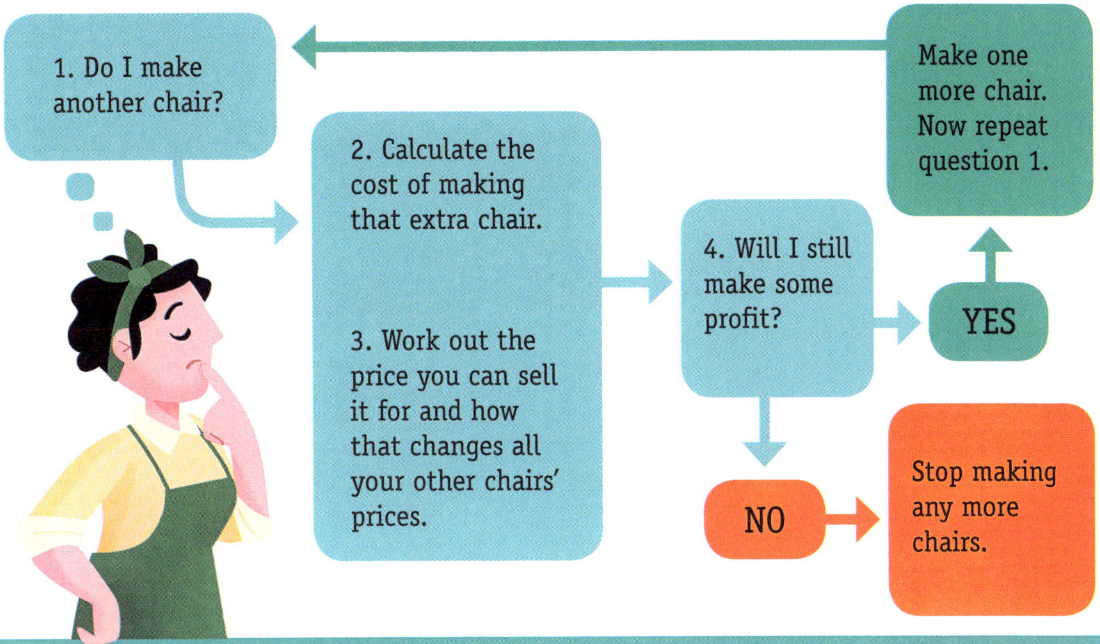

Every day, people make choices using marginal analysis, even if they don't realize it. For example: is it worth staying up an extra hour to play a new video game?

It's not just producers who make marginal decisions; consumers have to make them too. For example: is it worth eating one more burger?

Utility tends to go down the more you consume something. Eventually, having more stops being worth it, even if the price goes down.

Competition

Competition makes products cheaper for consumers and gives them more choice. It also makes the economy more efficient. Here's how a competitive market works:

If a business is doing well, it will tempt other businesses to have a go at producing the same product or service.

Competing businesses often lower their prices to attract buyers. Now the original business has to lower *their* prices, because they will sell nothing if they overcharge. This is called **price competition.**

Another way of attracting clients is to offer a better service, or to be more efficient. By using resources better and wasting less, businesses can gain an advantage over their rivals.

The price for failure is steep. A business that is not competitive will not last long.

So how do you defend yourself from competitors? Escaping from price competition is what drives firms to try new ideas and sell better products:

Technology

By inventing a new technology, or product, businesses can leave the competition behind. For example, since the invention of the motor car, over 100 years ago, horse-powered transport has declined.

Quality

By making a better product, a business can distinguish itself from its rivals. If a business has a reputation for high quality, it can charge higher prices.

Productivity

More productive businesses make things more quickly and cheaply than their rivals. Henry Ford did just that in 1913, when he invented the **assembly line**...

Advertising

People are more likely to buy something they've heard of. So businesses that reach out to customers by advertising are likely to do better – even though it costs money to advertise.

Competition encourages the development of new, exciting ideas and better-run businesses, but it can also lead to businesses shutting down. This process is known as **creative destruction**, and many governments help people who lose their jobs because of it.

Monopolies

Imagine you owned all the chocolate in the world. You could decide exactly how much to sell, and set the price too. When a business has complete control over a market like this, it's known as a **monopoly**.

In a monopoly there is no competition, which usually means fewer, less varied products and much higher prices. It is another example of a market failure.

Some monopolies are created by governments or laws. For example, in some countries only pharmacists or taxi drivers with a government licence are allowed to operate.

Businesses can also create monopolies by buying up all their competitors.

But not all monopolies are bad. In some cases, they even make sense.

Imagine if eight water companies all wanted to lay pipes to supply water to your house.

Sometimes competition is inefficient or impossible. When this happens, it's called a **natural monopoly**. It's then up to the government to protect consumers to make sure they get a good deal.

A business that is very successful can create a monopoly. It can escape the challenge of its competitors by building barriers to defend itself.

These barriers are fine as long as they are *fair*. If a business is well run, or develops a good idea that other businesses can't copy, they deserve to continue to succeed – don't they?

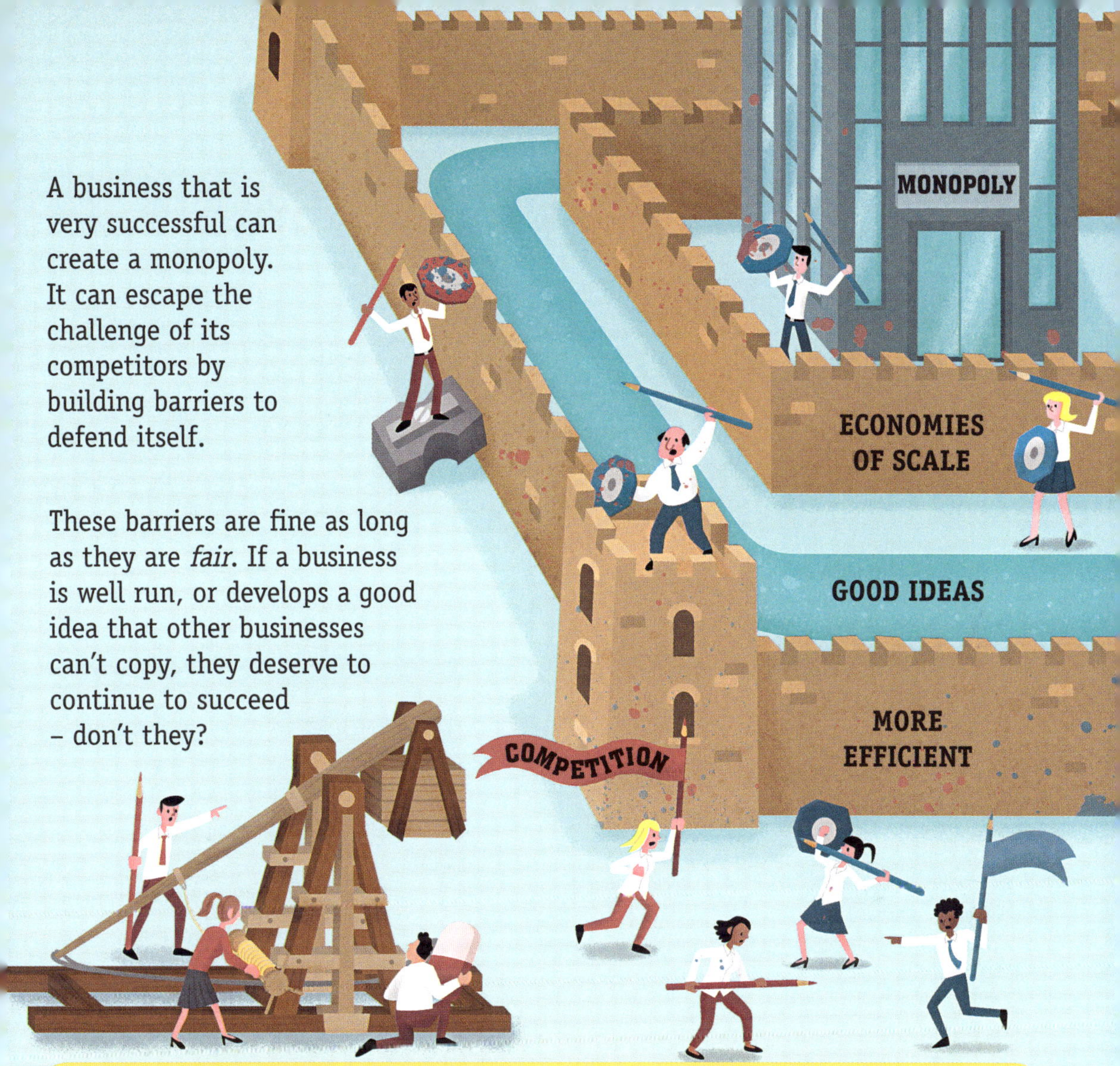

Regulating monopolies

In some cases, businesses seek to create *unfair* barriers to their competitors. It's then up to governments to **regulate** the market and ensure competitors have a chance to compete. Regulations known as **competition laws** make unfair barriers illegal.

In 1982, US telephone business AT&T, which owned all the telephone lines in the USA, was deemed to be an unfair monopoly by the government. It was forced to split into seven smaller companies, known as the *Baby Bells*, who had to compete with each other.

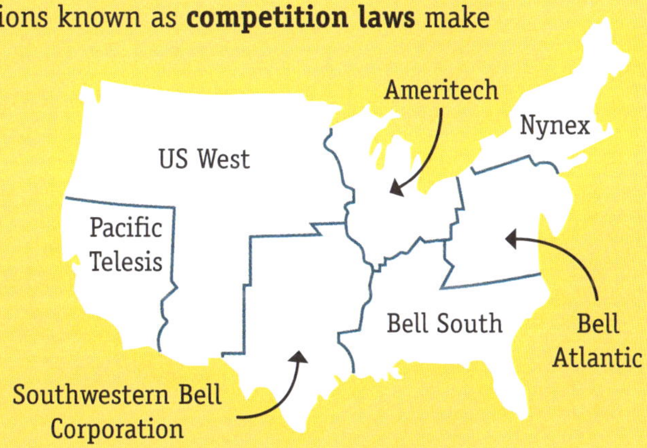

Oligopolies

Often markets are controlled not just by one, but a few large businesses. This is known as an **oligopoly.** Here's a (pretend) example:

Checkmates and *Knight's Move* are the two biggest chess-set manufacturers in a country. They don't have many competitors, so they mostly worry about competition from each other.

One business might want to undercut the other one.

But they know that the other business is likely to retaliate:

So what's the best thing for these businesses to do?

The branch of economics that models the way rivals interact is known as **game theory** (for more, see page 107). One of the methods game theory uses is mapping out the consequences of different decisions on a grid, like this one:

KNIGHT'S MOVE (columns) / **CHECKMATES** (rows)

	Knight's Move: keeps prices the same	Knight's Move: lowers prices
Checkmates: keeps prices the same	Knight = same profit as before Checkmates = same profit as before	Knight = a lot more profit Checkmates = much less profit
Checkmates: lowers prices	Knight = much less profit Checkmates = a lot more profit	Knight = less profit Checkmates = less profit

The model predicts that each business will make more profit if it lowers its prices. So *both* firms will end up lowering their prices and making *less* profit – unless they can somehow agree to keep prices high...

Big businesses sometimes make an agreement not to compete with each other in order to keep profits high. This is known as a forming a **cartel**. In many countries it is illegal.

How businesses affect the world

Markets are meant to help businesses and consumers agree on a fair price, but sometimes they fail to take everything into account. This kind of market failure is called an **externality**. Here are two examples.

Bee story

A beekeeper produces honey to sell. As well as making honey, her bees fertilize the farms all around her hives. This is a **positive externality.**

Local farmers grow extra crops, so they make more profit. But the beekeeper finds she can't get a good price for her honey... and in time her business fails, affecting everyone.

The problem is, the market price is only about the honey in each jar. It doesn't reflect the fact that the bees are doing useful work for the local farmers.

Banana story

A banana plantation uses big quantities of chemical fertilizer. Huge numbers of bananas are produced cheaply...

...but when it rains, the fertilizer runs off into local streams. Now river weeds grow so fast they consume all the oxygen in the water.

Without oxygen, many fish die and the local fishing industry begins to struggle. This pollution is a **negative externality.**

Changing incentives

When externalities cause market failure, it's often up to a government to try to fix things. Spending money is one solution, but the real goal is to change the way businesses – and people – behave.

Positive incentive

To help beekeepers, governments in some countries pay them a regular sum of money known as a **subsidy.** It might seem unfair on other businesses, but it's one way to make sure there are enough beekeepers around to help farmers grow healthy crops.

Negative incentive

Many governments force businesses to pay fines if they are damaging the environment. As long as the fine is big enough to eat into a producer's profits, it forces them to find ways to run their business without creating problems for the world around them.

Governments use incentives to influence the way consumers behave, too. Often they are trying to fix many externalities at once:

Positive incentive

By paying a subsidy to commuters to ride bikes to work instead of driving, a government improves air quality and public health.

Negative incentive

By charging commuters for taking their cars into the city, a government reduces air pollution and encourages them to walk or ride a bike.

Chapter 5: Economic systems

An **economic system** is a set of rules about how resources get shared out and exchanged.

In some communities, traditions and family ties determine how a harvest is shared out, or how things are made. But in most places, markets and governments have largely taken on these roles.

Governments also collect money from people and businesses, known as **tax**. Then they decide how to spend that money so it's shared out across society. Deciding how much tax to collect, and how to spend it, is a key part of an economic system.

How to share?

In your life, you probably come across different ways of deciding what to do with resources and how to share them out. They are examples of **economic systems** – even though people don't usually call them that.

Sharing goals

Just as at home or school, each country faces the challenge of how to share out resources. Here are some different goals a government might aim for when sharing things out.

Freedom

Everyone's different. People should be free to decide what they want and need.

Equality

People should have access to the *same* things and opportunities – no matter how much they need or money they have.

Healthy planet

It's really important that animals, natural resources and the climate aren't endangered by human actions.

Stability

In times of crisis, such as a natural disaster, the government might make decisions about what to make and how to share it out.

Getting richer

Making things that will make the country richer helps to improve everyone's life.

There's lots of debate about the best way of sharing out resources and running the economy. The next few pages will explore some examples of systems people have tried.

Markets in charge

One way for a government to run an economy is *not* to get involved at all. This is known as a **market economy**, and it was the system in place in Britain for part of the 19th century.

At the time, Britain was undergoing a big change, known as the **Industrial Revolution**.

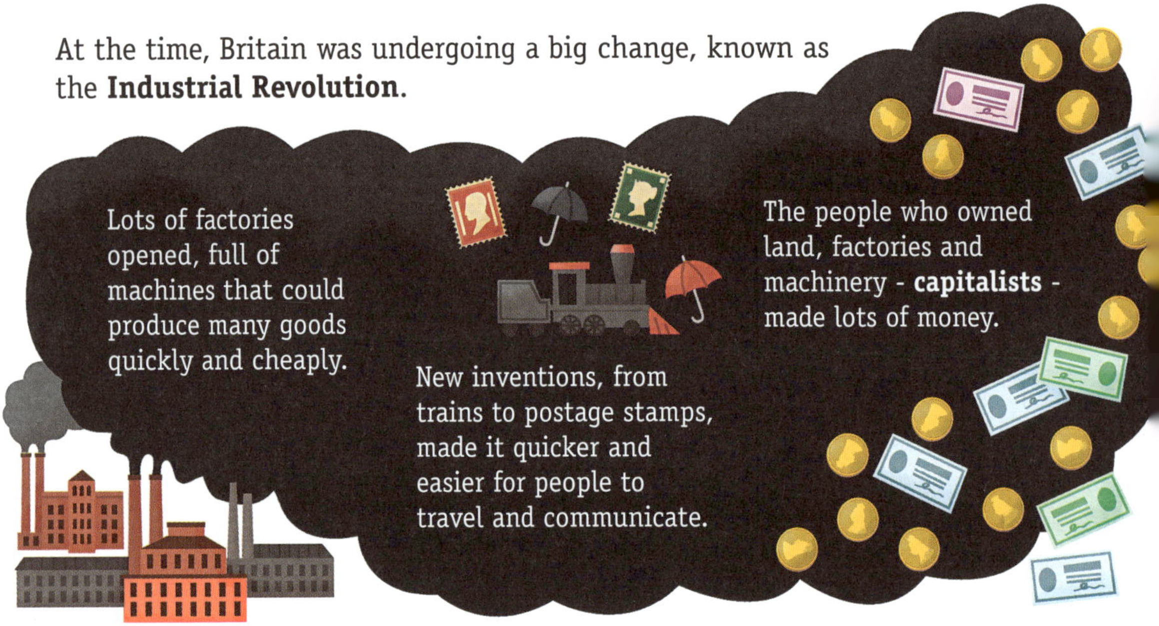

Lots of factories opened, full of machines that could produce many goods quickly and cheaply.

New inventions, from trains to postage stamps, made it quicker and easier for people to travel and communicate.

The people who owned land, factories and machinery - **capitalists** - made lots of money.

The industrial revolution brought prosperity for some, but by the beginning of the 20th century, a quarter of the country was living in poverty. The government's policy was described as ***laissez-faire*** – which meant 'leaving capitalists alone to run their businesses as they like'. The system was later named **capitalism**.

The government's decision not to help didn't resolve problems – if anything they got worse. It became clear that the system needed reform.

Government in charge

To try to fix capitalism, people around the world experimented with giving governments more power. One of the places that made the most drastic changes was Cuba in the 1960s.

A group of revolutionaries overthrew the Cuban government. They set up a system known as **communism**, with the goal of sharing the country's resources equally between Cubans.

They were inspired by the ideas of the German economist Karl Marx.

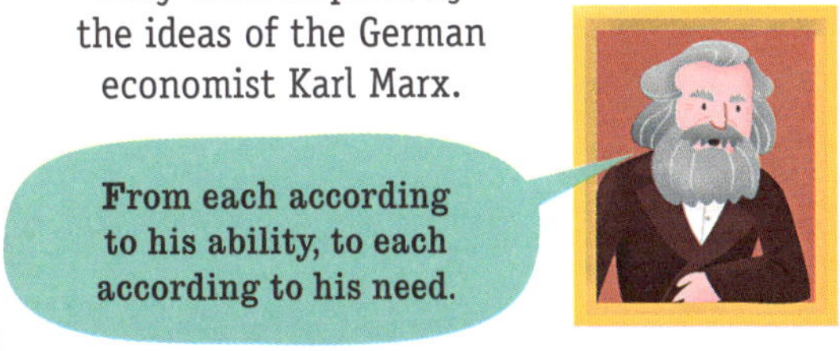

The new government created lots of economic plans – including one to manage food production. This is known as a **planned economy**.

The government also took over all the land, factories and businesses, which helped put the plan into action.

Although resources were mostly shared fairly, there were huge problems too...

It was hard to motivate people to work for the common good...

...and even harder to plan for all the things millions of people might want or need.

In practice, giving full control to governments *or* markets hasn't worked. Most countries have since tried to find a more balanced system.

Mixed economies

Nowadays, most countries around the world have some kind of **mixed economy** – where the government is responsible for some things, and the market for others. Here's *roughly* how it works.

Government

The government makes laws that guarantee people's *right* to own things, ideas and designs. It also sets rules about what businesses can and can't do.

The government also tries to manage the economy and set targets about things such as prices, unemployment and poverty.

It helps develop future businesses and industries by funding scientific research.

Markets

People have the right to own things, such as...

...and have the right to exchange them in markets, according to the laws of supply and demand.

The government also produces certain things that benefit all of society and are mostly paid for by taxes. These can include **infrastructure projects** such as building roads, and **public services**, such as waste collection, libraries and education.

What kind of government?

In practice, mixed economies vary country by country, depending on whether the government that's in power is 'big' or 'small'. This describes how much control a government takes over its economy, businesses and even individuals.

BIG government often means **MORE...**

Small government often means **LESS...**

...money spent on public services

...regulation of businesses

...laws about what people can and can't do

...taxes

How a government acts also depends on its beliefs about the best way to organize a society. The words **left-wing** and **right-wing** are sometimes used to describe these beliefs.

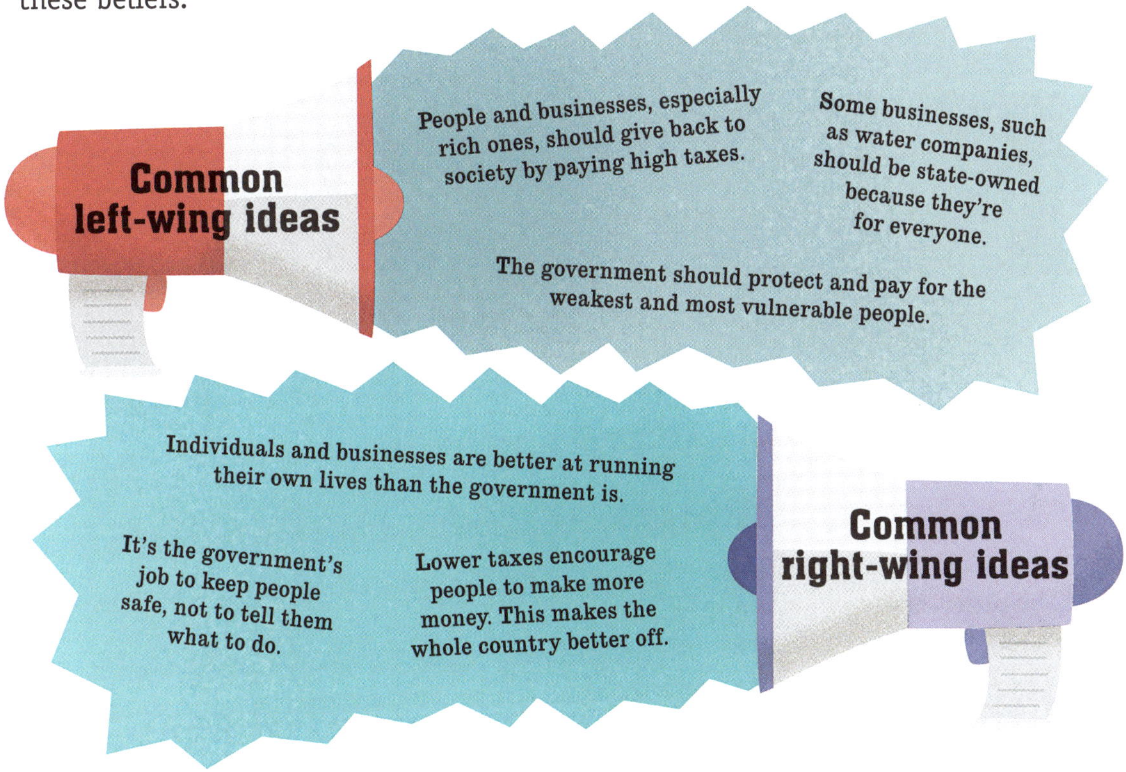

Most people *and* governments support a mixture of left-wing and right-wing ideas, and prefer a big government approach for some issues, but not others.

Left out

Governments often have to try to please different groups, who want or need different things, with a limited amount of money. Usually, they end up helping some groups, while others get left out – whether that's families, pensioners, students, people out of work or refugees like this family...

No country's economic system is perfect. You'll find some ideas for improving them in chapters 6 and 8.

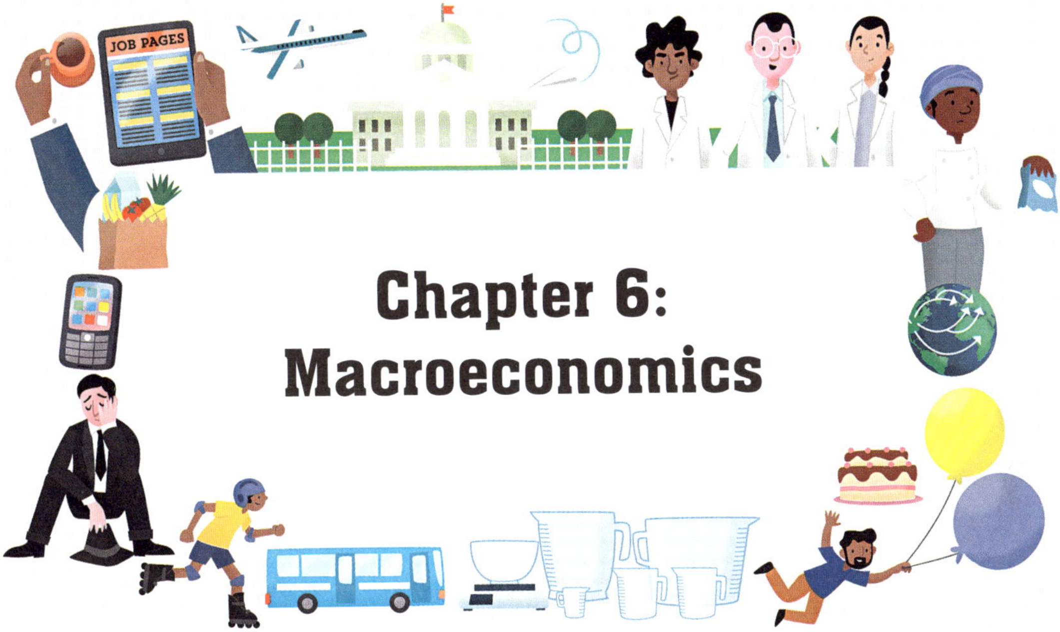

Chapter 6: Macroeconomics

Macroeconomics is about looking at the BIG picture – the economy as a whole.
Are people getting richer or poorer?
Are more businesses opening or closing?
Are things getting more expensive or cheaper?
And what can governments do?

The choices governments make about what to do (or not to do), are known as **policies**. When people vote on a new government, one big question they ask is, "Would their policies be successful?"

Big picture

In economics, you can look at a problem from the point of view of a person or business. For example, 'Why is it hard to find a job?'

Or, you can zoom out and look at what's going on in the whole economy. For example, 'Why are LOTS of people finding it hard to find a job?'

How are problems in an economy linked? What's caused them? What might fix or prevent them? These BIG QUESTIONS are what macroeconomics is all about.

Big choices

When it comes to issues that affect the economy of a whole country, there's not much one person or business can do. Generally it's up to governments to try to manage the economy to make sure it's working as well as possible. What the government does is a bit like what this baker does...

The baker has a vision of the perfect cake.

Each government has an idea of what the perfect economy looks like. For example, plentiful well-paid jobs, top-quality schools and hospitals, a clean, healthy environment...

There are lots of different recipes the baker can try in the quest for the perfect cake.

Government ministers can try all sorts of different ideas and policies suggested by economists.

Making the cake then requires careful measurement. So does managing an economy, except instead of flour, you measure things like unemployment.

However grand the vision, bakers and governments are limited by the ingredients they've got and the environment they're working in.

Sometimes things go mostly to plan, and sometimes they really don't...

Of course the economy *isn't* a cake, and managing it is a big responsibility. The decisions people in power make have huge consequences on people's lives – much more than a burned cake.

Measuring the economy

Government economists measure as much of the economy as they can, to spot patterns and problems that might need fixing. An important measure is the value of everything produced in a country over a period of time. This is known as **Gross Domestic Product** (**GDP**).

One way to work out GDP is to add up how much has been spent on everything that's been produced in a country in a year. For example, the GDP of the US in 2018 was made up of...

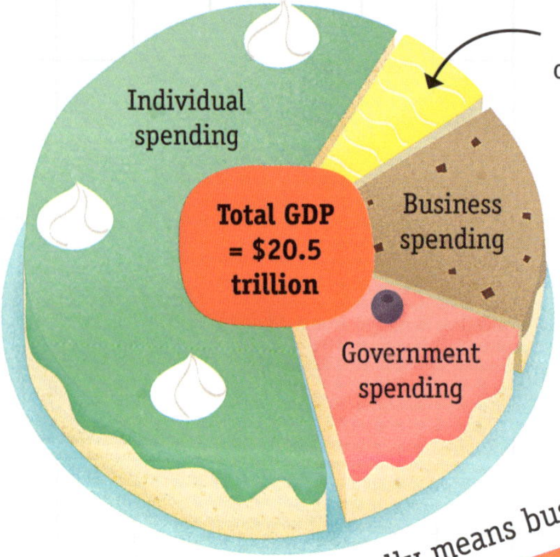

This is the difference between spending that comes *into* the country from people abroad and spending that goes *out of* the country on foreign goods.

An increase in GDP usually means businesses have been producing more.

Businesses are making more money, so they tend to spend more.

This creates more jobs and workers feel more confident about the future.

With more people spending and earning, the government makes more money in taxes. So it can spend more as well.

More production and spending can create a positive cycle where people are generally better off. If GDP increases for more than six months, the economy is said to be **growing**.

Not the only goal

Governments often set themselves the goal of increasing GDP, with the hope that it will make people better off and improve their quality of life. But GDP only measures things that have a price, so focusing on it can lead to forgetting LOTS of other really important things, such as...

Free work

GDP doesn't take into account all the work parents and carers do at home for free, such as teaching kids to read, or doing housework.

Environment

Nature does a lot of essential work for free, too. For example, forests clean the air we breathe, but they only become valuable in GDP terms if they're sold and chopped down.

Inequality

A rich country with high GDP can still have lots of poor people, if the riches aren't shared out fairly.

A fall in production and spending can create a negative cycle, where people are generally worse off. If GDP falls for more than six months, the economy is said to be in a **recession.** Most economies follow a pattern of good times followed by bad ones.

More measurements

As well as GDP, economists measure all sorts of other things to get an idea of how the economy is affecting people's lives. These are known as **economic indicators**.

Are things getting more expensive, or less?

This is measured by looking at how the price of a typical shopping basket of goods changes over a period of time.

Prices almost always increase over time. This is known as **inflation**. People don't tend to notice if prices creep up slowly, but they do if things get more expensive quickly.

If prices are decreasing, it's known as **deflation**. It sounds great, but it often means people stop spending – nobody wants to spend money *now* on something that will be cheaper tomorrow.

How many people are out of work?

The number of people who want a job but don't have one is known as **unemployment**.

Governments generally want to keep unemployment low, but there will always be some people without jobs.

How much are people earning?

This is measured by monitoring weekly average wages, which tend to increase a bit every year.

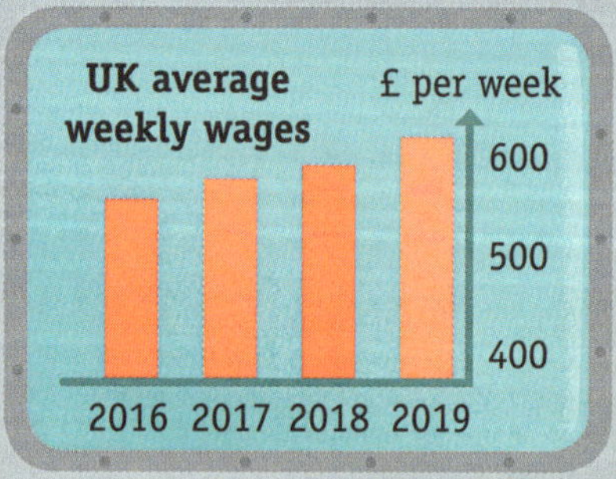

Wages are often compared with inflation. If *wages* don't increase as quickly as *prices*, people will end up poorer.

ALL these numbers are constantly changing, so the official figures only ever show a moment in time.

What can governments do?

Governments can use certain tools, such as **taxes**, to try to manage the economy. It's up to a government to decide what to tax and how much to collect.

In most countries today, individuals and businesses pay tax on what they *earn* – whether that's wages or profits.

They may also pay tax on what they *own,* such as property, and what they *buy* (the price of most things you buy includes a sales tax).

Governments use taxes to try to make the economy...

...greener, safer, healthier.

Taxes can be used to increase the price of things that might be damaging to society, and discourage buyers.

...bigger.

Cutting taxes, for example for businesses, means they have more money to spend, make and hire. Helping businesses can make the economy grow.

...fairer.

Most governments charge higher earners more tax, to pay for things that mostly help poor people (see more on the next page).

Finding the right BALANCE with tax is tricky.

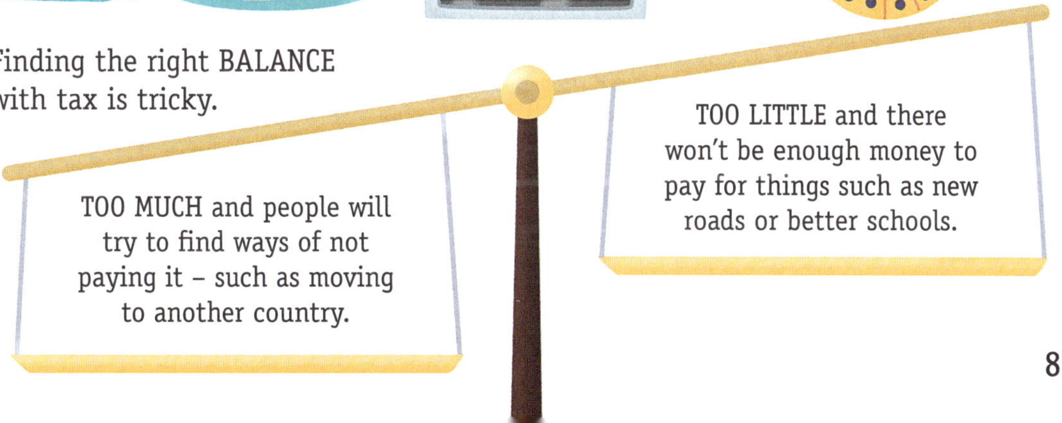

Government spending

A major job of government is to choose how to spend its money. These are some of the things they can spend it on.

Social protection

Supporting people struggling due to unemployment, disability, old age or all sorts of other reasons.

Public services

Services everybody needs such as education, healthcare, policing.

Infrastructure

Building and maintaining things such as roads, bridges and internet cables.

Governments can use spending as a tool to make the economy...

...greener.

The government can spend money on things that do not cause pollution, such as wind turbines.

...fairer.

Spending money on things that give all people better opportunities and good quality public services, whether they are rich or poor.

...more productive.

For example, by spending money to improve internet speeds.

Government borrowing

Governments often want to spend more money than they can collect in taxes, so they increase their funds by *borrowing* money, often from a bank or another country. But a government can only afford to borrow so much, because they have to pay that money back, including extra money, known as **interest**.

In 2018, the US Government spent **$4.1 trillion...**

...of which **$390 billion** was spent paying back interest it owed.

All governments borrow money and over time this can get *really* expensive. So governments have to find a balance between spending, printing and borrowing.

Interest rates

It's not just governments that borrow money; businesses and individuals borrow too. Another tool the government can use to steer the economy is to change **interest rates** – the amount banks charge for borrowing money.

The government works with a national bank, often known as the central bank, to do this.

Increasing interest rates makes it more expensive to borrow money, while decreasing them makes it cheaper.

Lowering interest rates can help to boost the economy by encouraging people and businesses to borrow more, and then to spend more.

In practice

Nobody knows exactly what will happen when a government uses any of these tools, because there are so many other factors to think about. For example, here's why cutting interest rates might not have the effect a government expects.

So people in government have to make their best guess at what will work. Even with the best intentions, they can't seem to stop economic crises from occurring every decade or so.

Crisis!

Economists study past recessions in order to try to avoid repeating mistakes in the future. One of the worst, the Great Depression, started in the USA and spread all around the world.

Most economists at the time thought that unproductive businesses would fail and the rest would start rehiring and the economy would recover. But for years, it didn't. A British economist, John Maynard Keynes, came up with an explanation.

Why would businesses start hiring if nobody's spending?

→ The government should do the opposite of what everyone else is doing and **SPEND** money, for example by building houses.

→ This creates jobs and boosts incomes.

→ When people have jobs they will start spending again.

For over a decade after the depression, US President Roosevelt did just that, spending huge sums on building projects and creating jobs. But he also printed lots of money, reduced interest rates and raised taxes – so it's hard to know exactly what caused the economy to recover.

During the Great Depression a fall in *demand* was one of the triggers of the crisis. But sometimes, a crisis is triggered by a fall in *supply*.

As recessions throughout the 20th century showed, there is no neat and easy solution for solving crises. Governments and economists often end up having to choose between two bad options.

People at work

Most people around the world spend more time at work than they do with their families. It's work that turns seeds into food, wood into paper and ideas into inventions. Work is a huge market, and here's how the market for work *works*.

The rules of work

To protect workers, governments set and enforce rules that make working fairer and safer. These are known as **workers' rights**, and they include the right...

Some rules increase the cost of work.

So governments have to consider the costs and benefits of each rule.

Unemployment

According to the laws of supply and demand, in theory people would only ever be out of work temporarily. In THEORY...

If the demand for work drops... → ...people lose their jobs. → So workers are willing to work for less. → Wages fall, making it cheaper to hire. → Employers are able to hire again.

But, in REALITY, in most countries there are always people out of work, sometimes quite a few and some for a long time.

People don't always live in the places where businesses are looking for workers.

When businesses are struggling, managers find it's easier to simply fire *some* workers, rather than cut wages for *all* workers.

Unemployment depends on how the rest of the economy is doing.

There's often a mismatch between the skills workers have and the skills businesses need.

Being out of work is really tough financially, and it often affects people's mental and physical health badly, too. So it's one of the big challenges governments tackle. Here are some of the things that can help.

Poverty

Most people agree that everyone should have the chance to have a decent life. Yet in reality, some people have so little that they struggle day-to-day. Measuring poverty is the first step to making sure the economy is working for everybody, not just the rich.

Who is poor?

Look at these families living in India, the UK and the USA...

What these families show is that poverty isn't just a number. The family in the middle earns more than 60 times the family on the left, but they're both unable to meet their basic needs. The family on the right has no income, but has earned lots in the past, and probably will do in the future, too.

One definition of **poverty** is not having enough money to take part in the society you live in. In a study carried out in the UK, people said this meant not having enough money for essentials such as...

But it also included things such as...

By this measure, in the UK, just over 1 person in 5 is living in poverty.

Poverty trap

Making the most of your talent and creating a secure life takes that much more skill, willpower and luck if you're poor. On the flip side, once you're rich it's easier to stay rich. Here's the difference being born rich or poor can make...

Poverty is a huge waste of potential and deeply unfair. Left unchecked, the gap between rich and poor, known as **inequality**, tends to increase.

Here are some popular policy ideas that some people believe can help. It's not just about sharing around, but changing the conditions that keep people poor.

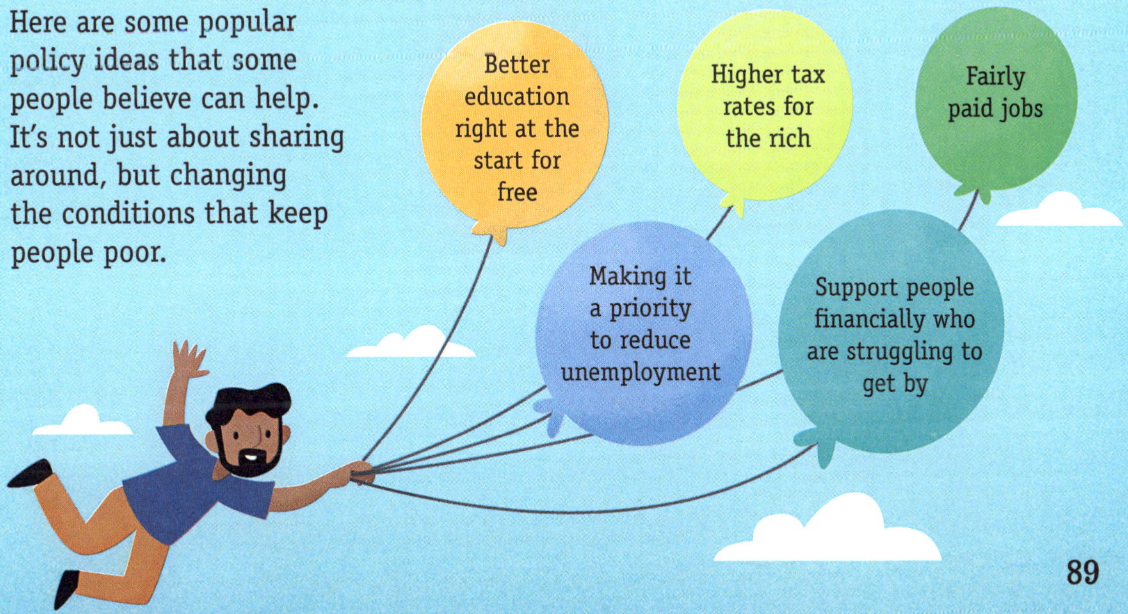

Chapter 7: International trade

For thousands of years, ships have crossed stormy seas, caravans have tramped across endless deserts and ox-carts have trundled down pot-holed roads. All that enormous effort was worth it so that people could trade, not just locally, but with people from around the world.

Trade gives people greater choice, lowers prices and brings essential resources to places where they might not be available. Trading over long distances makes markets more efficient and increases competition. But, despite all those benefits, the very idea of trading across borders can be controversial.

Imports and exports

Some countries produce certain goods more cheaply than other countries. **Trade** means exchanging these cheap goods for other countries' cheap goods.

Goods *bought from* another country are known as **imports**.

Goods that are *sold to* another country are known as **exports**.

For example, France makes blue cheese more cheaply than Japan. Japan produces TVs more cheaply than France. It makes sense for French cheesemongers to make extra cheese to export, and for Japanese engineers to make and export extra TVs. Consumers in both countries will end up with better things, and cheaper, too.

Long distance trade is not easy. There are many logistical barriers that make it harder and more expensive to move large amounts of goods across borders (for example, cheese).

Other barriers are intentionally put up by countries to make trade more difficult, such as charging a border tax, or **tariff**.

Tariffs protect local businesses by making it more expensive for foreign businesses to compete with them.

Tariffs or free trade?

Politicians are often tempted to use tariffs. Tariffs make it harder for foreign businesses to sell their goods, which pleases local businesses and wins votes.

Although this might seem a good idea, there are problems with tariffs. Many economists believe that governments should do everything they can to remove them, and promote a low-tariffs policy, generally known as **free trade**.

Since 1945, free trade economists have been winning the argument. Despite the controversy, many countries have dropped most tariffs and become more open and more linked together – although all countries still keep some barriers to trade. This is part of a process known as **globalization.**

Why free trade works – in theory

Many economists believe free trade benefits everyone because of an elegant economic theory called **comparative advantage**, invented two hundred years ago. Here's how it works...

Imagine that Liz and Carrie have been shipwrecked on a desert island. They have two main tasks: collecting coconuts and catching fish to survive.

Carrie is very good at these jobs. She can catch 20 fish a day *or* collect 20 coconuts a day.

Liz isn't so good at either job. She can catch 2 fish *or* 18 coconuts a day.

Carrie is better at producing both coconuts *and* fish. So is it actually worth her sharing the workload and the food with Liz if she is simply better at doing everything? The surprising answer is **YES**, because of what it *costs* her to do the work.

Whenever Carrie spends time collecting 1 fish it costs her the time she could have spent collecting 1 coconut.

Whenever Carrie spends time collecting 1 coconut it costs her 1 fish.

Whenever Liz spends time catching 1 fish it costs her the time she could have spent collecting 9 coconuts. That's **expensive**.

Whenever Liz spends time collecting 1 coconut it costs her 1/9 of a fish. That's **cheap**.

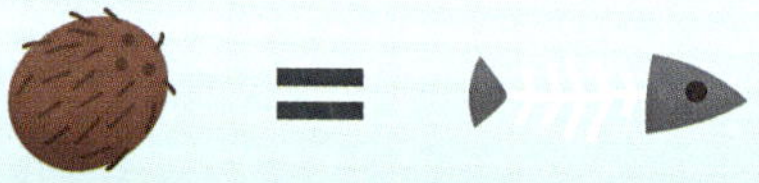

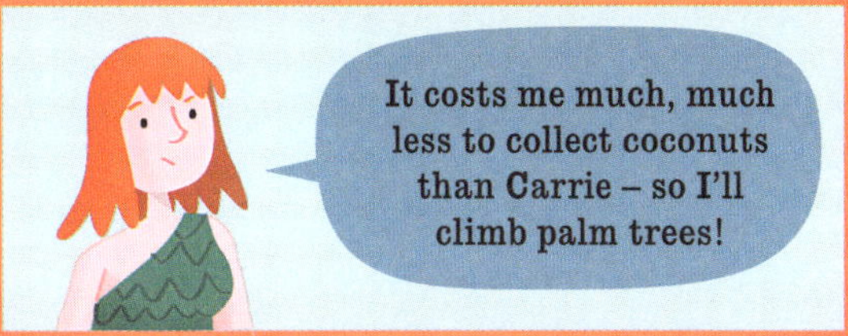

Although Carrie is a little faster at collecting coconuts, Liz has a much lower opportunity cost when she collects them. This is called a **comparative advantage.** It means the best way to collect food on the desert island is for each of the castaways to *specialize* in producing whatever leads them to give up the least and then trade for what they don't have.

This is how much food is produced after 10 days if they *don't* specialize and trade.

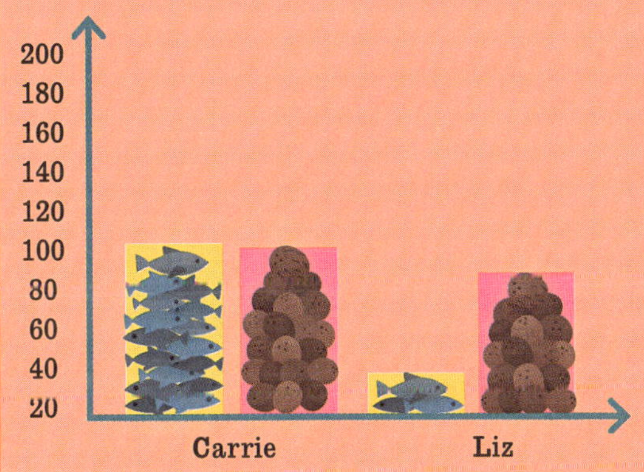

After 10 days they would have 110 fish and 190 coconuts.

This is how much food is produced after 10 days when they *do* specialize and trade.

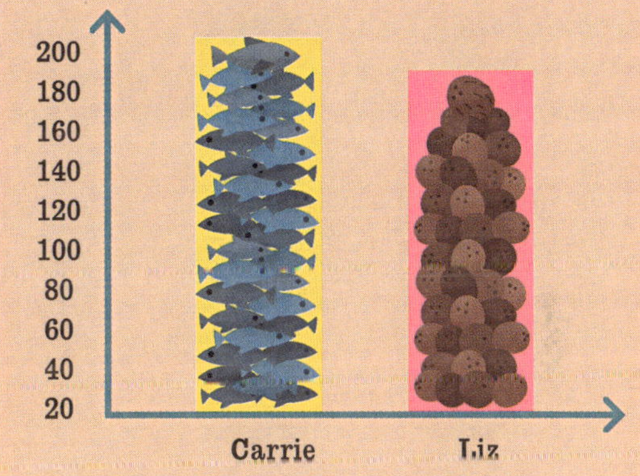

After 10 days they would have 200 fish and 180 coconuts.

Comparative advantage works on desert islands and it works in the real world as well. If every country is free to produce what they make most efficiently and trade for what they can't produce so efficiently, more things get made overall, of better quality, and cheaper.

But this is only possible if countries trade freely with each other. In theory, free trade makes life cheaper and better for *everyone*.

Reasons for barriers

All governments want *some* control over what is sold in their country, so they often still keep some tariffs and trade barriers.

It can be very hard for a new business to compete with well-established ones. Here's an example from 60 years ago...

For fifty years, the South Korean government protected many infant companies with tariffs. Today, these have become world-class competitors.

Some industries could be dangerous if they were controlled by another country.

Most governments – and people – agree that there are certain things no one should manufacture or sell. At least, not to just anyone. Many governments demand that products do not harm the environment, are safe for children, and have safety warnings on them. These are known as **non-tariff barriers.**

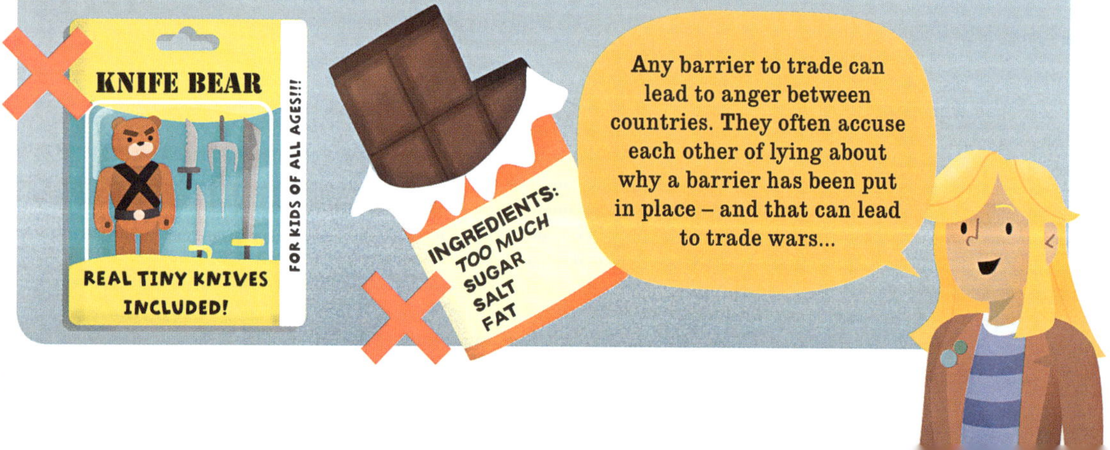

Trade wars are risky

If a government sets high tariffs, other countries are likely to respond by bringing in tariffs of their own. Your tariffs might stop imports from coming in, but they will stop your exports from leaving, too.

If rival countries bring in higher and higher tariffs, it's a form of conflict called a **trade war**. Trade wars are difficult to win, because everyone suffers. A famous example occurred during the Great Depression.

In 1930, American farmers and manufacturers were struggling. To help them, the government quadrupled tariffs on 900 imported items.

The tariffs worked. American imports of foreign goods plunged 66%.

But other countries retaliated with tariffs of their own. American exports plunged by 61%.

International trade ground to a halt. By 1934, American GDP had halved and world trade had shrunk by 66%. Thousands of firms went out of business, and millions more people became unemployed. It was a global disaster.

Trading blocs

Sometimes, groups of countries sign free-trade agreements with each other, forming **trading blocs**. Examples include the EU in Europe, or MERCOSUR in South America. All members agree to trade freely with each other. Sometimes, blocs also agree to put up joint tariff and non-tariff barriers to make trade with non-members *more* expensive.

Some trading blocs are simply to do with trading goods and services. Others, such as the EU, allow people and money to move around freely as well. People can live and work in any member country, and be paid and pay taxes where they live.

Sometimes a country may believe that another country or bloc has acted unfairly. If this happens they can appeal to the **World Trade Organization** (WTO), an international organization that provides rules for settling trade disputes and negotiating new agreements.

Globalization

Globalization is a way of describing a huge economy that includes practically the whole world. In recent years this global economy has grown enormously, partly because of free trade, but also for two other simple reasons: **containerization** and **communication**.

70% of the world is covered in oceans – so the best way to move things around is by ship. Around the world, thousands of large cargo ships carry almost anything you can think of, inside metal boxes called **containers**.

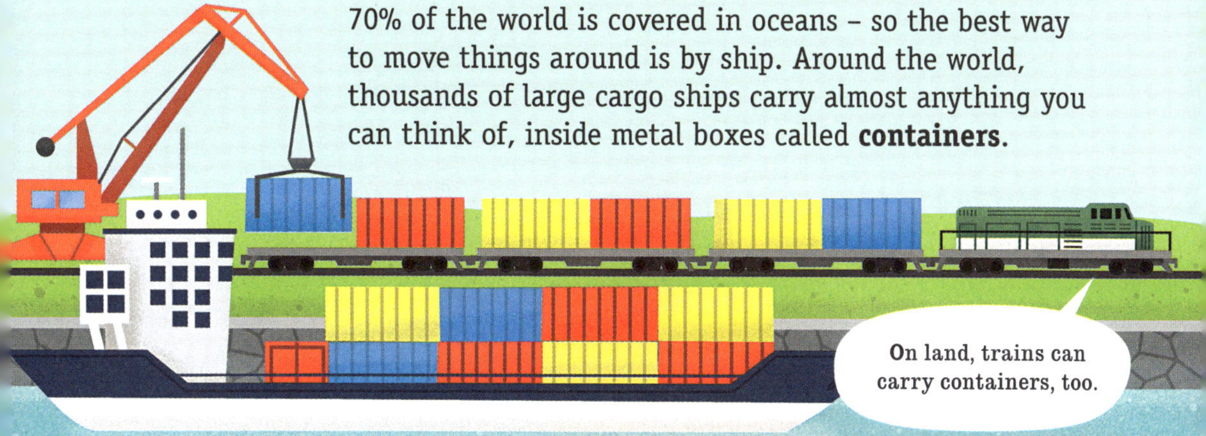

In 1945 it used to take a week to load and unload cargo ships. Now, because of the container system, it takes just 6 hours to unload much bigger ships. This efficiency means that global trade has exploded in the last 70 years.

With the invention of the internet and email, it takes no time at all for people on the other side of the world to talk. Running a global business is easier than ever, and large businesses can coordinate production across many countries.

Globalization – winners and losers

WINNER: lots of people

Although the world's population has grown enormously, the number of people living in extreme poverty has actually gone *down*.

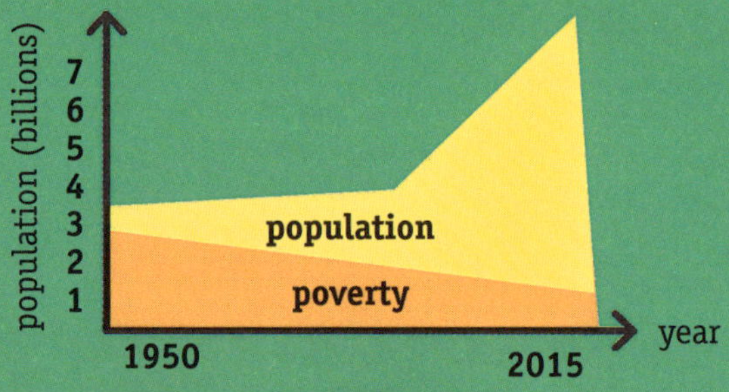

LOSER: independence

International trade rules and agreements often restrict what policies or laws a country can use. Other countries will stop trading with countries that break the rules.

LOSER: accountability

Because the world's biggest companies operate in many countries, it is sometimes hard for individual countries to make them follow rules or pay a fair amount of taxes.

WINNER: technology

Trade allows countries to specialize in what they do best, because they no longer have to produce everything they need. Over the past fifty years this focus has been a big factor in the world's rapid technological development.

In a more connected world, good ideas and innovations spread much faster. After gunpowder was invented by the Chinese, it took 300 years to reach Europe. This would not be the case today.

WINNER: development

Globalization has brought new jobs and opportunities to places such as China, India and Indonesia. Billions of people in these countries have been lifted out of extreme poverty.

LOSER: some workers

Businesses often move factories abroad to countries with cheaper workers. The workers left behind often struggle to find new jobs or retrain. Without help from governments, small towns and even whole regions can find globalization a painful process.

LOSER: carbon emissions

More trade means more production and transportation. This creates more carbon dioxide, which has caused our current climate crisis.

LOSER: small countries

Big trading blocs can get great deals for themselves... ...but this means smaller countries get the bad end of the same deal, so it's hard for their economies to grow.

WINNER: cooperation

For trade to flourish, countries must cooperate with each other. Working together, they can tackle big issues such as migration and climate change.

LOSER: *too* specialized

Sometimes countries (espccially poorer ones) are forced to specialize in exporting a single commodity such as gold, coffee or bananas. But it is risky to rely on just one export. The country is very vulnerable if prices, or people's tastes change.

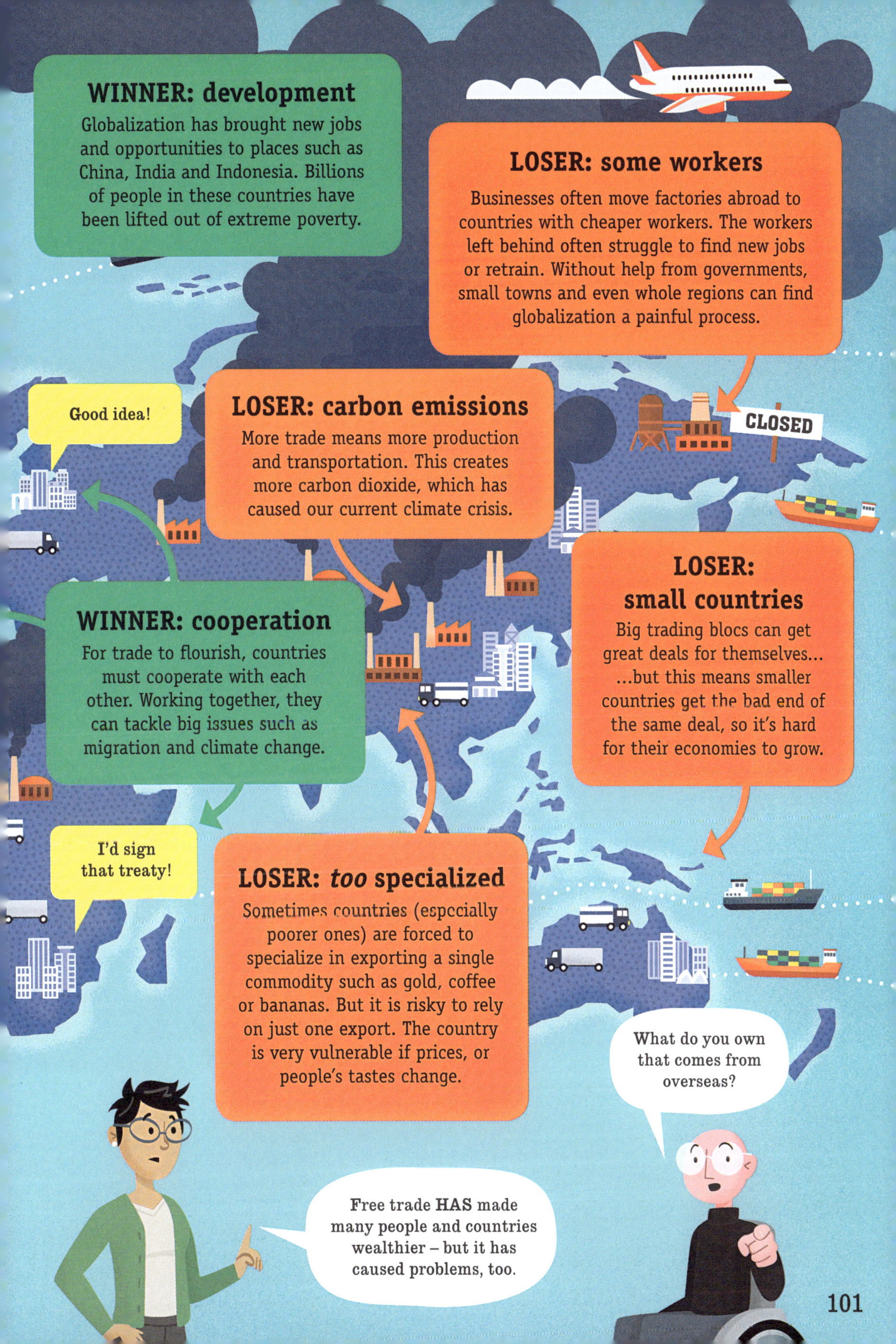

Chapter 8: Big questions (and a few answers)

There is almost no limit to the questions economics can tackle. Economists use their skills to analyse the problems, both big and small, that face the world today.

This chapter explores just a few of these questions, as well as asking what type of answers we should be looking for.

Can economics help save the planet?

When fossil fuels such as oil and coal are used, they give out carbon dioxide, a gas that warms the planet. We have known this for decades, but are still using more and more fossil fuels each year.

There's no time for despair because there's still time to change. If enough people CHOOSE to change their spending habits, markets and businesses will respond.

Individuals can...

Choose not to fly. Plane travel is the fastest growing source of carbon dioxide pollution.

Eat less meat. Farming animals consumes enormous amounts of resources and land.

Repair things instead of throwing them away. This saves resources.

Choose locally produced goods, even if they are more expensive. This cuts transport pollution.

But the biggest and most important choices will have to be made by *societies.* Only governments can pass laws or raise taxes to change EVERYONE'S incentives. Here's one idea: bringing in a global tax on the use of fossil fuels.

This is called a carbon price.

If the carbon price is high enough, using and producing fossil fuels would become too expensive to be profitable. This would be hugely unpopular with...

- Oil companies, who couldn't sell oil cheaply any more.
- Countries that rely on fossil fuels for exports.
- Businesses – and people – that rely on using cheap fossil fuels.

The people who don't want these changes to happen often make an economic argument. They say "It's too expensive to change, people will lose their jobs." But there's a powerful economic argument for finding alternatives to fossil fuels.

The Stern Review of the economics of climate change estimated that the cost of dealing with climate change now **= 2% of global GDP.**

The review estimated that the cost of waiting decades to deal with climate change **= 20% of global GDP.**

How do wars start?

Since the time of our earliest ancestors, wars have started for a wide variety of political, historical and even psychological reasons. But most wars have had important *economic* causes too.

Resources

War was an important part of the Roman Empire's economy. Rome benefited greatly from luxury goods, mines and grain-producing regions that it conquered. Today, countries fight to control valuable resources such as oil fields.

International trade

In the 19th century, the British Empire made vast profits selling a highly-addictive drug called opium to China.

When the Chinese Emperor banned the opium trade to protect his people, the British invaded China twice, in 1839 and 1856, in order to keep their drug-pushing operation going.

Scarcity and corruption

One of the causes of the Syrian civil war, which began in 2011, was a major drought. Syria's water-starved farms failed. Farmers fled to cities, but even there, food and jobs were in short supply.

On top of *that*, people were angry with the government for unfairly taking and distributing jobs, food and resources.

In 2011, mass protests began against the government. The government responded with violence and civil war broke out.

How to stop wars

One reason that economists studied **game theory** (see page 63) was as a way of predicting how to win a nuclear war. It turned out that winning involved *not fighting at all.*

Between 1945 and 1991, relations between the USA and the Soviet Union (Russia and other states) were extremely tense, partly because both countries had deadly nuclear weapons.

Here's where game theory came in. A famous game had two sides choosing whether to betray the other or cooperate.

The striking lesson from the game was that if you couldn't trust the other player, the most logical outcome was *always* to betray.

So both sides knew the most logical step for their enemy was to start a surprise nuclear war.

According to the theory, the only way to prevent an attack was to build *so many* bombs that both nations knew neither side could survive a war.

This was described as a deterrent.

The deterrent took away any incentive to betray the other and helped them to cooperate.

Some economists believe that wars can be stopped by global trade too.

Why is technology so important?

People often get really excited about new gadgets – some even camp overnight by a shop to be the first to get their hands on a new phone. But *nobody* gets more excited about technology – even the humble electrical washing machine – than an economist.

Since its invention over 100 years ago, the electrical washing machine has...

...saved SO MUCH time, especially for women doing chores at home. This has freed up time for women to get paid work outside the home.

...changed the kinds of jobs women do. In the 1870s in the US, around 50% of working women were employed as domestic servants, while under 1% are now.

New machines, ideas and ways of doing things can change the way people live. New technologies also allow people to make more with less, which is how economies grow. Governments can encourage this by...

...providing infrastructure like broadband cables.

...funding research.

...protecting ideas with laws, so people can create new things without worrying they'll be stolen.

What about jobs?

In most economies, about 10% of jobs are destroyed each year by new technologies and about the same number are created. But when a factory closes in a town, a whole community can become unemployed, and those individuals pay the cost – unless governments support them.

Throughout history, people have worried that eventually technology will wipe out more jobs than can be created – but so far this has not been the case.

Is inequality ok?

Economists aren't the only ones who can answer economic questions. For example, American philosopher John Rawls explored people's feelings about inequality by getting them to imagine an ideal world.

1 In this world, there will be two groups of equal sizes, called 'richer' and 'poorer'.

2 YOU will get to live in this world, *after* you've answered the question – 'how rich should each group be?'.

3 Then, a flip of a coin will determine which group you go in.

In lots of countries, people taking part in the exercise tend to design a world with inequality, where the rich earn a bit more than the poor – but not too much more. Here are some of their reasons.

It's only *fair* if people who work harder or better are rewarded for it.

Yes but, when a company's managers earn hundreds of times more than an unskilled worker, that's *unfair*. There's only so much more a manager can achieve in a day!

Inequality is also *motivating*. Hard work, good ideas and taking risks needs to be rewarded, otherwise people wouldn't bother.

But knowing you're at the bottom can be *demotivating*, especially if you think you'll never do well, however hard you work.

Ok so *some* inequality is good, but not too much.

Interestingly, these imaginary, but still unequal, worlds were much more equal than the *real* world is. And more equal than most people realize, too. A 2017 study in the US showed that people thought the richest 20% of the population...

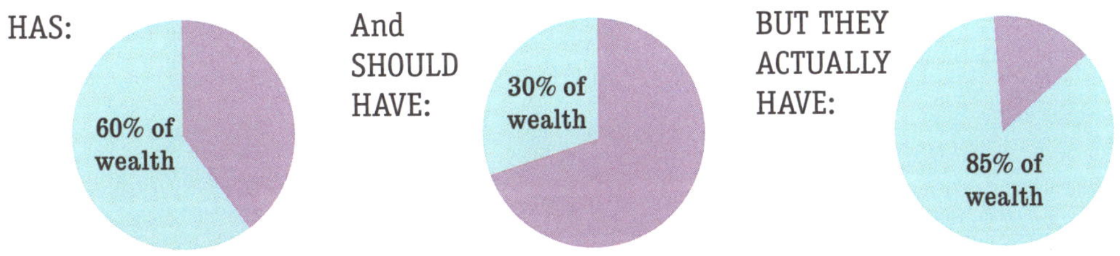

Even if people think *some* inequality is ok, this seems unfair. Do you think everyone in your country has a fair chance to become rich, successful or happy?

Are we running out of resources?

The Earth can only replace some of the resources we use each year. A group of researchers called the Global Footprint Network calculate the day each year we start using resources that won't be replaced.

In 2019, it fell on July 29th, the earliest day yet. It means that right now we are using up the Earth's resources 1.75 times faster than they can be replaced.

The group calculates how much we use by looking at *everything* we consume. They include resources such as the forests' capacity to suck up carbon dioxide. They also calculate how many Earths we'd need if *everyone* had the same lifestyle as people in some of the richest countries in 2019.

United States	5.0 Earths
Australia	4.1 Earths
Russia	3.2 Earths
Japan	2.8 Earths
United Kingdom	2.7 Earths
China	2.2 Earths
Brazil	1.7 Earths
India	0.7 Earths
World Average	1.75 Earths

It is unlikely that we will ever need five Earths. As the demand for scarce resources rises, their price will increase. This should encourage people to use different resources and develop new technologies. But because we only have only one Earth, some people are suggesting another fix: find a new planet.

The solar system contains more resources than we could ever hope to use. Although space travel is extremely expensive now, it is quite possible that as technology improves, it will soon become efficient and effective to harvest asteroids for minerals, comets for water and even set up mines on the Moon.

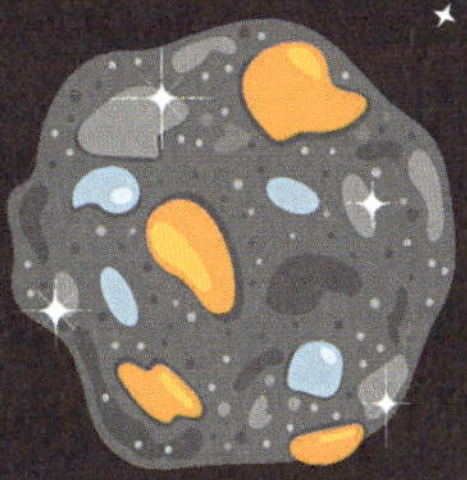

Psyche 16 is an asteroid that lies between Mars and Jupiter. It is thought to be made entirely of metal – mostly iron, nickel and gold. The asteroid is estimated to be worth around $700,000,000,000,000,000,000. That is a fortune, enough to give each of the 7.6 billion people on Earth about $92 billion dollars each.

Is moving to Mars a good idea?

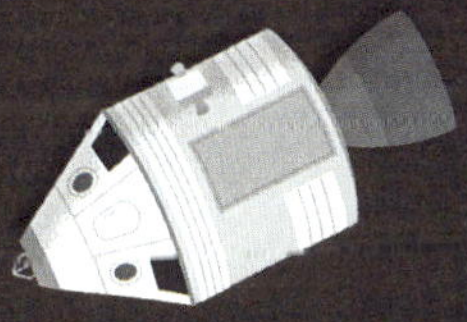

The economic case for sending humans to Mars is a little harder to make. Because Mars is so far away it costs *a lot* to get there, especially if you need to carry things with you. There will always be cheaper ways to get resources from space.

But maybe that shouldn't stop us trying. Although the original Moon landings didn't result in any permanent settlements (yet), the enormous investment in space exploration has produced many inventions that have made life on Earth better.

- solar panels
- hand-held vacuum cleaners
- memory-foam mattresses
- CAT scanners
- scratchproof glass
- wireless headphones
- in-ear thermometers
- laptop computers
- computer mouse
- LED bulbs
- water purifiers
- baby milk formula

So many questions...

Economists have considered many questions, some of which you might not even think count as economics. For example:

What's the best month of the year to be born in?

In the northern hemisphere, if you were born in September, you are in luck. Researchers have discovered that September babies are more confident, more likely to go to university and the least likely to go to prison.

In most countries, the school year starts in September, so September babies are the eldest in their classes. Especially in the earliest years, that little age advantage can make a big difference and provide a lasting confidence boost.

The same principle also applies to sports. Professional soccer players in Europe are much more likely to be born in January, for example, as January is the start month for age-levels in soccer.

In America, pro baseball players are more likely to be born in August for the same reason.

What causes famines?

When a town, region or country doesn't have enough food to feed its people, it's known as a **famine**. Indian economist Amartya Sen analysed many famines and discovered something surprising.

People can starve even if plenty of food is being produced, as famines are usually caused by problems with food distribution.

Sen himself lived through a famine in Bengal in the 1940s. There, despite a better than average rice harvest, millions of people died. This was because labourer's wages couldn't keep up with rising food prices.

Sen was awarded the Nobel Prize for economics in 1998 for his ground-breaking work.

Should you stick to your first guess?

Studies have shown that in tests, 75% of students believe the first answer they think of is most likely to be right.

Unfortunately, they are *wrong*. One hundred years of experiments have demonstrated that people who trust the little voice in their head telling them to change their answers tend to improve their scores. Changes to answers are more likely to be from wrong to right, than the other way around.

Why are Instagram influencers so successful?

Influencers are ordinary people who use social media to market their lifestyle and sell products. The influencer economy is worth BILLIONS of dollars worldwide.

Oddly, one of the main reasons for their success was discovered over a hundred years ago by an eccentric American economist called Theodore Veblen.

He suggested that people like buying things to show off their wealth and aspire to buy things they can't afford. He called this **conspicuous consumption.**

In the past, people were just trying to impress their neighbours – but on social media, successful influencers reach an audience of *millions*. Many businesses have recognized the advertising power that this brings.

Here's how influencing works:

Businesses often give an influencer expensive items for free.

The influencer wears them in a video. Their fans see a person who seems pretty ordinary wearing cool, luxury glasses.

The fans want to copy the influencer. They buy a pair for themselves.

What gets left out?

Whether it's people deciding how to spend their money, businesses choosing who to hire, or governments trying to manage an economy, some people or things often get left out.

Informal markets

Some workers and businesses are invisible: they're not officially registered and they don't pay taxes. This makes it harder for the government to measure the economy, and they can't regulate these businesses and protect workers.

Women...

Ignoring certain groups can lead to governments making unfair decisions. For example, if the government cuts spending on pre-school education it tends to affect women more than men.

...and race.

When people don't have the same opportunities, wages and rights because of their gender or race, it's known as **discrimination.**

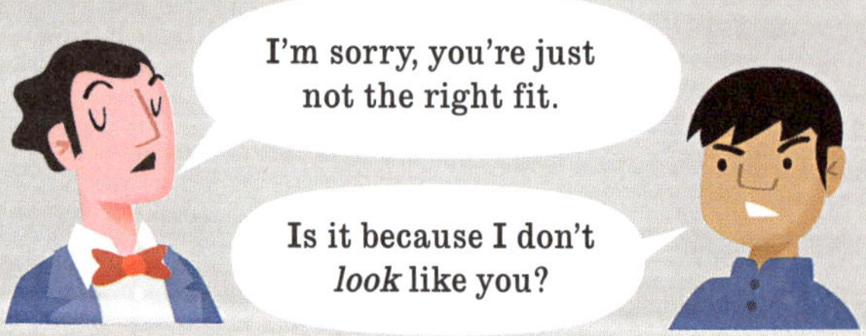

This kind of discrimination can lead to higher unemployment in certain groups, and businesses losing out on people's talent.

Banks

Until recently, economists often ignored banks when creating models of how a country's economy was working. Partly this was because banking is complicated, but mostly because they assumed banks, overall, simply get on with their job – helping people to save and borrow money. And this seemed to work until a banking crisis began in 2007 that affected the world economy.

Lots of American and European banks almost collapsed after taking huge risks and losing lots of money.

→

The banks stopped lending, businesses closed and people lost their jobs and homes. There were recessions in many countries.

→

Economists struggled to make models of the consequences of the crisis and to suggest solutions.

Nature

It's easy to take the work nature does for granted, but *all* production depends on it for resources – and to turn waste *back into* resources. Here are some examples.

Trees turn polluted air into clean air.

Soil filters and cleans water, and allows most of our crops to grow.

Predators eat the bugs that destroy food crops.

If the way people consume and produce creates too much waste or uses too many resources, it threatens the work nature does *for* us. Economists call these externalities (see page 64) and are studying these 'invisible' parts of the economy more and more.

Big questions

Some economists debate BIG questions such as 'What is a successful economy?' Here are some different answers.

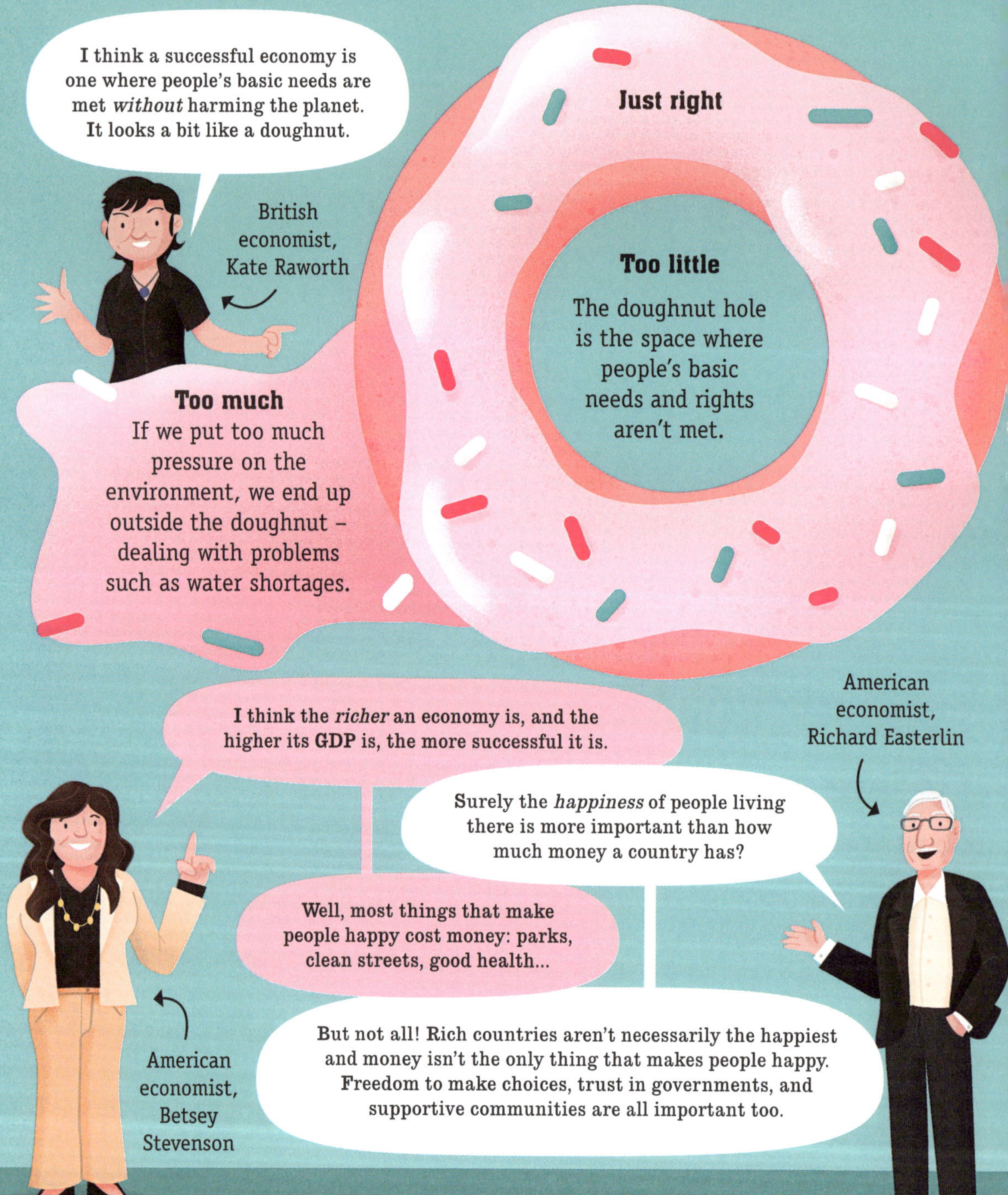

There isn't one right answer to this question. Often governments try to work towards all these definitions of a successful economy.

Small questions

Other economists focus on much smaller, more specific questions. In 2003, Indian and French economists Abhijit Banerjee and Esther Duflo helped set up Poverty Action Lab. The lab tests practical solutions to problems such as: How do you get more people to use mosquito nets to prevent them from getting malaria?

The PROBLEM: Malaria is a disease transmitted by infected mosquitoes. In 2017, there were 219 million cases and around 435,000 people died.

Sleeping under an insecticide-treated bed net is a really effective way of preventing malaria, but lots of people don't have one.

The QUESTION

What's the price which gets most people to use a net?

Free?

Are people more likely to use it if they've paid a tiny bit for it?

The Poverty Action Lab's approach is to look for **EVIDENCE** that a solution will actually work, before recommending it.

We're copying the main method doctors use to test medicines – randomized controlled trials. We set up this test so that similar people are randomly given a free net or one costing 60 cents.

We wonder if more people will choose to use a net if they have to pay for it, as it'll seem more valuable.

The TEST: In Kenya, to test how the price of a net affected how people used them, participants were randomly presented with option A...

...or option B.

The RESULT: 65% of people who were offered option A accepted it, compared to only 15% for option B. People used both nets just as much, whether they were free or not. So it was *actually* more efficient to give the nets out for free.

Making sense of the world

The world is big, changing and complicated. Economics is about finding ways of making sense of it. Here are some tips and techniques to help you do this, from using numbers to questioning facts.

Compare

It's hard to know how big or small a number is when it's by itself, so try to compare it to something else.

This sounds scary, but compared to some other animals, crocodiles present very little risk to humans. Mosquitoes carrying diseases kill around **400,000** people each year.

Divide

One way of making a big number more meaningful is to divide it by a total – often the whole population. For example...

But when you divide it by the number of people in each country, China produces one and a half times less carbon emissions *per person* than Iceland does. This may change how you think of the problem.

Extreme scales

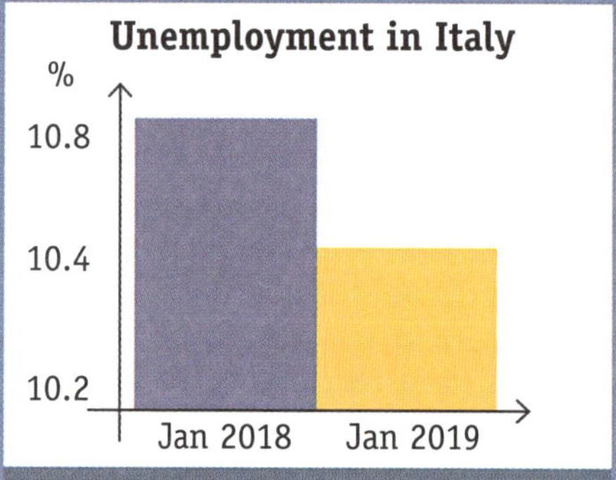

This graph makes it look like unemployment has halved in a year, but in fact it's dropped by just **0.4%**.

Missing or old data

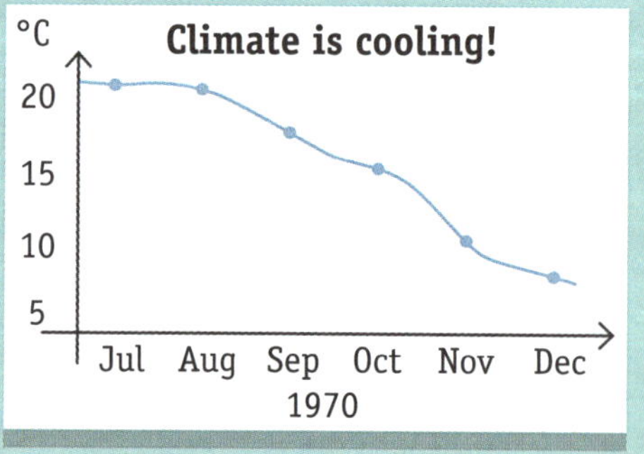

This graph shows the temperature cooling, but only for half the year from summer to winter, which is just what you'd expect. The data is also around 50 years old.

Be careful about making a **generalization**, or a broad statement about a group of people, things or countries.
This is a very violent country. Every day, the news is full of criminals. We must spend more money on police officers.
Actually the crime rate is falling, and has been for the last 20 years.
Always check the facts before jumping to conclusions.
Be ready to change your mind. This means you're open to new ideas; it doesn't mean you're easily led by others.
Actually, I think you'll find that the tooth fairy doesn't have to pay taxes.
How dare you disagree with me! I'm not friends with you any more.
It's because she uses money for charitable purposes.
Mmm, I hadn't thought of it that way.
Don't blame people or businesses for their choices – find out *why* they made them.
Think about what their **incentives** were.
If you want to change their choices in the future, think about how to change their incentives.
If you don't change their incentives, they'll probably just make the same bad choice again.

What next?

Economics is very complicated – but now you have the tools to understand it and start *using* it in your own life...

To make your own choices...
Let's go to that town meeting tonight!
...and make powerful choices together.
If we all act as one, there's nothing we can't achieve.
We need to live without destroying the planet.
We'll need to design policies to help us do that.
Economics will help us understand what might and might not work.
Even if there's still so much we don't know.
But that's **OK**. Economics isn't going to **FINISH** *ever* – there will always be more questions.
Which means we are going to need **LOTS** of great new ideas.
Including from you! What do **YOU** want to study next?

Glossary

This glossary explains some of the words used in this book. Words written in *italic* type are explained in other entries.

capital anything that helps you *produce* things more efficiently, such as money, but also complex technology or even clever ideas.
capitalism an economic system in which private individuals and businesses control production rather than the government.
communism an economic system in which government takes control of production, with the belief that this will be fairer for everyone.
cost how much money a business spends on *production*.

demand how many people want to have something.

economy any community of people who consume, *produce* and *trade* things together.
externality a cost that is not borne by the producer but by the people around them. It is a market failure because the product's price doesn't reflect its true cost.

GDP Gross Domestic Product, the total amount of wealth generated by all the people and businesses in a country.
globalization the process of countries and businesses becoming more connected around the world.

incentive a reward that encourages people to make a particular choice.
inequality when some people or countries are wealthier, on average, than other people and countries.
inflation when prices for things go up over time and money loses value.
infrastructure road networks, power grids, police forces and other things that people in a community all rely on but rarely pay for directly.
interest an amount of money that people, businesses or governments agree to pay back to anyone they borrow money from, on top of the total amount borrowed.
interest rate a number, usually decided by a central bank, that tells lenders what amount of *interest* they are meant to charge.

labour *any* work that people do when *producing* something, whether it's physical work, thinking up ideas, or even telling other people what to do.

macroeconomics the study of choices that affect a whole country, or even the world.
market *any* place where people or businesses buy and sell things: from shops, to offices, to the internet.
market failure when something is unfair or unsafe for buyers or sellers in any *market*.

microeconomics the study of choices made by businesses, households and small *economies.*
mixed economy when governments *and* businesses produce things.
modelling using simplified versions of reality to test out ideas and find answers to questions.
monopoly when a single business controls a *market.*

oligopoly when just a few business control a market.
opportunity cost any choice a person makes means they've chosen not to do other things. The choices not taken are called an opportunity cost.

poverty when people do not have enough money to afford basic needs such as food and shelter.
production the process of making a *resource* into something, typically to *trade.*
profit the money gained by a business after *costs* are subtracted from *revenue.*
public services things provided for everybody by a government, paid through *taxes.*

regulation rules that governments set up to make markets work fairly, and to stop businesses from becoming too powerful.
resources anything people need to survive, and to use for *production.*
revenue the money a business earns by *producing* something.

scarcity the fact that there isn't enough of most *resources* and products to meet *demand.* It means that people have to make choices about what they want and how to share.
specialization when a person, business or country concentrates on *producing* some things and not others.
subsidy an *incentive,* in the form of money, paid by a government to people or businesses.
supply the amount of something available to be bought in a *market.*
surplus when a person, business or government has more of a *resource* or product than it needs.

tariff a tax that must be paid to a government if you want to sell a product in their country.
taxes money that individuals and businesses pay to the government
trade buying and selling *products* in a *market.*
trade war when two or more countries put up *tariffs* against each other's products.
trading bloc when two or more countries agree to share certain rules affecting their *markets,* such as shared *tariffs* or *regulations.*

unemployment the amount of people in an *economy* who don't have a job at a particular time.
utility a calculation of the value that people place on different choices.

Jobs in economics

Studying economics means trying to make sense of how lots of things work, from people to markets to governments. People who study economics often end up working in all sorts of jobs – many of them extremely well-paid, and some of them incredibly powerful.

accountant helps people keep track of exactly how much money they have earned, saved and spent – for individuals, businesses or even governments.
actuary determines how likely different events are to happen in the future, for example how long a person might live.

business development helps businesses and other organizations find ways to grow, and helps to improve relationships between businesses so they can all grow.

chief executive is in charge of running a business or organization.
civil servant works for governments to help them carry out policies and run the country efficiently.

data scientist researches all kinds of information, analyzes what that information contains, and presents it to people, for example to test how well *policies* are working.

economist studies economics, writes about economics, and often teaches it, too.

financial analyst studies markets, businesses and government regulations to predict what effects these will have.
forecasting analyst studies a particular industry, such as shipping, to determine how efficiently it could operate.

investment analyst studies markets and profits to help people and businesses decide how best to invest their money.

management consultant helps businesses and other organizations find ways to work more efficiently.

policy maker comes up with and tests ideas on how to make the world work better, or more fairly.
politician represents the opinions of people or of a political party, and turns policies into law. Around the world, many Presidents and Prime Ministers trained as economists.

quantity surveyor advises or oversees all levels of building projects.

stockbroker buys and sells stocks and shares at a stock exchange on behalf of clients, as well as advising clients on what to buy or sell.

Index

Acknowledgements

Written by
Lara Bryan & Andy Prentice

Illustrated by
Federico Mariani

Edited by
Alex Frith

Designed by Jamie Ball
& Freya Harrison

Economics experts:
David Stallibrass,
First Principles Economics
Pedro Serôdio,
University of Middlesex

Series editor: Jane Chisholm

Series designer:
Stephen Moncrieff

First published in 2020 by Usborne Publishing Ltd., Usborne House,
83–85 Saffron Hill, London, EC1N 8RT, United Kingdom.
Usborne.com

USBORNE

MONEY

FOR BEGINNERS

Written by
Eddie Reynolds, Matthew Oldham
and Lara Bryan

Illustrated by
Marco Bonatti

Contents

Usborne Quicklinks

For links to websites where you can visit a virtual bank, see money from around the world, watch video clips about how money works and find games and activities to help you manage your money, go to the Usborne Quicklinks website at

www.usborne.com/quicklinks

and type in the keywords 'money for beginners'.

Children, please ask a grown-up before going online and follow the internet safety guidelines at the Usborne Quicklinks website. Children should be supervised online.

What is money?

Even people who deal with money as part of their job, such as bankers, accountants and economists, don't all agree what money actually *is*. The simplest (but slightly incomplete) answer is that it's anything that's accepted as payment.
In theory, this means all kinds of things.

Unfortunately, not many people will accept stickers or carrots as payment. Instead, there are two forms of money that most people use every day – **cash** and **electronic money**.

Cash is another word for coins and banknotes. Typically, it's handed to somebody in exchange for something else – in this case, Raj's video game.

Each coin and note belongs to a specific set, known as a **currency**, that can only be spent in certain parts of the world.

Unlike cash, electronic money (or e-money) isn't a physical thing – it's money stored electronically. Anyone with a **bank account** has e-money. Different devices can be used to access e-money to pay for things.

When you pay with e-money, no physical money changes hands. Instead, the e-money is sent from the bank account of the person paying to the account of the person (or business) selling.

Behind the scenes, the process of moving e-money from one account to another can be quite complicated.

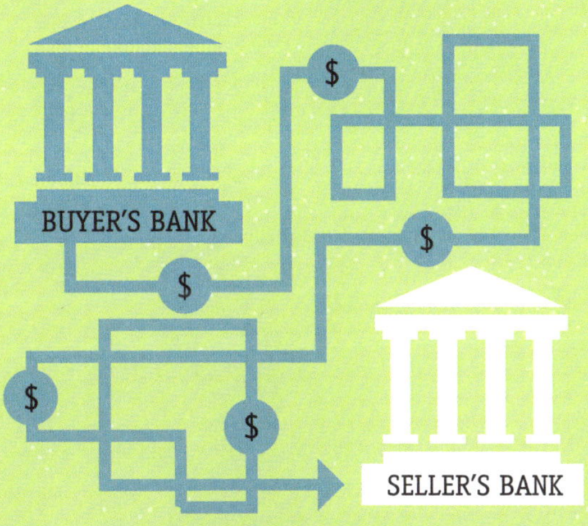

How money moves

Money flows between people constantly. When money moves from one person to another, it's known as an **exchange** or **transaction.** Here are the main ways it happens.

Earning

Most people **earn** money by doing a job that somebody **pays** them for. Find out more in chapter 4.

Spending

People **spend** money they earn on things they need, such as food and electricity, and stuff they want, such as books and treats. There's more on spending in chapter 5.

Taxation

People can't keep all the money they make. Everyone has to give some to the government to help pay for **public services**, such as schools and hospitals. This is known as **taxation.**

Donating

Some organizations and charities rely on people **giving** them money. Giving money to a cause is known as **donating.** Find out more in chapter 5.

Investing

Investing is when someone spends money on something to make *more* money from it eventually.

There are many different ways to invest. Find out more on pages 78-81.

Borrowing and lending

When people can't afford to do something, they can sometimes **borrow** money from somewhere else, such as a bank.

Lent money is known as a **loan**. All loans have to be paid back. There's more about borrowing money in chapter 4.

All these transactions and exchanges take place between people, businesses, organizations, and even governments. *Most* money moves in this way, but not *all* of it...

Stealing

Another way money moves is when it's stolen, which is of course **illegal**. In the last year alone, hundreds of billions of dollars worth of money was stolen worldwide. There's more about money crimes on pages 66-67.

Money around the world

Nobody knows *exactly* how much cash and e-money there is in the world. It exists in so many different currencies that it's hard to calculate. In 2017, the US government estimated that there's slightly over **80 trillion US dollars** out there. That amount changes every day.

If you had 80 trillion US dollars (US$), you could buy...

Canadian, US and Bolivian dollars are different **currencies**, even though they're all called *dollar*. There are lots of other currency names too, such as the euro (€), which is used in 19 countries in Europe.

There are currently 180 currencies in use across nearly 200 countries.

A single unit of one currency, such as 1 US dollar, is rarely worth the same as one unit of another currency, such as 1 Bolivian dollar.

In China the main currency is the yuan. In March 2021, 1 yuan was worth...

...around 11 ruble – the currency used in Russia.

...around 8 denar – the currency used in North Macedonia.

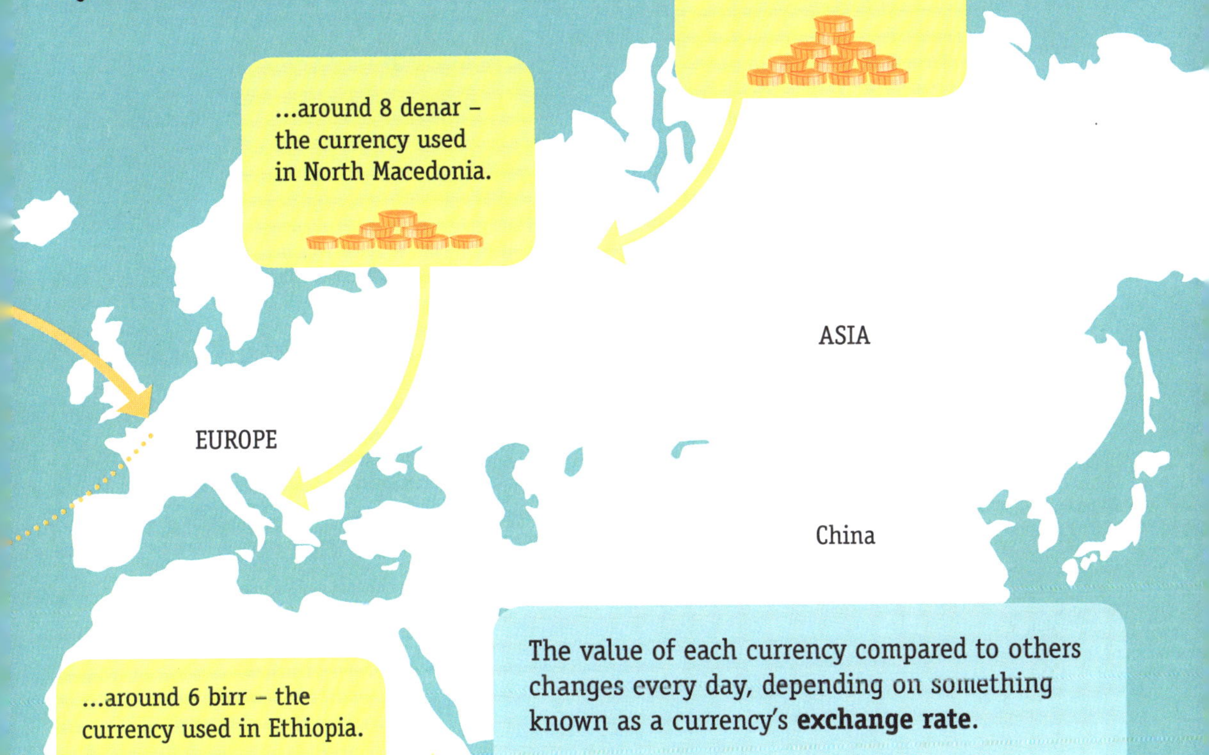

...around 6 birr – the currency used in Ethiopia.

...around 2 rand – the currency used in South Africa.

Turn to pages 20-21 to find out why exchange rates change all the time.

The value of each currency compared to others changes every day, depending on something known as a currency's **exchange rate**.

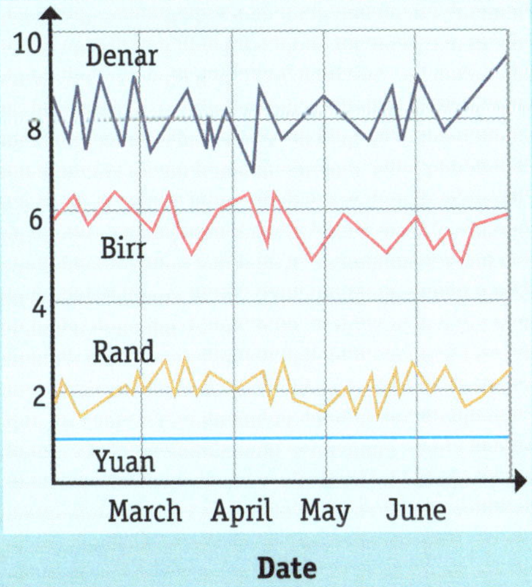

Throughout the rest of this book, prices and amounts of money are all shown in the same currency (US dollars), to make them easier to compare.

Money customs

People follow all sorts of rules when they handle and talk about money – often without realizing it. These change over time, and vary from country to country, and even family to family.

In some places, such as a supermarket, prices tend to be set...

...and in others they aren't. Discussing a price is known as **negotiating**.

Sometimes, everyone pays their share...

...at other times, one person may pay for everything.

Giving a bit of extra money in exchange for someone's service, is known as a **tip**.

Americans expect big tips – 20% is typical. In parts of south-east Asia, tips are rare.

In Korea and Japan, people hand over money and gifts using two hands, as a sign of respect.

Talking about money

Lots (and lots!) of people worry about money, regardless of how much or little they feel they have. Sharing information with people you trust can be a good way of picking up useful advice.

But talking about money is sometimes seen as rude. This is because it's often a personal, even emotional topic.

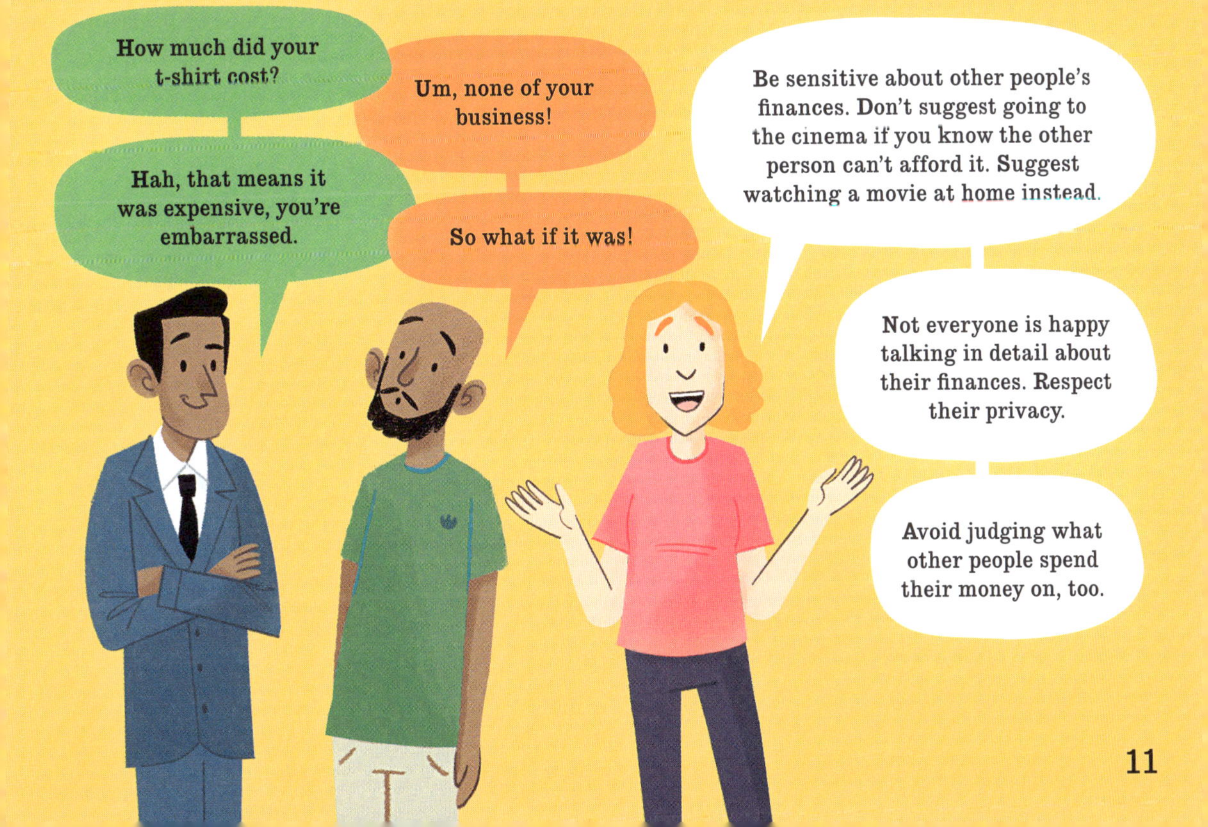

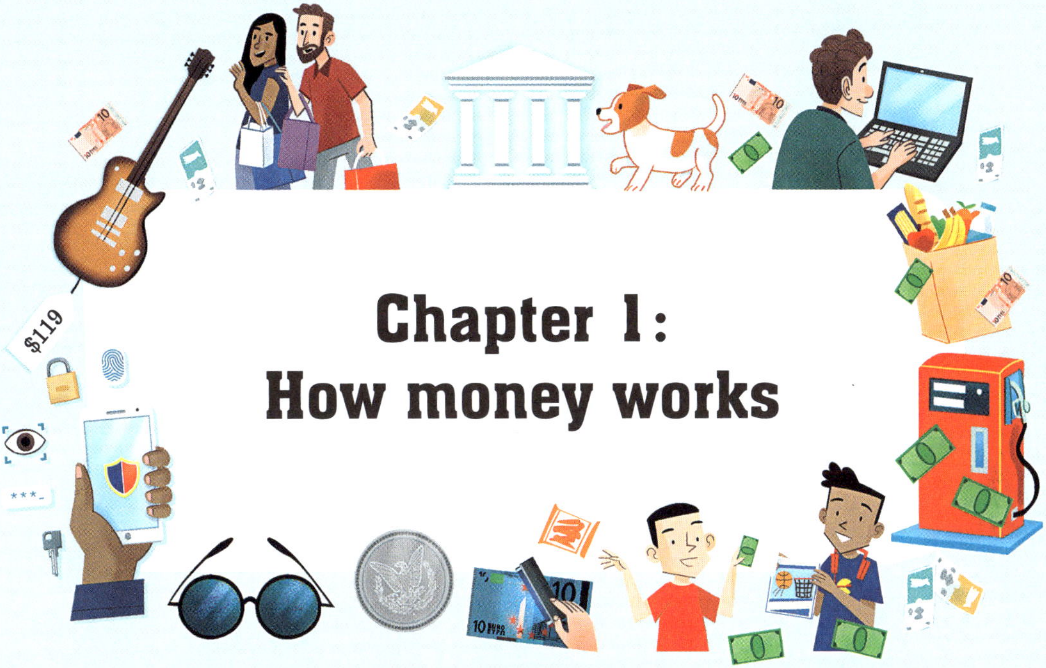

Chapter 1: How money works

Money is everywhere – whether you think of it as pieces of metal, sheets of paper, or as numbers in a bank account. And yet, most people use it every day without thinking about what it is or how it works.

You can't use just *anything* as money. It has to have some very specific features to make it valuable. Read on to find out more.

What's money for?

Money is for buying things, isn't it? Well, yes – but it has other uses, too. If it was just about buying something, you might not need money at all...

This way of buying something is called **bartering**, and you don't need money to do it. But how can you barter if only one person has what the other one wants?

This is where money comes in handy. People nearly always want money, so you can nearly always use it to buy what you want.

Experts say that when people use money to buy things and trade with each other, they're using it as a **medium of exchange**. But there are other ways to use money. You could also *save* it to use at a later date. Or *collect* it until you have more.

When money is used in this way, experts say it's being used as a **store of value**. It's only possible to *save* money because it keeps on being worth something.

People also use money to *measure value*, in the same way they use minutes and seconds to measure time. This makes it easier to work out what you can afford to buy, and to compare how much different things are worth.

Experts call this using money as a **unit of account**.

Easy money

Money would stop working if it was difficult to use. It's no coincidence that cash and e-money are used all over the world, but carrots, say, aren't. Money has certain attributes that make it excellent at what it does. The things that work best as money are...

Portable

(Easy to carry around)

Uniform

(Each piece in each currency that's *worth* the same also *looks* the same.)

Divisible

(Pieces worth amounts small enough to pay for things of any price)

Durable

(Won't break or rot)

In practice, even cash and e-money aren't *perfect*. Notes can tear, coins can wear down, credit cards can snap, and computer failures at banks can make e-money disappear. But most of the time, all these work just fine.

Liquid money

Money flows easily from person to person and from business to business. Nearly everyone is happy to accept it as a form of payment, so it can be used to buy nearly anything. This quality is known as **liquidity**.

The value of money

Money isn't valuable in the same way as food, shelter and water – humans *can* live without it. Coins, banknotes and e-money only have value for a few specific reasons:

1.

It's the law. Today's money is what's known as **fiat money**. This means it's only valuable because governments have set laws that *say* it's valuable.

To help people trust these laws, most governments share responsibility for the money in their countries with a separate organization known as a **central bank**. Find out more about central banks in chapter 6.

2. Central banks and governments limit the money supply.

Imagine a world in which photographs of cash could be used as cash...

This may *seem* fair, as everybody gets money. But if that happened, the original coin – and the photos of it – would *lose all value*.

If everyone could create unlimited amounts of money, people wouldn't *need* it from each other, so they wouldn't exchange it for things.

In the real world, where only a limited amount of money is available...

There's only one coin to share between three, so the coin is in demand, making it valuable.

3. Cash can only be made in specific places, under very secure conditions.

To make it hard for people to create their own unlimited supply of money, coins and notes are designed to be easy to identify, but difficult to copy exactly. Here are some typical design features.

However clever the designs, criminals can still produce fake, or **counterfeit**, notes and coins. But it's very difficult. If a banknote has all the features of a genuine banknote, it's almost certainly been made legally. So you can *trust* it.

Digital value

Although e-money doesn't have a physical form, we still trust it has value for the same three reasons.

1) E-money can be exchanged for cash, which the central bank and government have declared valuable.

2) There are rules limiting how banks create it, and how *much* they can create.

3) It's possible to produce *fake* e-money, but the hacking knowledge required to do this makes it just as hard as counterfeiting *physical* money.

Currencies

Money isn't the same everywhere. Each country will usually have its own type of money, called a **currency**. People and businesses from that country will expect to be paid in the local currency.

Sometimes you need to get money in another currency – whether it's for a family trip abroad, or a business making an international deal.

To exchange one currency for another, you need to know how much the currencies cost in relation to each other – this is what's known as an **exchange rate**.

You can exchange different currencies at a business called a foreign exchange bureau. It's also often possible to do this at a bank or post office. These places usually display the relative value of each currency on boards like this:

This board shows how much 1 US dollar is worth in other currencies.

Places that exchange currencies make money by buying them at one rate and selling them on for more.

EXCHANGE RATES

DATE 07.10

TIME 14.40

		WE BUY	WE SELL
EURO	EUR	00.89	00.77
UK POUND	GBP	00.83	00.72
MEXICAN PESO	MXN	19.38	16.79
BRAZILIAN REAL	BRL	03.70	03.28
CHINESE YUAN	CNY	07.03	06.77

The time and date are shown, because exchange rates change all the time.

People with euros who want US dollars, need to pay €0.89 for $1.

Every currency in the world has a unique 3-letter code name.

People with US dollars who want euros, only get €0.77 for $1.

A currency's value changes all the time, depending on how many people want it – the higher the demand for it, the higher its value.

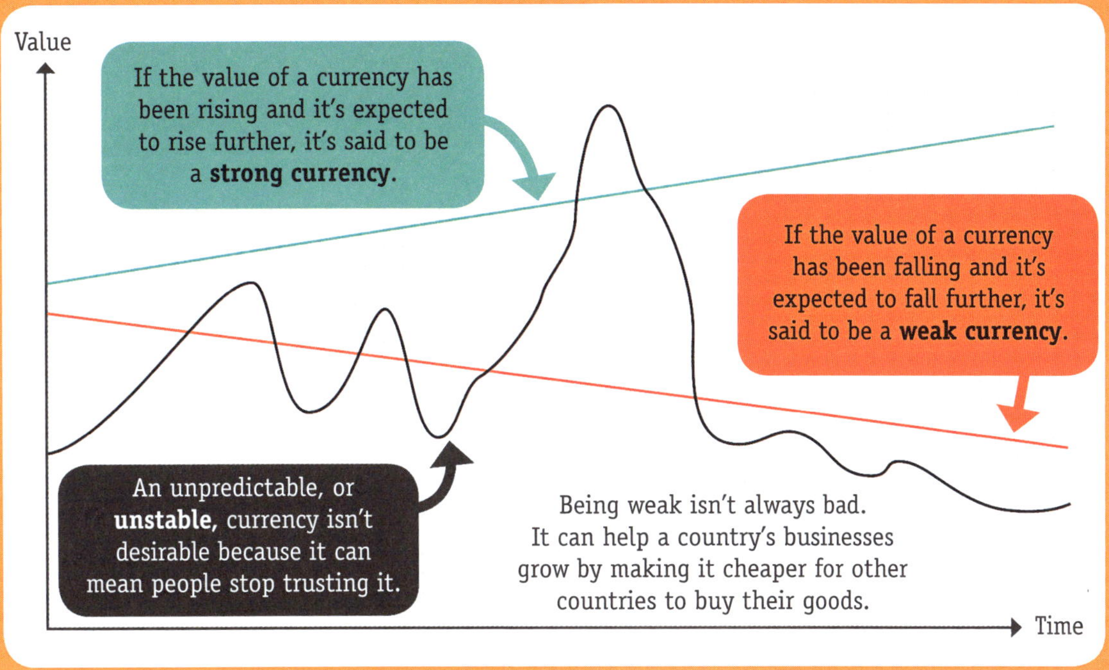

There are several reasons why some currencies are in more demand than others.

Valuing trust

A currency's value depends on how much people trust that country's government. If people don't, the value of that currency will go down.

Strong business

The more business a country does, the higher the demand for its currency.

Political decisions

Governments decide how much new money to create. If they reduce the amount, their currency will become rarer, which may make it more expensive.

If a currency is both strong and stable, it's likely to become a **reserve currency**. This means that banks and governments buy that currency to store their wealth. Today, the world's most dominant reserve currency is the US dollar, but countries also use the euro, UK pound and the Chinese yuan.

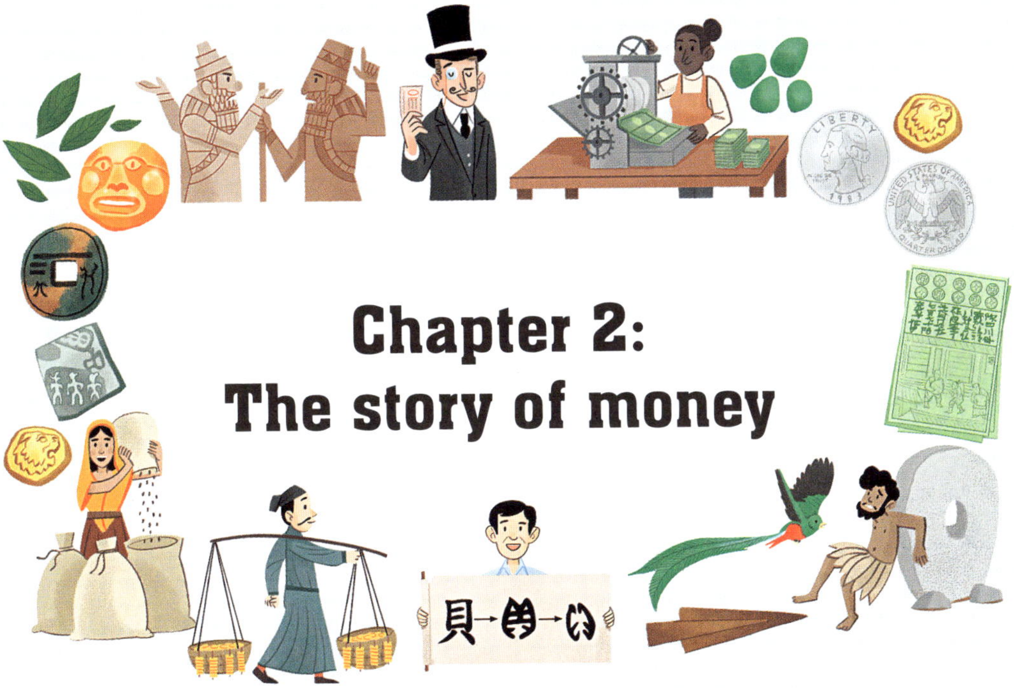

Chapter 2: The story of money

Money has been used for at least as long as people have been able to write things down. We know this because many of the oldest examples of writing are receipts and lists of things people owed each other.

It's likely, however, that some form of money existed long before this – before it even had a name. As an idea, it seems to have occurred to people all around the world, rather than spreading from one place to another.

But how did it end up in the form it has today?

Not quite money

The oldest surviving evidence of people using money to trade goods comes from Mesopotamia (modern-day Iraq), around 9,000 years ago. Before this, historians think people used a mixture of methods to trade with each other.

Sometimes people had the right things to barter with, but they weren't ready at the right times, so they made promises to each other instead. This sort of promise is also known as an **I.O.U.** (short for "I owe you").

Although no one used the word "money" to describe these promises and transactions, all the ingredients of money were there.

Definitely money

We know Mesopotamians used these things as money because they wrote down records of debts they owed each other, and how these debts were paid. This is some of the earliest ever writing. Records show they used a grain called barley to measure small sums, and silver to measure larger amounts. They may have even used barley seeds and slivers of silver as coins – although none survive.

Funny money

At least since Mesopotamian times – and all over the world – people have used a variety of things in the same way we use cash today. These simple forms of money varied wildly...

These forms of money were often desirable in some way, and had their own value.

But many of them also had drawbacks, too.

Some forms had fewer drawbacks than others. For instance, cowrie shells were both rare and desirable. They were also **portable**, **durable** and came in a fairly **uniform** size.

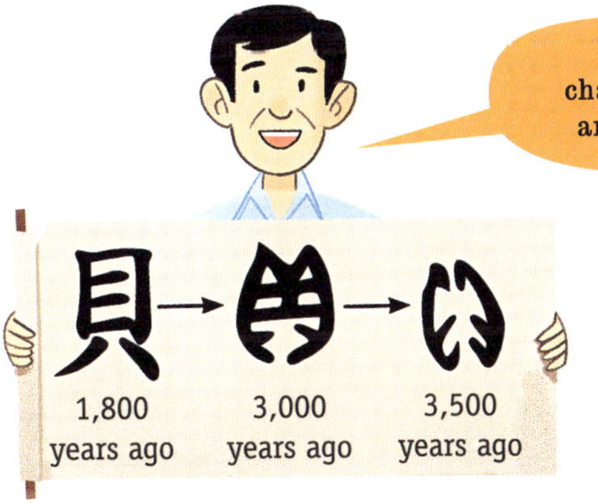

In China, cowrie shells were such a successful form of money, people started to make bronze copies to use as well.

Bronze copies were first used around 2,400 years ago. These small, man-made, metal objects had a lot in common with another, much more recognizable form of money that was already being used in China, and beyond – **coins**.

The rise of the coin

Money has taken many different forms throughout history, but some things have been used more widely than others. Over time, small flat discs, made from certain metals, especially **gold** and **silver**, came to be used across the globe.

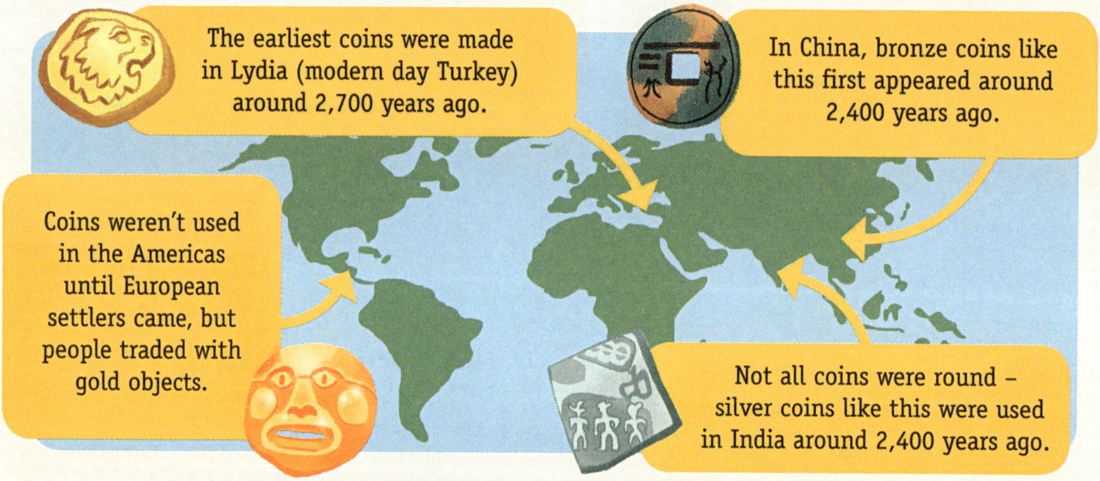

Gold and silver were the perfect materials to make coins – rare enough to be precious, but not *too* rare, so almost anyone could have a little.

Gold and silver were too valuable to use for everyday business, so people also made coins from other, less rare metals, too.

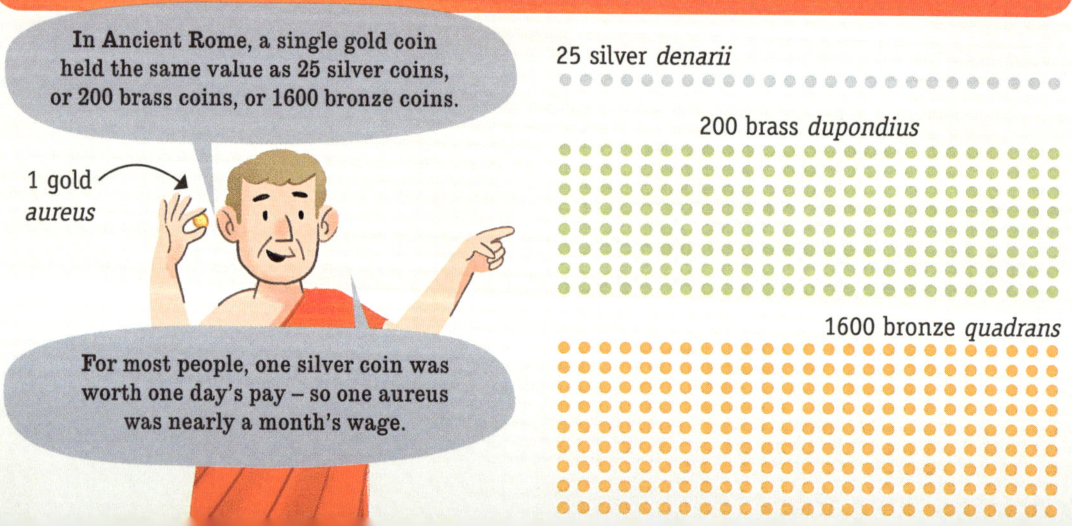

Coins were made, or **minted**, by local rulers and governments who used them to collect taxes. They had to be recognizable, so people could feel confident spending them and accepting them. Many features of coins haven't changed since they were first used, around 2,700 years ago.

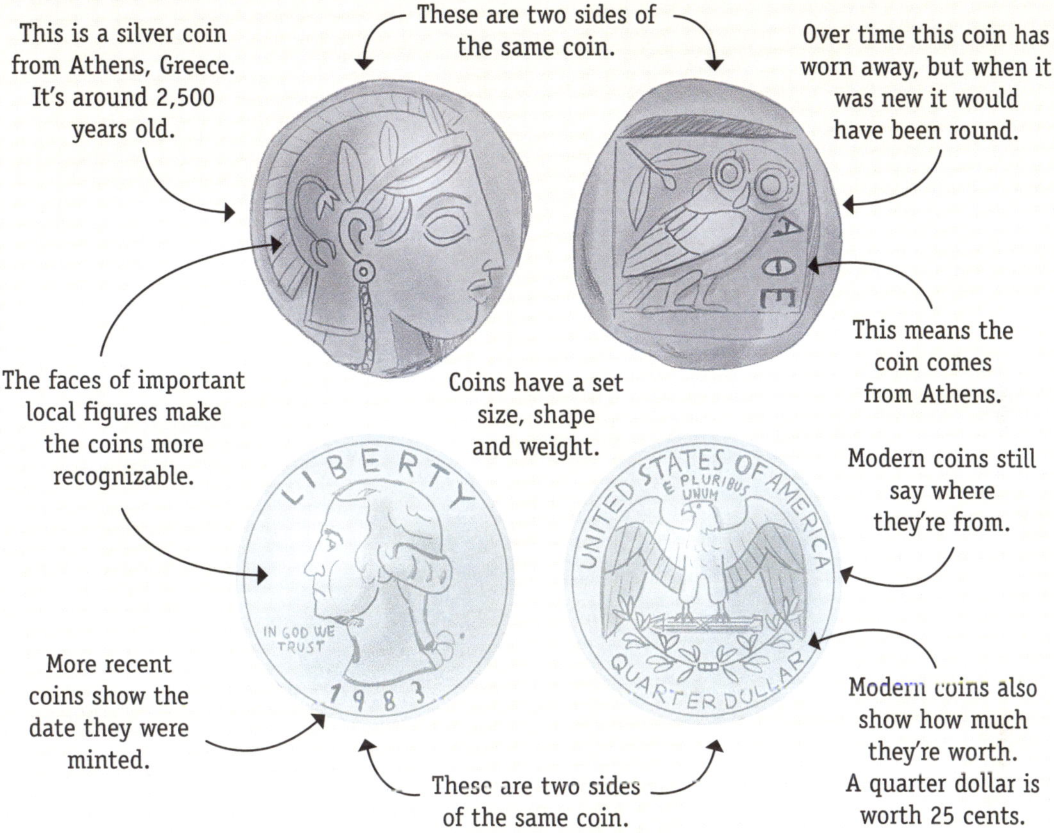

This system worked well for over a thousand years, but coins weren't perfect. They were heavy to carry in big quantities and, worse, people could steal them. People found creative ways to cheat with coins, too.

Banknotes

One of the major problems with coins is that people often needed lots of them to pay for expensive things. Then, around 1,000 years ago, people came up with a new way to handle large sums of money.

To solve this problem, bankers in China offered to store people's coins in secure vaults. They would then issue paper receipts, called *Jiaozi*, to show how much people had stored. Instead of reclaiming their coins, people used these receipts to pay for things – whoever had the receipt could then collect the coins.

Jiaozi were the world's first **banknotes**. China was the first country to develop cheap ways of making paper and printing, so it was in a unique position to create this form of money.

Each bank designed and produced their own Jiaozi. Like banknotes today, they had elaborate designs to make them as hard to copy as possible.

Jiaozi weren't perfect. They were only ever used to represent really large sums of money, so most people didn't use them. They were easier to copy than coins, too. Banks at this time were risky businesses. If they failed, their customers would be left with worthless receipts for money they couldn't reclaim.

It took a while for this system to catch on. It was even abandoned for around 400 years. But in time, China began printing standard notes that worked in all the major banks – a system that survives to this day.

Not worth the paper it's printed on

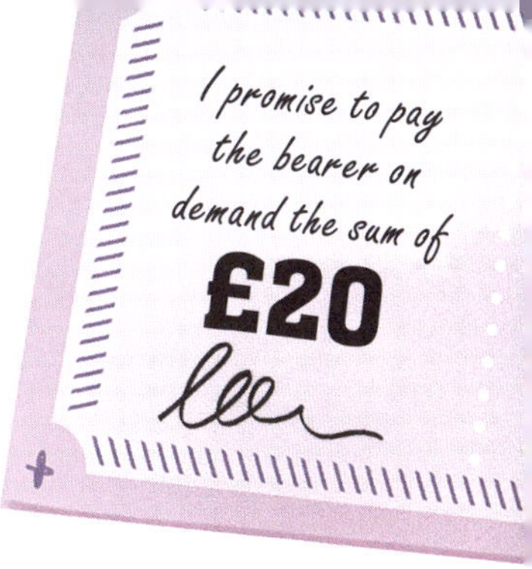

Modern banknotes still look as if they're receipts, just like Jiaozi. In some countries, the signature of the chief banker has been printed next to a sentence that says:

"I promise to pay the bearer on demand the sum of...".

But if you took that note into a bank to "demand" to be paid, they wouldn't do anything. That's because all money today is fiat money – it isn't linked to a store of coins, or gold, or anything else. Fiat money gets its name from the word *fiat*, which means "let it be done" in Latin – it's only valuable because the government says so. This hasn't always been the case...

Governments discovered they'd printed more money than could be matched by ALL the gold in the world. But they also realized this *didn't matter* – so long as people kept trusting banks.

The gold standard soon became a thing of the past. It ended for good in 1971 when the USA became the last country to stop using it. Banknotes were no longer linked to anything else. The age of fiat money had begun.

Money in all its forms

Money isn't just about cash or e-money. It is, at heart, a promise that most people trust. Over the centuries, people have developed at least three other ways to turn promises into money.

Debts

...are money that someone promises to pay you in the future.

In this example, Julie and Rob are using debt as money. Instead of paying Rob back in money, Julie has agreed to take on his debt instead.

Debt is often described as something you *have* – when you have debts, you owe money. But it's also something you can *buy*.

When you buy debt, you're owed money by a debtor. This can be valuable because debtors usually pay back an extra fee called interest (see page 60). Buying debt can be risky because debtors aren't always able to pay you back. But if they are reliable, this risk is very low.

One type of low-risk debt that people can buy is called a **bond**. This sort of debt typically lasts a very long time. It's usually sold by governments or big companies who are very likely to be able to repay the money in the future.

Stocks and shares

...are money that you've paid to own a small part of a business.

If you own one or more *stocks*, it means you have a *share* in the business's profits. If the business is doing well, you might get regular payments from it, or you could choose to sell your stocks, hopefully for more than you paid.

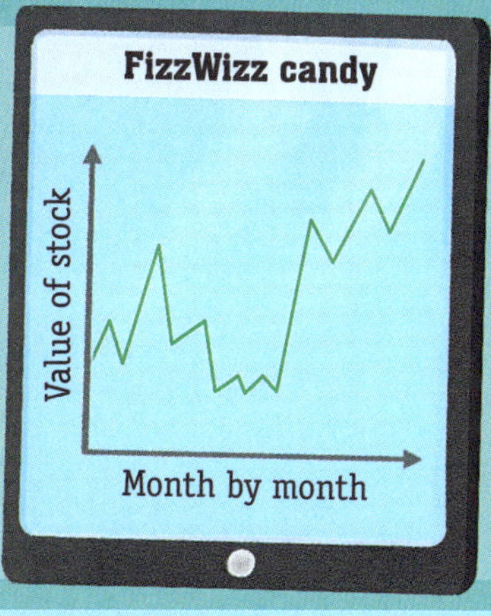

Derivatives

...are promises of money based on the value of some other thing, such as a stock, or debt, or just something people produce, such as wheat.

These two people are discussing a kind of derivative known as a **future**.

Debts, stocks, derivatives and other forms of money are all known as **financial instruments.** You can exchange them with other people *as if* they were money. Most people who work in banks – especially the highest paid ones – advise rich customers on how to get even richer by buying and selling financial instruments.

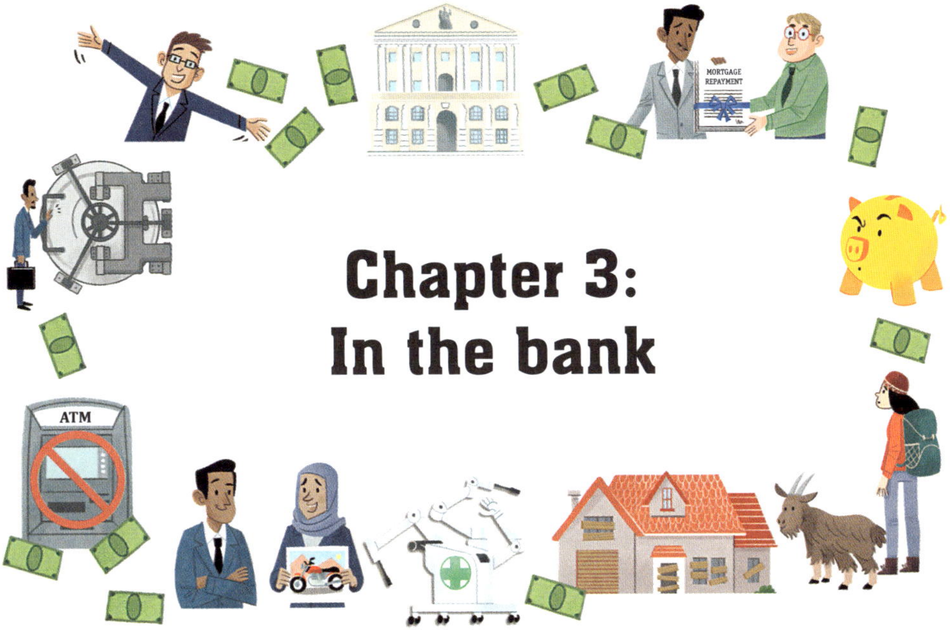

Chapter 3: In the bank

Many people's first experience of banking is storing money in a **piggy bank**. But, as you save more money, you might need to put it in a **commercial bank** instead. This is because commercial banks are safer and more convenient.

But a bank is more than simply a piggy bank for grown-ups. Banks do lots of things that piggy banks can't. They **lend** people money, and to do so they **create** new money out of nothing. If this sounds a bit like magic, that's because, in some ways, it *is*.

This chapter looks at what different types of banks do, why and how they do it, and some of the effects they can have on the world.

Where's my money?

Almost all adults put, or **deposit**, their money in a bank. But they rarely think about what happens to that money. This is partly due to misleading language people use when they talk about banks.

For a start, people usually visit just one branch, or office, of their bank. But big banks often have lots of branches in cities and towns around the world, and online, too.

So if you ever hear someone say...

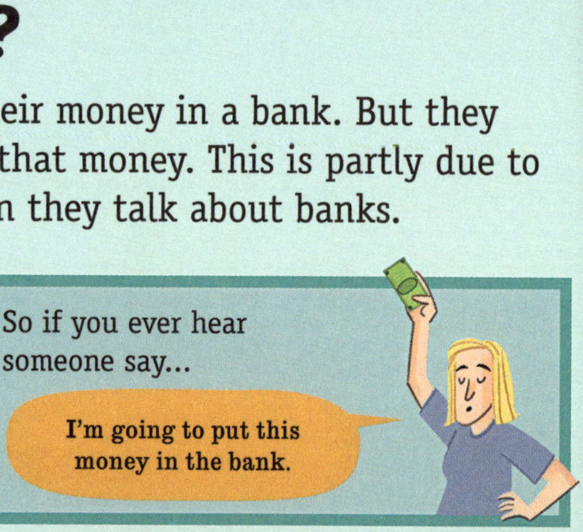

...it might sound as if the branch they go to will then keep this deposit there, in a box of cash with the depositor's name on.

In reality, that's *not* what happens. When you deposit money, it becomes part of a big "pool" of deposits and earnings that belong to ALL the branches of that bank.

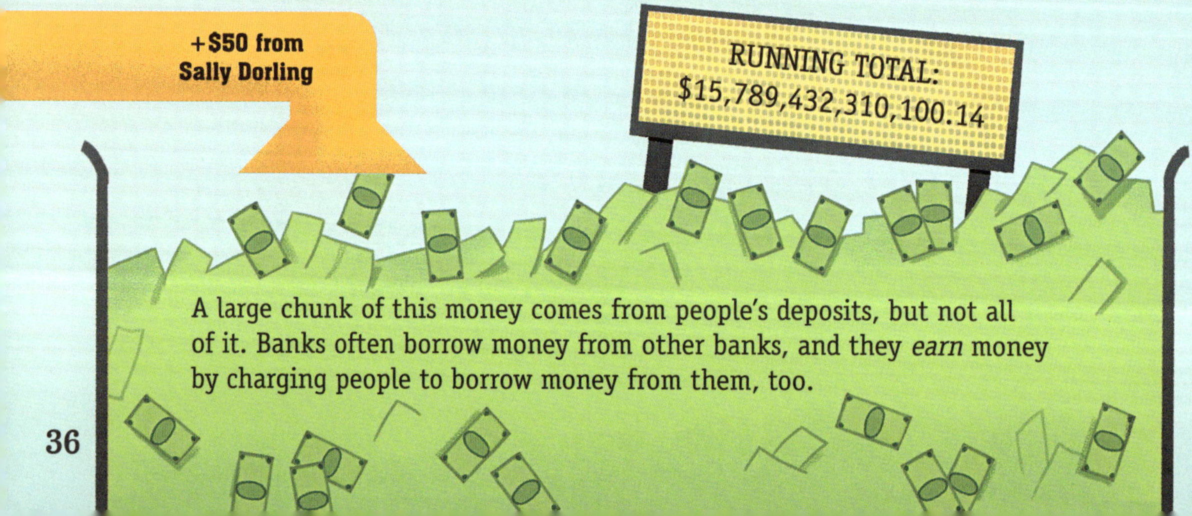

A large chunk of this money comes from people's deposits, but not all of it. Banks often borrow money from other banks, and they *earn* money by charging people to borrow money from them, too.

Once your money is in the pool, a number of things might happen to it. For example...

It gets spent

A bank is a business. Like all businesses, a bank spends money all the time to pay for the day-to-day running of the bank, and to help it grow and improve.

It gets stored

Banks *don't* need to store the full amount of money that has been deposited. It's very unlikely every customer will **withdraw** all their money at once.

Instead, most banks keep *some* cash in a super-secure vault in the bank...

...*some* in another bank, known as a **central bank**...

...and the rest in **ATMs***, or **cash machines**, where customers can withdraw it.

*ATM means *Automated Teller Machine.*

Why people want banks

Even if you start out keeping money in a jar or **piggy bank**, sooner or later, you'll most likely move it to a bank instead. This kind of bank is known as a **commercial** or **retail** bank.

Because...

It's safe and secure

Banks keep money safe from criminals. Bank computers are protected – it's extremely difficult for hackers to steal people's details. And the vaults where banks keep cash are very secure too, with security cameras in every room.

You can track it

When you deposit money in a bank, the bank keeps track of how much you spend and how much you have left. A **bank account** is a record of how much money you have available. There are several different types of account.

There are many ways to spend it

When you have a bank account, you can pay for things with a debit card, online or with an app on your phone. You can also use the card to withdraw cash from an ATM.

Your money grows

As you know from the previous page, banks *use* the money you deposit. They may thank you for your deposits (and encourage you to deposit more) by adding money to your account at the end of each month or year. This is known as **interest**. Many people save money for the future this way.

Borrowing money

When people, businesses and governments need money to buy something they can't afford, a bank might agree to lend, or **loan**, them money. People borrow money from the bank for all sorts of reasons.

Unfortunately, loans aren't free. If a bank agrees to lend you money, you have to pay back the amount of the loan, plus some extra on top. This is called **interest** too.

Banks will only lend you money if they decide they can trust you to pay back the full amount, plus interest. Find out how they decide on page 62.

Why do banks charge interest?

Banks charge interest for lots of reasons. It's the main way they make money. It's also a safety net if things go wrong – interest from successful loans helps make up for money lost on loans that people don't pay back. There's another big reason, too – interest helps stop money from losing value over time. Find out more on pages 98-99.

How banks create money

Another misleading word people use when talking about banks is *lending*. Banks don't actually lend money they *already have* – they **create** the money to lend, as if by magic. Here's how it works.

Zak needs a loan of $50,000 from the bank to start up a business.

After reviewing his application, the bank thinks Zak's business idea will work well. So it agrees to lend him the money.

The bank creates NEW e-money by typing $50,000 into a computer and adding it to Zak's account, while also noting down $50,000 as missing from the bank's own money.

The +$50,000 and the –$50,000 are just numbers on a computer – they cancel each other out with every dollar that Zak pays back, until the bank is missing nothing. But before Zak has to do this, he has $50,000 to spend on his business. He can then use the money the business makes to pay the bank back.

A risky trick?

Around 97% of all the money currently in banks has been created this way. It exists as numbers in people's bank accounts, and debts owed in a bank's own accounts. The rest is cash, created by governments.

But if there's more e-money than cash, what would happen if everyone wanted all of their money at once?

If everybody decided to take out their deposits, it wouldn't be possible. This has never happened on a worldwide scale – most people only take out very small amounts of cash. But it HAS happened to individual banks...

When lots of people withdraw their deposits all at once, it's known as a **bank run**, or **run on the bank**. If a bank runs out of cash, it can no longer function, because it can't pay back its depositors. People lose trust in the bank, so stop depositing money there. That means the bank has almost no money to spend.

Bank runs can be prevented by...

Borrowing cash. If a bank is low on cash, it can borrow it from other banks.

Setting limits. Banks can stop people taking out more than a certain amount each day.

Insuring deposits. Some governments promise to pay depositors their money if the bank can't. This stops people worrying as much if banks are low on cash.

Other types of bank

Not all commercial banks work the same way. **Islamic banks**, which can be found all over the world, have alternative ways to help people buy things, and still make a profit. One of the main things that's different is how they work with interest.

According to Islam, interest is immoral because it can grow over time. This puts unfair pressure on the borrower.

One of the ways Islamic banks get around charging interest is known as *murabaha*. Here's how it works.

This method means the customer agrees a price with the bank that can't be changed. The bank still gets to make a profit, but there's no interest involved, so the debt can't grow bigger.

Most people trust banks and use them regularly, but some people choose to store and borrow money elsewhere. Here are some common alternatives.

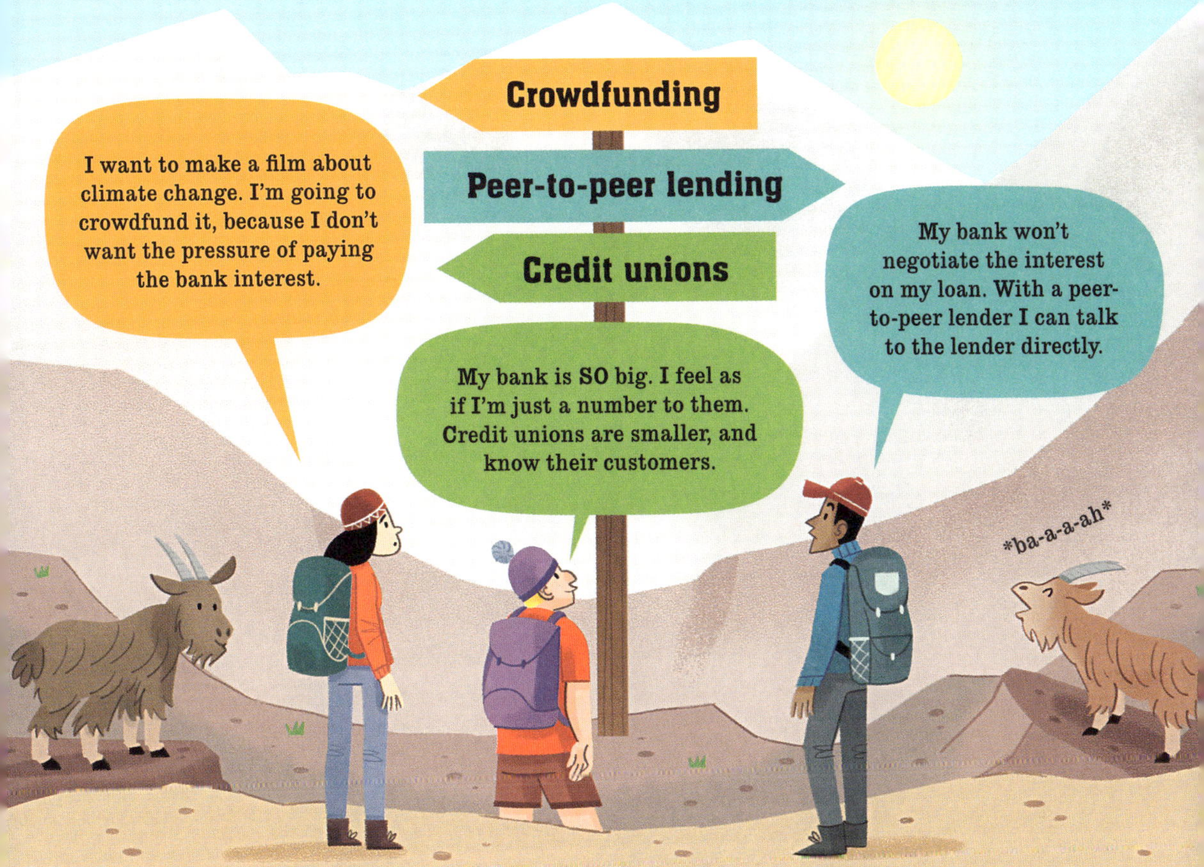

What do these terms mean?

Crowdfunding involves presenting an idea to the public, often on a crowdfunding website. People who think it's a good idea can help to pay for it. In return, you offer these people a reward when the project is finished. For example, in this case, a copy of the film. If you can't raise enough money, you usually have to give it all back.

Credit unions are like small, simple banks. Instead of customers, they have *members*, who all have a say in how the union is run. If a member wants to borrow money, the union will lend them other members' deposits, and will charge less interest than most banks. In some places, organizations known as **building societies** do this too.

Peer-to-peer lenders are companies that put people who want to *lend* in touch with people who want to *borrow*. Lenders see requests from potential borrowers, and can choose who to lend to. Lenders don't need to charge as much interest as a bank to make a profit, because they don't have extra costs to cover, such as paying staff and running a business.

Offshore banking

When businesses or people earn money, they have to give some of it to the government, as **tax**. But which government? Some avoid paying tax by having a bank account in a country where the government doesn't demand much tax. These places are known as **offshore tax havens.**

Denise, a wealthy businesswoman and investor, isn't happy with how much tax she pays.

If Denise sets up a shell company, she can open a bank account for it in the tax haven, then make sure money she earns from her investments goes straight to that account. Tax would be charged on her earnings as if the earnings were made there. In the end, she'd pay *much* less tax.

Famous tax havens include the British Virgin Islands in the Caribbean, and the Channel Islands between France and the UK. Tax havens are often heavily criticized. Here are some reasons why.

Governments worldwide lose around $700 billion in tax each year.

If governments had more money from tax, they'd have more to spend on people in need.

But businesses and investors help people in need, too. If I have more money to invest, the businesses I invest in have more money to create jobs, or make their products cheaper.

Hmm... but even if that's true, it's still not fair. If I have to pay taxes, why shouldn't a rich person, or a big business?

You shouldn't! Personally, I vote for a government that cuts taxes for everybody.

Well how do you expect governments to fund things like schools and roads then?

The banks often keep depositors' identities and money activities secret.

I've heard that some offshore banks don't check where depositors get their money from, or how they spend it.

That's often true, and it's a good thing. Checking where the money comes from would breach our customers' privacy.

But if you don't check at all, it makes it easy for criminals to hide stolen money. And terrorists have been known to fund wars and violence through tax havens.

But that happens so *rarely*. Is closing the banks going to stop them? And besides, we also help people in danger keep money safe from criminals and terrorists.

How do you know that it happens rarely if you don't even check?

Some researchers have estimated that around 10% of the world's wealth is in tax haven bank accounts. If that was split between everybody in the world, each person would get over $1,000. That's more than people earn in a year in some parts of the world.

Behind-the-scenes banks

There's another kind of bank, known as an **investment bank**, which you're unlikely to come across in your day-to-day life. Most of them are in skyscrapers in big cities, and they do a very important job. They help businesses and governments find funding for really, *really* expensive projects.

Imagine a business called RoboDoc, which makes robots for hospitals. It needs funding to keep growing and to manufacture more robots, but it's not sure where best to get it.

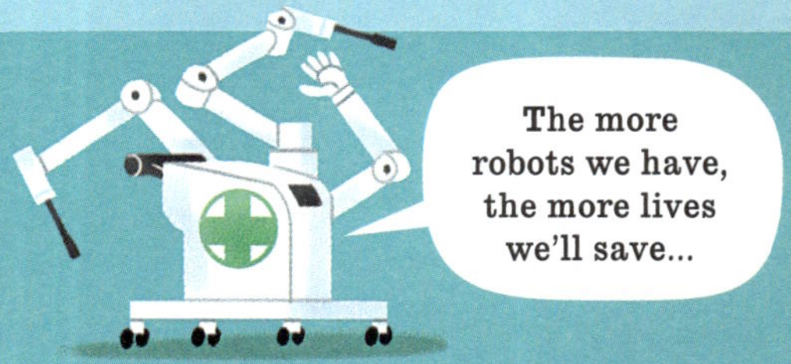

An investment bank might suggest that a business does one of the following things...

Banks often lend to governments and businesses. The downside: they often charge lots of interest.

It's often possible for a business to make money by using its earnings to buy shares, bonds, derivatives and debts.

Sometimes businesses go on sale. Buying another business may cost lots of money, but it often means acquiring a bigger team and more resources for making products.

This usually means finding people to buy shares in the business. These shares can then be traded with other investors.

Investment banks might not only *advise* clients what to do – they can do it all for them, too.

Go to page 32 for a quick reminder of what these are.

Shares are sold to investors through **stock exchanges.** The people who help companies and investors buy and sell shares are known as **stock brokers.**

When an investment bank steps in to buy shares it can't sell, it's known as **underwriting.**

Investment banks are good at these jobs, because they work closely with lots of different companies and investors all the time. They have an excellent overview of who is interested in buying shares, and which shares sell well.

Investment banks charge LOTS of money for this service – hundreds of thousands, or even millions of dollars. But for companies it's often worth it. It would be much harder to find funding for big projects without investment banks.

Banks in crisis

Useful though banks are, they can be dangerous for society if they're run badly. In the years before 2008, commercial and investment banks played a central role in what became a global financial crisis. Here – in short and much simplified – is what happened.

In a bid to make more money, commercial banks in the US began offering mortgages to more and more people. Many of these people were unlikely to be able to pay back the loan and the interest.

The banks knew this was risky. If people couldn't pay them back, the banks would lose money. So they *sold* the bad debt to other organizations – usually investment banks.

Now, when borrowers repaid loans, the money went to the investment bank that bought the debt.

The investment banks knew this debt was risky, too, so they bundled up the mortgage repayments with more reliable debt and sold it to investors. This was sometimes illegal.

Every month, investment banks and investors would share the profit from mortgage repayments. The more people took out mortgages, the more this profit grew.

This system seemed to be working. Houses kept going up in value. People sold their old houses for more than they paid for them, paid off their mortgages, and took out new mortgages on more expensive homes...

...until house prices stopped rising. Many people could no longer pay off mortgages by selling their homes. Huge numbers of people were in debt that they simply couldn't repay.

This was a disaster. Commercial banks couldn't sell any debt to investment banks. Investment banks had no repayments to pay to investors. Everybody in the chain was losing money, and losing trust in each other. The consequences were dire.

There was less money around. People lost their jobs, and many couldn't afford basic necessities. When this happens on a large scale over a period of time, it's known as a **recession**. This one was a BIG one.

Banks and investors all over the world were involved, so the recession spread beyond the US to other countries. BILLIONS of people were affected.

Anger at the banks

By mid-2008, some banks had lost SO much money they were forced to shut down. Others stopped lending, which meant people and businesses couldn't borrow. In some places, governments opted to save banks that were close to failing, by giving them LOTS of tax money. People were angry.

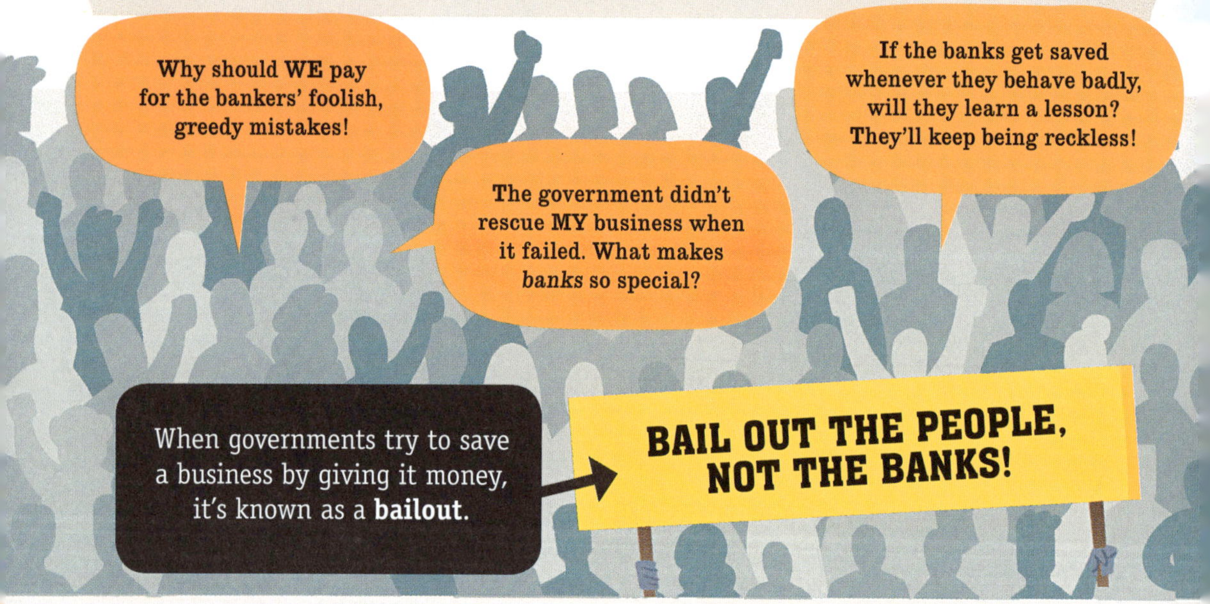

When governments try to save a business by giving it money, it's known as a **bailout**.

Though many people were angry that the bailout happened, not everybody was against it.

Even though the causes of the crisis were unclear, many people directed their anger at the banks and bankers.

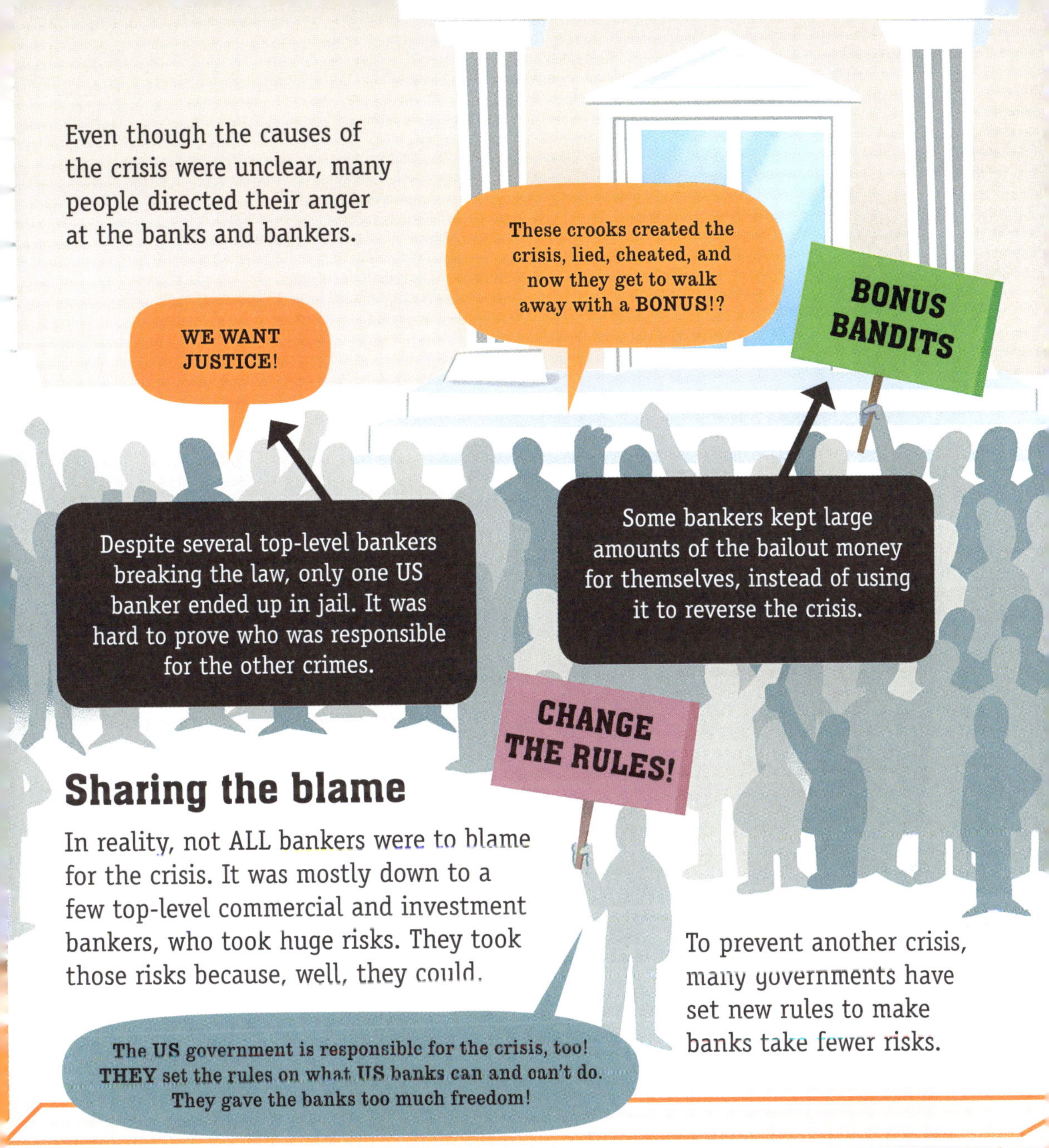

Despite several top-level bankers breaking the law, only one US banker ended up in jail. It was hard to prove who was responsible for the other crimes.

Some bankers kept large amounts of the bailout money for themselves, instead of using it to reverse the crisis.

Sharing the blame

In reality, not ALL bankers were to blame for the crisis. It was mostly down to a few top-level commercial and investment bankers, who took huge risks. They took those risks because, well, they could.

To prevent another crisis, many governments have set new rules to make banks take fewer risks.

Will history repeat?

Probably, but nobody knows for sure when or how. The UK central bank's website says: "History shows that there are two things we can be sure of when it comes to financial crises: there will be another one, and the next one won't be the same as the last."

Understanding how banks work, and monitoring what they do, can make it less likely there will be another crisis as big as the 2008 financial crisis.

Chapter 4: Earning and borrowing

Have you ever wanted to buy something that you couldn't afford? There are two common solutions to this problem: **earn** some money, or **borrow** some.

There are literally millions of jobs you could do to earn a living, and they would all earn you different amounts. But even people who earn lots and lots have to borrow money from time to time. So many things wouldn't be possible without borrowing, such as buying a house or starting a business.

Earning your way

When you're a child or teenager, you might be given **pocket money** or an **allowance**. But once you grow up, you'll probably need to *earn* money by doing a job that somebody pays you for.

There's more than one way for teachers, bus drivers, sandwich tasters and cat trainers to set up their work lives. For example...

Cat trainer Kayla is an **employee** at a cat training company. She...

...is paid an agreed amount of money every month, known as a **salary**.

...is guaranteed to be paid money, as long as she works for her employer.

...gets some paid time off each year, but has to work the same number of hours each week.

Cat trainer Nico is **self-employed**, or **freelance**. People (his **clients**) pay him to do one-off jobs caring for their cats. He...

...earns different amounts every month, depending on how much work he does.

...is not guaranteed paid work. He has to find clients.

...can register as a **business** and pay employees to work for him.

...doesn't get paid time off, but can decide how many days and hours he works.

The job hunt

Most people try to find a job that will pay them enough money to live on. But this isn't the only thing people think about when they look for a job.

Before starting a job, the **employee** and the **employer** have to agree on what the job will involve. They usually both sign a set of papers, known as a **contract**, to show that they're both happy with the arrangement.

CONTRACT

A contract usually shows...

- How much you'll get paid.
- How many hours you'll work.
- How much time you can take off.
- What to do if you're sick.

Employer's signature: ....

Employee's signature: ....

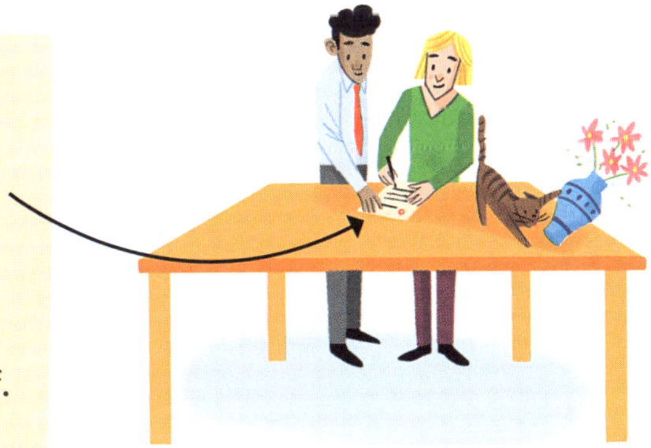

If you think the arrangement in the contract is unfair, it might be worth asking for – **negotiating** – a better one. You'll find some top negotiating tips on page 118.

High pay, low pay

Some people are paid more than others, whether it seems fair or not. For example, top footballers are usually paid much more than gardeners. This is because salaries are partly influenced by how rare a person's skills are – the **supply** – compared to how many employers want those skills – the **demand**. Here's how it happens.

Like anybody with a job, gardeners and footballers are paid to provide skills that their employers need.

But some skills are harder than others, so fewer people can do them.

The number of people with top-class football skills is low, but there are lots of teams that want those skills, so teams compete for players.

In contrast, the number of people who can grow vegetables is higher than the number of gardeners needed, so gardeners compete for employers.

How low does it go?

To protect workers, many governments have made it illegal for employers to pay employees less than a particular amount. This is known as the **minimum wage.** The minimum wage tends to be smaller in countries where basics such as food and clothes cost very little.

For example, in Israel, bread costs...

The minimum wage is $1,446 per month.

In Albania, bread costs...

The minimum wage is $212 per month.

Economists and politicians often disagree on how effective a minimum wage really is at protecting citizens.

On the one hand...

On the other hand...

Many employers pay more than the minimum wage, because they believe they'll attract better staff by paying more. But sometimes employees have to campaign to get better pay. Here are some ways they might go about it.

Join a union

Trade unions are groups of workers. They campaign for workers' rights and organize protests known as strikes to encourage employers to improve pay, working conditions or overall fairness.

Tell the media

For example, if a woman is paid less than a man for doing the same job, she might tell a newspaper. Public embarrassment can make employers change their ways.

A helping hand

There are many different ways you can **borrow** money from a bank or lending company. Each way is suited to a different situation where people need money that they don't yet have.

Borrowing small amounts

If somebody needs money to make a quick purchase before they can afford it, they might use a **credit card**.

How it works: a credit card company or a bank pays for your purchase. You then pay them back later – usually within 60 days.

If you don't pay back on time, the bank or company charges **interest**, so the amount you owe goes up.

Many banks let you spend more than you have in your account. This is known as an **overdraft**, and you have to pay it back – with interest.

Some bank accounts, especially for students, give customers interest-free overdrafts, but always up to a limit.

Borrowing large amounts

Imagine two people come across a large, empty warehouse that nobody is using...

But they don't have enough money in the bank to rent the warehouse, buy chocolate-making machines, and pay staff. So they'll have to apply for a **loan** at a bank or lending company.

One week later...

The lender usually carries out checks to see if the borrower can be trusted to pay back the loan, plus interest.

If the lender says yes, the borrower and lender have to sign a contract, which states...

...how much is being borrowed.

...a deadline for the borrower to pay it all back.

...how much interest is charged. (See next page for more about interest.)

People sometimes give the lender their personal belongings if they don't have money. This is known as **paying with collateral**.

Paying for money

Usually, when you borrow money, you have to pay interest. The amount depends on something known as the **interest rate**, which is a percentage of the amount you borrowed. Here's a simplified example of how it might work.

5% of $10,000 is $500.

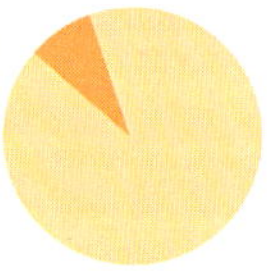

$10,000 + $500 = **$10,500** This is the total the van buyers have to repay.

With this kind of loan, you only *fully* own what you've bought once you've paid it *all* back, including the interest (but you can use it in the meantime).

It can take decades to pay back loans. This is partly because some loans (for example to buy a house) are very big, but also because banks like long loans. Long loans with regular repayments mean they have a steady stream of money coming in.

Interest that grows

Most people pay off debts in regular, monthly chunks, including a bit of interest each time. If you delay or miss a payment, you can sometimes end up owing much more than you started with. That's because you have to pay off interest on the bit of interest you *didn't* pay. Each month you leave the debt unpaid, the more the interest goes up.

It's a lot like the way a snowball gets bigger more quickly the longer you roll it. For example...

Compound interest can be a terrible thing if it grows for too long – people end up owing very large amounts.

But it can be a good thing too. Most savings accounts *pay* compound interest. So if you leave money in a savings account and don't touch it, your savings will get bigger and bigger, by more and more each year.

German-born scientist and thinker Albert Einstein is supposed to have said about compound interest...

Credit ratings

Most banks and loan companies won't lend money to *everybody* who asks, because some people might not pay it all back. Lenders use a scoring system called a **credit rating** to estimate how risky it is to give somebody a loan.

This flow chart shows some of the things that affect a person's score, and what it means for their borrowing.

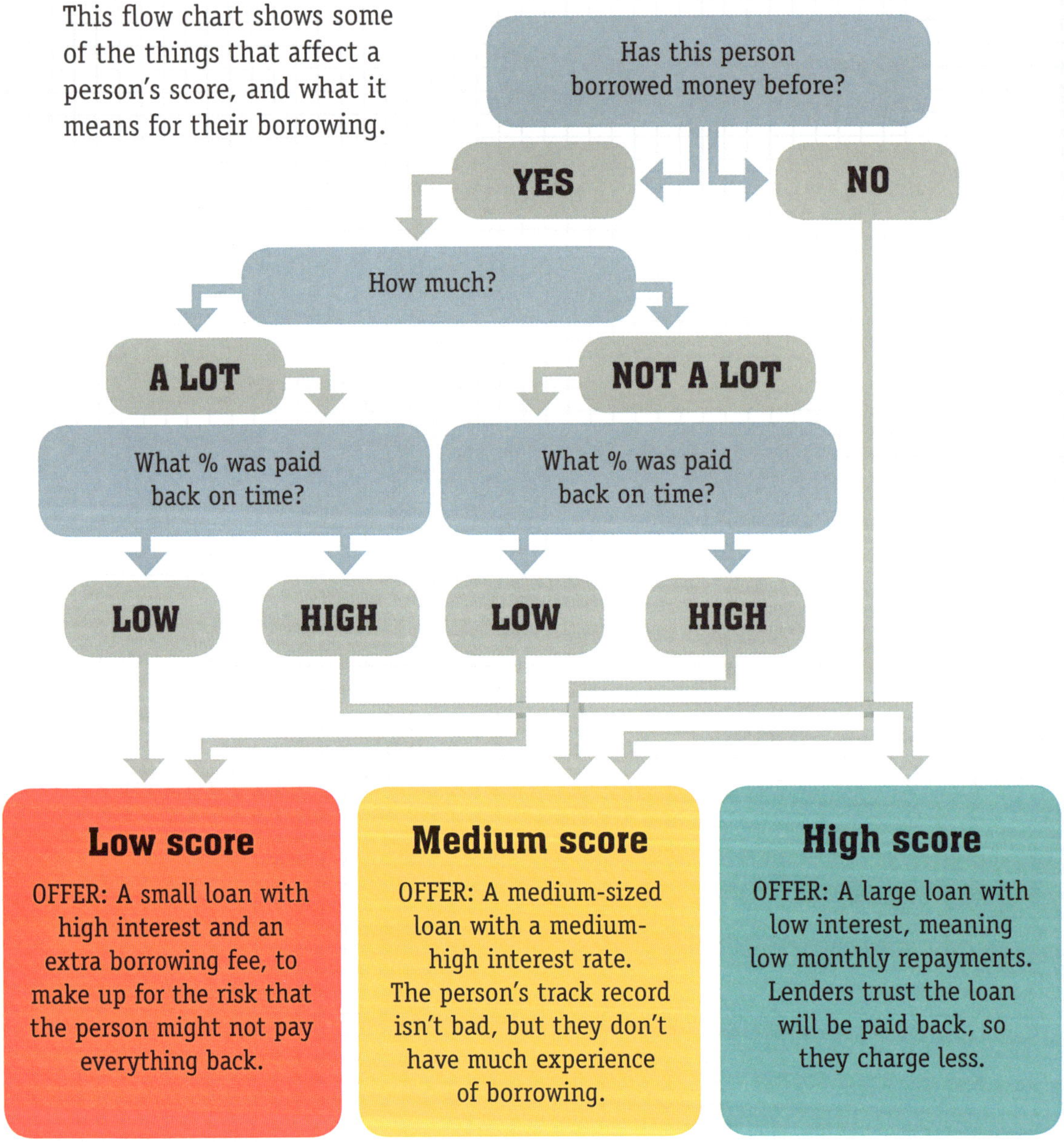

A person's score might also be affected by how much debt they're already in, and how regularly they pay their rent or any other bills on time.

Banks support credit ratings, because it helps them decide who to lend money to. But some people are against the system, because it makes it easier for wealthy people to get more money, and it can make it harder for poor people.

If you have a *very* low score, a bank might refuse to lend to you at all. Low scorers sometimes turn to illegal lenders, known as **loan sharks**, who don't worry about credit ratings. This is a bad idea, for many reasons. Here are some of them.

VERY high interest

Loan sharks often charge such a high interest rate that some people are never able to pay the loan back.

Pressure

If the interest is too high to repay the loan, some loan sharks persuade people to take out *another* loan to pay off the first, often with an *even* higher interest rate.

Intimidation

Loan sharks have been known to turn up at people's homes to threaten them. They can even be violent if you can't pay them back.

Managing debts

When people borrow money, they usually manage to pay it back – eventually. But unexpected things can happen to anyone, and sometimes debt can spiral out of control. However, even when debt starts to feel unmanageable, there *are* ways out.

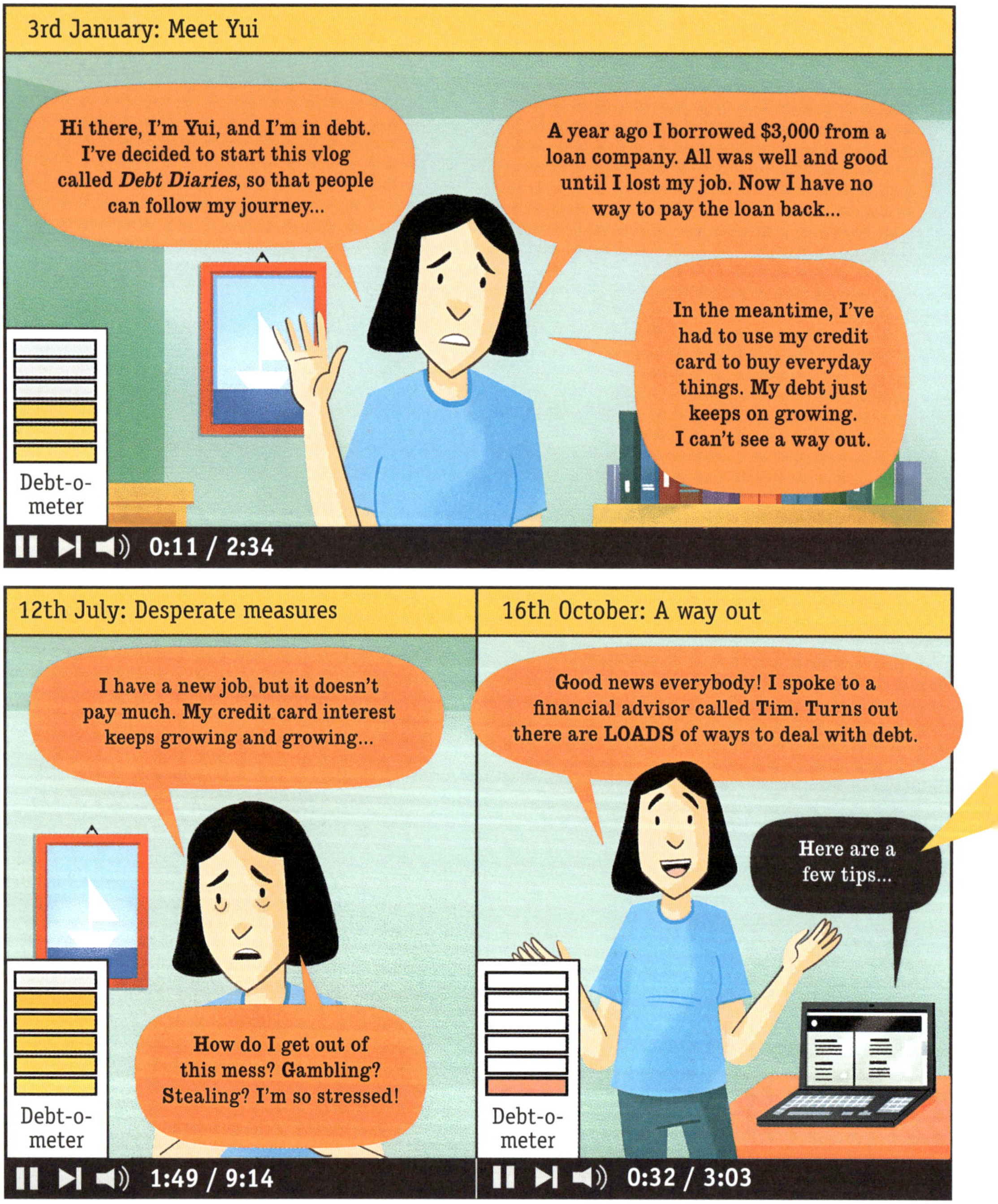

Fri 09:37

http://www.tims-money-tips.com/

TIM'S MONEY TIPS

"With over 20 years of professional experience, I'm the one to trust when it comes to managing your money!"

Less for longer

Talk to the lender to see if you can pay back in smaller chunks over a longer time.

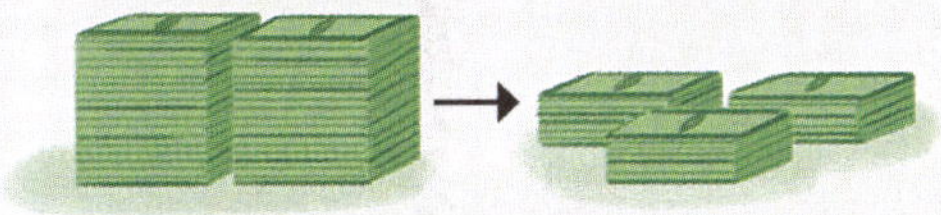

Freeze the debt

Lenders always want their money back, but they're sometimes happy to wait. Ask for a break in repayments for a month or two.

Package it up

Some people owe things to many people and companies at the same time. It can all be a bit confusing. One option is to take out one big loan to pay off those debts, so it's easier to manage.

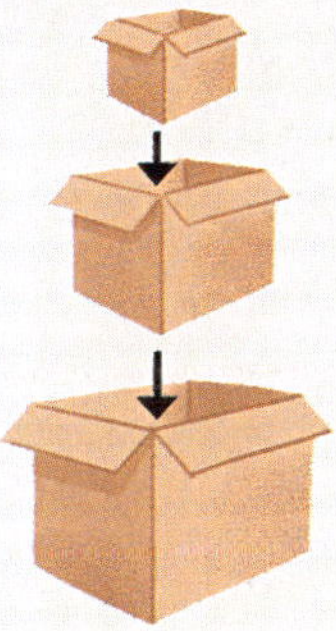

Write it off

If there's no way you can pay lenders back, some of them might let you off part of your debt. They'd rather have some money than none. This is known as *writing off* debt.

Ask for help

In some places, local governments might also give money to people with unmanageable debt problems.

A last resort

If somebody is in lots and lots of debt and there's no way they can pay it all back, they might apply for **bankruptcy**. This means all their debt is written off. It's a last resort, because even though it takes away some stress, people often have to pay off what they can in collateral. Going bankrupt limits how much you can borrow in the future, and in some places, it even limits the sorts of jobs you can do.

Illegal earning

Money is often at the heart of a crime, whether it's pickpocketing or lying about income to avoid tax. Here are a few examples of ways people try to steal money – sometimes successfully.

Theft

Theft is when you take something from somebody without their permission, often using force. For example, a bank robbery.

Fraud

Fraud is when a criminal tricks somebody into giving them money, or into letting them use money they got their hands on illegally.

For example, **embezzlement** is when somebody uses money that a business has given them control over for their own personal gain.

Money laundering is a type of fraud, too. It's when somebody disguises where their money came from to make it look as if they got it legally.

Phishing is when somebody tries to get money or sensitive information, such as people's bank account details, often by sending links to fake websites.

In 2017, staff at a Canadian university were sent emails claiming that a company it owed money to had new bank account details.

They paid over $8 million into the account, which turned out to belong to a fraudster, not an actual company.

Card fraud means illegally obtaining and using somebody else's debit or credit card details to take their money, or to sell the card details to others.

In 2007, two men in London installed hidden cameras by ATMs so that they could collect card details from people using the ATMs, including their passwords. They managed to collect the details of over 19,000 people.

Protecting money online

The tricks, scams and thefts that happen in real life take place online too. So it's worth being careful about any purchases you might make online and the kind of information you share.

Here are some ways businesses can tempt you into spending money online.

Free trials

Lots of websites and apps offer to let you try their product for free. But all free trials end, and often automatically start charging you.

"Virtual" money

When you buy things with "virtual" money inside a game world, it sometimes actually costs you real money too.

Expensive add-ons

Some games and apps are free up to a point, but then charge you to get to a new level, or for certain features.

It might be dishonest to trick you into overspending like this, but it's not against the law. However, it *is* illegal to trick you into sharing personal information. This is **phishing**, and it can allow someone else to pretend to be you, and spend your money. Here are some of the forms it can take.

An official website

Hackers can make identical copies of official websites, in order to trick people into handing over their login and credit card details.

A pop-up

BIG REWARD!
Congratulations, you have been selected for a special prize!
-
Click below to claim!

OK

Clicking on "OK" here will cause harmful software to download.

A suspicious website

A web address in a format you don't recognize

Requests for personal details

A link in a message

Links in text messages or emails can lead you to a webpage that asks for your details.

Safety tips

Of course not all links and pop-ups are malicious, but it's not always easy to tell. Here are some tips to avoid getting tricked.

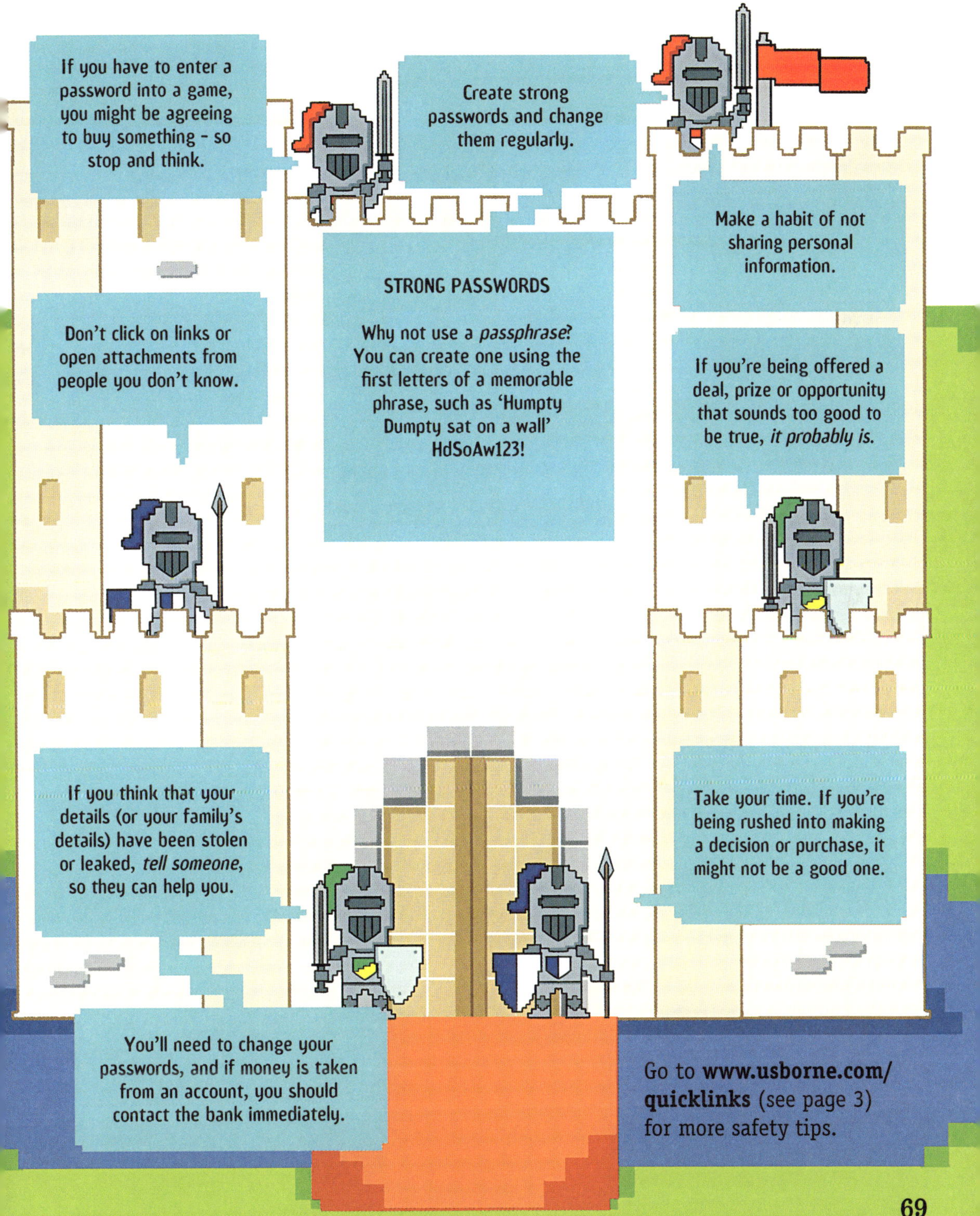

If you have to enter a password into a game, you might be agreeing to buy something – so stop and think.

Create strong passwords and change them regularly.

Make a habit of not sharing personal information.

Don't click on links or open attachments from people you don't know.

STRONG PASSWORDS

Why not use a *passphrase*? You can create one using the first letters of a memorable phrase, such as 'Humpty Dumpty sat on a wall' HdSoAw123!

If you're being offered a deal, prize or opportunity that sounds too good to be true, *it probably is.*

If you think that your details (or your family's details) have been stolen or leaked, *tell someone*, so they can help you.

Take your time. If you're being rushed into making a decision or purchase, it might not be a good one.

You'll need to change your passwords, and if money is taken from an account, you should contact the bank immediately.

Go to **www.usborne.com/quicklinks** (see page 3) for more safety tips.

Chapter 5: Spending, growing and giving

Once you have some money, you can start **spending** it – hooray! But before you rush off and spend it all, it's useful to know how to **manage** your spending. It's easy to fall into a habit of spending too much, and this can make your life very tricky.

It's often wise not to spend *all* of your money. Instead, by **saving** and **investing** you might be able to grow your money into *more* money. Or, you could use your money to help other people, by **donating** it to a cause that you support.

Budgeting

No matter how much money you have or will earn, it's a good idea to plan what you're going to do with it. One way to do this is to write a list of where your money comes from, and how you aim to spend it. This is known as **budgeting**. Here's an example.

Some people budget weekly, or every few months.

Money in (and where it comes from)

An extra way to earn money outside of work

Money out (and where it goes)

A list of your spending goals is known as your **budget**.

A list of what you end up spending is known as your **accounts**.

Monthly finances

Income:

Salary from job	$3,600.00
Clothes sold online	$120.00
TOTAL	$3,720.00

Expenses:

	Aim to spend	Actually spend
Taxes	$900.00	$900.00
Rent + bills	$1,020.00	$1,020.00
Transport	$260.00	$250.00
Food	$200.00	$300.00
Leisure	$940.00	$830.00
Savings	$400.00	$400.00
TOTAL	$3,720.00	$3,700.00

This person stuck to their budget – their income was bigger than their expenses. When people overspend, it means their expenses are bigger than their income.

Keeping track of spending is important. It helps you work out whether you're likely to stick to your budget.

Spending wisely

To stick to a budget you usually have to limit your spending. Most people can't afford to buy everything they want, whenever they want it. Here are some tips on how to spend wisely and spend less.

THE DAILY SAVER

27th May, 2019
95 cents

Ms. Piggybank's spending secrets

Buy out of season

Coats and scarves are cheaper in summer. Buy things well before you (and everybody else) will need them.

Comparison shop

Look in several shops and browse online to see if anywhere sells what you want cheaper than other places.

Shop with a list

Many purchases people make are unplanned. That's not always a bad thing. But if it happens all the time, your spending can rocket. Plan your purchases in advance and limit your impulse buys.

Discount codes

Some websites offer discount codes for when you shop online. Always search for discount codes before you buy.

Walk, walk, walk

If you can get somewhere safely and quickly without hopping on the bus, why not save your bus fare by walking instead?

Overspending

Even if you budget carefully, it's still easy to spend more than you planned.

Sometimes people overspend because they have to.

Other times, people spend too much money carelessly, and businesses often encourage them to do so. Here are some of the ways they do it.

Special offers make people more likely to buy things.

Businesses place **advertising** almost anywhere to tempt customers to buy products.

Some companies post glowing but **fake reviews** of their products online.

Others offer customers **discounts**, sometimes just for posting a positive review.

Expensive accidents

Often when people have to make large payments, it's because something unexpected has happened. Luckily, it's sometimes possible to get *somebody else* to cover the cost of repairs and replacements. This is the world of **insurance**.

Jake buys a new home and has to protect it against some of the things that *might* one day go wrong.

An **insurance company** offers to pay for any repairs in case of fire or flooding...

...above a certain price...

...in exchange for Jake paying the company $90 per month...

...and only if the fire or flood isn't Jake's fault.

A pipe in Jake's house burst. The kitchen flooded. Jake proved to the insurers that it wasn't his fault, and that repairs cost $10,000. The company covered the costs.

People can buy insurance to cover the costs of almost anything unplanned.

Missing a flight 

A sick pet 

Tripping over 

Insurance companies can afford to cover these costs because the total monthly payments from all their customers come to more than the amount they spend on things going wrong. But most try to avoid covering costs, by making it hard to prove the accident *wasn't* your fault.

Sorry sir, we won't pay to replace what was burgled. You posted on social media that you were on holiday. The burglars might have seen your post and known you weren't home.

Growing money in a bank

Money isn't just for spending. You can use it to make even more money. One way to do this is by depositing it in a bank account that earns interest. It's a handy way of earning a bit more and saving for the future. Here's how it works.

If you've read chapter 3, you'll know that your money doesn't just sit in a bank account doing nothing...

The amount of interest you receive is a percentage of the money in your account. This is known as an **interest rate**. Different types of account have different interest rates. If you don't spend your money, it will grow by different amounts, depending on the type of account you put it in.

Current accounts tend to have lower interest rates than savings accounts. Why?

Current accounts are designed to make everyday spending easier.

Most people use their current account several times each week, so the amount in the account changes often.

Savings accounts are designed to help people save and grow their money.

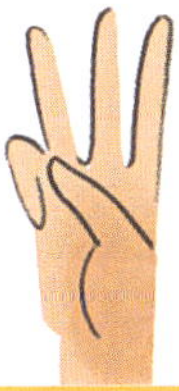

It's harder to use money in a savings account to pay for things, so the amount in the account changes quite rarely.

Banks need *reliable* sources of money so that they know how much they can lend out or invest.

The amount in savings accounts changes less than current accounts, making savings accounts more reliable. So banks try to encourage people to open them by offering higher interest rates.

Growing money by investing

Another way of "growing" money is by **investing** – spending money on something, hoping to make a profit from it later. Anything you buy or own that can you sell on is known as an **asset**. Here are three examples of assets that Reena could invest in...

Precious things

Some expensive things can become even more expensive over time, such as houses, artwork, or precious objects. But it's never guaranteed.

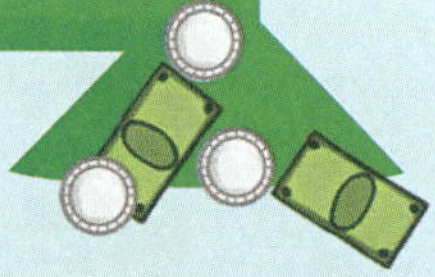

Selling an asset in the future – if it's worth more – will make Reena a profit.

Bonds

Bonds are debts you buy from companies or governments (see page 32).

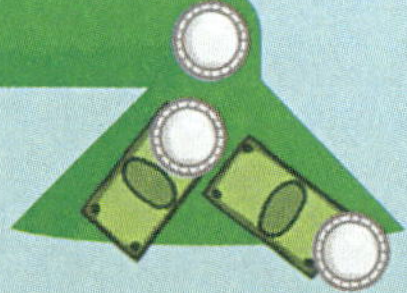

The company or government promises to pay the debt back by an agreed date (usually years in the future) *plus interest*.

Shares

A **share** is a small part of a company (see page 33).

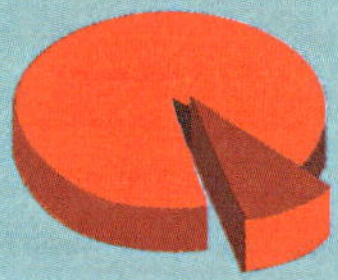

If a company does well, the value of its shares goes up...

Reena might make money from shares in two ways.

1. Selling her shares for more than she paid – usually when the company is doing well.

2. Receiving regular payments from the company's profits, known as **dividends**.

Earning without working

A few people are able to invest enough money to make a large regular income from their investments – even after they've paid taxes on it. Twenty years on, Reena has continued to invest and save, and now she wants to stop working.

She has...

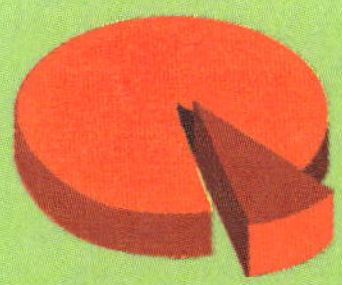

...$500,000 invested in shares, which earns her $19,000 a year.

...$1,000,000 in a savings account, which earns her $40,000 interest a year.

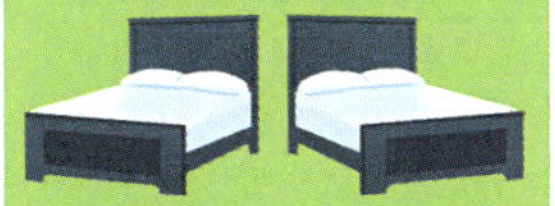

...two apartments that people rent from her, which earn her $20,000 a year.

Most people will never earn enough to make all these investments. But even people with a little wealth can *gradually* invest more over many, many years. With a lot of time, effort, and a little luck, they might make enough from their investments to stop working, like Reena.

A note of caution

Investments can be risky and they're never *guaranteed* to keep making money.

For example, a business you have shares in might fail and stop paying dividends, or the interest on your savings account might drop.

Over time, prices tend to rise due to a process known as **inflation** (find out more on page 98).

As prices rise, your money buys you less. In ten years' time, $79,000 might be worth much less than it is now.

Buying and selling shares

Most bonds and shares are traded by people known as **stockbrokers** through places known as **stock exchanges**. Companies and investors tell stockbrokers how many shares or bonds they want to *sell*. Other investors then negotiate a price with the brokers before *buying*.

Stock exchanges are full of screens with up-to-date share price information. Investors find this information online, in newspapers, or by talking to brokers.

Risky shares

Shares are risky investments – they can *lose value* just as quickly as they *gain value*. Reena has shares in *Sunny Juice Corporation* and keeps an eye on them. She talks to her stockbroker when she has questions.

Another way Reena could minimize risk is by spreading her investments across lots of companies.

That way, if one company's share price starts dropping, but the others rise or stay the same, her losses won't be too huge. This is called **diversifying**. Reena can diversify on her own, or she can invest in a **mutual fund** – a company that diversifies *for her* and takes part of the money those investments earn.

Good shares, bad shares

Some people think certain investments are harmful. Others disagree.

Raising money for a cause

You don't have to be rich to give money to a good cause. People often raise money for charity by organizing events or activities that people can pay to take part in. This is known as **fundraising**.

Fundraising is hard work, and it's a good idea to get help. You could start by asking a family member or a teacher. Then use the questions and tips below to plan your event.

What could my event or activity be?

- Quiz night?
- Basketball tournament?
- Sponsored run or bike ride?
- Car boot sale?

Do I need anybody's permission?

- School's permission to host a charity gig
- Local council's permission to fundraise on the street (with a grown-up)

Tips and tricks

There are lots of fundraising techniques that make people more likely to donate. Here are just a few, with examples of how you might use them to raise money for a stray dog charity.

Have a clear target.

Give incentives.

How can I spread the word about my event?

- Advertise in the local newspaper?
- Make posters?
- Announcement in school assembly?
- Create event on social media?
- Set up a crowdfunding website (see page 43)?

What costs might there be? Make sure you raise more than you spend.

- Paying to hire a room (for example for a quiz)?

ROOM FOR HIRE

- Buying materials (such as snacks for the basketball teams)?
- Invitations and thank you notes?
- Promotional materials to let people know about your event?

Emotional stories are often more persuasive than facts and figures.

This is how lonely Sniffles found a loving home...

Every year, 100,000 stray dogs end up in shelters...

Have multiple ways to donate and share the information.

If you can't come along but want to donate and tell your friends, visit the charity's website, click donate, and send the link to everyone you know!

Choosing a cause

Is it more important to protect animals or provide people in dry parts of the world with fresh water? There are so many charities out there that need donations. How do you choose one over any other?

There's no right or wrong answer to the question, "Is one charity better than another?" There are many different reasons to donate to a charity, including its relevance to you and how effective your donation would be.

Philanthropy

For very wealthy people, donating large one-off amounts isn't always the most effective way to use money for good. Instead, setting up organizations known as **philanthropic foundations** allows them to make large, *regular* donations to good causes.

Philanthropic foundations are largely funded by the money that grows from a wealthy person's investments.

Azim Premji, Indian businessman and philanthropist

The money that grows from investments provides a large, regular source of funding. That means foundations (and any institutions that foundations fund) have a reliable income, so they can keep on doing their work for a long time.

The foundations set up by Scottish-born businessman Andrew Carnegie still help fund hundreds of libraries around the world. He helped set up those libraries with the vast fortune he made in the steel industry.

Is giving always good?

Charities and foundations play vital roles in improving people's lives worldwide. But not everybody agrees that *all* types of philanthropy and donations are good. Here are some reasons why.

Some people prefer to donate to charities and foundations that help solve the *causes* of a problem, not just the *effects*.

Some people think you should only donate money to the poorest and most disadvantaged in the world.

Funding for foundations can come from profits from investments in companies that exploit people.

Some people say that companies should spend charitable money on running their own company more fairly, rather than giving money away to other causes.

Giving money isn't as simple as "always good" or "always bad." There are different ways to give, and different organizations to donate to. It's a good idea to research each option before giving money, to decide which you think will help most.

Chapter 6: Governments and money

Money doesn't just move between banks, businesses and people – it's also used by governments. They get LOTS of it from taxes – often billions, if not *trillions*, of dollars. Then they spend this money on **public services** such as schools, roads and the police.

One of the main jobs for every government is to decide how to manage **taxpayers'** money. Even small choices have big consequences – if a government closes a library or builds a playground, it won't make much difference to the total amount it spends, but it can have a huge impact on people's day-to-day lives.

How taxes work

Almost everybody in every country has to pay some taxes. Most governments set out to collect them in a fair way, but people often disagree about what it means to be fair.

Types of taxes

Throughout history, governments have charged taxes on many things. For instance, around 300 years ago, men in Russia had to pay taxes if they had beards. Today, the sorts of taxes people pay don't vary much from country to country. Here are some of the main types, but they're not all used everywhere.

Tax on money that people earn is an **income tax.**

Tax on money that businesses earn is a **corporate tax.**

Workers and businesses both have to pay **social security** – money that specifically goes to healthcare and public retirement schemes.

Tax on things that people buy is a **sales tax,** or **Value Added Tax (VAT).**

Tax on things people leave behind when they die is an **inheritance tax.**

Tax on your possessions and money is a **wealth tax.**

Tax on goods imported from abroad is a **tariff.**

Making taxes fair

Taxes are often calculated as a percentage of the total value of something, such as your income. This percentage is called the **tax rate**, and it's designed to make the tax system fairer.

Governments often set higher tax rates for higher earners. This is called a **progressive tax** because the tax rate *progresses*, or increases, as people earn more.

It might seem unfair to tax people different amounts, but imagine if everyone paid $10,000 a year instead...

When governments tax everyone the same amount, it's called a **regressive tax** because the rate *regresses*, or decreases, as people earn more.

Taxes and choices

Often governments use taxes to change the way people spend their money.

Charging high taxes on certain products or services will make them more expensive and *discourage* people from using them.

Charging low taxes on products or services will make them cheaper and *encourage* more people to use them. This is what's known as a **tax break**.

Tariffs discourage people from buying foreign goods and encourage people to trade within their own country.

Spending public money

Governments use money from taxes to pay for jobs and services that many people take for granted. If they didn't, we'd have to organize these things ourselves. It's up to each government to decide how much it can afford to spend and what services it should provide.

Here are some examples of what a government might buy with money from taxes.

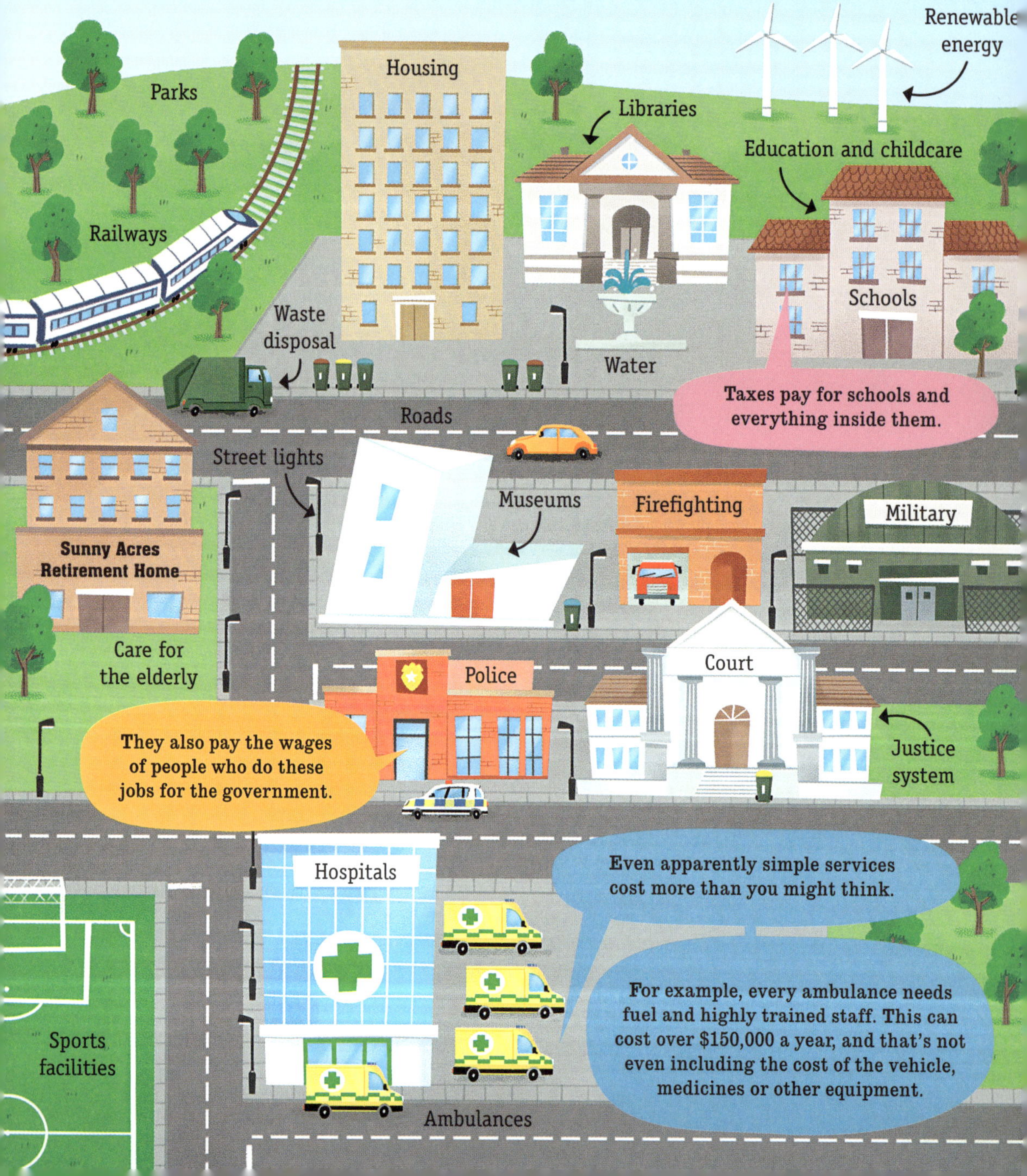

How to get more

If a government raises more money in taxes than it spends, it has a **surplus**. However, nearly all governments do the opposite – they spend more money than they raise, which leaves them with a **deficit**. When this happens most governments choose between two options, but both of them carry risks.

1) Borrowing

A government can borrow money from banks and other lenders. The total amount a government owes is called the **national debt**.

Most governments have a reliable source of income, from taxes, so banks like to lend them money. Borrowing money from banks can be an effective way for a government to raise funds quickly, so both sides are happy...

...but it's not sensible in the long term. Banks demand interest on the money they lend, and this can be very expensive. For example, in 2018, the US government spent around $390 BILLION of tax money, *just to pay back interest it owed.*

2) Printing money

If a government runs out of money, it can simply create more of its currency to pay for things. This might seem like an easy solution, but it's dangerous because a government maintains the value of its currency by *limiting* the money supply (see page 18).

This doesn't stop many governments from printing more money. Some do it because it's easier than raising taxes. Others do it for another, more complicated reason – find out more on page 101.

A *temporary* deficit isn't always a bad thing. Everyone relies on services the government provides – from roads and schools to hospitals and emergency services. If a government simply stopped spending when it ran out of money, it would be extremely damaging for both people and businesses.

Talking about tax

People often disagree when it comes to tax. Some think governments should raise taxes and spend more public money. Others want them to lower taxes and spend less. Here are some of their reasons.

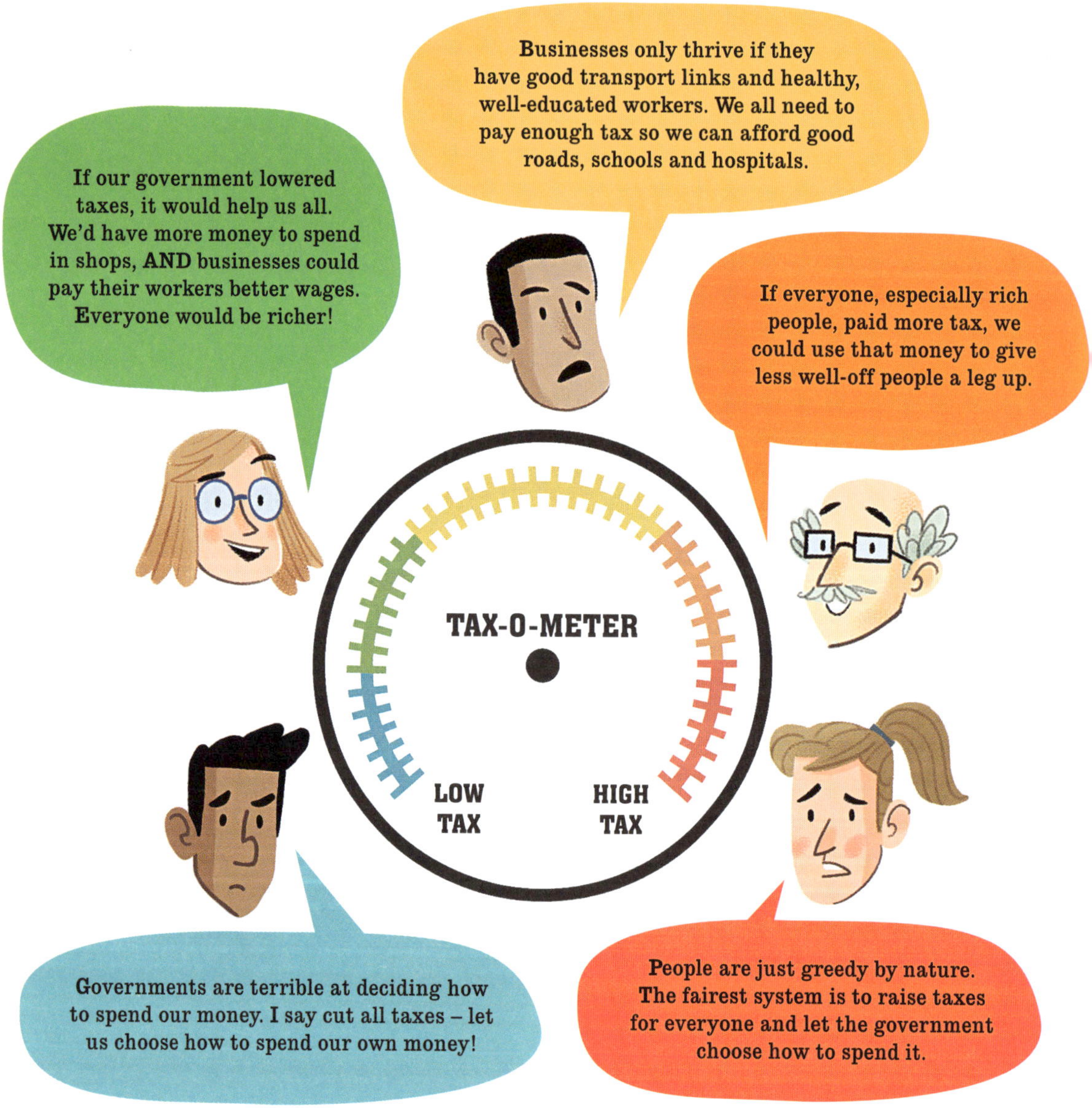

Many people feel very strongly about how much money they want to pay the government in tax. In countries where people can vote, it's often one of the main reasons why people support one particular political party rather than another.

Welfare

The support a government provides for its citizens is known as **welfare**. Almost every political party agrees it's good to spend *some* money on welfare, but it's harder to decide how much, or who deserves it.

*Some local governments in Canada and Finland have experimented with a scheme known as a **Basic Income.** Here, governments continued to *collect* taxes, but only from the rich. At the same time they also paid *everyone* a salary that would cover essential living costs, no matter how much they earned. Basic Income is an attempt to make welfare fairer – *everyone* gets the same amount, but only people who can afford it pay taxes. So far, experiments haven't shown if this can work across a whole country.

Keeping track

Most governments control how much they tax and spend – but they *don't* control what people do with their money. The way people spend affects how much money a country makes and where this money ends up – what's known as a country's **economy**. Each government keeps track of the economy so they can try to keep it stable.

One measure of a country's economy is called **Gross Domestic Product** or **GDP**. It's the total amount that all the goods and services in that country could be sold for – assuming people paid a fair price.

There are many sorts of goods and services. They all count towards GDP...

GDP can be misleading. If lots of people live in a country, they'll produce lots of goods and services. This means a big country will often have a higher GDP than a small country, even if the small country makes more money for its size.

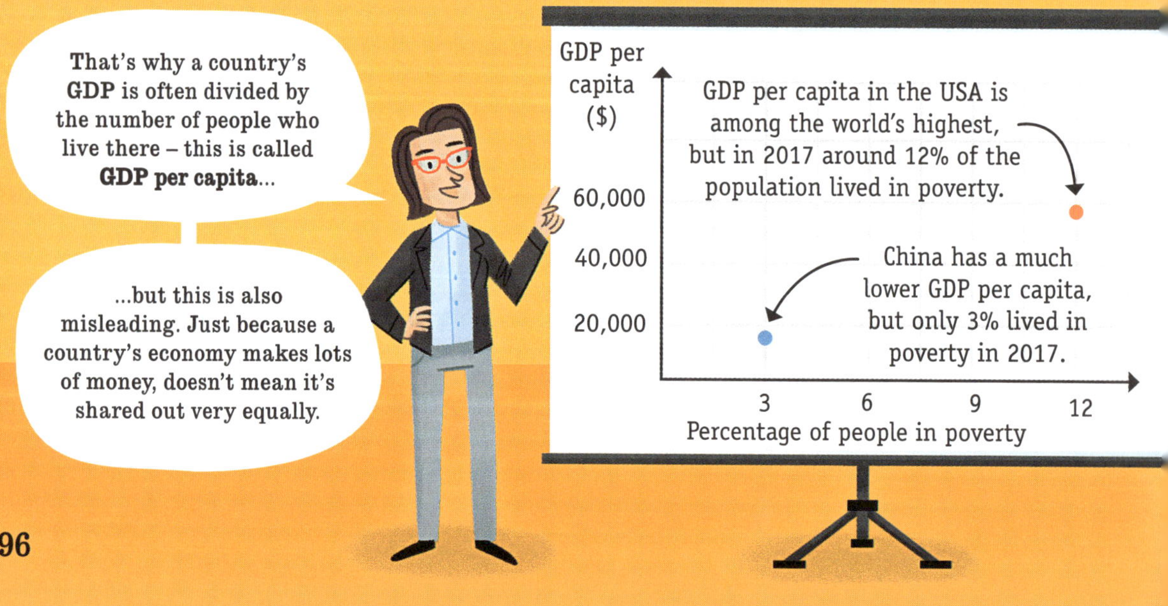

Price watch, wage watch

To get a better idea of how the economy is doing, governments track the prices of things people need to buy, and how much people earn.

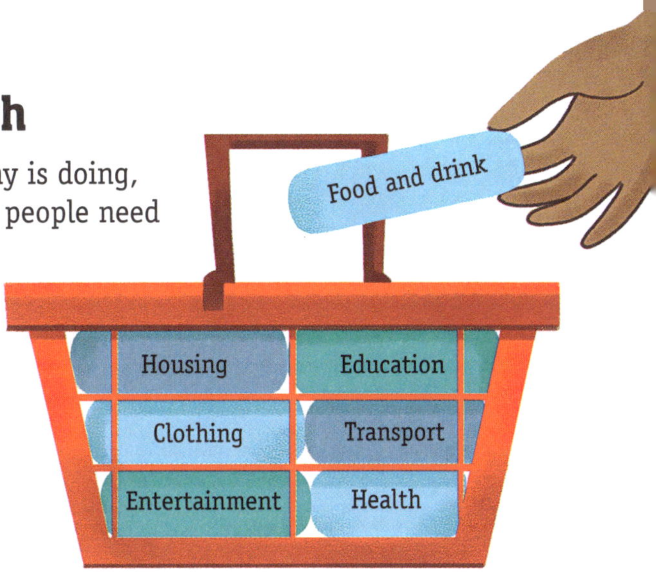

It's impossible to monitor the price of *everything*, so governments focus on an imaginary shopping basket of things most people buy. Over time, these prices nearly always go up. When this happens, it's called **inflation**.

Governments also track how many people have jobs (the employed) and how many don't (the unemployed). They monitor people's wages, too: people will end up poorer if their wages don't go up as quickly as prices.

If wages and prices rise at the same rate...

...nobody really notices, and everyone can keep buying the things they need.

But, if wages *don't* go up as quickly as prices...

...people end up worse off because they can't afford to buy as many things.

Managing the economy isn't an exact science, and economists argue about the best way to do it. But there are three ideas that most agree on:

Spending is good! The more people spend, the more money businesses make, the more they can afford to increase their wages.

Employment is good! People with jobs earn money to spend and pay taxes. And they're usually happier.

Inflation is usually good, but not *too* much, and not *too* quickly.

The importance of inflation

Prices can rise and fall for many reasons. If they go up in just one shop, it's not necessarily due to inflation and it probably won't affect many people. Inflation is when prices go up in most shops, in most places. It affects everyone, especially if it's out of control.

When inflation happens too quickly, wages can't keep up and money loses its value.

People stop being able to afford many things. They're forced to make different decisions.

Although a lot of inflation causes problems, governments still aim for a *little*. One reason for this is because the opposite can be *really* bad. If prices fall, it's known as **deflation**. That might sound appealing, but it has serious consequences.

Deflation encourages people to spend less. Businesses end up losing money, people lose their jobs – and this in turn means everyone ends up spending even less.

Governments and central banks

Governments need help managing the economy of their countries. Most work alongside a national institution called a **central bank** to help commercial banks and influence how much people spend.

In many ways, the central bank acts as a bank for commercial banks.

All commercial banks have an account with the central bank. The money in this account is known as its **reserve**. The central bank lends money to commercial banks. The interest it charges is known as the **base rate**.

Commercial banks depend on loans from the central bank. These loans protect commercial banks from many of the risks they face – for instance if their investments fail or their customers borrow money and don't pay them back.

The central bank doesn't take many risks, so it's always able to lend money to commercial banks if they run into trouble. By providing this safety net, the central bank helps everyone trust the whole banking system.

A country's central bank is often **independent** of its government, but they both share their plans with each other and work together. One of their main projects is to manage inflation, so it stays at a steady rate. Turn the page to find out how they do this.

Managing inflation

Managing inflation is difficult because, in most countries, businesses are free to set their own prices. There are, however, a few ways in which governments and central banks can make a difference.

If inflation is too high...

The central bank can **raise** the base rate, which is the interest it charges on loans to commercial banks.

Now it's more expensive for commercial banks to borrow from the central bank.

Commercial banks are more likely to raise their own interest rates, to cover these extra costs.

It becomes more expensive for people to borrow money from commercial banks.

This encourages them to save instead of spend...

...which is bad for businesses.

So they respond by freezing their prices – or even lowering them.

Inflation **decreases.**

If inflation is too low...

The central bank can **lower** the base rate.

Commercial banks lower their interest rates to attract customers.

People and businesses have more to spend.

Businesses put up their prices to increase profits.

Inflation **increases**.

Sometimes inflation is so low, changing the base rate doesn't help.

When this happens, the government and central bank can step in by creating new money, a process known as **quantitative easing**.

First, the government borrows money from commercial banks.

Then the central bank creates new money to repay the commercial banks.

The base rate is so low, commercial banks won't earn any interest if they hold onto this new money.

They invest it and loan it.

People have more money to spend.

Businesses increase their prices.

Inflation **increases**.

Taking control

There isn't just one way to manage a country's economy. Some people would like the government to have more control, so it can decide what happens to everyone's money. Others would like the government to leave the economy alone, and do nothing.

Total control

If a government had *total* control over the economy, we might not need money as we know it at all.

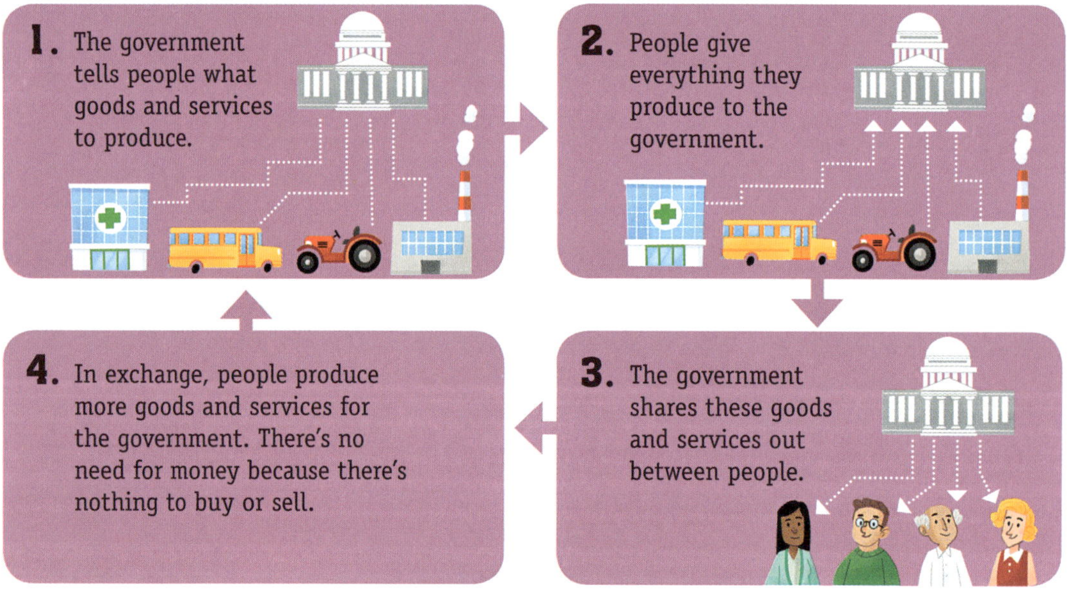

How much control?

In reality, no government has abolished money, or taken complete control over its country's businesses and trade. But equally, no government has left the economy completely alone. There are different degrees of control governments can take. What do you think is best?

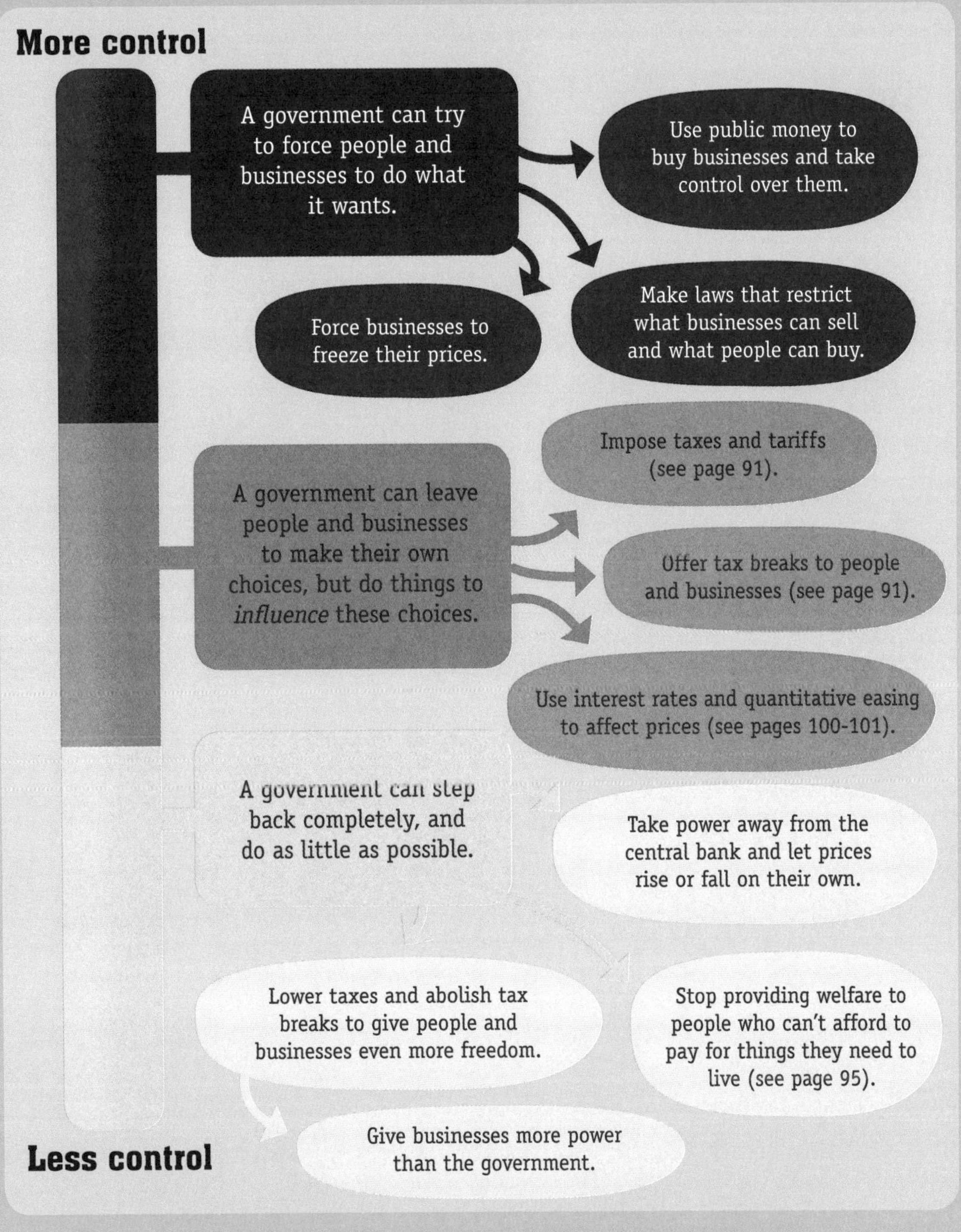

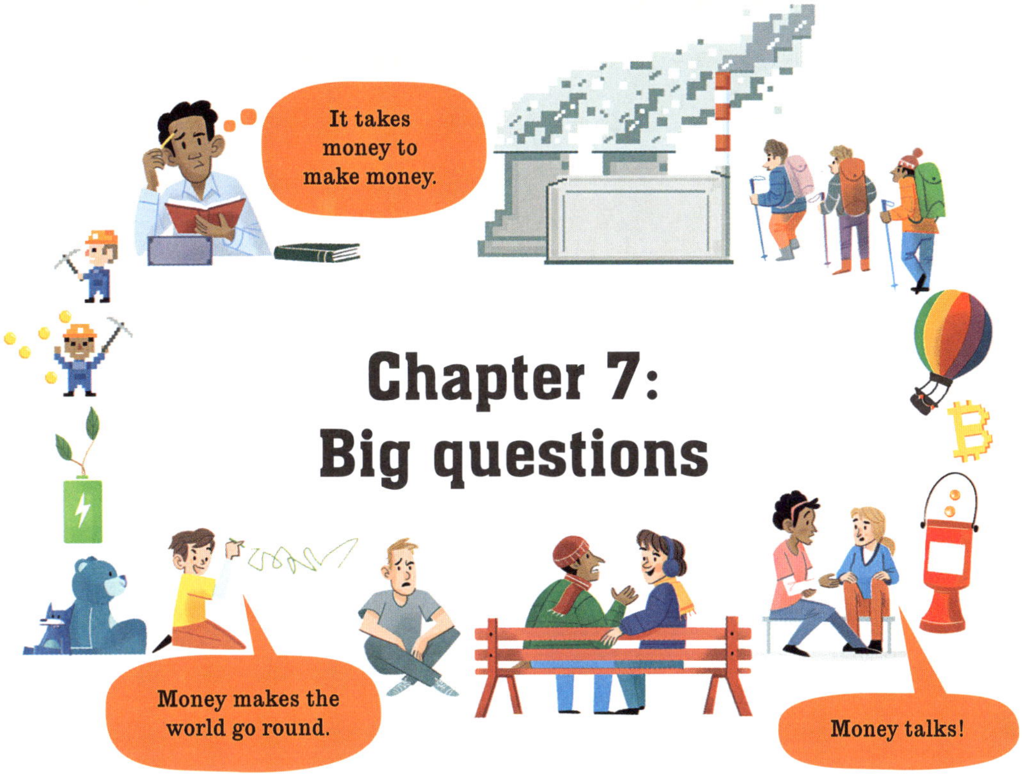

Chapter 7: Big questions

According to countless stories, songs and even religious beliefs, money can be both the source of great sadness, as well as a route to finding happiness. But is this because of money itself – or is it all to do with the way people behave when they have too much, or too little of it?

No one knows the answer to this question, but in this chapter you can find out some of the ways people have tried to tackle problems relating to money, happiness and equality. To begin with, try to imagine a world in which people manage without money at all...

Do we still need cash?

More and more people no longer use cash to pay for things. They prefer to use a mobile phone or bank card instead. At this rate, some countries, such as Sweden, are forecast to become cashless in the next 10 years. So do we need cash at all?

Paying with e-money...

✓ ...is often **quicker**, because neither side needs to count out coins or change.

✓ ...is **cheaper**: paper money costs a lot to produce and distribute.

✗ ...makes your money more **vulnerable** to attack from hackers.

✗ ...requires electricity, as well as an **expensive** device and the internet to work.

Cash...

✓ ...is **simple** and **accessible** – you don't need a bank account, phone or the internet.

✓ ...works in a **crisis**, such as a flood, because it doesn't need power or a network connection.

✗ ...makes people and businesses carrying it **vulnerable** to robbery.

...is **private**. You can spend cash without it leaving a digital record of what you're up to.

On the flip side, it's hard for the police to trace criminals who use cash.

The key advantage of cash is that *everyone* can get their hands on it, even if they don't have an address, a bank account or a phone. Without it, about 1.7 billion people in the world wouldn't have access to money.

Do we need money at all?

Some people believe that money makes the world less fair – rich people inherit money without having to work for it. But there are alternatives to money that are much less easy to hoard. Could any of them replace money entirely?

Now imagine, for example, that you could pay for *everything* with time...

Nobody here is actually paying with their time. They're just trading units of time – in much the same way people pay with money. Maybe the problem we need to solve isn't money, but how we use it? Or maybe we've just not come up with the right alternative?

What about cryptocurrencies?

A cryptocurrency is a digital currency that is created, exchanged and kept safe using codebreaking – or **cryptography**. The first, known as **Bitcoin**, was created in 2009. Since then, many more have been made.

In February 2011, one virtual "coin" of Bitcoin (or **₿**1) was worth $1. By December 2017, **₿**1 was worth $19,783.

Here are two of the main reasons why they became so valuable.

Nobody is in charge

Most currencies are created and monitored by governments and banks. Cryptocurrencies are only created and exchanged by the people who use them (find out more on the next page) – no one else is involved.

Not everybody trusts banks or governments, especially since the 2008 financial crisis. Many people are excited by the idea of a currency that avoids them.

No secrets

There's a public record of every Bitcoin that has ever been created, and every Bitcoin transaction, known as a **blockchain**. Each entry on the blockchain is given a coded "fingerprint" that can't be changed.

This makes cryptocurrencies difficult to steal or counterfeit. If there's no record of a transaction on the blockchain, you know it's fake.

The system that protects Bitcoin is very secure. Hackers *have* found ways to steal Bitcoins, but it's very difficult, and often more expensive than it's worth.

Highs and lows

Twelve months after one Bitcoin was worth $19,783, its value had fallen to $3,183. The value of cryptocurrencies goes up and down regularly, and often drastically. As well as being unstable, there are other disadvantages, too.

They're hard to get and spend

There are two ways to get Bitcoins. You can buy them from somebody who has some, but that can be quite expensive. Or you can create your own by cracking a code...

Before a Bitcoin transaction is added to the blockchain, somebody has to crack a code. This is known as **mining** for Bitcoins.

The codes are so complicated, the code-crackers, or **miners**, have to use expensive, extra-powerful computer hardware.

The miner who cracks the code first is rewarded with new coins. A record of these coins appears on the blockchain.

Even if you manage to get some Bitcoins, they can't be spent everywhere. Not very many people or businesses accept Bitcoins as payment, and you can't exchange Bitcoins for another currency at a bank.

They're environmentally unfriendly

In November 2017 it was reported that Bitcoin-mining hardware worldwide used up more power than the entire Republic of Ireland did that same month.

That power was created by burning fossil fuels, which cause pollution.

Some people argue that cryptocurrencies aren't the problem – the power source is. If cleaner forms of energy were available, miners wouldn't produce as much waste.

Can money buy happiness?

Psychologists and economists have worked together to try to find out whether money and happiness are linked. One theory says it depends on the *kind* of happiness. You can imagine these as two different mountain peaks.

These are the results of a survey of 1,000 people in the US. What do *you* think?

Are rich countries happier?

Being richer tends to make people happier. But is it enough just to live in a country where most people are rich? This chart uses data collected by the World Bank to compare how rich a country is with how satisfied its population is.

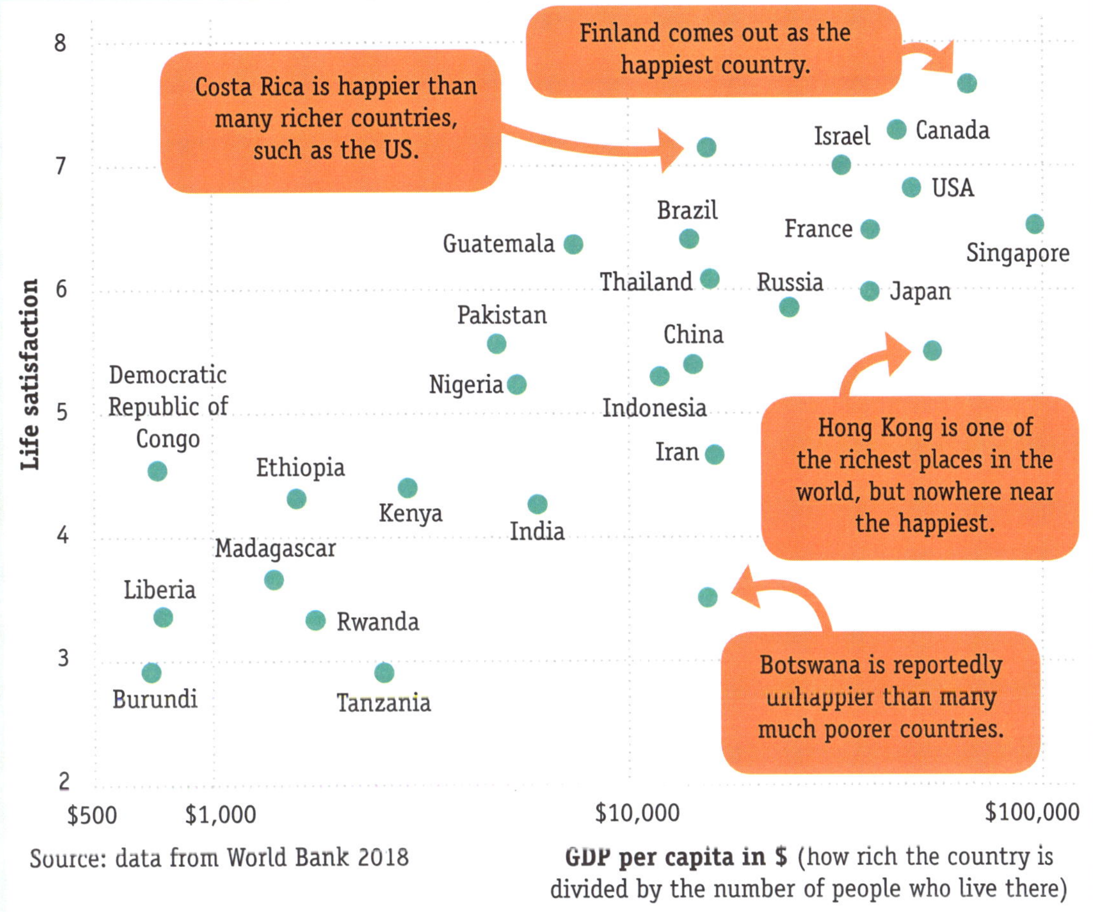

This chart only provides a very simplified overview of what it's like to live in a country. But one thing it *does* suggest, is that even if richer countries *tend* to have more satisfied populations, this isn't always the case. So money isn't the only thing that makes people happy...

Is inequality bad?

Inequality is everywhere. Sometimes it doesn't matter – some people can wiggle their eyebrows, while others can't. But other times it seems really unfair, such as when some people have more money than others. When it comes to money, shouldn't we all be equal?

Imagine, for example, paying students in a school from a big pot of money. Here are three ways of sharing it out.

1. Everyone is paid the same, no matter what grades they get.

2. Only students with the top grades are paid, to encourage everyone to work hard.

3. Everyone gets something, but the better you do, the more money you get.

Which option would you choose? Would you choose any of them?

Lots of people tend to be ok with *some* amount of inequality – as long as it's not too extreme and everyone has a fair chance of reaching the top.

In practice, it's hard to control how much inequality there is. In fact, the gap between rich and poor in most countries around the world is getting bigger – in some places faster than others. This happens for all sorts of reasons.

Money makes money

If you already have money, it's easier to make even more money from interest on savings and big investments.

Discrimination

When people don't have the same opportunities, wages and rights because of their gender or race, it's known as **discrimination.** It's often illegal, but it's a fact of life for many people.

Salary gap

People with power can, and do, give themselves big rewards, including the biggest salaries.

Tax havens

Wealthy people often find ways of paying less tax – making them richer and their governments poorer (see more on page 45).

There are as many different opinions about how to keep inequality in check as there are people.

Rich people create jobs and opportunities, so if we help *them*, we help everyone. The money trickles down.

It might help a little if the rich give money to the poor, but I think it's better to make sure we're all given equal opportunities from the start.

Poor people should take power from the rich!

If we forced everyone to share out their wealth more equally, we'd all be better off!

Dishonest money

One reason people like money so much is that it doesn't just allow you to buy *things*. It also has the power to open doors and influence *people*. So how do we make sure that it's not used for dishonest ends?

Money has the power to motivate people to change the world.

It can be used to influence the government, too.

Many people would agree it's OK to offer prize money to encourage innovation, and that it *can* be fair to hire lobbyists to influence governments. But both these ideas can be abused, and this is known as **corruption**. In most countries, governments set up anti-corruptions laws, but they don't always work.

Paying to get around a rule or to get preferential treatment is known as **bribery**.

Bad for everyone

Corruption is unfair: it means people with more money have more power than other people. It's also dangerous because it weakens people's trust in governments and businesses.

Turning on the light

Corruption thrives behind closed doors, where people can act in secret. Governments can try to tackle it by...

...making laws that allow citizens and journalists to force organizations to share what they're up to, known as **freedom of information (FOI) laws.**

...making sure law courts are free to try people – however rich or important they are.

...paying officials a fair wage, to make it less tempting for them to accept bribes.

...making sure people are open about when they're being paid to do something. For example, YouTubers need to say if they're being paid to promote a product.

...making lobbyists share information about what they do and how much they spend. This makes it easier to spot if corruption is taking place.

But if there are too *many* rules, people and businesses might struggle to follow them, and governments might struggle to keep track of everyone. So occasionally, *getting rid* of rules and paperwork can help too.

Protesting with money

When people decide not to buy something in protest, it's known as a **boycott**. That might seem like a small thing, but when lots of people act together it has a big impact. Here's a famous example.

At the beginning of the 20th century, India was under British rule. Britain made lots of money out of India – for instance, by taking control of its fabric industry.

1. Buy cheap cotton from India.

2. Ship it to British factories, and turn the cotton into fabric.

3. Sell that cloth at a high price in India and around the world.

Political campaigner Mohandas Gandhi encouraged Indians to boycott British products, in particular cloth, and make their own.

Nobody knows exactly how many people stopped buying British cloth, but as the boycott spread, more and more people began to support the independence movement. Many more years of protests eventually helped bring about Indian independence, in 1947.

This kind of protest – with money instead of violence – inspired many other people fighting for their rights all around the world.

The spinning wheel became a powerful symbol of Indian independence, even shaping the design of the Indian flag.

Consumer power

Consumer power is the idea that consumers can influence the decisions businesses make. Here are some more ways people do this.

Switch

Instead of not buying something, you can switch to a seller you prefer. Losing customers sends a signal to the seller.

Write

Writing a letter or social media post to a company lets them know about the issues their customers care about.

Donate

Give money to support organizations that campaign to make businesses behave better – for example by looking after the environment.

How to negotiate

One day, you might find yourself in a situation where you need to discuss a price in order to get a better deal. This is known as **negotiating**. Here are some tips for how to negotiate effectively – whether it's a phone contract, a faulty item in a shop or even a salary.

How to become a billionaire

One billion dollars is A LOT of money. To count to one billion, one number every second, would take over 30 years. How does anybody get their hands on that much money?

The billionaire baby
Wealth inherited from family

Starting money: Lots
Time taken: Rapid
Risk: Low
Success chances: High

The investor
Invested money until it grew into billions

Starting money: Medium
Time taken: Slow
Risk: Very high
Success chances: Low

The inventor
Invented something that kept on selling

Starting money: Varies
Time taken: Varies
Risk: Medium
Success chances: Very low

The entrepreneur
Businessperson who runs a big company or a few

Starting money: Varies
Time taken: Slow
Risk: High
Success rate: Low

Although anybody can become a billionaire, in practice most are over 55, grew up in a wealthy country, and around two thirds went to university.

There are no strict rules for how to earn a billion. You often hear about people who start with little and end up with lots – but that's because they make good stories. In reality, many billionaires have lots to begin with.

How much is enough?

Imagine you and four friends are each asked: "How much money would you need to live comfortably and happily for the rest of your life, with no other income?" Whoever writes the smallest amount gets the money. What number would *you* write?

You'd have to choose an amount *high enough* for you to buy basic necessities, but *low enough* to stand a chance of getting the money at all. How much somebody needs to live comfortably will vary from person to person.

There's no right answer. It's also extremely unlikely you'll ever have to make this decision. But the question forces you to think of the lowest amount possible that would be "enough" for you. It'll probably be less than a billion!

What next?

By now you should have a sense that there isn't only one correct way to manage your money. Nor is there only one way to talk about it or even *think* about it. That's because money is an intensely personal subject. It's about how you relate to other people – your future plans, the work you do and, most of all, the promises you make.

At the same time, money is something that connects you to everybody else on the planet. As it changes hands from person to person or from business to business, another link is added to a chain of transactions that stretches back for thousands of years, reaching all over the world. This is why money matters.

Glossary

This glossary explains some of the words used in this book. Words written in *italic* type are explained in other entries.

asset any valuable item, such as a house or car or *bond* that can be sold to turn it into *liquid* money.

bank see *commercial bank* or *investment bank*

bank account a record of money deposited in a bank.

current account money you can access easily, at any time.

savings account money you can only access sometimes, but that should earn greater *interest* than a current account.

bankruptcy when a person is unable to pay their debts, and his or her possessions are sold off to pay back *creditors*.

bartering exchanging one thing directly for another, without using money.

billionaire someone whose total wealth adds up to at least 1 billion of their *currency*, for example $1,000,000,000.

bonds long-term *debts* sold by governments and big businesses.

boycott when many people agree not to spend money on a certain product, or a range of products made by certain businesses.

budget a written list of all income and expenditure, either for a person, a business or a government.

cash money in the form of coins or banknotes.

central bank a single bank that works closely with its country's government to control a *currency*.

collateral *assets* that *creditors* can collect from a person or business if they cannot repay a *debt*.

commercial bank a bank set up for individuals and businesses to save their money and apply for *loans*.

contract a written agreement, for example an employer agreeing to pay a particular *salary* in exchange for an employee doing a job.

costs money a business spends before it can sell its products.

counterfeiting making fake banknotes or coins.

credit money borrowed from a bank or business, that becomes *debt*.

credit card a card that allows a person to pay for things with *credit*.

credit rating a system used by banks to decide which customers they will give *loans* to, and at what price.

creditor a person, bank or business that *loans* money to another person.

cryptocurrency a digital *currency* that is created, exchanged and kept safe online, using mathematical and codebreaking techniques.

currency a system of money in general use in a particular place, such as British pounds or US dollars.

currency exchange swapping one kind of currency for another.

debit card a card that allows a person to pay for things by linking directly to a *bank account*.

debt money that is owed to a person, *bank* or business, typically to be repaid with *interest*.

national debt money that is owed by a government to other governments or *banks*.

deficit when a business or government spends more money than it takes in.

deflation when prices in a country go down, on average.

derivatives any form of money whose value is derived from another form of money, such as a good, a service or an *asset*.

diversifying investing in several different things to minimise risk.

e-money an electronic form of *cash*.

economy the amount of money in a country, and how much that money is moving around within it.

finance to do with money, or the management of money.

financial instrument a *contract* between people, banks or businesses that relates to *cash*, *assets* or *derivatives*.

fraud lying to another person with the aim of getting them to give you money; usually a crime.

funding money needed for a business or project.

fundraising asking for money, usually to help pay for a charity or other good cause.

future a type of *derivative*, in which one person promises to pay an amount based on something that hasn't happened or doesn't exist yet.

GDP Gross Domestic Product, the total amount of *wealth* generated by all the people and businesses in a country.

gold standard an old system of money in which the value of a *currency* was linked to the value of a certain amount of gold.

inflation when prices in a country go up, on average, and when the value of a *currency* goes down.

insurance paying a small amount of money to a company that will help you pay back a large amount, in the event of an unpredictable event happening, such as an accident.

interest extra money you have to pay back to someone you have borrowed money from, and money that banks pay to customers with deposits.

compound interest interest that adds to a *debt* if you don't pay off the exisiting *interest*.

interest rate the proportion of a *loan* that is charged as *interest*.

investing spending money on something, such as artwork or a *share* in a business, that you hope will increase in value.

investment bank a bank that governments, businesses or wealthy individuals use to raise money for expensive projects.

liquidity the more easily money or *assets* can be collected and spent, the more liquid it is said to be.
loan money given to a person or business that has to be paid back, usually with *interest*.
loan shark a business or person that gives out *loans* illegally, often charging very high *interest*.

market a place where people can buy and sell things, or the people a business hopes to sell to.
mortgage a *loan* that allows a person to buy a house or other building and pay the *debt* back over many years.

overdraft spending more money from a *bank account* than you have in that account.

quantitative easing when a government creates money, through *loans* from a *bank*, with the aim of increasing *inflation*.

philanthropist a person who gives away large amounts of their money to good causes.
poverty when people do not have enough money or income to afford basic needs such as food and shelter, and cannot get *loans*.
profit money gained by a business on top of what it costs to run that business.
public services things such as *welfare*, provided for everybody by a government, paid through *taxes*.

recession when the *economy* or *GDP* of a country gets weaker over a period of time.
regulations laws that make sure *banks* and businesses can't take big risks with other people's money, and to stop businesses from becoming too powerful.
retail bank see *commercial bank*

salary regular payment for doing a job, typically paid each month.
securities any form of *financial instrument* that one person can buy or sell to another, such as *shares*.
shareholder someone who owns *shares* in a business, and who can receive a portion of any *profits*.
shares parts of a business that are owned by different people.
stock market place where *stocks* and *shares* can be bought and sold.
stockbroker a person who is allowed to buy and sell in a *stock market*.
stocks another word for *shares*, although it technically describes a set of many shares.

taxes money that individuals and businesses pay to the government, to be spent on *public services*.

wage payment for doing a job.
wealth the amount of money a person or business has, including *assets* and *cash*.
welfare money paid by governments to provide basic services for people who cannot afford them.

Index

Acknowledgements

Written by
Eddie Reynolds, Matthew Oldham
& Lara Bryan

Illustrated by
Marco Bonatti

Edited by
Alex Frith

Designed by Jamie Ball
& Freya Harrison

Money experts:
Museum on the Mound*, Edinburgh*
Martina Collett,
South Thames College, London
Young Money, *(part of*
young-enterprise.org.uk)
Madalena Leão,
Treasury policy advisor

Series editor: Jane Chisholm

Series designer:
Stephen Moncrieff

First published in 2019 by Usborne Publishing Limited, 83-85 Saffron Hill, London EC1N 8RT, United Kingdom. usborne.com

USBORNE

POLITICS

FOR BEGINNERS

Contents

Chapter 6: Big questions 95

Sometimes what matters most isn't who's in charge, or what they stand for, but what they're actually going to do to fix the world's problems...

What is politics?

People often use the word politics to talk about who runs the country and how. But 'politics' actually covers the way people make decisions about how to work together in all kinds of groups, big or small.

Here's an example of a (smallish) group: a sports team.

The group has some common aims...

...but not everyone agrees on how to achieve those aims.

The group may not always agree, but they need to work together, because they want to do well.

Groups deciding the best way to work together is what politics is all about.

Most groups have a way of organizing themselves, so decisions get made in the same way each time.

This is called a **political system**.

Sometimes, people in the group will want to change the system.

That's politics too.

Groups such as sports teams can be described as **societies**. In societies, not everyone can get their own way all the time. They have to have a system so that they can make decisions and get along. That's why politics is so useful.

Politics is everywhere

When people talk about politics, they're usually talking about *large societies*, such as entire countries. In those societies, the word politics can refer to almost any aspect of day-to-day life.

Education

- What should people learn in school?
- Should school be optional?
- Are teachers paid enough?
- Should school be free? What about university?
- Should everyone have to learn a foreign language?

Foreign policy

- Should we do business with enemy countries?
- Is it always good to give aid to other countries?

War

- Should we ever go to war?
- What should the army do when there's no war?

Health and welfare

- Who should pay for doctors and hospitals?
- Who's in charge of caring for the elderly?
- Should going to the dentist be free?
- Might it do more good to tackle poverty first and healthcare second?

Environment

- Should people pay more tax if they have a car?
- Should we fly in food from other countries?
- How many wind farms should we build?
- Should we combat climate change, even if it hurts the economy?
- Should we pay people to use less electricity?
- Should we have to pay for plastic bags?

Work

- Should we give money to people who don't have a job?
- Should parents all get time off work during school holidays?
- How much is a fair wage?
- At what age should people stop working?
- Do we need people from other countries to move here and work?

Transport

- How old should you be to drive?
- Should bus rides be free for kids?
- Does our city need a new airport?
- Should wearing a cycle helmet be compulsory?

Economy

- Who should be allowed to borrow money from a bank?
- How much tax should people pay?
- Is our society too unequal?
- Should governments control how much things cost?
- What's the best way to make people better off?

Housing

- What's the best way to help people who are homeless?
- Is renting a flat too expensive?
- Who should be in charge of building houses?
- Do we have enough homes?

Culture

- Should newspapers be allowed to publish whatever they want?
- Who gets to choose what's shown on TV?
- Should museums be free to all visitors?
- How can we get more young people playing sports?
- Do we want more tourists to visit us?

Law and order

- Should police officers carry guns?
- Is it fair to make smoking illegal?
- Who should be allowed to get married?
- Who decides how long a prison sentence should be?

Who's in charge?

'Who's in charge?' is one of the biggest political questions in large societies. The answer is important, because whoever's in charge gets to tell everyone what to do. You don't always have to do what someone else tells you to, but it's hard to say 'no' to people who have *power* or *authority*.

A person with *power* can force you to do things by making you scared.

A person with *authority* doesn't have to force you, usually because you're part of a bigger group that has already agreed that he or she is allowed to tell you what to do.

Who has authority?

In a fair society, the people in charge need to have authority, not just power. The political system will only work if most people agree that those in charge are *allowed* to tell everyone what to do.

Think about all the people who might tell you what to do. How many of those actually have authority? What do you think?

Parents

Head teacher

Team captain

Prime Minister

Facebook friends

Armed robber

Bullies

Younger brother and sister

Police officer

What is a government?

In a big society such as a country, the answer to the question, 'Who's in charge?' is usually: the government. The government can be a single person or a group of people, but it nearly always has the final say in decisions about how the society is run.

All governments are different. For example...

Until the end of the 1700s, France was ruled by a ***king***. People believed that the king's authority came from God.

In the Middle Ages, the town of Siena in Italy was ruled by a ***council*** of business people which changed every two months.

In Ancient Sparta, there were ***two kings*** from two different royal families.

The Luba Kingdom in Central Africa was ruled by lots of ***chieftains*** and ***one king***.

The people in a government need to have authority if they're going to tell everyone what to do, and trust that people will accept it. But where does a government's authority come from? It could come from tradition, a *higher* authority, a popularity contest, or perhaps it's a choice based on wisdom...

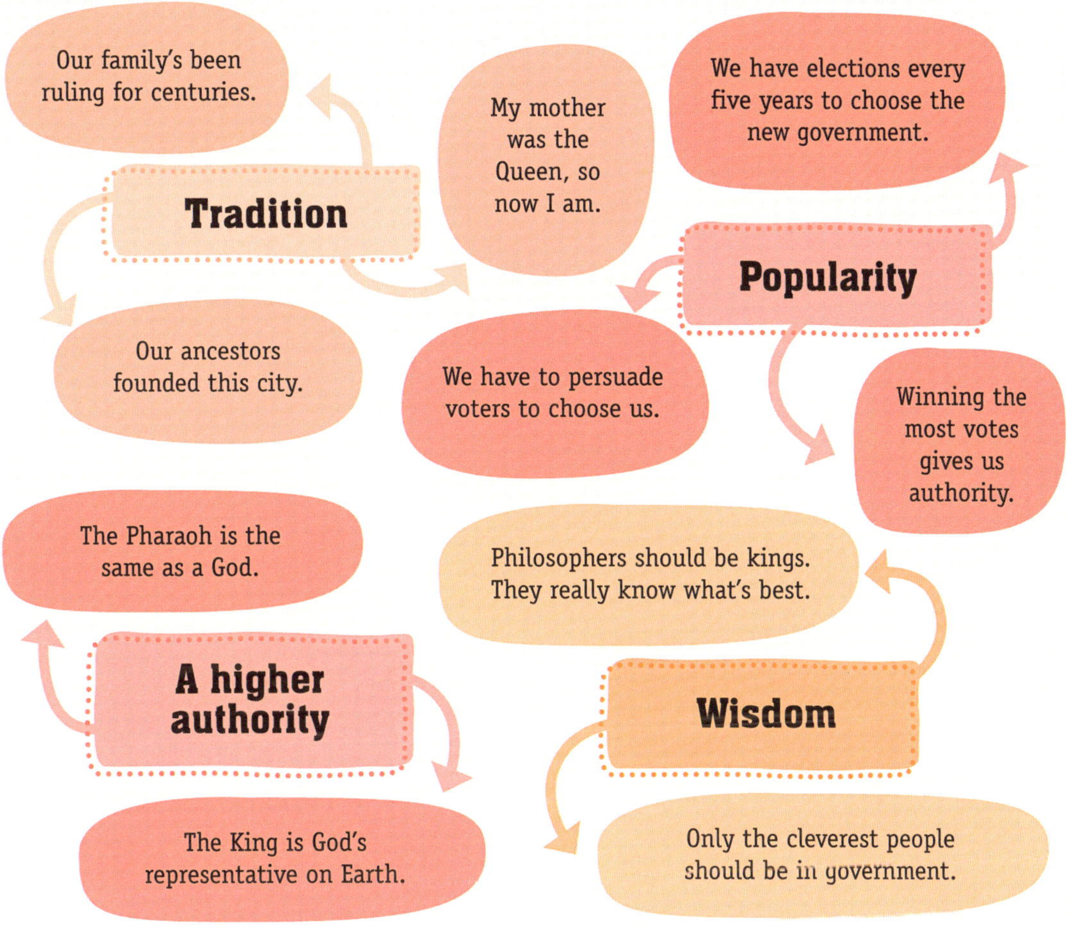

If a government is claiming to have authority, it needs to have a good reason – and that reason needs to be accepted by most (if not all) of the people in society. A government with both those things is known as a **legitimate government**.

Sometimes, people *don't* accept that the current government is legitimate, and want a change. They might protest, demand reforms, or start a revolution – which could lead to a *new* government.

Chapter 1: All kinds of governments

Throughout history, people have argued about what kind of government is best for their societies. Governments have changed too – either gradually over time, or suddenly when one group of people decides they've had enough of the current type of government.

This chapter will explain some of the different kinds of governments in the past – from the very beginning of something called **democracy** in Ancient Greece, to rebels in America who helped to elect the first President of the United States.

Ancient democracy

When the city of Athens in Greece was first founded, it was ruled by the wealthiest people who lived there; other Athenians had no say. Around 2,700 years ago, people demanded changes so they could rule themselves. This was the beginning of the world's first **democracy.**

Anyone who was a citizen could take part in government. But who was a citizen?

In Greek, the word *democracy* means 'rule of the people'. But citizens had to be free men, over 20 years old, and both parents had to be born in Athens. This meant only 10-20% of the people who lived in Athens were citizens.

The political system was made up of two main bodies: the **Boule** (or Council) and the **Ecclesia** (or Assembly).

Citizens
(around 6,000 men)

Boule
500 members, chosen by random draw

- decides when the Ecclesia meets
- decides what will be discussed
- comes up with new laws

Ecclesia
All citizens encouraged to attend

- discusses big issues
- accepts or rejects the laws decided on by the boule

This is how a session in the Ecclesia might have looked, during a debate on whether Athens should go to war.

The Roman Republic

Meanwhile, in Italy, Rome was becoming a great city, ruled by kings. In 509BC, wealthy families, known as **patricians**, rebelled against the latest king. They set up a new form of government, called a **republic**, which means a government without a king or queen.

In the king's place, the patricians chose two **consuls** to do the job of ruling Rome.

Consuls

Having two meant that neither one got too powerful.

The consuls' power was limited by...

The Senate

This was a body of patricians who advised the consuls.

Tribunes

These were representatives of the ordinary citizens, known as **plebians**.

The three parts were linked to make sure that no person or group had too much of the power.

This is sometimes known as a system of **checks and balances**. It means each part of government has its power limited by the other parts.

Dictatorship

In an emergency – such as a rebellion, invasion or war – the Republic had special rules in place. The Roman people could elect a **dictator**: someone who could temporarily rule however he liked, with no checks from the Senate or Tribunes.

But dictatorship didn't always go to plan. The last dictator of Rome was Julius Caesar, who refused to step down. He made himself dictator for life (cut short by an assassination plot). Today, dictatorship is almost always seen as a bad thing.

Empires and emperors

The Romans became more and more powerful, conquering land beyond Rome and building up an empire under Roman control. But in Rome itself, the system began to collapse, and in 27BC, the republic was replaced by rule under an emperor.

The land the emperor controlled grew until it covered much of Europe. This is how it looked at its biggest, 1,800 years ago.

The Roman Empire was split into regions known as **provinces**. Roman officials known as governors were assigned to each province.

The emperor ruled from Rome and had complete authority. His 'decrees' – public pronouncements – automatically became law.

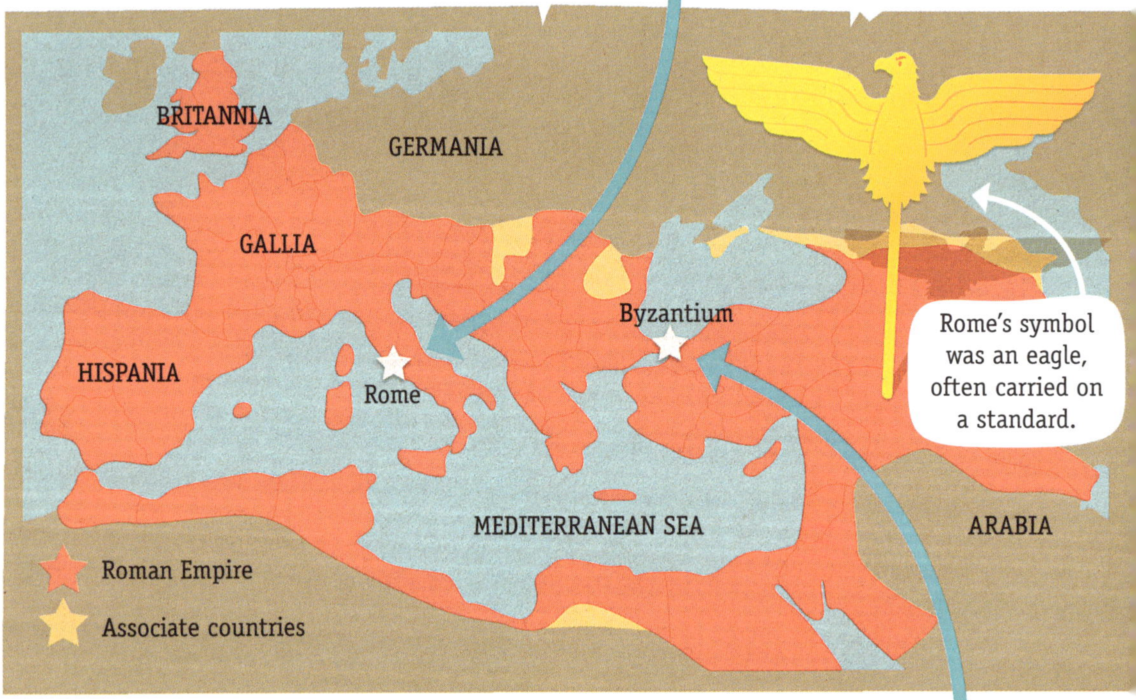

People living in the provinces outside of Rome itself had to pay taxes to the emperor, but actually they had quite a lot of freedom to live their lives.

The Roman army protected the empire's borders, and conquered ever more land. Eventually, the empire got so big, it was impossible to rule from Rome. In 285, it was split into two, ruled by two emperors in two different cities.

The Roman government was in charge of a huge area and a huge number of people, many more than most governments today. This is how they did it...

China: from empire to meritocracy

Meanwhile, large parts of Asia were ruled by an emperor, too. Emperors often gained power through military might, but the actual work of government was done by highly trained people called **civil servants.** From the 7th century, civil servants were chosen by exam. Only the very best passed the exams – this system is known as a **meritocracy.**

In Europe, before the 19th century, people got government jobs if they were members of ruling families, a system known as **nepotism**. But the Chinese system eventually inspired European governments to give people jobs based on merit instead. But meritocracy has its own problems...

Feudalism

In 1066, a ruler named Harold was crowned king of England. But a rival, William of Normandy (in France), thought *he* should be king. So he sailed to England, fought and killed Harold, and took the crown for himself. He earned the nickname 'William the Conqueror'.

William had to find a way to rule England, a foreign country where no one had any reason to be loyal to him. His answer was **feudalism**. This was a version of **monarchy** – rule by king or queen – that continued in England for hundreds of years. This is how it worked:

This system sounds quite peaceful, if unfair on the peasants. But in fact, some people tried to rebel against William. His power as king had no limits – so he could get away with whatever he wanted, and often used violence to control any rebels.

Absolute monarchy

Absolute monarchy or **absolutism** describes a government where all of the power is in the hands of a king or queen, a style of politics common in 17th and 18th century Europe. One of the most famous absolute monarchs was King Louis XIV of France (1643-1715). He used all kinds of tricks to hold onto as much power as he could.

War glory

Louis spent lots of money making France's army the strongest and most modern in Europe, and sent them to fight his enemies so he could secure France's borders.

Image

Louis built a grand palace, and commissioned portraits that made him look like a powerful ruler.

Money

Louis updated France's tax system so that more money went straight to him.

Intimidation

Louis used his power to crush his opponents within France, especially people who disagreed with his Catholic faith.

Loyal advisors

In the past, the king's advisors came from *noble* families – rich and powerful people. Instead, Louis hired less wealthy people. That meant they relied on the king for their position in society, so were less likely to disagree with him.

Divine justification

When Louis was born, his parents had been trying to have a baby for 23 years. So people thought he was a gift from God, and Louis believed it too. He claimed that God had given him the right to rule.

Centralization

Before Louis, remote places in France often had their own laws and tax systems. Louis brought the whole country under the control of the central government.

Controlling the nobles

Louis' biggest problem was to see off challenges from France's noble families. Powerful nobles had rebelled against Louis' father, and there were riots in Paris. Louis needed to find a way to stop these nobles from getting too powerful, or too likely to rebel against him. So, he ordered the troublesome ones to come to live at his palace in Versailles, where he could control their lives.

Self-government

Around 300 years ago, the government in Britain controlled colonies on the east coast of North America. In the 1770s, one influential group of people who lived there, known as **Patriots**, argued this was unfair. They began demanding the right to govern themselves.

In 1773, the British changed how tea was taxed, without asking American colonists. This led to an act of rebellion known today as the 'Boston Tea Party'.

Britain controlled 13 regions, known today as *states*. After the Boston Tea Party, Patriots in each state started making their own alternative governments, and refused to obey British rules. The 13 states declared themselves independent from Britain in 1776, and the **War of Independence** began.

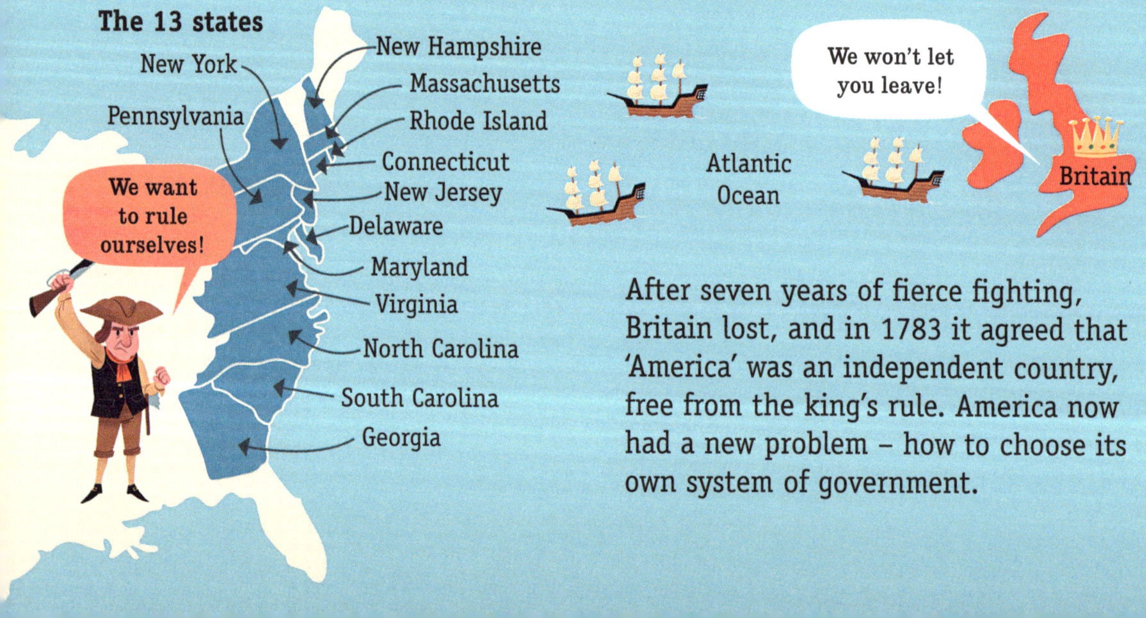

After seven years of fierce fighting, Britain lost, and in 1783 it agreed that 'America' was an independent country, free from the king's rule. America now had a new problem – how to choose its own system of government.

A new constitution

During the war, each state had its own **constitution**, which was a set of rules to organize how their state government would be run.

In 1787, representatives from the thirteen states, known as the **Founding Fathers**, met in Philadelphia, Pennsylvania, to discuss a new constitution for a *national* government for their new nation, the **United States of America**. Here are three of the Fathers, who took inspiration from three systems:

James Madison | Alexander Hamilton | Benjamin Franklin

In 1788, the Founding Fathers combined these ideas and agreed their new constitution. In 1789, after lots of arguing, they added a list of ten amendments, written in a document known as the **Bill of Rights**.

The **Constitution** said there should be an elected president, appointed judges and a House of Representatives and Senate. See more on page 42.

The **Bill of Rights** made sure the rights of individual people – and the states – were respected, unless those people were slaves, or Native Americans...

Representative democracy

The United States' new constitution created a system of government called **representative democracy**. But it wasn't very similar to how democracy had looked when it first started, in ancient Athens.

Ancient Athens
(Direct democracy)

USA
(Representative democracy)

America was a much bigger and more complicated society than Athens, so direct democracy would have been very difficult to organize.

But there was a more fundamental reason too. One of the Founding Fathers, John Adams, called it...

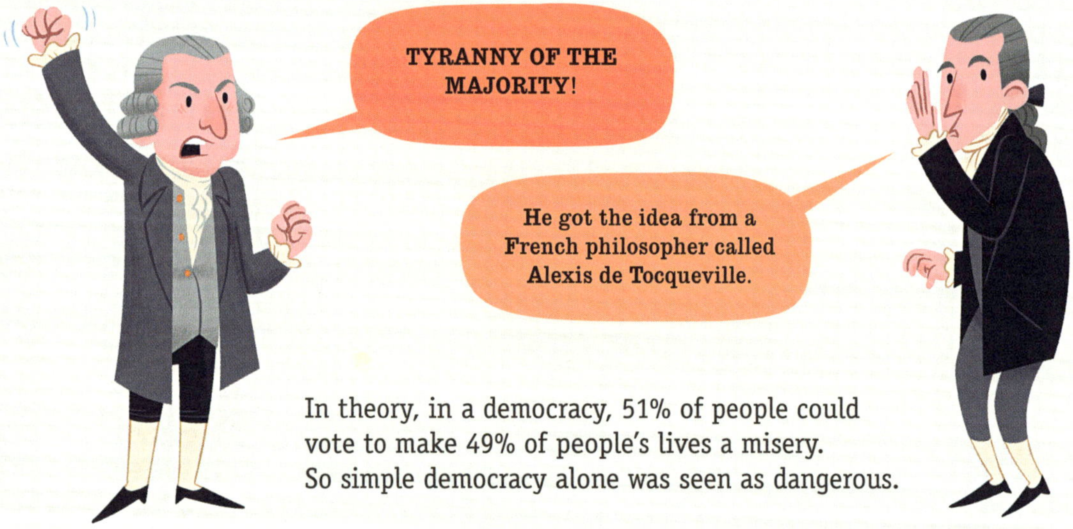

In theory, in a democracy, 51% of people could vote to make 49% of people's lives a misery. So simple democracy alone was seen as dangerous.

To prevent a tyranny of the majority, the American constitution created several branches of government, and included checks and balances – just as the Roman Republic had done. To read more about the American system, see pages 42-43.

Most countries in the world today are representative democracies (although they have differences between them). Here are some of the reasons for preferring representative democracy to direct democracy.

The perfect representative?

You might not know who they are, but you probably have representatives. You could think of them a little like a servant you've sent to buy you things you need from a shopping list...

...but many people – including the Founding Fathers – said representatives ought to do *more*. They should be wise enough to make decisions for you *better* than you can yourself. That's the theory, anyway...

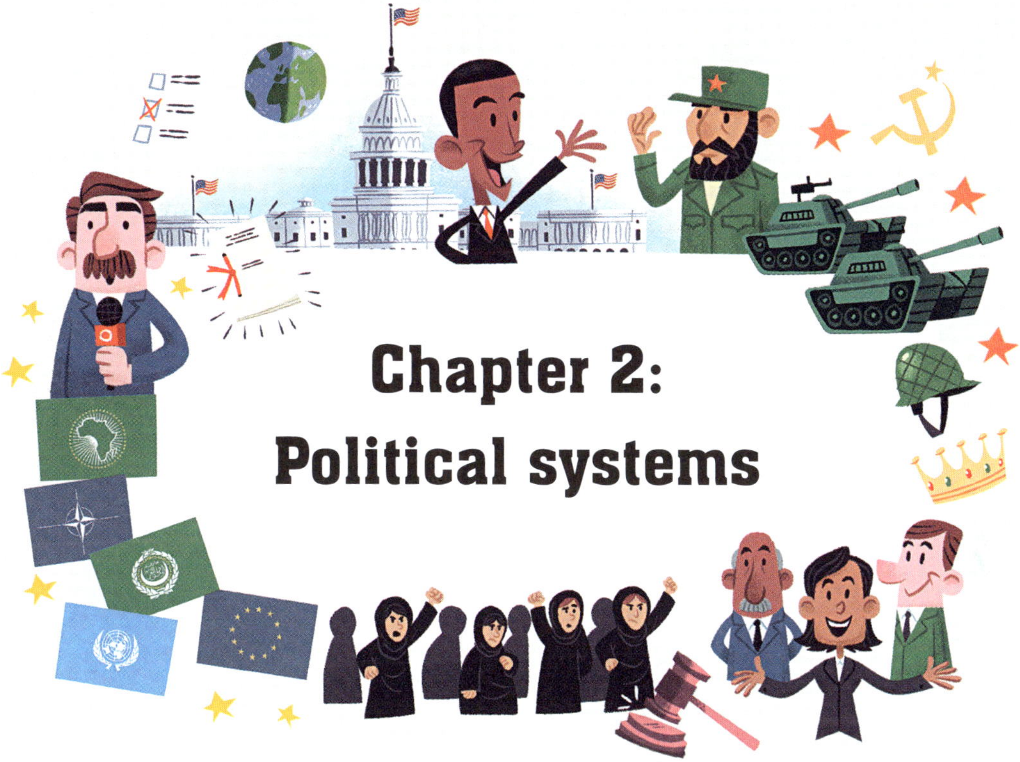

Chapter 2: Political systems

A **political system** is a set of basic rules about government, such as who gets to be in charge, how they are chosen, and how a government divides up its many responsibilities. Most systems are designed to hold together a **state** – the word for an independent country with its own government.

No country has a perfect political system. Sometimes, arguments about how to change the system have led to wars and revolutions. And some people think it'd be better to do away with government altogether.

Types of political systems

In your life, you deal with all sorts of different political systems, even if people don't describe them like that.

At home...

It's a little like an *absolute monarchy* – often with two monarchs (see pages 22-23).

At school...

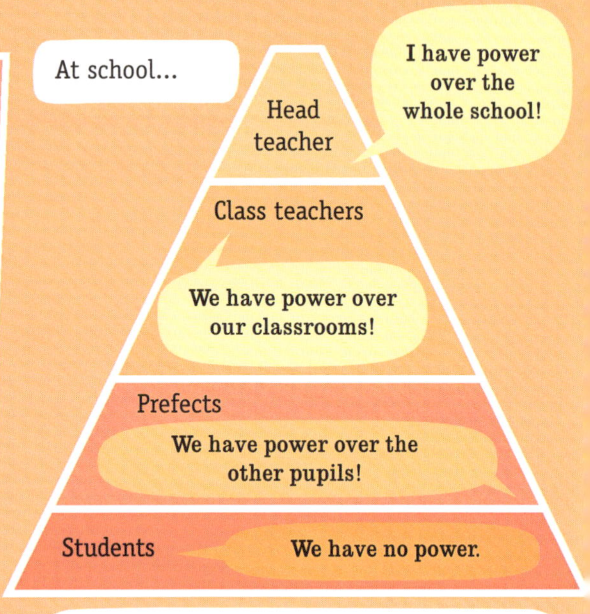

It might feel like *feudalism* (see page 21).

At times, it can feel as if there's no system in place at all...

Creating a system

Most states are made up of different groups of people. So, systems have to balance the need to be fair to each group with the need to keep everything running smoothly. Some systems were invented by giving very different answers to some basic questions.

Who chooses the rulers?

- The strongest should rule.
- Citizens choose them in regular elections.
- No one *chooses*. Rulers inherit their position.

Who sets the laws?

- A group of politicians, such as a parliament
- Everybody gets to vote on each new law.
- A king or queen.

Who's the head of the army?

- The army looks after itself, independent of government.
- The king or queen
- The government

Who judges the law?

- A team of judges, picked by the government
- The government
- Religious leaders
- A team of judges chosen through an election

Most political systems claim to have the same ultimate goals – to keep citizens safe from attack, to help them settle arguments between themselves, and to make life better. The next few pages will explore some examples of the systems people have tried.

Authoritarian systems

Until the 1800s, most states were ruled by a single very powerful leader. Today, states with this kind of government – either a single person called a **dictator**, or a small committee – are known as **authoritarian** states. These leaders have power to make their own laws, often designed to help them keep power. Here are some examples:

No opposition

Many dictators came to power after an election. It suits them to pretend they still run a democratic country – but they don't want to lose any future elections, so they set new rules to make sure no one else can win.

Watch everyone

Some authoritarian leaders employ huge numbers of spies, to watch and listen to everyone around them – and report back to the leader.

Control the media

All TV, radio and even internet broadcasts must be approved by a state **censor** – someone who can remove any stories that the leader doesn't want citizens to know about.

No gatherings

National police are allowed to disperse any public gatherings of groups larger than a family – to prevent people from plotting a revolution.

The strictest dictators use laws to demand total obedience, and even hero worship, from their citizens. States with these laws in place are described as **totalitarian**.

No criticism

Anyone who speaks or publishes ideas that criticize the leader, or the state as a whole, can be arrested and imprisoned.

Kim Jong-un inherited his father's role as Supreme Leader of North Korea in 2014. This country is often described as a totalitarian state.

Army rule

Sometimes, a country's military chiefs seize power. These chiefs may decide to stay in charge until they feel the country is ready for an election – which may take decades.

A government controlled by the army is often known as a **military junta**.

Argentina was governed by a series of different military juntas five times between 1930 and 1983.

God's law

In some countries, spiritual and religious leaders are in charge. They often have support from huge numbers of people, more than any army.

A political system based on religious laws is known as a **theocracy**. These laws can be as strict as any dictator's laws.

In Iran in 1979, devout Muslims deposed the government and declared their spiritual leader, Ayatollah Khomeini, to be the new ruler.

Fascist dictators

One political movement, known as **fascism**, grew popular by appealing to people's love of their country. But they did it by preaching hate for foreigners, and bullying people into voting for them.

The world's first fascist party was founded by Benito Mussolini in Italy in 1919. In 1922, he was elected as prime minister. In 1925, he declared himself dictator.

Communism

During the 20th century, several countries tried to set up a new system known as **communism**. In theory, it required everyone to share possessions – food, clothing, housing – equally. In reality, although communist governments brought about great changes, none managed to set up a perfectly equal society.

The key ideas of communism were developed by a German philosopher named Karl Marx, in his book *The Communist Manifesto*, published in 1848.

During the 20th century, determined leaders in several countries gathered people who were inspired by Marx's ideas. Each helped overthrow an existing government, often an authoritarian one, and worked to set up a communist state.

Class war

Marx and others described European societies as being made up of groups called **classes**. Monarchs and lords were the *upper class*. People who owned factories or had well-paid jobs were the *middle class*.

Communism was intended as a system to fight for the rights of the *working class* – people who did most of the work, but were paid very little.

Political leaders such as Lenin gained great support from the working class.

By gathering and protesting in massive numbers, communists were able to imprison, execute or banish most of the upper class.

New leaders – people who championed the working class (but were often themselves from the middle class) – took over.

Houses previously owned by wealthy, upper class individuals were now taken over by the government.

Middle and working class people couldn't sell their wares – instead, they gave everything to the government...

...who then shared it around.

The system relied on people working hard, and not cheating. But when times were hard, people *did* cheat.

Communist leaders had to cope with famine and war. To try to make their system work, they used exactly the same tactics as totalitarian dictators, and often carried them out even more ruthlessly...

Rule of empire

For much of the 19th and 20th centuries, many European countries invaded other countries around the world, creating giant nations known as **empires**. The countries they conquered didn't have their own governments, and were known as **colonies** or **dependencies**.

This map shows some of the European colonies around the world, in the early 20th century.

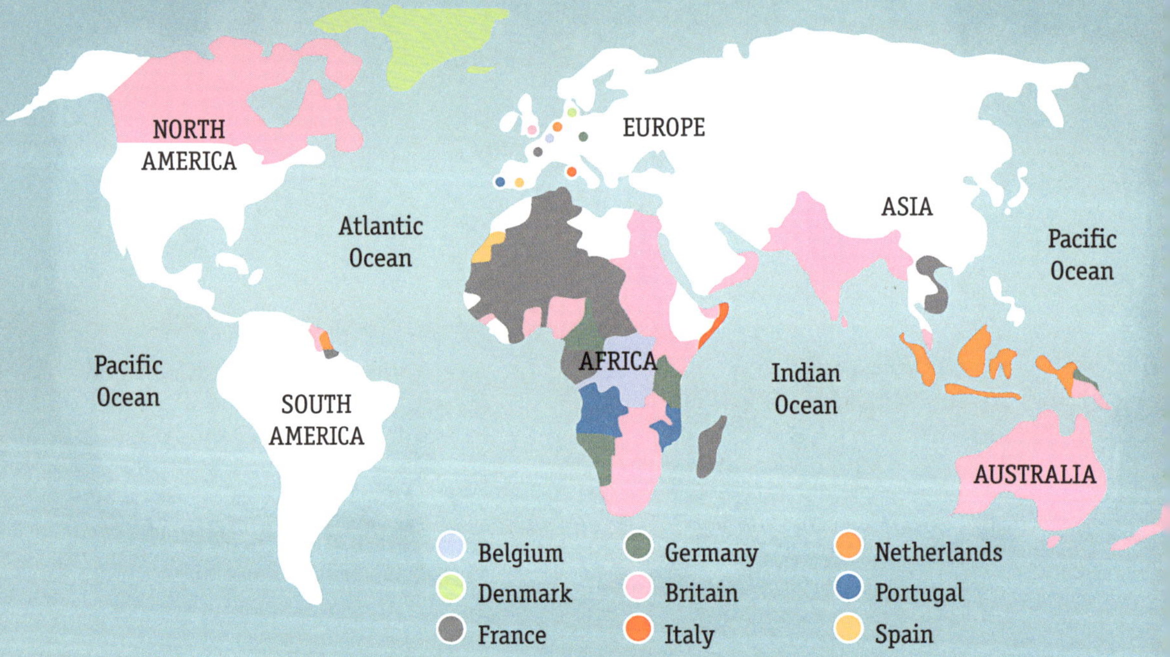

Empires used different systems to keep control in their colonies, such as:

Direct rule

The ruling nation imposed its own system of government on the country.

For example, the main government in France ruled all French colonies.

Indirect rule

The ruling nation hand-picked locals to be in charge of their country – as long as they did as they were told.

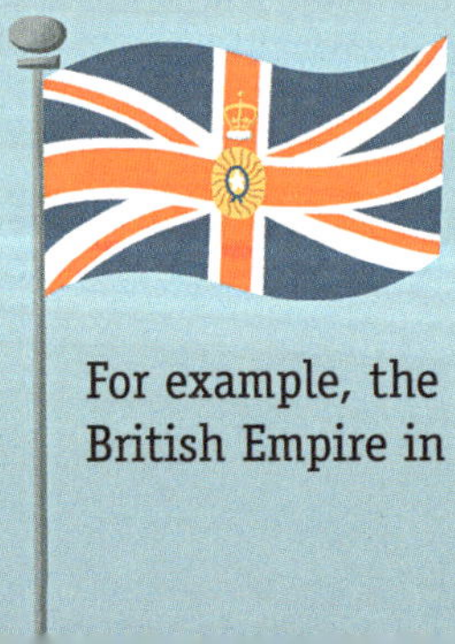

For example, the British Empire in India

Settler rule

Europeans moved into the colonies and formed their own governments, with no input from locals.

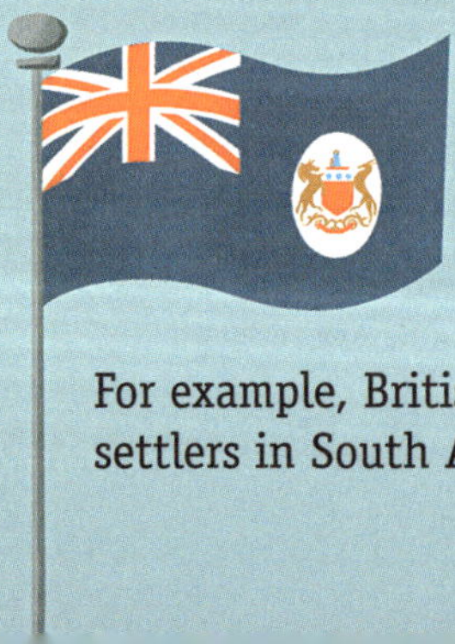

For example, British settlers in South Africa

Empires and violence

Europeans often built up their empires by military conquest, and ruled in an authoritarian way. They believed their way of life was superior to the ones they encountered in their colonies, and even believed it was their duty to 'civilize' the people they met. But mostly they wanted to make money from crops or mineral treasures in each colony, and to gain power to compete with other empires.

Empires used a variety of methods to keep power in their colonies.

Language and religion

All government business was conducted in the language of the ruling empire, making it hard to overturn the system from within.

Often, people were forced to adopt the empire's culture, too, for example by converting to a new religion.

Border confusion

Empires made treaties with each other – and not with locals – to draw up borders. Communities living on both sides of the new borders were split apart.

Seizing land

Rich settlers took control of the best land, so they could make money for themselves – and keep locals from getting rich from their own resources.

Making new enemies

Ruling governments sometimes appointed local leaders from minority groups. These minorities often ended up being hated by rival groups.

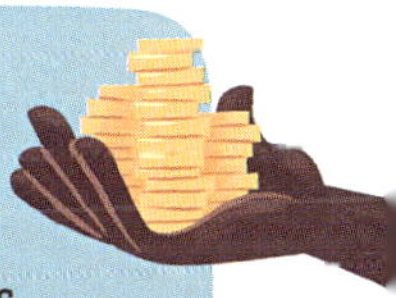

Taxation without benefits

Most colonies had to pay taxes to the ruling government. Often, these taxes were spent in other parts of the empire, taking money away from the colony itself.

The end of the empires

During the 20th century, many colonies successfully campaigned and fought for independence. Meanwhile, countries around the world began to agree that empires were not a legitimate form of government. However, many former colonies are still struggling with the after-effects of colonization. Find out more on pages 75, 90, and 101.

The democratic process

Most countries today are **democracies.** Just as in ancient Athens, a democratic political system is designed to let citizens influence the way their country is run. Here's how it works in the most common version, known as **representative democracy**.

Citizens

(Everyone who is allowed to vote – find out more in chapter 3)

Everyone gets to vote for a representative in a contest, called an **election.**

Elected representatives*

In government, groups of elected representatives get together to debate policy ideas...

...and turn them into proposals for new laws, called **bills.**

The media

(internet, TV, radio, newspapers)

News outlets explain the debates, and hire experts to give their opinions on new policies and bills.

Many news sources try to sound neutral. But in fact, each has its own **bias** – when people mix facts with opinions.

Citizens

People react to the news in different ways, creating something called **public opinion**. Of course, there's usually more than one opinion...

Elected representatives

Representatives often react to public opinion (and the media) before they vote to turn a bill into a new law. If they ignore all opinions, or side with an unpopular one, they may lose their jobs at the next election.

*in the UK, they're called MPs.

Sometimes, governments decide that a decision is so important – or has so many supporters on opposite sides – that they ask everyone to vote on it. This is known as a **referendum**.

Referendum on voting age

Should we lower the voting age to 16?

YES ☐ ☐ NO

Some smaller countries, such as Switzerland, hold referendums for lots of decisions. The Swiss system is a modern example of **direct democracy**.

Majority rules

Many democracies use a simple system: whoever or whatever gets the most votes wins. This is called a **majority**. But sometimes, the majority winner might not actually be what *most people* want. For example...

You can find out more about voting and elections in chapter 3.

Sharing power

Representatives have to work together to make all kinds of decisions. To prevent any one person from having too much power, most democracies split up the government's responsibilities across three groups, often called **branches**.

Executive branch

Carries out – or **executes** – policies and laws.

It's often a single person, such as a **president** or **prime minister**, with the help of a group called a **cabinet**.

The executive branch usually has to approve any new laws, and can often propose them – but it can't *create* them. That's the job of the legislative branch...

Legislative branch

Makes new laws and gets rid of old laws (called **legislation**), and discusses **policies** – ideas for how to make society work.

The legislative branch is usually made up of elected representatives, split into groups known as **political parties.** People in rival parties often disagree with each other.

Judicial branch

Makes sure the other two branches aren't breaking any rules, especially rules from a national constitution.

Ensures that everyone in the country, including the leader, obeys the same set of laws, or faces the same punishments.

Usually made up of a small group of **judges** – expert lawyers – who are appointed, not elected.

How the three branches work together

In the legislative branch, new laws are debated...

This part of the process is what people often think of when they hear the word 'politics'.

After the debate, there's a vote...

In the executive branch, laws are put into action...

In the judicial branch...

This is the part that makes sure no one person, or branch of government, can do whatever it likes.

Democracy in the USA

One of the world's most famous political systems is the one used by the United States of America. Authority is shared between three sections: a leader, called the **President**, and two groups of representatives called **Congress** and the **Supreme Court**.

What the President does

- responsible for ensuring that laws and policies are put into practice, and appoints a Cabinet to help with this.
- appoints new judges to the Supreme Court.
- in charge of the armed forces.
- can approve – or refuse – new laws.

The President is chosen by an election every four years, voted for by everyone* in the country. Currently, presidents can only serve two terms.

The President and Cabinet work in the White House, in America's capital city, Washington, D.C.

What Congress does

- suggests, debates and – if enough people agree – can send new laws to the President for approval.
- divides other areas of responsibility between two separate groups, called the **House of Representatives** (or **House** for short), and the **Senate**.

The House is responsible for setting up new taxes, or suggesting changes to old tax laws.

The Senate is in charge of approving people the President picks for the Cabinet (and other jobs), and makes agreements with other countries.

All members of Congress are chosen by elections within their separate states.

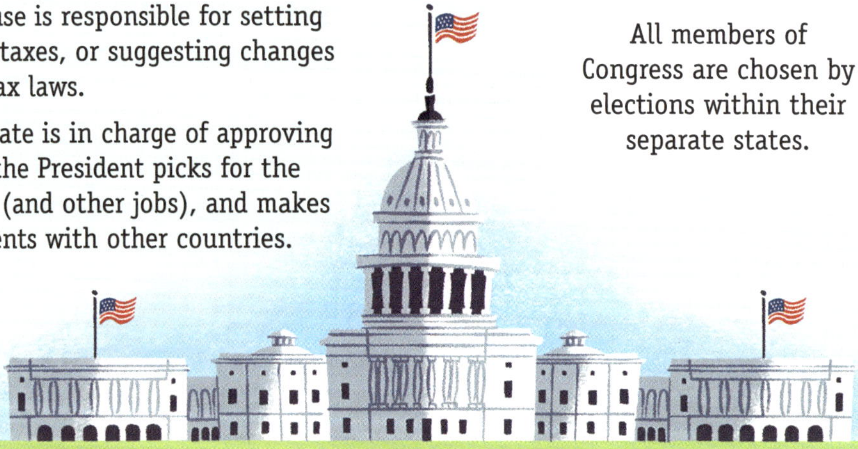

Both groups meet in the Capitol Building, also in Washington, D.C.

*Not quite everyone. Find out more on page 60.

What the Supreme Court does

Decides whether or not new laws might go against the Constitution (see page 25).

Led by a judge called the **Chief Justice**, and up to eight Associate Justices. New Justices are appointed by the President whenever there is a vacancy.

This is the Supreme Court Building, also in Washington, D.C.
In most countries, government buildings are in the capital city.

(Not) Getting things done

For 250 years, America's system of checks and balances has – so far – helped prevent any one person from abusing his or her power. But the same system can sometimes make it difficult to make *any* changes.

Democracy in the UK

The UK is officially ruled by a monarch – the *executive* – but real political power belongs to the *legislative* branch, known as **Parliament**. A similar system is used in many countries, such as Canada, Australia, Spain, Norway, Sweden and Japan. Here's how it works in the UK:

Monarch

A king or queen calls on Parliament to meet – but doesn't actually have any say in what happens there.

Houses of Parliament

Two groups of people, called **Houses**, meet to debate and vote on new laws.

House of Lords

Over 1,000 people, known as **Lords**, can suggest amendments to laws, and can vote against laws passed by the Commons. Most lords are chosen by MPs, and none are elected.

House of Commons

650 **Members of Parliament** (**MPs**), who are elected every five years. MPs debate laws. If more than half agree, they can make new laws and scrap old ones.

Government and Opposition

Most MPs belong to a political party (see page 56). If one party has more than half of the MPs, they form the **Government**.

The party with the second-most MPs is known as the **Opposition**. They argue against government ideas and stop them doing whatever they like.

Prime Minister

The leader of the political party with the most MPs becomes the **Prime Minister** – the most powerful politician in the country.

Cabinet

The Prime Minister appoints some MPs, known as **ministers**, to be responsible for different areas of government policy, such as health or education.

Inside the House of Commons

People called recorders take careful notes of everything that is said.

Speaker

An MP who runs the House, and chooses who can speak.

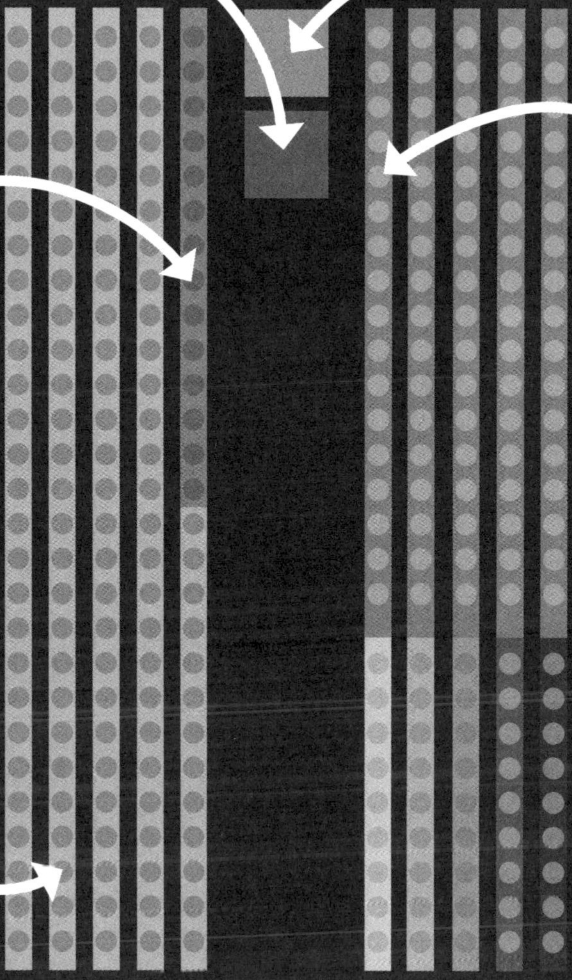

Front bench

The Prime Minister and other Cabinet ministers sit here.

Opposition front bench

The leader of the Opposition is in charge of challenging the Prime Minister to defend policy decisions, and help make sure he or she is running the country properly.

Back benchers

Most MPs don't have a specific role. They are supposed to vote the way their party leaders tell them (but don't always).

Independent MPs and MPs from other parties.

Ayes and Noes

When MPs vote on any new laws, they have to walk along one of two corridors, called **lobbies**, that lead behind the rows of benches on either side of the speaker.

AYES

People who vote 'yes' are counted as 'ayes to the right'.

NOES

People who vote 'no' are counted as 'noes to the left'.

Gallery

Where spectators and journalists can watch.

For most debates, only some MPs are present. MPs who live and work nearby are summoned by an electronic bell to tell them when it's time to vote.

Running a country

Governments decide how a country should be run. But putting those decisions into action is a job for non-politicians known as **civil servants.** Here's how it works in the UK.

Minister or Secretary

(A member of the cabinet with responsibility for one area, such as education)

Responsible for turning policy ideas, such as improving school attendance, into practical suggestions.

Civil servants

Write up specific ideas into a document called a *White Paper.*

Experts

A few experts help write the Paper; lots of experts read it and suggest improvements.

Civil servants

Civil servants re-draft the Paper to turn it into a *Bill of Parliament.*

Parliament

MPs hold a debate about the Bill, and vote on whether or not to turn it into a new law.

Civil servants

If the Bill becomes a law, civil servants explain the details to every school, such as...

At schools

Navigating the system

A system in which civil servants run the day-to-day business of government is often called a **bureaucracy.** It means, 'rule by people who sit behind desks'. Bureaucracies have strict rules about who civil servants can help, and what they can and can't do. Sometimes, navigating the system can be a slow process...

In the past, civil servants often tied bundles of papers together using red tape. Today, people often refer to 'red tape' when they're talking about the difficulty of getting help in a bureaucratic system.

Local politics

Political news is mostly about what's happening in national government. But often the things that affect people's daily lives the most have to do with their home towns or regions. This is the world of **local government**.

National government

(sometimes called central government)

- Makes laws and decisions that affect the whole country.
- Controls and spends an enormous amount of money.

Local government

- Can make laws and decisions that only affect a small area – as long as they don't go against national laws.
- Controls and spends a smaller amount of money.

Federal politics

Many of the biggest countries in the world, such as the USA, Germany, Brazil and Russia, are known as **Federal Republics**.

'Federal' means a country is made up of independent states that have their own governments, who agree to follow some laws set by a national government. 'Republic' means a country has an elected leader – such as a president – instead of a monarch.

One Federal Republic, India, is the largest democracy in the world. It's home to over one billion people. Here's how each person is able to have representatives.

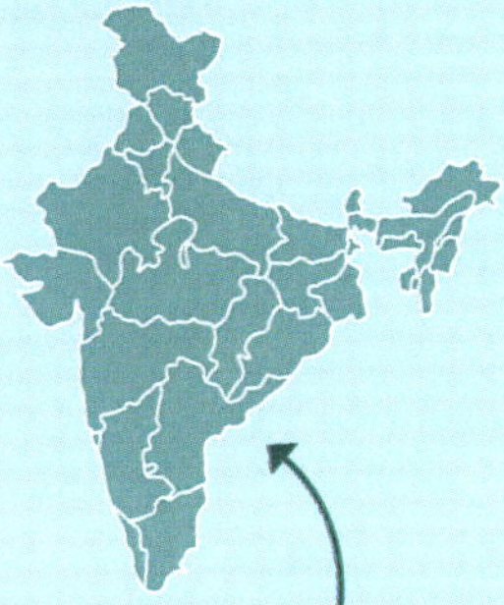

India is divided into 29 *states* and 7 *union territories.*

Levels of government

A president signs off laws and decisions made by a central parliament.

Parliament is made up of representatives chosen after nationwide elections.

Parliament is led by a prime minister, who leads the party with the most seats in parliament.

Jawaharlal Nehru was India's first and longest serving prime minister.

States (and most territories) have their own governments, made up of representatives chosen in state elections.

State governments collect taxes and make laws just for their state.

Most states are divided into smaller sections called *districts*, many of which have their own government, too.

Within some districts there are even smaller governments...

The biggest cities are governed by *councillors*.

Rural places are governed by groups called *Gram Panchayat*.

International politics

To avoid wars, governments from different countries often make agreements with one another, called **treaties.** Most aren't just about war – treaties can make it easier for people to move around, or trade goods, or share information. Sometimes, groups of countries go even further – forming international organizations with common aims and interests. Here are a few examples:

The United Nations (UN)

Nearly every country in the world is part of the UN. Known as member states, they all agree to follow its rules, and to work together to help promote global goals.

UN flag

People called **delegates** from each member state work in the UN Headquarters in New York City.

Interpreters translate speeches through headphones, so everyone can understand.

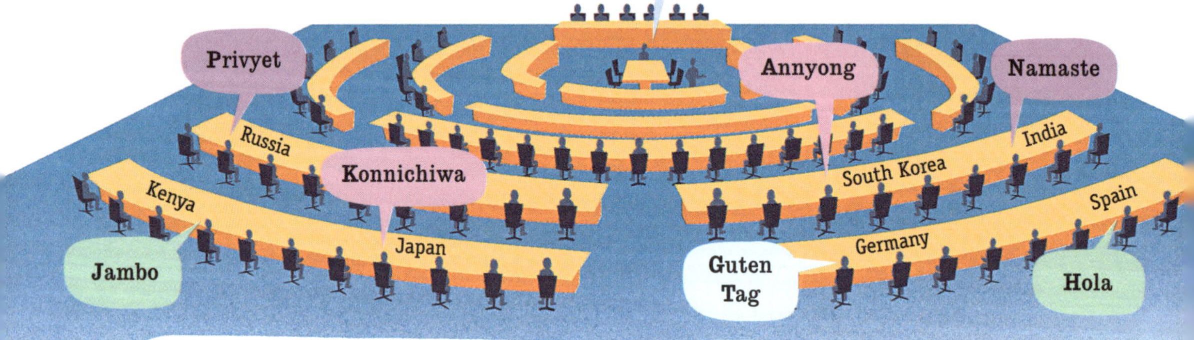

Global goals

- maintaining peace between countries
- protecting the environment
- promoting equality and fairness in all societies
- giving aid, such as food and shelter, to places that have suffered from natural disasters or war

Global authority

Five member states – China, France, Russia, the UK and the US – have more power than the others. They're known together as the **UN Permanent Security Council.**

If all five agree, the Council can authorize military action against a country, or impose **sanctions** – making it illegal to trade goods with that country.

The European Union (EU)

Most European states have agreed to share their resources, allowing people to live, work and trade across the Union.

EU flag

The EU has its own parliament, too, based in Brussels and Strasbourg. Citizens from each member state elect representatives to vote in the European Parliament, for example on how to spend the money each state provides.

The Arab League

An alliance between most countries in the Middle East and North Africa, to help protect each other and to share resources.

Arab League flag

North Atlantic Treaty Organization (NATO)

A military alliance between most countries in North America and Europe, who agree to help defend each other, and to share resources including weapons.

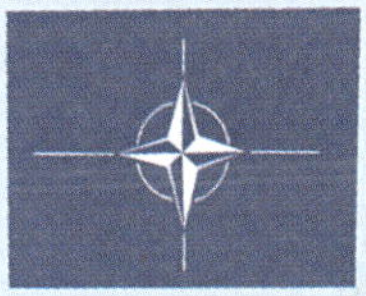

NATO flag

The African Union

An alliance between most countries in Africa to promote unity and peace, and to set up an international system of trade.

African Union flag

Homes away from home

Most governments send officials, called **ambassadors**, to live and work in foreign countries. It's their job to negotiate with the government in that country.

What if there was no system?

Some people think everyone would be much better off if there was no political system at all – an idea known as **anarchy**. What do you think?

A perfect world

Some thinkers, often called **political philosophers**, challenge political systems by presenting ideas they think should form the basis of a society's politics. Here are some famous examples from around the world, and across the centuries.

Confucius, China, 5th century BC

Plato, Athens, 4th century BC

Ibn Khaldun, North Africa, 14th century

Thomas Hobbes, England, 17th century

Jean-Jacques Rousseau, France, 18th century

Jeremy Bentham, England, 19th century

Thomas Paine, England/USA, 18th century

Hannah Arendt, Germany/USA, 20th century

Chapter 3: Elections and voting

Governments don't stay in power forever, even though some would like to. If there was no way to get rid of a government, it could do whatever it liked, with no consequences. In democracies, if you don't like the way a government is doing its job, you can change it by **voting** in **elections**.

Elections

In most elections, people put themselves forward as **candidates.** This is known as **standing for election.**

In some elections, the winner is put in charge of the whole country. Other elections choose candidates to be in charge of smaller local areas.

Candidates usually stand for election as part of a **political party** – a group with a shared set of goals or values – who compete to be in charge of the national or local government. Here are some examples of major parties around the world.

Asia

India: Bharatiya Janata Party, Indian National Congress

Japan: Democratic Party, Liberal Democratic Party

South Korea: Democratic Party of Korea, Liberty Korea Party

Africa

South Africa: African National Congress, Democratic Alliance

Ghana: National Democratic Congress, New Patriotic Party

Algeria: National Liberation Front, National Rally for Democracy

Europe

France: Socialist Party, Republicans, En Marche

Germany: Social Democratic Party, Christian Democratic Union

United Kingdom: Labour Party, Conservative Party, Liberal Democrats

North and South America

Argentina: Justicialist Party, Radical Civic Union

USA: Republicans, Democrats

Mexico: Institutional Revolutionary Party, Party of the Democratic Revolution

Some parties use symbols to represent them. For example, in the UK, the Labour Party uses a rose, the Conservative Party, a tree, and the Liberal Democrats, a bird.

Before an election, candidates, and the parties they belong to, try to persuade people to vote for them. This is called a **campaign**. Parties usually put together a list of **policies** – the things they're planning to achieve if they win.

First, candidates tell everyone their party's policies.

Candidates give interviews and go around the country talking to people.

(People aren't always pleased to see them.)

On election day, voters mark who they're voting for, either on paper or electronically.

In some elections, voters mark several candidates, putting them in order from best to worst.

After the votes are counted, the winners are announced, and the winning candidates start their jobs as politicians. This is called **taking office**. (This sometimes doesn't happen until a few months after the elections.)

Who gets your vote?

People base their choices on all kinds of reasons. Some people base their vote on their opinion of an *individual candidate*. This could be because of what the candidate has done or promises to do... or for slightly... fuzzier reasons.

Often, people pick a *political party* and stay loyal to that party in every election. Everyone has their own reasons.

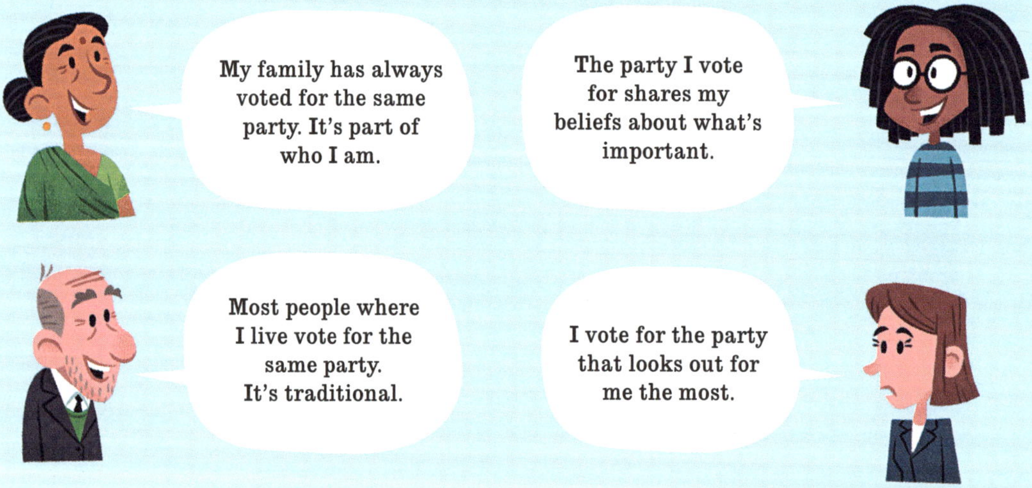

Someone who votes for different parties each time is sometimes called a **floating voter** or **swing voter**.

You might have heard the terms *left-wing* and *right-wing* used to describe politicians and parties (and people). Some parties describe *themselves* as left- or right-wing. Other people think the idea of left and right is old-fashioned.

Common left-wing ideas

People should pay lots of tax, especially rich people.

The government is the best at providing things such as healthcare and transport.

The government should make laws to protect the rights of weaker people and groups in society.

Society should change, to become fairer.

Common right-wing ideas

Taxes should be low.

Individuals and businesses are better at running their own lives than the government is.

The government shouldn't interfere too much in people's lives.

Traditional values are important and rapid social change can be harmful.

A lot of people have views somewhere in the middle – or agree with some left-wing and some right-wing ideas. And a lot of parties don't fit into these categories at all. (There's more in chapter 5 about this.)

Political parties change over time. Sometimes, if there's a big disagreement about something, they split into several new parties.

There are also **single issue** parties, which campaign about one thing, such as protecting the environment.

Who can vote? Who can't?

To vote you have to be on a list called an **electoral register**. Most adult **citizens** can vote, and some non-citizens can too.

A **citizen** is someone born in a country, or who's become an official member of the country after living there.

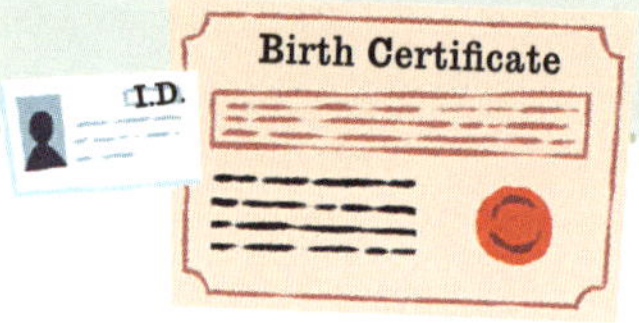

I'm an adult. Can I vote in the next election?

Are you a citizen of the country where you live?

NO → Is it a general (national) election?

- **YES** → Sorry. Only citizens can vote in general elections in most countries. (You *may* be allowed to vote in local elections.)
- **NO** → You may be able to vote in local elections.

YES → You may be able to vote in local elections. Are you in the military (army/navy/air force)?

- **YES** → Depending on where you live, this might be a problem. In countries such as Egypt and Venezuela, people in the military can't vote.
- **NO** → Are you in prison?

This is because of a worry that, if soldiers get too involved in politics, they might try to take over.

Are you in prison?

- **YES** → Sorry. In countries such as Russia and the United Kingdom, prisoners can't vote.
- **NO** → Have you *ever* been in prison for a serious crime?

Have you *ever* been in prison for a serious crime?

- **YES** → Oh dear. In some countries, such as the US, this can mean a lifetime ban on voting.
- **NO** → Congratulations! You can vote. Unless someone tries to stop you (see pages 64-65).

In some countries, such as Australia, if you're eligible to vote, it's against the law NOT to vote. You might have to pay a fine if you don't.

Who counts as an adult?

In most countries, you can't vote until you're *at least* 16. Usually, the voting age is 18.

Votes for (not quite) all

It's been a long struggle for many people to be allowed to vote. The right to vote is sometimes known as **suffrage**. This timeline shows which national governments were first to give the vote to women – and other groups who'd been left out of voting before.

1800s

In 19th century democracies, you had to be a property holder to vote. And you had to be a man. So only reasonably well-off men could vote.

This rule was dropped in most places during the mid-1800s. For example, in France, most men, rich or poor, could vote by 1848. (But French women had to wait almost a hundred years longer.)

1893 New Zealand

First country in the world to give all adults (including women) the vote.

1906 Finland

First country in Europe to give women the vote. Women could not only vote – they could stand for political office.

1929 Ecuador

First country in South America where women could vote.

1931 Sri Lanka

(known as Ceylon until 1972)

First country in Asia to extend voting to women. Sri Lanka was also the first country in the world to elect a female prime minister, in 1960.

Suffragettes

Women who fought for the right to vote in the 19th and 20th centuries were called **suffragettes**. They used a mixture of tactics – from chaining themselves to railings outside politicians' houses to smashing windows and planting bombs.

Women at war

During the two world wars women took on typically male jobs while the men went off to fight. This led to more support for female suffrage. **British** women got the vote in 1928, after the First World War, while in **France**, women got the vote in 1944, near the end of the Second World War.

1945 **Senegal and Togo**

The first countries in Africa to give women equal voting rights. But the people they were voting for were under French control, because these countries were **colonies**...

Decolonization

After the Second World War, some countries that had been previously ruled by foreign powers gained freedom. This process is known as **decolonization**.

1947 **Pakistan &** **1950** **India**

India and Pakistan were both ruled by Britain, as part of the British Indian Empire, until 1947. They then became separate, independent countries and introduced votes for women soon after that.

Racism and voting rights

People from certain racial groups have historically been barred from voting in many countries – for example, black people and Native Americans in the USA. Across the world, the fight for equal votes for all people, regardless of race, has been long and hard.

1960 **Canada**

First Nations people in Canada – those descended from the original inhabitants – didn't get the vote until 1960.

1965 **USA**

In theory, black men gained the vote in the 19th century, and black women could vote from 1928, but racist laws were passed in some parts of the country to try to stop black people from voting. In 1965 the Voting Rights Act was passed, to protect black voters in all parts of the country.

1967 **Australia**

The country's aboriginal population (that is, people whose ancestors were from Australia and the islands around it) finally gained the vote, long after the rest of the population.

Nelson Mandela became president in the first fully democratic election in South Africa.

1994 **South Africa**

After the end of a racist system called **apartheid**, which gave white South Africans more rights, black people gained the right to vote in national elections.

When voting goes wrong

For most adults, voting is a simple, easy process. In some extreme cases, things get more complicated – but don't worry, problems like the ones below are fairly rare, and are illegal in most countries.

Keeping voting safe

To make voting freer, safer and fairer, many countries have **secret ballots**, and some have **election monitors**, too:

Secret ballots

If voting is completely anonymous, and your vote doesn't have your name on it, then it's harder for people to try to bully or threaten you into voting a certain way. They will never know how you voted.

Election monitors

These are people who go to polling stations and anywhere that votes are being counted. They keep an eye on things and make sure no one's cheating. Election monitors sometimes belong to international organizations such as the Organization for Security and Cooperation in Europe (OSCE).

A watchful media

If reporters keep a sharp eye on the government, politicians and other community leaders, this can help warn people about attempts to meddle in the results of an election.

For example, in the 1970s, journalists discovered that US President Richard Nixon had spied on his rivals during an election campaign. He was forced to resign and a new election was called.

Ordinary people on social media sites can help share information about illegal or immoral election activity, too, such as voter intimidation or bribery.
Read more about the media and politics on pages 108-109.

Electoral systems

Each country has something called an **electoral system**. This is a way of working out how many elected representatives a party gets after an election, and how a government is formed. There are three main systems: **proportional representation**, **majority** and **plurality**.

Proportional representation

Proportional representation, or PR, is the most commonly-used system in national elections around the world. Each political party wins a share of available positions, usually known as **seats**, in the country's parliament or assembly, matching the share of the vote that each party has won.

Over 90 countries use some form of PR for their national elections, including Germany, Sweden, Italy, South Africa and Japan.

Let's say there's a national election and there are four parties competing for 500 seats. The election results turn out like this:

Here's how 500 seats would be shared out between the parties under a PR system:

In real life, it's often more complicated than that. Many countries set a minimum limit, called a **threshold**. If a party gets under, say, 5% of the votes, it won't get any seats at all. The spare seats have to be shared by the bigger parties, often using a mathematical formula.

Minority governments

If any one party has more than half the seats, they can form a government. But, under PR, it's rare for any party to manage this, meaning it's hard for one party to form a government – or at least, a government that's able to get anything done.

For example, if the Peach Party from the opposite page formed a government, the other parties could work together to stop them making a law.

A government with fewer than 50% of the seats is called a **minority government.** Minority governments don't tend to be very effective. But there's another option...

Working together

The most common type of government under PR is known as a **coalition.** That just means a government made up of representatives from two or more parties.

Parties sometimes form coalitions with other parties that they have a lot in common with.

Forming a coalition usually involves making deals and agreeing to compromise. Coalitions can happen even between parties with strong disagreements.

Plurality and majority systems

As well as PR, other electoral systems include **plurality** voting and **majority** voting. Around 80 countries use one of these systems, including the USA, Canada, the UK, France, Nigeria and India.

Plurality

Whoever gets the most votes wins, even if it's just one more than the person in second place.

Used in: UK general elections

Majority

The winner needs a majority – more than 50% – of votes. If there are more than two parties this usually means several rounds of voting.

Used in: French presidential elections

While Proportional Representation allows multiple representatives to be elected at a time, plurality and majority voting only allow one winner in each race. This is useful for when you need just one winner, such as in a presidential election.

Imagine a country is electing a president. Three candidates stand, from three parties. These are the percentages of the total votes that each wins.

This means *more than half* of citizens voted for someone other than the winning candidate.

But which is the best?

No electoral system is perfect, but each has strengths and weaknesses. Here are some of the arguments for and against them...

Plurality systems are best because they tend to avoid minority governments and coalitions. It's simpler for a government to make decisions if all its representatives are from the same party.

Simpler, maybe, but plurality systems are often unfair. *Most* people might end up voting for one of the losing parties, so a lot of votes are basically wasted, and only a few people get what they want.

Well, **majority** systems solve that problem. The winner always gets more than 50% of the votes. So at least 50% of voters end up getting someone they had a role in electing, even if it wasn't their first choice.

It's still not fair on people who vote for smaller parties. They never get represented! In Proportional Representation, a vote for a small party isn't automatically wasted.

That can be a good thing. Sometimes small parties hold dangerous, extreme views.

Well, large parties can have dangerous views too, especially for people in minority groups, such as immigrants*.

But it's harder to hold elected representatives to account for their dangerous views or actions under Proportional Representation, as you don't tend to vote for individual candidates, and it's harder to vote *out* politicians who do or say bad things.

Ah, but the *party* still has to hold their representatives to account. They may not even have to wait for another election!

OK, but you're leaving a lot up to the parties in your system. It's all rather complicated to understand, and comes in so many versions. In plurality and majority systems, you vote for individuals and there's only ever one winner. Simple.

*See pages 110-113

Chapter 4: Political change

You may have to wait until the next election to vote out a government you don't like, but voting isn't the only way to bring about political change.

You can also try to change a politician's mind about a policy, or persuade them that the policy will lose them votes at the next election. There are lots of ways to do this, from writing letters to your representatives to staging a protest march.

In extreme circumstances, such as a dictatorship, people sometimes use far more drastic and less peaceful methods to bring about political change.

Putting politicians under pressure

In between elections, organizations called **pressure groups** try to persuade the government, or other representatives, to create new laws or change existing ones. Here are some types of pressure group:

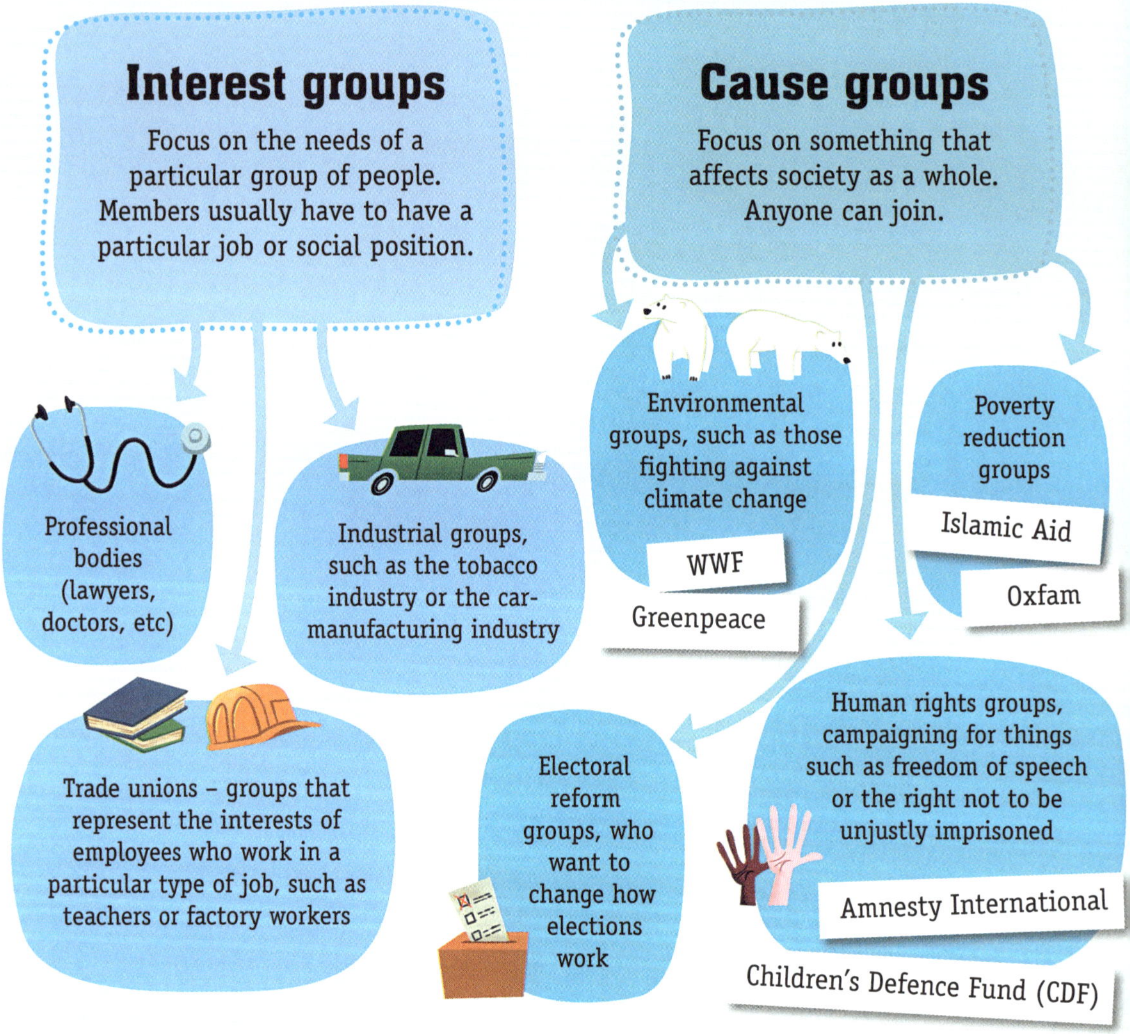

Pressure group tactics include...

- organizing protests (see page 74).
- gathering signatures in petitions.
- paying lawyers to challenge laws.
- putting out adverts to spread their message and gain more supporters.
- getting celebrities who agree with their messages to act as spokespeople.
- organizing meetings with politicians, to try to influence them directly.
- persuading the media to champion a message.

Loitering in the lobby

Trying to influence representatives about particular political issues is often called **lobbying.** The word is thought to come from the lobbies or hallways of the UK Parliament, where MPs and Lords gather and chat before debates.

Pressure groups can hire professional lobbyists to help them persuade politicians to vote in a particular way. Groups with more money to pay for lobbying are often more likely to get their voices heard, so the lobbying process isn't fair.

If a pressure group is very rich or powerful, it can be *anti-democratic.* It means the government is likely to do what small groups of people want, which isn't necessarily in the best interests of most voters.

RESIST! PROTEST!

When you think your government is doing something wrong, one way to tell them is to join a **public protest** – a gathering of people with a message that they want to get across. Here are some famous protests from the last hundred years or so.

We want voting rights and jobs!

Where and when? 1960s USA, where black people in many places had to live separately from white people, as second class citizens. A series of protests became the *Civil Rights Movement*, fighting for black rights.

Protest: The 1963 March on Washington

What happened next: The Civil Rights Movement led to the 1965 Voting Rights Act (see page 63) and other legislation to combat anti-black discrimination.

Movements

One-off protest marches rarely change anything. But when a single protest spawns *new* protests, and people form into groups to campaign for something, this is sometimes called a **movement**.

When a protest involves walking from one place to another, it's called a **march**.

People also protest by refusing to move from a place – for example, standing in front of bulldozers if they don't want buildings torn down.

WARNING: protests don't always end well. Sometimes, police use violence to break up protests and, in some countries, protesting itself is a crime. Some protesters become violent, too.

We want independence!

Where and when? 1930s India, which was under British rule

Protest: To protest against Britain's control of salt production, a political campaigner named Mohandas Gandhi led a march to a beach and gathered grains of salt. Collecting salt was illegal, so this was an act of **civil disobedience** – breaking the law as a protest.

What happened next? Gandhi was arrested, but soon released. Years of protests eventually helped to bring about Indian independence.

Give us democracy!

Where and when? Communist China, 1980s

Protest: In 1989, students led a pro-democracy protest in a place in Beijing called Tiananmen Square.

What happened next? The Communist government sent in tanks and many protesters were killed. China did not become a democracy although, over time, it adopted an economic system known as **capitalism**, see pages 86-87.

In spite of the successes of the Civil Rights Movement in the 1960s, black people still suffer from unequal treatment in the USA. The **Black Lives Matter** movement is currently campaigning about police violence against black people, and other forms of discrimination.

Revolution!

When the people of a country take power from the government, that's a **revolution**. Some use violence, while others are peaceful.

How to start a revolution

First, you need an unpopular government – almost always an undemocratic one that's hard to get rid of by other means. For example...

...**Iran**, 1970s

(The deeply unpopular Shah was overthrown in 1979.)

You also need an immediate crisis – or several – that whips up people's anger to a fever pitch, so that they can't bear things the way they are. For example...

...**France**, 1780s

(The French Revolution began in 1789. King Louis XVI was executed in 1793.)

Then, you need people who are prepared to stand up to the government... and even die to bring about change.

Cuba, 1953 – revolutionary leader, Fidel Castro, led a band of rebels against the government.

Many of them died, or were captured and tortured. But others took up the struggle, and Castro's fighters finally beat the government in 1959.

What next?

For a revolution to succeed, it helps if the army and police decide to take the side of the revolutionaries. For example...

Tunisia, 2010-11

When people were protesting against the president, during the Tunisian revolution, the army refused orders to shoot at them.

The revolution lasted a couple more months, until the dictator-like president was removed.

Often, there's a charismatic leader who's good at persuading people to take action and put their lives at risk. For example...

Toussaint Louverture
(Haitian revolution, 1790s)

Emiliano Zapata
(Mexican revolution, 1910)

Lenin
(Russian revolution, 1917)

People also need to know what they want to replace the old government with. Democracy? Communism? Theocracy?

After our president stepped down, a temporary government took over. By the end of 2011, we had our first free, democratic elections. I hope we'll remain a democracy.

Tunisians queuing to vote in a Presidential election in 2014

(New democracies can be fragile.)

What can I do?

As an individual, it can feel hard to know where to start to change the world. Problems such as poverty, homelessness and pollution can feel impossibly huge. But there's a lot you can do, even if you're not old enough to vote. Even just discussing politics with your friends and family can change the world, by changing people's minds.

Here are some things you could try:

Write...

...to your local political representatives and to journalists about things that matter to you, and encourage your friends to do it as well.

Join...

...a political party, a campaigning organization, such as Greenpeace, or take part in a local campaign, such as saving a local library, school or hospital.

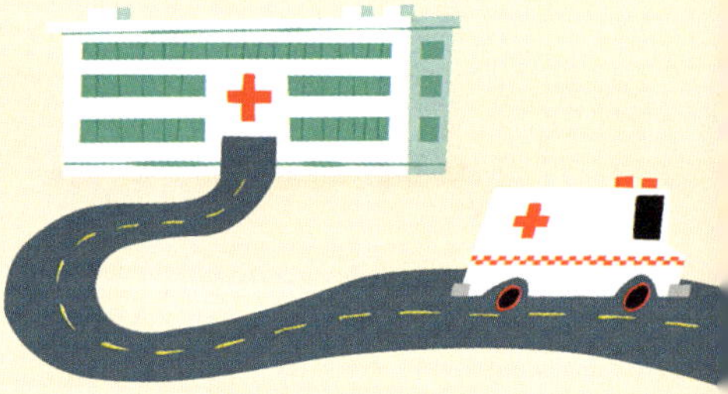

Stand...

...for election in a Youth Parliament. These are organizations that elect young people and focus specifically on issues that affect children and teenagers. They don't run countries, but governments do consult them. It's also great experience if you want to become a politician later.

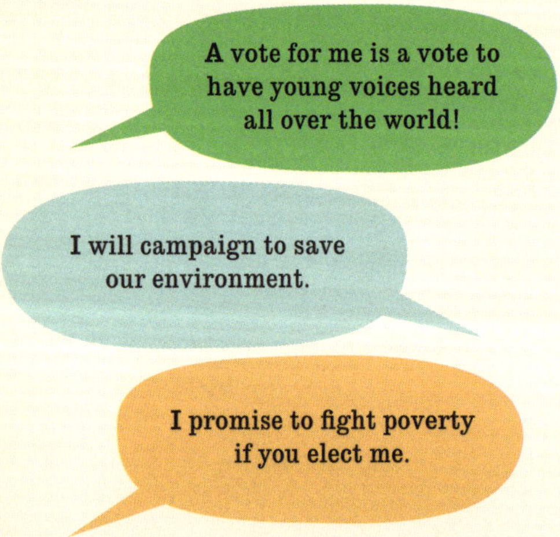

Debate...

...with your friends. Schools often have debating societies, where you argue for and against an idea. Debating helps you learn to explain your ideas clearly, and how to listen and argue with people who have different ideas. Find out more on page 118.

Pester...

...adults in your life about political issues you care about. It'll sharpen your debating skills, and you might even persuade them to change who they vote for, or to bother voting at all.

Read, watch and listen...

...to the news. In order to change the world, you need to know what's happening in it. Although, always beware of bias and try to read a variety of news sources, for balance.
Find out more on pages 108-109.

Don't buy...

...products from companies whose actions you disagree with. For example, you could avoid buying burgers from a fast food company if you know they treat their workers badly, don't pay their taxes or use child labour.

This is known as **boycotting**. If enough people boycott a company, it is more likely to change. But make sure you do your research, as a lot of accusations fly around online that aren't true.

Ask...

...questions and try to understand how your country works. The more you know, the better equipped you'll be to try to change things.

And, if you're eligible where you live:

Vote...

...in elections. It can feel as though one vote makes no difference, but every vote adds up to make a *big* difference.

Become...

...a politician. It's not a job for everyone, and it takes a lot of hard work and mental toughness. But you never know. Perhaps you're the future leader of your country?

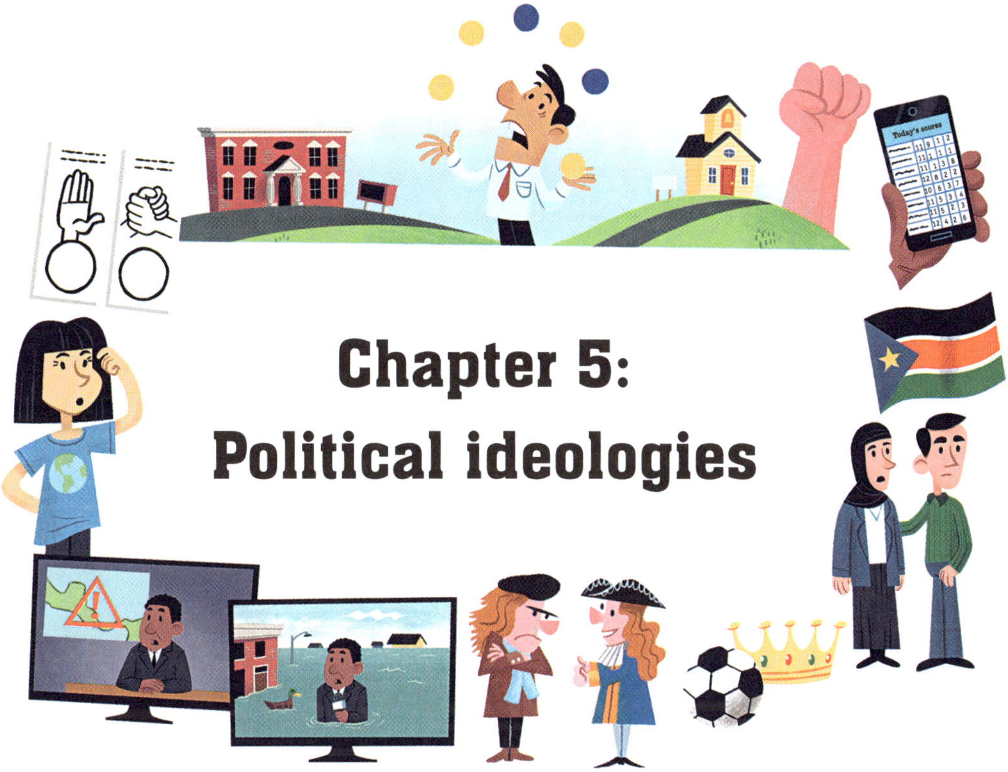

Chapter 5: Political ideologies

Most politicians have to make promises to get elected. For example, they pledge to make society better, or fairer. Across different parties, most politicians say they want the same thing: that everyone should have a fair chance at succeeding in life, no matter whether they were born into the richest or poorest family.

But politicians and political philosophers often have very different beliefs – or **ideologies** – about what 'succeeding' means, and about the best way to organize a society so that it really is fair to everyone.

Fixing society's problems

Politicians take on one of the hardest jobs in the world – trying to make everything better for everyone, as quickly as possible. Often, they have to try to please different groups who want – or need – very different things, and they don't have unlimited funding, either.

Being a politician is a little like being a juggler. Each ball represents an important need for society. The more balls that get added into the mix...

...the more likely it is that one will be dropped.

Finding solutions

Politicians and political philosophers can try to make the world better in two very different ways.

Left and right, big and small

Political parties are often driven by a particular ideology that explains their policies. Often, that ideology is part of a range that people describe as stretching from left to right (see page 59).

Where do you sit?

The political terms *left* and *right* come from the 18th century. In the French National Assembly, revolutionary politicians sat on the left of the King, while his supporters sat on the right.

Who should pay for society?

The meanings of left and right have changed over time, and vary from country to country. But, roughly speaking, left-wing ideologies promote the idea that the government should intervene to help people, while right-wing ideologies believe individuals or communities are better off looking after themselves.

(This discussion could continue for hours – and it often does.)

Liberals and conservatives

Left and right ideologies are often about the economy. But some people are more concerned with *cultural values*, such as laws about marriage and families, religious freedom, and what children learn in school.

How big should a government be?

'Big' government doesn't mean it just has a lot of people in it. It often means the amount of money a government spends (and how much tax it asks people to pay). But it can also mean, 'how much does it interfere in people's lives?'

Big government can mean...

- Lots of laws about businesses, making sure employers pay fair wages and don't rip off their customers
- Laws forcing people not to take risks, for example wearing a cycle helmet
- Lots of public services, such as free healthcare
- Lots of police, and a secret service with the power to spy on citizens – potentially making everyone safer
- High taxes

Small government can mean...

- Limited power for police and spies
- No laws telling people how to live their own lives, only laws ensuring people do not harm each other
- Fewer laws about businesses, making it easier for new businesses to become successful quickly
- Low taxes
- Fewer or no public services

Capitalism and socialism

In 19th-century Europe, a change, known as the **Industrial Revolution**, swept through society. Lots of factories opened, full of machines that could produce goods very quickly, and some people started making lots of money. These changes led to the development of two new ideologies: **capitalism** and **socialism**.

Capitalists believed that the changes could only be a good thing.

But *socialists* thought that the Industrial Revolution was in fact harmful to the biggest section of society: the workers.

Socialists imagined a completely new way of organizing things.

Some socialists tried running fair factories – but most couldn't make enough money or provide enough jobs. Extreme socialists, called commmunists, tried changing entire societies (see pages 34-35).

Socialist or capitalist? Take the test.

Start here

People should be free to earn as much money as they can, as long as they do it legally.

NO → That's not fair! Some people will end up with lots more money! → **You're a *pure socialist*.** Society works best when all earnings are shared.

YES → Is it fair that some people get very rich while others stay poor?

NO → Lots of rich people have an unfair advantage, such as money from their parents. Governments need to share some of that wealth. → Should governments share out all of the extra money rich people earn?

YES → You're a *pure socialist*.

NO → If people can't make money from the work they do, they'll stop working very hard. → Governments need to give businesses room to succeed or fail. But should governments leave all businesses alone?

YES → Businesses *don't* need laws to force them to be kind. If they don't treat their staff well enough, they'll fail. → You're a *pure capitalist*.

NO → Businesses *do* need laws, or else they may treat their staff badly. → Should governments run any companies themselves, paid for by taxes?

NO, none → **You're a *mixed capitalist*.** Businesses are more efficient than governments, but they need laws to stop them from exploiting people.

YES, some → There are some things so many people rely on, it's safer for governments to have some control – such as power lines or trains. → **You're a *social democrat*.** Capitalism allows businesses to run well, but isn't suitable for everything.

(Is it fair that some people get very rich while others stay poor?) **YES** → Most rich people deserve the money they earn, and they create jobs, too. → **You're a *pure capitalist*.** Society works best if people are free to make money.

Nationalism

A country that is run by its own government is officially called a **state**. A **nation** is something different – it's used to mean a group of people who have a similar culture, history or language, and who feel linked to a particular place (but doesn't always describe an independent state).

Your nation is probably part of your everyday life. It's why...

...the teams you support are probably part of a national league.

...your lessons are probably in the same language as at the school down the road.

...the stories about your country usually come first on the news.

But which nation you belong to isn't always that clear-cut.

Sometimes, nations are linked to **ethnic groups**. This means groups that are – or at least, feel they are – descended from the same group of people.

Nationalism, internationalism and patriotism

Nationalists believe governments have more responsibility to help people from their own nations than people from other nations. That doesn't mean they think we have *no* responsibility towards people in other countries...

For example, if there's a flood in our country...

But if there's a flood in another country...

Some people believe that's unfair, and that we have an equal responsibility to help *all* human beings, no matter where they live. You could call these people **internationalists.**

Feeling *proud* of your country or nation is known as **patriotism.** You don't have to be a nationalist to be patriotic. You might be an internationalist who thinks we should treat everyone equally, but still feel proud when you sing your national anthem.

Nor do you have to be patriotic to be a nationalist. You might think your country isn't anything special, but still think it's wrong to help people in other countries *before* taking care of all the people in your own country.

One state, more than one nation

Often, there is more than one nation within a single state.

For example, the United Kingdom is a state that has its own government. But within the state, there are at least four nations.

The nations are...

- Northern Ireland
- Scotland
- England
- Wales

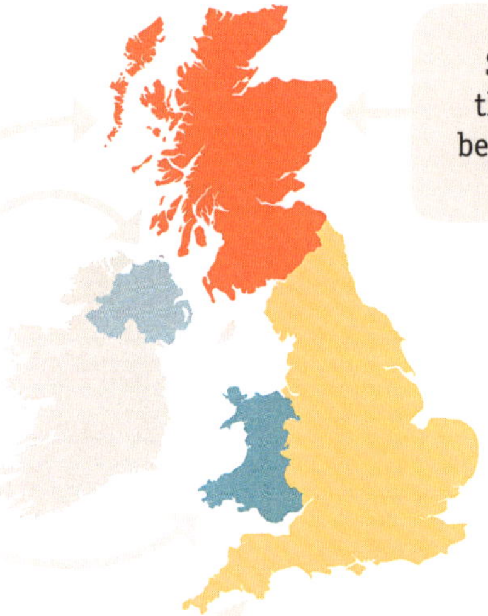

Scottish nationalists think Scotland should become a separate state.

Northern Ireland, Scotland and Wales have their own national parliaments that run things such as health and education. But a central parliament makes decisions for the whole United Kingdom.

Some parts of the UK, such as Cornwall, are home to nationalists who want their region to be recognized as nations, too.

A new country for South Sudan

Nationalists who want to form their own independent states are known as **separatists.** There are separatist movements all over the world. In 2011, after decades of civil war, people in southern Sudan got the chance to vote on becoming independent from the rest of Sudan.

The ballot paper looked like this.

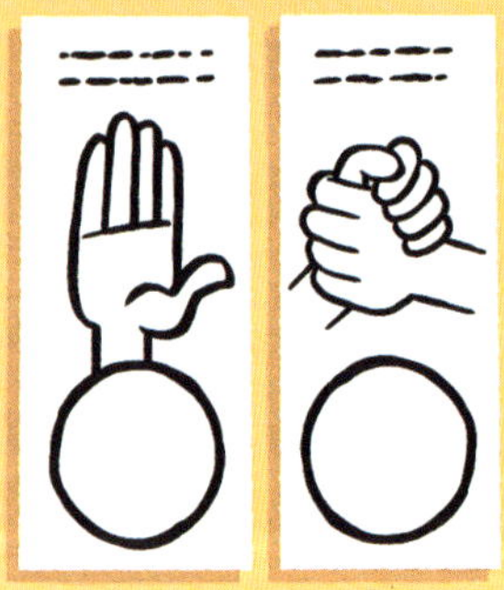

99% of voters said they wanted to become a new country: South Sudan.

A capital city, a flag and a national anthem were chosen.

Other countries accepted or 'recognized' South Sudan...

...and a new state was formed.

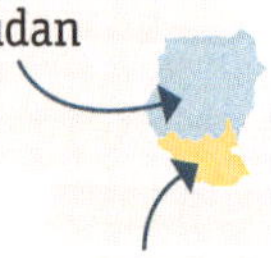

Nationalism and violence

Yugoslavia was a group of nations that, together, formed a communist state after the Second World War. But in the early 1990s, Yugoslavia split apart into separate states. In one, Bosnia and Herzegovina, three rival nationalist parties won shares of the vote, and formed a coalition. But they all wanted different things...

The Bosnian Party of Democratic Action

The Serbian Democratic Party

The Croatian Democratic Union of Bosnia and Herzegovina

The coalition soon broke down into war. In one of the worst cases of violence, more than 8,000 Bosnian Muslims were killed by Serb forces at a town called Srebrenica†. This kind of deliberate massacre of a particular ethnic group – people who share the same culture or ancestors – is called **genocide**.

In 1995, the leaders of each group signed an agreement which ended the war and created a new system of government.

Bosnia and Herzegovina is still a single state, but has two separate parts which have quite a lot of independence.

- The Federation of Bosnia and Herzegovina – mostly Bosnian Muslims and Croats live here
- The Republika Srpska (pronounced 'serp-ska') – mostly Serbs live here

So far, this new system has been successful in preventing violence between nationalist groups.

†Say 's-reb-ren-eats-uh'

*Say 'crow-ats'

Where do you stand?

This chart shows some examples of political ideologies, and lists a few of the ideas they promote. Most people – and most political parties – support some ideas from more than one part of the chart.

You might like some **left-wing** and some **right-wing** ideas, and prefer **big government** for some issues, but not all (see pages 85-86).

Communists

Government should provide all services, and control all industry.

Socialists

Government should provide services such as healthcare, education and electricity – and these should be paid for by taxing the rich more.

Left wing

Shared responsibility

Social democrats

Governments should allow people to make a profit, but it should also spread out some of the country's wealth, and run some services (see page 87).

Left liberals

Governments should *make* laws to protect all people, regardless of race, gender, religion and sexuality. But they should also *reduce* laws that restrict people's choices, for example by legalizing drugs.

Left-wing anarchists

No one should be allowed to own private property, and there should be no government at all.

Left-wing libertarian

Personal property is OK, but no one should own so much of anything that they have power over other people.

Big government

Government control

Fascists

Some ethnic groups are superior to others, and the superior groups have a right to dominate the inferior ones.

Conservatives

A stable society is the most important thing. Governments should preseve a society's way of life and not change things too fast.

People in different countries often don't agree on where the political 'middle' is.

Individual responsibility

Right wing

Classical liberals

Governments should protect all people's rights to be free, and taxes should be low – because taxation is a kind of government interference.

Capitalists

Governments shouldn't make too many rules about how people make money and run their businesses. People should buy services such as health, security and education from private companies.

Individual freedom

Small government

Right-wing anarchists

Private property is a moral right but governments should not exist.

Chapter 6: Big questions

Political ideologies often attempt to answer a single big question: how should society work? But many people turn to politics to answer more specific and detailed questions about society.

This chapter explores just a few of those questions, from 'Can war ever be justified?' and 'What is terrorism?' to 'Is freedom of speech always a good thing?' and 'Am I a feminist?'

Is there such a thing as human rights?

Human rights are rights we *all* have *simply because we're human.* **Rights** mean how a person should be treated – for example, with kindness – and can mean things a person is entitled to have – such as clean air to breathe. Most people agree that governments everywhere should respect and help preserve human rights.

In 1948, the United Nations signed a document called the **Universal Declaration of Human Rights.** Here are some of the things it said.

In theory, everyone has human rights. But some people argue that theory isn't good enough. In practice, you need someone with power who will stick up for you – otherwise talking about human rights doesn't mean much at all.

Hannah Arendt and statelessness

During the Second World War, lots of people were forced to leave their homes. One of them was Hannah Arendt...

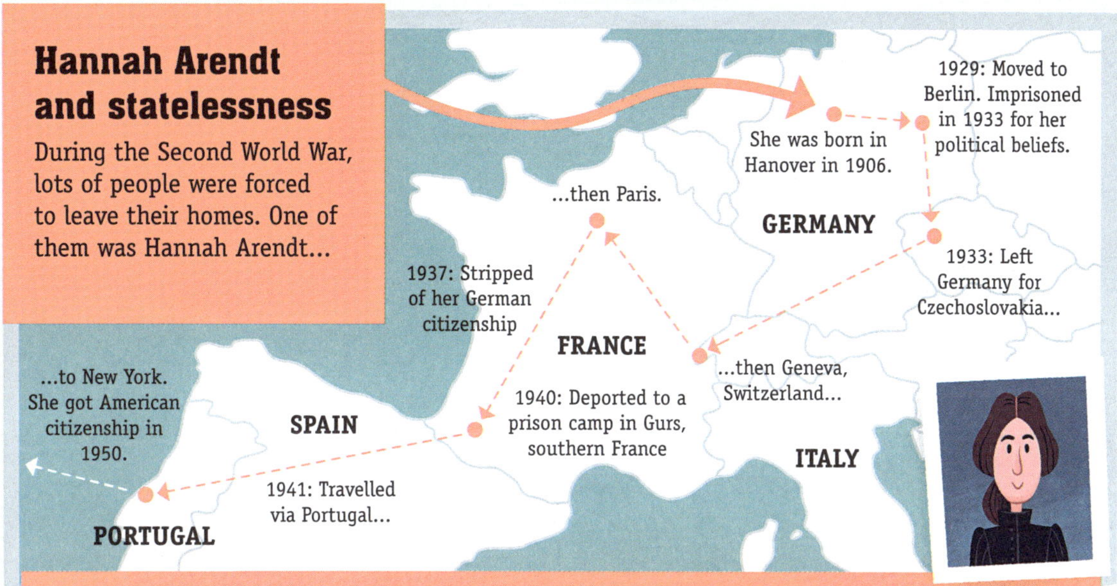

Arendt described her experience as **statelessness.** She argued that what people call *human* rights are really just rights you have as a citizen of a state. If your state abandons you, there's no one else willing to defend your rights.

Today, there are still millions of stateless people. Most of them don't have the rights the Universal Declaration promises. Does this mean there *isn't* such a thing as human rights?

How far should we be willing to go to protect human rights? Should we be willing to go to war, for example...?

Can war ever be justified?

If two people have a fight, they can be judged using their nation's laws. But when *countries* go to war, it's a matter for **international law**.

War happens when political relations between two or more countries get so bad they start using soldiers, bombs and guns. Virtually everyone agrees that war is the worst possible solution to a problem. But, on rare occasions, the UN* Security Council will agree – under terms of international law – that war *is* justified.

International law isn't all written down in one place. It's a mixture of treaties and agreements made between countries.

Why do you want to go to war?

I want to get more money or more land for my country.

Another country has invaded *me*! I want to defend myself.

I think another country is getting too powerful.

I want to prevent human rights abuses in another country.

✗ This may have seemed reasonable to absolute monarchs 400 years ago. But now, it's seen as **aggression**, which is illegal in international law.

✗ Making sure no one country gets too powerful might make sense. But this is not considered a good enough justification for war by most people today.

✓ If another country has committed an act of aggression, it is legal (and justified) in international law to declare war to stop them.

? This is where it gets complicated. Some people think that it's not only justified, it's a *duty*. Other people think human rights can be used as an excuse for powerful countries to tell weaker countries what to do.

And it's also possible that the reason a country *claims* they've gone to war isn't the real reason at all.

*United Nations, see page 50.

Two wars in Iraq

Twice in the past 30 years, a group of countries has declared war on Iraq.

The First Iraq War

1990
Iraq invaded Kuwait. Iraq's president, Saddam Hussein, announced that Kuwait was now a province of Iraq.

The UN demanded Iraq leave Kuwait. When Saddam refused, the UN authorized its members to go to war.

1991
Soldiers from 35 countries pushed Iraqi soldiers out of Kuwait. After just 100 hours of fighting, Iraq surrendered and the UN-backed group left.

The UN told Saddam to pay back Kuwait for the damage done during the war, and to promise to destroy Iraq's long-range weapons.

Over ten years later, in 2002, US President George W. Bush spoke at the UN. He claimed Saddam was abusing human rights and building deadly 'weapons of mass destruction'. The UN *didn't* authorize a war. But then...

The Second Iraq War

2003
The United States – with support from three other countries – declared war on Iraq, saying they had *proof* that Saddam Hussein possessed illegal weapons.

Within days, this group of four countries captured Baghdad, the capital of Iraq, and forced Saddam to run away. Many Iraqis celebrated, because Saddam *had* been abusing human rights.

A prominent statue of Saddam Hussein in Baghdad was pulled down in 2003.

With no stable government, Iraq fell into chaos. The group stayed to help, but many Iraqis thought these outsiders had no right to interfere, and so they fought back.

2006
Saddam was captured. He was accused of human rights abuses, including genocide, and executed.

2011
All four countries finally withdrew from Iraq. Later in that year, it was discovered that Iraq had never owned the illegal weapons it was claimed.

Most people think the First Iraq War was justified. It's harder to say about the Second. Some say Saddam had violated UN rules and had abused human rights. But many suspect that the coalition wanted to get rid of Saddam because he was too powerful. And some think they *really* wanted control of Iraq's oil.

Why are some countries poor?

Although there are poor people in all countries, some countries have very high overall levels of poverty, meaning most people can't meet their basic needs. There are many causes of this, from natural disasters to problems in society and government.

Economic crisis

A country's **economy** means the amount of money, jobs and things it produces. If the economy starts to fail, a lot of people end up without jobs.

Corruption

Politicians who are **corrupt** may steal tax money. They may also run their countries badly, too. Find out more on page 115.

War

Wars can be very expensive for governments while they're happening, and rebuilding after a war costs a lot of money too.

Natural disasters

These destroy homes and businesses, instantly plunging many people into poverty.

Why are some people richer than others?

Why are some people so poor they can't afford food, when others in the same country have so much money that they can buy a wristwatch or a necklace that costs the same as a house? There are all sorts of reasons.

Money makes money

The more money you start off with in life, the easier it is to make more. So rich families become richer over the generations.

Lack of education

It's usually easier to get a well-paid job when you have lots of skills and qualifications. In many countries, education costs money, so it's harder for poor families to escape from poverty.

Luck

Some people end up in the right place at the right time to make money. For example, working for a company when it first starts to become very successful.

Some politicians think poor people could become rich if only they worked harder. Others think society needs to make people share their wealth – see the debate between capitalists and socialists on page 87.

Should rich countries help poor countries?

Rich governments often give money to the governments of other, poorer countries. This is known as **foreign aid.** But that money often comes with strings attached...

I'm from the government of a rich country.

I'm from the government of a poor country – one of your ex-colonies.

We know your country is recovering from all sorts of difficulties, not all of them your fault. We'd like to help.

Okay... that's patronising, but it'll help. We're going to spend it on a new power station. We really need a better electricity supply.

You didn't read the small print, did you? We think power stations aren't environmentally friendly, so you can't spend our money on that.

But it's our money now! Can't we decide what's best?

I'm sorry, but we just don't trust you to spend it responsibly. *We* want it spent on protecting the environment.

Hang on a minute. What about all the damage *your* government did to our environment when you were exploiting our resources?

Perhaps we shouldn't give you the money at all. Your government is corrupt, so half of it won't make it to the people who need it.

Well, maybe we don't *want* the money if it means you'll try to control how we run our lives.

What is terrorism?

Terrorism is the name for a type of violence that targets ordinary people and aims to make everyone in a society feel scared.

What do terrorists really want?

They want to make everyone afraid, so they can get their own way. They're a little like pressure groups, but they use violence and fear instead of peaceful protests.

What kinds of things do they want to make people do?

Some terrorists describe themselves as **freedom fighters**. They usually want independence for a nation that's part of another country (see pages 90-91). Other terrorists might want to change the way people live their lives, based on their beliefs.

How do people become terrorists?

Terrorist leaders often try to recruit people using a process known as **radicalization**. It involves gradually getting the person – often a teenager or student – used to extreme ideas, for example through social media, by playing on their hopes and fears.

What about extremists? What does it mean when someone's called that?

An **extremist** is someone whose views are so extreme that they will do anything to put their point across – usually including violence.

What kind of thing do extremists believe?

Some, called **fundamentalists**, base their views on twisted versions of religious beliefs. Others, for example **white supremacists**, believe that white people are superior. But there are other types, too.

How common is terrorism? Should I be scared?

Not very common at all. In most countries, far more people are killed or injured by road traffic accidents. The reason terrorist attacks make news headlines is because they're unusual.

What are governments doing to stop terrorism?

One thing most governments do is check people's bags and clothing at airports, to make sure no one brings weapons onto a plane.

So that's a good thing, right?

Checking people at airports makes it much harder for terrorists to cause harm. But it can lead to **profiling** – stopping specific groups of people more often, based on race or where they're from. Profiling is unfair.

What else are governments doing to keep us safe from terrorists?

In some countries, police have the power to arrest someone they suspect of being a terrorist, even if they don't have much proof.

That's not fair on the innocent people they arrest!

I disagree! I think that's a fair price to pay if it prevents terrorists from murdering people. I also think it's OK that some spy agencies are allowed to listen in on phone calls, or read private messages.

I don't want them to read mine!

It's a difficult balance. Many people think privacy is more important. But government spies and police agencies have used their powers to prevent deaths, and to arrest dangerous terrorists. I think it's worth sacrificing my privacy.

What is prison for?

In most countries, people who are convicted of serious crimes are sent to prison for years, or even for life. But taking away someone's liberty is a big step, and societies have to justify doing it.

Here are some of the main reasons societies give to justify putting people in prison.

Incapacitation

Getting criminals off the streets so they can't hurt people or commit more crimes.

Deterrence

Putting people off breaking the law, by making them scared they'll be caught and put in prison.

Rehabilitation

Making criminals less likely to commit crimes in future, by helping them and teaching them new skills in prison, so they can make money legally.

The reasons above are all practical – they either aim to prevent future crimes, or get dangerous people off the streets in the present.

Any other reasons?

There's another reason a lot of people believe in, even if they don't admit it: **retribution**. This means punishing criminals because they *deserve* to suffer for what they've done. Politicians who promise to be 'tough on crime' can appeal to people who believe in this.

Problems with prison

Not everyone thinks that these reasons are good enough. There are a lot of arguments about why prison doesn't work, or isn't fair.

Locking up a bunch of criminals together just means they can swap tips about how to commit crimes more sneakily in future!

Prison is very, very expensive. We should spend that money on funding *education*, to help people avoid a life of crime in the first place.

Prison sentences are racist! In the US, for instance, a black man is likely to get a 20% longer sentence than a white man for the same crime. For example, a five year sentence might turn into a six year one for a black man.

I get that prison is meant to be unpleasant but it's *really* dangerous. Too many prisoners live in fear of violence from other criminals... and even guards.

Here are some alternatives to putting criminals in prison.

Restorative justice

Getting criminals to meet their victims, apologise and do something helpful for them. This can also reduce the likelihood of someone commiting another crime.

Retraining

Taking a class can help some criminals learn to change their ways – for example, driving courses for speeders or drunk-drivers.

Monitoring

Wearing an electronic tag that allows the police to track where criminals go, so they can't get up to too much trouble... ...in theory.

Community service

Doing work that makes life better for people, such as picking up litter and removing graffiti.

What is freedom of speech?

Freedom of speech – also known as **freedom of expression** – is the idea that people should be able to share their ideas without fear of being arrested.

When a government or another powerful group limits someone's freedom of speech, it's called **censorship**. This might mean banning certain books, or stopping people who are considered dangerous from speaking in public places.

The word *censor* comes from the name of a government official in Ancient Rome whose job included keeping an eye on how Roman citizens behaved.

A Roman *censor*

Why do we need freedom of speech in politics?

Being free to share information – and ideas – allows voters to make decisions based on what's *really* going on. If people aren't able to report the facts, especially those that expose a government's failings, democracy won't work properly. That's why dictators love censorship.

Squashing free speech means dictators can tell people that everything is fine, even when they're committing terrible crimes – and no one is able to say otherwise. Using strict censorship also scares people from daring to speak up against the government.

Is freedom of speech always a good thing?

On the whole, freedom of speech is good for democracy. But many think there should be *some* limits to what you're allowed to say – or write, or sing – in public. Still, not everyone agrees on where society should draw the line.

Freedom of speech means I should be allowed to say anything I like!

Even if what you say puts someone in danger?

How can *words* put someone in danger?

Let's say you know where a team of soldiers are hiding. Should you be free to post that online and probably get them killed?

OK, maybe I shouldn't be allowed to post *that* kind of thing. But apart from that, I should be able to say what I want.

What about... if you go on TV and tell viewers to go out and kill people? Should that be against the law?

It depends... what if I say it as a joke? I'm not comfortable with the government or lawyers deciding what's funny...

OK, jokes are a tricky one. What if I wanted to say something horrible, such as 'All gay people are evil'? Some people call that *hate speech*.

Where do you draw the line on that, though? Are you going to start banning all opinions you disagree with?

What about if you spread harmful lies about someone? Should that be illegal?

It depends on the lie.

You like saying 'it depends', don't you? Has anyone ever told you you should go into politics?

How does the media affect politics?

The media is shorthand for the way people share information – TV news, the internet, print newspapers and magazines. In totalitarian political systems, the government controls the media but, in a democracy, a healthy, independent media is vital.

But there is also a darker side to the relationship between the media and politics, even in a democracy...

The good

The media can...

- dig up the truth and uncover secrets that politicians would rather bury, and let everyone know what the government is up to.
- help to keep citizens informed about politics – which laws are being passed, what's being debated, and where the country is heading.
- ask politicians challenging questions, giving the public a chance to see how they perform under pressure, and whether their ideas make sense when you look at them carefully.
- publish campaign promises during elections so people can make informed voting decisions.
- offer historical context: when something big is happening in politics, it's often similar to something that's happened before. The media can bring on experts who can draw historical parallels and help us understand the present.

The bad

The media can also...

- report the news in a **sensationalist** way. For example, making out political news stories to be more extreme than they actually are.

- show strong **bias** towards one party or set of beliefs. If the people who run a particular news site hold strong political beliefs this will affect which news stories they cover, and how they cover them.

- be corrupt. Journalists, broadcasters or newspapers might take bribes in order to report things in a way that puts a certain politician in a good or bad light. (Luckily, other journalists can work to uncover this corruption.)

- be influenced by their bosses, who pay their wages – even if they're not actually corrupt. Many news companies are owned by individual billionaires, who have strong biases, or something to gain from helping or harming certain political parties.

- allow extreme views to take hold. If an extremist is given enough airtime, people can start to think that person's views are OK.

What can you do?

As a reader and viewer, the best thing to do is to read and watch a wide variety of news sources, and to read beyond the shouty headlines. Ask yourself if the news source you're using is trying to get you to react in a certain way, by using emotional language instead of facts.

What is immigration?

People who choose to move to another country are usually called **immigrants**. There are many reasons to do this, from wanting better weather, to needing better job opportunities. People who leave their countries to escape wars or other dangers are known as **refugees**. Unlike immigrants, refugees don't really have a choice.

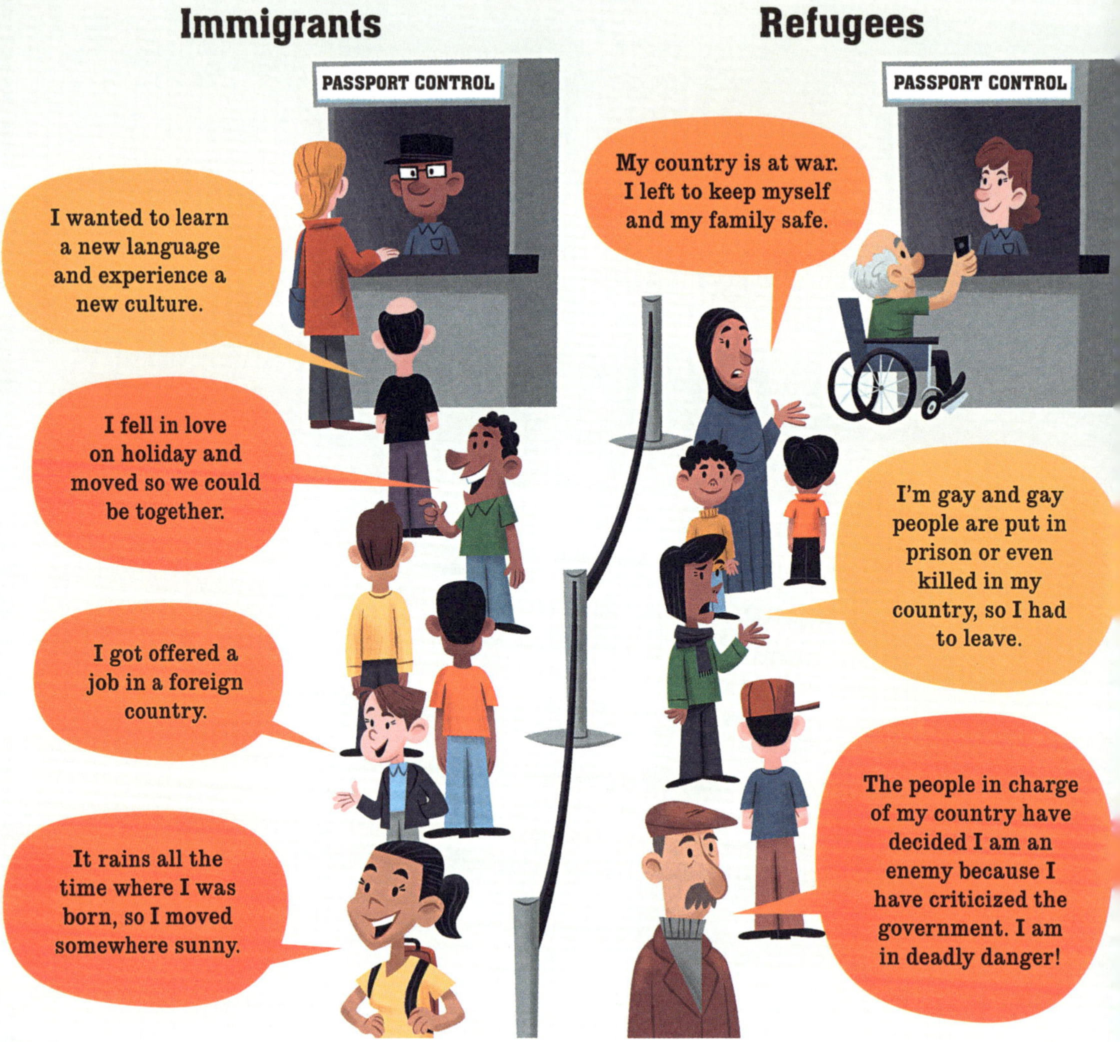

Most countries have strict rules about who they will let in as immigrants. Often, newcomers to a country have fewer rights, such as not being able to vote, or not being allowed to see a doctor for free. Refugees often have to work very hard to prove they are genuinely in danger, too. Even then, they may only be allowed to live in camps, not in proper homes.

Why are people against immigration?

Some political parties win votes by whipping up fears about the effects of immigration in their country, such as the idea that immigrants are 'stealing' jobs from locals. Some politicians also tap into a distrust of foreigners, known as **xenophobia**. Many of these fears aren't based on reality, but it's hard to persuade someone to change their feelings using logical arguments.

Immigrants are stealing our jobs!

Many immigrants only come to the country *because* they've been offered a job – a job no one in the country wanted.

Well, immigrants will drive down wages then, because they're willing to work for less.

Not if the government makes it illegal to pay low wages.

I don't feel like I'm at home in my own country any more. Immigrants don't know how our society works, and some don't share our values.

I think having immigrants from around the world has made our society better – especially the food! And remember, immigrants learn from our culture, too. A confident, peaceful society should be able to pass on its values, as well as learning new ones.

That sounds nice in theory, but it's not what I see happening around me. I was happy with the way things were.

Living with racism

Racism is a belief that some races are superior to others. People who hold racist views are likely to treat people of other races badly. You don't have to be an immigrant to experience racism – your family could have lived in a country for centuries and still be a victim of racist insults, and worse.

Most governments have laws to protect people from racism, such as not giving people jobs based on what they look like, or because their names sound 'foreign'. But it's very hard to create laws to prevent more subtle forms of racism.

Am I a feminist?

Human rights apply to everyone. But some groups, even very large ones, have often lived at a big disadvantage. For example, women and girls haven't always had the same rights as men and boys, and in lots of ways still don't.

Here are some of the questions that women often have to worry about more than men and boys – often depending on the part of the world in which they live.

People who recognize that women and girls are treated unfairly, and believe they should have equal rights and opportunities to men and boys, are known as **feminists.** If you believe that, you're a feminist, too – even if you're not a woman.

Is under-representation a problem?

When people from minority groups aren't seen or heard, it's called **under-representation**. For example, in Hollywood movies roughly 70% of all speaking parts go to men (usually white men).

In most parliaments around the world, there are far more male than female representatives. Under-representation in government often affects other groups of people, too, such as gay people, disabled people and ethnic minorities.

But is it a problem?

Who's responsible for the planet?

Humans have done terrible things to planet Earth, from dumping oil and pumping out pollution to causing climate change by burning fossil fuels. Most people agree society needs to fix this – but how can politicians help us protect the environment?

Politicians can make laws to reduce pollution and tackle climate change. For example, they could ban cars that burn fossil fuels, or at least raise taxes on them.

Ah, but politicians don't all **WANT** to make laws like that because lots of voters can't afford new cars, or they want to make money out of fossil fuels.

But there are lots of politicians who **DO** want to help. And, unlike us, they have access to scientists and other experts, who can advise them on how society as a whole needs to change, if we want to save our planet.

What about the fact that governments change every few years, and the next government could undo any laws the previous one made?

Good point. So maybe it's more important to lobby private companies, instead of government?

You don't even have to lobby a company to make it change. If enough customers simply stop buying their products it's a very powerful motive for a company to change its ways.

But shouldn't government work to encourage companies to change, rather than relying on people to protest?

That's a nice idea in theory. But governments are made up of people, and people can become corrupt. The news is full of stories about government officials being friends with companies that create pollution...

Is corruption inevitable?

Corruption happens when politicians use their positions in dishonest ways, to gain money or power. Corruption could be any of the following things.

Bribery
Agreeing to give someone special treatment in return for money

Extortion
Using threats or violence to get ahead in politics

Nepotism
Giving money or important jobs to friends and family

Blackmail
Using other politicians' secrets against them

Embezzlement
Stealing money that's supposed to belong to the government

Here's one example.

DAILY NEWS LOCAL NEWS WORLD NEWS SPORT WEATHER

SCANDAL IN BRAZIL

In 2014, Brazilian police launched an investigation into corruption. It was revealed that companies who had been paid government money for big construction projects were using part of it to bribe government officials. Billions of dollars were ending up in the pockets of politicians.

For the next two years, there were anti-corruption protests across Brazil. People carried yellow and green brooms, demanding that politicians stop stealing money that they had paid in taxes.

In 2016, President Dilma Rousseff was sacked. Many company bosses and politicians were arrested and had to pay enormous fines.

Protesters demand an end to corruption

How to argue

In life, you're likely to come across a lot of people you disagree with. Here are some tips for how to create a convincing argument... without hurting people's feelings.

1 Don't make it personal

Pick apart someone's *ideas* rather than saying anything about them as a person.

2 Back up your opinions with facts

To find the facts in the first place, read and watch the news, and read widely around subjects you care about.

3 Appeal to people's emotions

Although facts are important, humans are emotional creatures, so if you can tap into someone's fears and hopes, you're more likely to persuade them. Often, people need to have a personal connection to an argument – sometimes facts alone can feel cold and abstract.

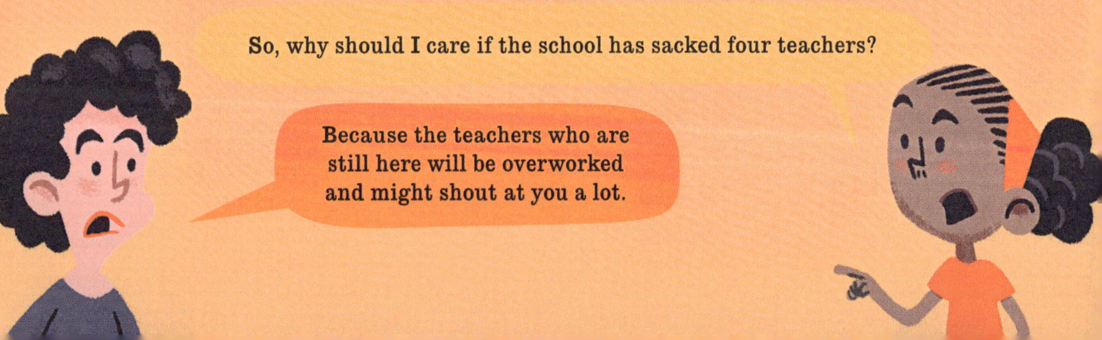

4 Look out for arguments built on lies

Sometimes, someone might be using a piece of false information as the starting point for their argument. For example...

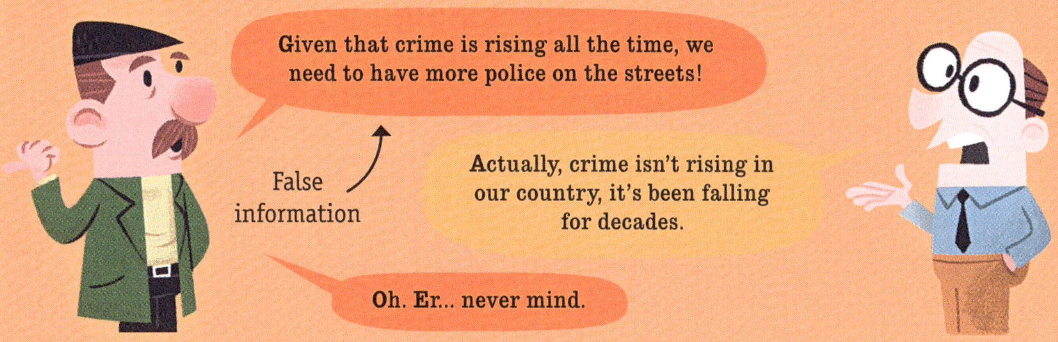

It's important to challenge any assumptions your opponent is making at the start, so they can't create an argument based on incorrect or out-of-date facts.

5 Don't lose your temper and shout

It's rude and disrespectful, and it will also make your arguments seem weaker, as you look like you're panicking and losing control.

Speaking passionately is fine; just don't yell.

6 Be prepared to change your mind

Sometimes, you might realize halfway through an argument that the other person might be right. That's OK. You don't have to keep arguing for the sake of it. Being honest about changing your mind can help others change their minds, too.

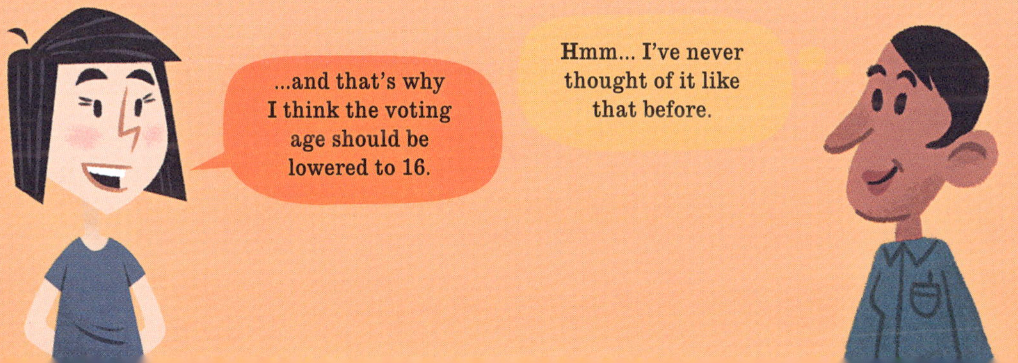

Learn to debate

One good way to learn how to have (and win) political arguments is to join a **debating society**. Schools and colleges often have these. In debates, people have arguments, following strict rules, and the audience votes on who wins.

Here's how a debate works...

Someone called the speaker reads out the suggestion – or **motion** – that's going to be debated.

The **proposer** presents an argument agreeing with the motion. She or he has few minutes to speak.

Then, the **opposer** speaks against the motion, with the same time limit.

Other people speak to back up both sides, then, after a summing up, the audience votes.

Many parliaments around the world use similar rules to debate before voting on a bill. So debating is very good training for a career in politics.

Some debates are about serious topics:

- should the death penalty exist?
- should we lower the voting age to 16?
- does social media make you more antisocial?

...but people practise using silly topics, too:

- who would win in a fight between a vampire and a werewolf?

What next?

Once you've finished this book, you'll probably know more about politics than the average person. But don't stop there. The world of politics is always changing. Watch and read the news to learn more.

Read about history. Spanish-American philosopher George Santayana wrote in his book *The Life of Reason*: "Those who cannot remember the past are condemned to repeat it." The more you know about political history, the readier you'll be to stop bad things from happening in the future.

Keep your eyes, ears and mind open. Ask yourself what you believe. Question those beliefs. Never passively accept what someone tells you. Vote, when you're old enough. Protest, if you disagree with your government. Write letters and emails to your representatives.

And even, perhaps, become a politician yourself...

Glossary

This glossary explains some of the words used in this book. Words written in *italic* type are explained in other entries.

absolutism a *political system* in which one person, such as a *monarch* or *dictator*, runs the country, with total control over everything.
anarchy when no one is in charge, or when there is no *government* at all.
authoritarianism a *political system* in which *government* has strict control, for example by outlawing freedom of speech.

ballot an *election* in which people vote, often using pieces of paper called ballots.
bias when the *media* or a *politician* discusses an issue from just one point of view.

cabinet a group of senior *politicians*, usually chosen by a *president* or *prime minister* to help run the government.
candidate a person who puts themselves forward to be elected as a *politician*.
capitalism an *ideology* that says the *economy* works best if people are free to set up businesses without too much interference from *government*.
censorship when a *government* tells people what they can and can't write or even say.
central government *government* that has authority over an entire country, usually based in the capital city.
citizen a person who is part of a *state*, often the state they were born in. Most adult citizens can vote and be *candidates*, and have to pay *taxes*.
civil servant someone who works for the *government* but is not elected. In many countries, civil servants have to be politically neutral.
coalition when two or more *political parties* work together to form a *government*.
colony a country ruled over by a *government* from another country.
communism a *left-wing political system* based around the idea that everyone should share resources equally, organized by a powerful *central government*.
constitution a set of rules, often written down, that outlines the basic *political system* of a *state*.
corruption when *politicians* use

their position of power to get money or or advantages for themselves.

debate a way to discuss competing ideas, often used in *parliaments*.
democracy a *political system* in which *citizens* can elect a new *government* every few years.
dictator the leader in an *authoritarian* system.
direct democracy a *political system* in which *citizens* are asked to vote on new laws as well as to elect *governments*.

economy the way that money moves in and around a *society*, and how a *government* manages that movement.
election when *citizens* all vote on who should be their new leader, or who should be in their next *government*.
empire a country that has conquered or taken over running other countries.
executive branch the part of *government* that approves new laws and is responsible for carrying out *policy* ideas.

federal republic a *state* made up of a group of smaller regions (often also called states), ruled by an elected leader.
feminism the belief that women and men should have equal rights and opportunities.
freedom of speech the right for people to say and write and share any ideas without fear of *censorship* or arrest.

government a group of people that run a country, often split across three branches: *executive*, *legislative* and *judicial*.
green politics *policies* or *protest movements* based around controlling human impact on the environment.

human rights basic things that all people should have acccess to, such as food, shelter and freedom from being harmed by others.

ideology the basis for a way of thinking about *society*, or a *political system*.
immigration when people who are originally *citizens* of one country, or no country, move countries.
independence being free from control by other people, organizations or countries.
international organization a collection of countries working together with a shared aim, for example the United Nations.

judicial branch part of a *government* responsible for deciding how to interpret laws, and who has broken them.

left-wing a broad *ideology,* usually defined by the belief that *governments* should impose high *taxes* and share resources between all *citizens.*

legislative branch part of a *government* responsible for discussing and agreeing on new laws and *policies.*

liberalism an *ideology* roughly defined by the belief that *governments* should not tell people how to live their lives, and should not spy on them.

local government governments within a country that are responsible for a small part of that country, such as a city.

majority the largest group of people in a country, or what a *political party* has if it has more than half of the representatives in a *parliament.*

media, the websites, TV shows, newspapers and any other way journalists and *politicians* talk to people in a *society.*

minority any group of people in a *society* who are fewer than the *majority* group – often at risk of being mistreated by that group.

monarchy a country ruled by a king, queen or emperor.

nationalism an *ideology* based on doing what is best for the people within a particular country or *state.*

parliament where *politicians* meet to debate *policies* and make laws. In some countries, it's called a congress, or an assembly.

patriotism an *ideology* based around feeling strong pride for your own country or *state.*

policy a specific idea a *government* carries out to improve *society,* such as an 'education policy'.

political party a group of people with a shared *ideology,* who try to get their *candidates* elected to a national *parliament.*

political system a set of rules that defines who can form a *government,* and what powers that government has.

politician someone who has been elected to their national *parliament,* and is able to *debate* and vote directly on new laws and *policies.*

president the leader of a *republic.* In some countries, a president is the most powerful *politician*; in others, her or his power is mostly ceremonial.

pressure group people who work together to try to influence *politicians*, for example by organizing a *protest movement*.

prime minister the leader of the *government* in some countries, usually in charge of the *legislative branch*.

protest movement a series of actions, such as marching or letter writing, to try to persuade a *government* to change the law.

public services things a *government* provides for its *citizens*, such as street lighting.

referendum a vote to answer a specific question, rather than an *election*.

representative democracy a *political system* in which *citizens* regularly elect *politicians* to represent their views in a *parliament*.

republic a country that does not have a monarchy, but is ruled by *politicians*.

right-wing a broad *ideology*, usually defined by the belief that traditional values should be upheld, and that *citizens*, not *governments*, are responsible for their own welfare.

socialism an *ideology* that promotes the idea that *society* can overcome inequality by letting *government* control services, such as education and healthcare, and using *taxes* to spread out wealth.

society a group of people, usually with shared values and aims. It can be small, such as a family, or large, such as a country.

state a country or collection of countries ruled by a single central government, often united by a shared culture and language.

suffrage the right to vote, usually applied to national elections.

suffragettes women who campaigned for the right to vote in the 19th and 20th centuries.

taxes money that *citizens* and businesses must pay the *government*, to be spent on running the country.

terrorist someone who performs acts of violence, often without warning and at random, to try to scare a *society*.

totalitarianism an extreme version of *authoritarianism*, in which a leader often demands that *citizens* worship them and obey direct commands.

treaty an official agreement between governments from two or more countries.

Index

Usborne Quicklinks

For links to websites where you can find out more about politics, governments, elections and voting with videos, virtual tours, activities and quizzes, go to the Usborne Quicklinks website at

www.usborne.com/quicklinks

and type in the title of this book. Please follow the internet safety guidelines at the Usborne Quicklinks website.

Here are some of the things you can do at Usborne Quicklinks:

- See inside the House of Commons in the UK
- Explore the similarities and differences between the UK Prime Minister and the US President
- Take a virtual tour of the White House in the US
- Find facts about political systems in India, Japan and other countries
- Discover leaders of every country in the world from ancient times to present day

Acknowledgements

Written by
Alex Frith, Rosie Hore
& Louie Stowell

Illustrated by
Kellan Stover

Designed by Jamie Ball &
Freya Harrison

Series designer:
Stephen Moncrieff
Series editor:
Jane Chisholm

Politics experts:
Dr. Hugo Drochon,
University of Cambridge
and Dr. Daniel Viehoff,
New York University

With thanks to:
Lupita Harris, John Pienaar,
Rachel Reeves MP, Nick Clegg MP
and The Earl Howe, PC

First published in 2017 by Usborne Publishing Ltd., Usborne House,
83–85 Saffron Hill, London, EC1N 8RT, United Kingdom.
www.usborne.com